THE LION AND THE UNICORN IN AFRICA

THE LION
AND THE UNICORN
IN AFRICA

*A history of the origins
of the United Africa Company
1787–1931*

FREDERICK PEDLER

With a chapter by
ALAN BURNS, G.C.M.G.

LONDON
HEINEMANN
IBADAN · NAIROBI · LUSAKA

Heinemann Educational Books Ltd
48 Charles Street, London WıX 8AH
P.M.B. 5205 Ibadan · P.O. Box 45314 Nairobi
P.O. Box 3966 Lusaka
EDINBURGH MELBOURNE TORONTO AUCKLAND
HONG KONG SINGAPORE KUALA LUMPUR NEW DELHI

ISBN 0 435 32680 5

Printed in Great Britain by
Richard Clay (The Chaucer Press) Ltd.,
Bungay, Suffolk

Acknowledgements and Sources

In venturing into history again after all these years it is appropriate that my first acknowledgement should be to those who taught me at Cambridge, and especially to Ernest Barker, Zachary Brooke, and Michael Oakeshott. It is pleasant to be reminded of those happy times.

I undertook this work after my retirement from the boards of Unilever Limited and N.V. and of the United Africa Company Limited, and I express my appreciation to all three of those companies for allowing me to use much material which belongs to them. To the United Africa Company thanks are also due for much valuable help with maps and illustrations.

I have been most fortunate in securing the collaboration of Sir Alan Burns, G.C.M.G., who is the author of chapter 9, which deals with the Royal Niger Company. During his service in Nigeria and the Gold Coast Sir Alan played a distinguished part in making the history of those countries, and he has been a pioneer in writing their history. My own copy of his history of Nigeria has sentimental value for me, since it bears the signatures of twenty members of the United Africa Company's staff in Gusau, who presented it to me when I left Africa to take up an appointment in London. Among many acts of kindness for which I stand in debt to Sir Alan was the hospitality which he extended to me on the first night which I spent in the Gold Coast after leaving the government service and joining the United Africa Company.

I wish to express my thanks to John Miles, M.A., who worked as my research assistant, and who was successful in discovering and elucidating a great deal of material; and to Monica Smallman, B.A., who carried out research for me in Bristol and London.

I owe a very special debt to J. J. Rankin, who wrote a history of the United Africa Company and its predecessors, which he completed in 1938. He had been a member of the staff of G. and A. Baker in Turkey, a company which belonged to the African and Eastern Trade Corporation. He secured promotion to be the agent of that company in the Canary Islands, from which post he retired in 1935. He then devoted himself to writing the history. His script provides no indications of sources, which professionals will deplore. He left a file of papers which indicates that he corresponded diligently with a great many people who had something to contribute. I know, however, from men who saw him at work, that he recorded much valuable material from orally communicated reminiscences of people who had acted their parts in the story, but who are no longer available for me. It was characteristic of the Liverpool houses which traded in the Bights that they engaged office boys at the age of 13 or 14 and continued to employ them as clerks for sixty years or more. There was no 'normal age of retirement'. These life-long servants had feudal loyalty to their house, and great pride in its origins. It was from such men as these that Rankin learned of the beginnings of Thomas Harrison, Hatton and Cookson, Pickering and Berthoud, and Woodin. Where possible, I have made every endeavour to investigate the origins independently; and in the stories of Richard and William King and of F. and A. Swanzy the sources have not been lacking. But some others have left no memorial—except in Rankin. In such cases I have accepted Rankin's account, because I am satisfied that he was a faithful and conscientious recorder.

Rankin enjoyed the closest co-operation of Alexander Alexander Cowan, at that time a director of the United Africa Company. A. A. Cowan went to Africa in the service of the Miller brothers in 1887, and from 1893 at any rate he was their confidant and counsellor. He was a leading actor in the formation and operation of 'the first pool', in the merging of Millers with the African Association, and indeed in everything with which Millers and their successors were concerned over half a century. Wherever Rankin is dealing with matters within the personal knowledge of Cowan, the hand of Cowan can be seen.

Most tragically, Rankin died as a result of a road accident shortly after he had completed his work, and although the United Africa Company took certain steps with a view to rounding off the work and arranging publication, these were overwhelmed by the outbreak of war. I have made a great deal of use of Rankin's material and I have acknowledged this in references. His work has been made available to serious research workers by the United Africa Company.

I am much indebted to Geoffrey Baker, formerly a manager of the United Africa Company, who made an analysis of the papers in the Public Records Office which relate to the Niger Delta in the years 1849 to 1893, which he has most generously made available to me.

I have resisted temptations and exhortations to provide background material and general comment; and as regards the industrial background of the story, I have done so with complacency because readers have only to refer to the excellent History of Unilever by Professor Charles Wilson, F.B.A., to whom I must express my appreciation for reading certain chapters and giving me much encouragement.

It has been a very remarkable experience and a great privilege for me to draw upon the memories of Sir Malcolm Knox and Cyril Beaumont, both of whom were in personal contact with Lord Leverhulme.

This book would never have been written without the most enthusiastic support and collaboration of many people who worked for the African and Eastern Trade Corporation and for the Niger Company, and who have shown themselves willing to go to endless trouble to help me. Some of them have written me letters, recorded interviews on tapes, sent me their diaries and other papers, or read and commented on the drafts of chapters. To all I express my deepest gratitude. The names are recorded below.

The list also contains the names of many other friends who have helped. To them also I am grateful for their generous assistance.

Anderson, A. I.
Arden-Clarke, P. A.
Baer, R.
Baeta, William T.
Barben, Jean
Barter, D. E.
Bâtard, André
Bauer, Professor P. T.
Bayley, A. M. C.
Berry, Fred
Binns, Victor M., O.B.E.
Birch, John P., C.B.E.
Blenkinsop, A.
Bloomfield, B. C., M.A., F.L.A.
Booth, Tom
Bracken, Benjamin
Bracken, J. R., M.A., B.Litt.
Bray, D. M., O.B.E.
Buckle, D. H.
Cake, Rosemary
Campagne, D. van Lookeren

Cato, K. A.
Cheneau de Leyritz, Jean
Chivers, L. F.
Cogle, Fred
Cole, A. A.
Cole, Lord
Cole, N. G.
Collinson, J.
Crookenden, H. C.
Davies, P. N., M.A., Ph.D.
De Blank, S.
De Haan, G. C.
Denyer, D. W.
Drew, Dan
Dunnet, Donald D.
Fage, Professor J. D.
FitzGerald, Sir Patrick
Fleming, Bob
Fox, R. T.
Fraser, Frank Lugard
Fromings, Joyce

Frorup, Daniel
Frorup, Madame
Frost, F. G.
Gilbert, Cecil
Gore Clough, Raymond, M.B.E.
Green, W. R.
Haak, A. A.
Hague, Jack A.
Hall, Denys
Hallett, E.
Hartje, H. G.
Hofman, Evert
Howarth, W. C.
Hüweler, Herr
Ingham, Professor Kenneth, O.B.E.
Johnston, J. W. W.
Jones, D. D.
Judd, E. C., M.V.O.
Kaye, E. D.
Keir, James
Kewley, Maurice
King, Edmund Poole
Knox, Andrew M.
Kuin, Dr. Pieter
Lane, Frank L.
Lesage, Raymonde
Livingston, Ethel
Loopuyt, Jan
Lunghi, A. J. A.
MacDermott, Alan
McKendrick, A. T.

MacPherson, Roy
Mallinson, Tom, O.B.E.
Martin, David
Ménard, C.
Minall, F. John
Muir, Rowland Huntly
Nixon, Alfred
Oliver, Professor Roland
Orris-Bird, A. C.
Osvalt, Jean-Jacques
Pardoe, Fred S., C.B.E.
Pointon, A. G.
Ralph, Miss E.
Roberts, W. W.
Rogers, Eric F.
Ruston, Clifford
Sedgley, D. E.
Sellars, W.
Sheldon, C.
Shepherdson, Glen
Smart, W.
Southall, Roger
Smith, Sir Arthur H.
Stephens, W. L.
Swanzy, Henry V. L.
Taylor, Dr. Kobina
Thorpe, E.
Wahid, Alhaji
Wallerston, George L.
Watson, Geoffrey
Whiteman, Neil
Wilson, Gordon H., C.B.E.
Winney, Margaret

My publisher deserves a special vote of thanks for being most helpful.

My wife has always been the first to read the typescripts, as they became available, and I am deeply indebted to her for a great deal of practical advice about style and presentation.

Table of Contents

List of Figures

List of Plates

Acknowledgements for Artwork

Frontispiece by Graham Spice

Endpapers by courtesy of Texoprint N.V. and the United
Africa Company International Limited

Fig. 2   Compiled from information supplied by Edmund Poole
King

Figs 3, 5, 6, 7, 8, 10, 11, 12   By courtesy of the United Africa
Company International Limited

The photographs are reproduced by kind permission of
the following:

Plate 3   From the painting by David Bates, 1860, in the
collection of the United Africa Company
International Limited

Plate 4   By courtesy of G. B. Ollivant and Company Limited

Plate 5   From a colour print in the collection of the United
Africa Company International Limited

Plate 6   From a colour print in the collection of the United
Africa Company International Limited

Plate 7   From the original painting in the collection of Edmund
Poole King

Plate 8   From *The Life of Mary Kingsley* by Stephen Gwynn,
Macmillan & Company Limited, London, 1932

Plate 9   From an original drawing in the collection of the United
Africa Company International Limited

Plate 10   From *The History of Unilever* by Charles Wilson,
Cassells and Company Limited, London, 1954

Plates 11, 12, 14, 18, 20, 21, 22, 23, 24   By courtesy of the United Africa Company International Limited

Plate 15   By courtesy of Kwesi Akumenya Cato, Director of the
United Africa Company International Limited

Plate 16   By courtesy of R. T. Fox

Plate 17   By courtesy of the National Portrait Gallery

Plate 19   Keystone Press Agency Limited

I

The State of Africa about 1780

This book is concerned with several different trading companies which were active in West Africa for many years. With hindsight it may be said that they had one thing in common, namely that they came together to make up the United Africa Company Limited, which was formed in 1929. During the previous half-century, a series of amalgamations had prepared the way for that event. These earlier combinations produced the Royal Niger Company, the African Association, the African and Eastern Trade Corporation, and the Niger group. The following pages are largely concerned with the processes through which those unions were accomplished. Readers may be assisted in following the story by the diagrammatic time chart on the following page.

The most ancient of these companies was Richard and William King, a firm which still exists under that name in the Cameroon Republic. The next to be formed was F. and A. Swanzy. By a strange coincidence, King took a lion for his trade mark, and Swanzy took a unicorn, so that between them they shared the two beasts which appear as supporters of the royal coat of arms in England. It is appropriate that a book about West African trade should bear a title derived from trade marks, because trade marks were a tremendous feature of the West African market. In relation to its size, there were probably more registered and 'used' marks there than in any other part of the world. African middlemen and customers attached the greatest importance to the trade mark which was on the merchandise offered to them.

The founders of the two companies, Richard and William King and F. and A. Swanzy, first went to Africa in the ninth decade of the eighteenth century, and this chapter will include a brief description of the state of affairs at the time of their arrival. It will also include a description of palm oil, and how it is produced; for without some knowledge of that commodity readers would be unable to appreciate what Africans contributed to the growth of the trade with which this book is concerned.

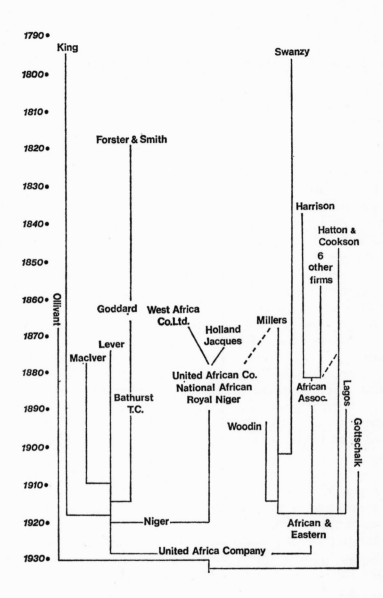

Fig. 1. Diagram of routes by which the principal predecessor firms reached the United Africa Company

The ninth decade, 1780 to 1790, was a period of great activity for the slave trade. About 64,000 slaves were being carried across the Atlantic every year, of which the British share was about 38,000.[1] The slaves were supplied by African dealers in the ports of West Africa. European trading captains purchased them, for shipment across the Atlantic, under a system of barter in exchange for merchandise of European manufacture. There had been a tendency for the main activity of the slave trade to move eastwards. By 1785, though the Gold Coast was still exporting about 10,000 slaves a year,[2] the traffic was more intense in the region of the Volta river, Lagos, and the Niger Delta. In the countries to the west of the Gold Coast trade in African produce was beginning. Ivory was important, and gold, hides, beeswax, and timber counted for something; but the mainstay of the trade was palm oil, a raw material which at that time was used in Europe principally for making soap, though it had many industrial applications in the manufacturing processes which were beginning to be undertaken in Europe and especially in Britain.

Since this book is very largely the story of palm oil, the reader had better be informed without delay, what it is. The oil palm, *elaeis guineensis* (see plate 1), is indigenous to West Africa. It requires rainfall of between eighty and a hundred inches a year, and a marked dry season is detrimental. The soil should have a high clay content to retain moisture. The palm requires a temperature around 90 degrees Fahrenheit (32 degrees centigrade) and a humidity around 90 per cent. Harvesting of the fruit is continuous throughout the year, with a seasonal peak from March to May. The fruit grows in a bunch, which contains several hundred fruits. Each one of them is rather like a date, in so far as it contains a nut, the kernel of which is the commercial palm kernel, and a pericarp which may be compared with that portion of the date which is eaten. The palm oil is expressed from the pericarp. A different oil is also now secured from the kernel, but this was not an article of commerce in Thomas King's days. Palm oil is a red liquid which is traditionally used by Africans as food, as an illuminant, and for making soap in combination with ash.

The oil-palm tree reaches a height of about 40 feet, and the village boys learn to climb the trees, using locally made ropes

[1] Fage, J. D., *An Introduction to the History of West Africa* (Cambridge University Press, 1955) p. 75.
[2] ibid., p. 84.

3

around the tree and the body of the climber to give a purchase. The cutter climbs the palm and cuts down the ripe fruit bunches, collects them, and takes them to his home. The fruit is detached from the bunch and placed in a large cauldron containing water, which is boiled. The women attend to this part of the work. The steamed fruit is placed in a wooden mortar, where it is pounded with a heavy wooden pestle. The young men of the family do this work. The pounding reduces the fruit to a pulp consisting of the fruit fibre (containing oil) and the nuts. The women and children separate the nuts from the fibre by hand. The fruit fibre is then placed in a rope net, which is twisted, using a stick to give leverage; and this wrings out the oil from the fibre. The remaining fruit fibre is boiled in water, and the oil which rises to the surface is skimmed off. There are, however, many variations on this theme. For instance, sometimes the fruit mass is placed at one end of a canoe, and mashed by treading with the feet. The canoe is then tilted towards the other end, where freed oil collects.[3]

In modern parlance the phrase 'West Africa' has come to include the vast savannahs of the sub-Saharan region; but at the end of the eighteenth century that area, which contained a number of powerful Moslem states, was more closely in touch with the Mediterranean than with the Atlantic coast. Camel caravans crossed the desert with merchandise and with pious pilgrims on the *haj* to Mecca; but hardly anybody crossed the great belt of forest which separated the savannah from the coast. It was infested by tsetse flies which carried the sleeping sickness. Europe was vaguely aware of the culture of the 'Sudan' below the Sahara, from the ancient writings of Ibn Batuta and Leo Africanus; but more direct information was shortly to become available, for Mungo Park's first journey of exploration began in 1795.

By that time, however, Thomas King and James Swanzy had already gone to Africa, and the West Coast was to them literally the coast, and the states and communities which had access to it. These included some powerful kingdoms, such as Ashanti, Dahomey, Oyo, Benin,[4] and Congo; and many town-states, notably among the Ewes and on the Niger Delta, organized for the slave trade. In other areas, such as the Bristol Coast (which is now called the Ivory Coast) the political units seem to have been smaller and less sophisticated; but the people were keen traders and came out in their canoes to

---

[3] United Africa Company, *Statistical & Economic Review*, No. 25 pp. 45–7, No. 3 p. 1.
[4] Fage, op. cit., pp. 87–98.

exchange goods with any European ship which cast anchor off the shore.

The Africans who occupied the coast welcomed European traders—albeit these were at that time mostly slave traders— because since the contact with Europe had begun, 300 years earlier, they had come to regard trade as their main resource. They offered their services as middlemen between the trading ships and the vast areas of supply and demand in the continent behind them. In their position of first contact with the traders, they were better able than the inland peoples to purchase firearms, and this conferred upon them a special position of power. They welcomed the trading ships providing that the ships' captains paid comey, a form of tax which will be described in the following chapter.

However, though the traders were welcomed in the ports, they were not allowed to go inland. In any case, the health hazards were so formidable that in general the seafaring visitors preferred to stay in their ships. On the River Senegal the French, and on the River Gambia both French and British, had established posts some distance from the sea, but this was hardly an exception to the general rule, for these navigable waterways were, for this purpose, to all intents extensions of the coastline. In the Seven Years War the English captured all the French positions on the Senegal and Gambia Rivers, and by the Treaty of Paris which brought that war to an end in 1763, all these places remained in English hands except Goree, which was to be restored to France. The English joined their new acquisitions to their existing posts on the Gambia River, and tried to set up a 'crown colony of Senegambia'. However, it was not successful and came to an end when war broke out again with France in 1778.[5]

Though the European merchants might not go inland from the coast, they had built on certain parts of the seaboard no less than forty-three forts. Most of these were on the Gold Coast, where the configuration of the coastline lends itself to the construction of buildings on promontories or on cliffs overlooking the sea. No forts were ever built in the Niger Delta or in countries to the east thereof. Dutch, Danes, Portuguese, and French, were established in this way, and a dozen of the forts were English.[6] The English 'castles' (as the major ones were called) were maintained by a statutory body known as the Company of Merchants Trading to Africa. This was

[5] ibid., p. 74.

[6] Lawrence, A. W., *Trade Castles and Forts of West Africa* (London: Cape, 1963).

the organization of the slavers, and it owed its status and constitution to an Act of Parliament of 1750. Before that date the castles in Africa had been maintained by the Royal African Company, chartered in 1672. This had received a subsidy from the Treasury, but did not prosper, and in 1750 it went bankrupt and was put into liquidation. Parliament then had to provide for the control of the castles, and the Company of Merchants Trading to Africa was formed for this purpose. The Act of 1750 provided that all British subjects carrying on trade with West Africa should be members of the Company of Merchants Trading to Africa. It was expressly stated, however, that trade should be free to all, the only obligation being the payment of a fee of £2. The merchants of London, Bristol, and Liverpool (who had paid their fee) elected three members each to a committee of nine, to which the affairs of the Company were entrusted. The institution had to change the character of its activities when Parliament, by an act of 1807, made it illegal for British ships to engage in the slave trade; but it survived until 1821 when the administration of the forts was transferred to the governor of Sierra Leone.

In the very decade in which this story opens there had appeared in West Africa an enterprise launched from Britain which was happily in sharp contrast with the grim forts, bristling with cannons towards the Africans on shore and no less towards enemies of European race at sea. The forts had dungeon-warehouses to accommodate the slaves pending shipment. They were equipped to export human beings out of Africa into captivity. But this new enterprise was devoted to bring human beings back to Africa, to freedom. The settlement at Freetown was established in 1787 and land was acquired by purchase from a Timne chief for the use of the 'free community of settlers, their heirs and successors, lately arrived from England and under the protection of the British government'. The 'settlers' were, of course, persons of African descent.

The language of trade was in general pidgin English. Although it is unlikely that any European visitors realized it at the time, it is now seen that this was a language consisting of a largely European vocabulary coupled with grammatical and phonological features of African languages.[7]

It must be emphasized that at the period when this story opens, the British interest in Africa did not take the form of colonies. 'Not

---

[7] Dalby, David, *Black through White: Patterns of Communication*, Hans Wolff memorial lecture, African studies programme (Indiana University, 1970).

until the last years of the nineteenth century was Britain really prepared to accept the notion that the fulfilment of her aims in West Africa would involve the establishment there of new British colonies. Until that time she tried to stick to her belief that colonies involved an unnecessary and unrewarding expenditure of money and effort, and indeed, as we shall see, on a number of occasions endeavoured to reduce her political commitments in West Africa, leaving her traders and missionaries to do their work unsupported by government.'[8]

[8] Fage, op. cit., p. 107.

2

Richard and William King

John King set up in business in Bristol in 1695. He came from
Broad Chalke in Wiltshire and was afterwards Mayor of Bristol. He
traded with the West Indies, and the firm was nearly a century old
before its African connection began. This was started by Thomas
King (see plate 7), the founder's grandson, in dramatic circumstances.[1] Thomas was apprenticed to a timber merchant in Bristol,
a good man in whom he could find no fault, but he found his work
very dull and when war broke out with France in 1778 he longed to
take part in the fighting. He was nineteen years of age.

The story of this book begins in a ferment of colonies becoming
independent. The thirteen American colonies took up arms against
King George's men in 1776. Englishmen were deeply divided over
the merits of this dispute, and in 1774 the electors of Bristol had
chosen as their representatives in Parliament two men who were
opposed to the government's policy towards America. These were
Edmund Burke and an American-born merchant named Henry
Cruger. Edmund Burke was the eloquent spokesman of those
Englishmen who sympathized with the Americans. However, in
1778 the French saw fit to intervene on the side of the Americans,
and this had the effect of rallying British opinion behind the
government in the war against the traditional foe. At the next
general election (1780) Burke and Cruger lost their seats. Bristol
was enthusiastic for the war. Immediately Bristol citizens fitted out
fourteen privateers, while eight Bristol merchantmen took letters of
marque, which entitled them to carry arms and to attack ships sailing under the flags of the king's enemies, without incurring the
penalties of piracy.[2] Of all the privateers the finest was the *Lyon*,
owned by a syndicate which included the name of Sydenham Teast.
Teast was an experienced operator, for he had fitted out privateers
against the French in the War of the Austrian Succession and in the

---

[1] From the family records of Mr. Edmund Poole King.
[2] Powell, J. W. Damer, *Bristol Privateers and Ships of War* (Bristol: Arrowsmith, 1930).

Seven Years War. He placed the following advertisement in the newspapers:

For a Six Months Cruize
Against the perfidious enemies of Old England
The Ship LYON
PRIVATEER
John Shaw Commander
Compleat frigate built

Mounting 32 carriage guns 10 of which are nine-pounders on her lower deck with Swivels Cohorns etc, and is intended to carry 180 men.

Gentlemen officers, Seamen and able bodied Landsmen willing to enter on board this ship are desired to apply to the Commander on board the ship now lying in Mr. Teast's dock, at his House in Prince's Street, Three Queens in St. Thomas-street, Jack of Newberry in New-street without Lawford's Gate, George and Dragon on the Quay, Prince of Orange near the Gibb, or to Mr. William Randolph one of the agents of the said Ship at his House on Redcliff-Parade, where the greatest Encouragement will be given.

This ship is full frigate built, and in every respect compleat for the intended purpose of a Cruizer; her Accommodations for the Crew in any season of the year (equal to any of His Majesty's cruizers) undeniably good and comfortable—The abilities of the Commander from several years experience in the two last wars, both as a seaman and officer, are well known to the most valuable part of the British community, the TARS OF OLD ENGLAND. She will certainly sail with the utmost expedition.[3]

Thomas King could not resist the appeal of this advertisement. His own paternal dwelling was in that same Redcliff Parade where William Randolph was waiting to give him 'the greatest Encouragement'.[4] He wrote to his father, Samuel King, in the following terms. Since readers may enjoy the spelling no less than the substance of this communication, it has been left as it stands in the original:

Honoured Sir   Bristol 6 Oct 1778
    It grieves me to think that I'm oblig'd to take this way of informing you, what I shou'd be asham'd to tell you oraly 'tis

---

[3] Felix Tarley's *Bristol Journal*, 1778 (26 September; 3, 10, 17 October), Bonner and Middleton's *Bristol Journal*, 1778 (26 September; 3, 10, 17, 24 October).
[4] Poll-books of Bristol.

9

what I've well & long consider'd & am not in the least doubt that 'twill prove a greater advantage to me, than ever any fault with Mr. Garnets; farr from it for I declare I'd rather serve him than any man living; but in this Bussiness I cannot any longer, for private reasons which you shall know by first Opportunity. Perhaps you think this Spirit of Privateering is got into my head but be assured Dr Sir it is not, I'm in a situation (let it appear ever so flattering to you) that will tend more to my ruin than advantage. You gave a very good premium with me, I'll confess, but I've to good oppinion of Mr. Garnett to think that He'll keep it all, however let that be as it will I'm certain you have too great a regard for your family to think of sacrificing everything that's dear to me for the sake of a few paltry Pounds and when you come to see the affair in a clear light, you'll have no objection to that which can only make me happy. You'll please to remember long before you put me here, I always had an Inclination to go to Sea, but my Mother being so very timorous, I never dar'd mention it without incurring Her and your displeasure; however 'tis what I was made for & let my Fortune or fate turn out as it will I never can be happy till I've your consent to go. It makes me shudder when I think on't of giving the best of Parents a moments uneasiness on my Account; notwithstanding my inclination is rose to such a pitch, do what I will I cannot stifle it, which if you do I'm certain of your consent, & if I don't forever after prove your dutiful son, than let me be treated as the most abandoned Wretch living; hoping for your approbation & forgiveness which you'll please let me know by an Advertisement in Thursday's Bristol Paper to this purpose omitting names; If the Gentleman who wished for his friend's consent in a particular undertaking will meet him (at an specified place you choose to mention) he shall have what he wish'd for in his letter dated 4th October 78 As I have not discovered my retreat, or my intentions to my most intimate friends, hope you'll carry this on with the utmost secrecy. However after what I've said if you will not grant my request let me thank the tenderest of parents.

I am sir your undutiful son at present

Thomas King

PS If my retreat should happen to be discovered now and my intentions be prevented, next time I'd take a more sure way.[5]

[5] From the original manuscript in possession of Mr. Edmund Poole King.

The 'retreat' was not hard to find, and Samuel King was able to send his reply to his son without adopting the ingenious suggestion of placing a notice in the newspaper. Notwithstanding poor mother 'being so very timorous', from a patriotic merchant adventurer of Bristol there could be only one answer, and Thomas embarked in the *Lyon* with his father's consent and blessing. The *Lyon* did in fact sail with expedition, as the advertisement had promised, but after some weeks at sea she met two French warships, which were not quite the kind of craft she was seeking. However, she made good her escape in a lively action, and was back in Teast's dock at Bristol for Christmas celebrations and minor repairs. Sailing again in the new year of 1779, she took a Bayonne privateer and a large Spanish ship from Havana carrying indigo and specie. She took the French *Valiante* and two Spanish ships, *Nuestra Senora de Los Dolores* from Buenos Aires carrying specie and furs, and *Nuestra Senora del Merced* from Havana carrying sugar and specie. Then she was sold by auction and her gallant commander, John Shaw, retired from active service and was appointed Havenmaster of Bristol.

The profits of such successful operations must have been considerable, and they were divided among the owners, officers, and crew. No record has been found of the profit of this voyage, but it is of interest to recall that an earlier Bristol privateer, Captain Woodes Rogers, who sailed with the famous Dampier as his pilot, came home with prize money amounting to £170,000.[6] Thomas King would have his share from the profits of the voyage of the *Lyon*; and although the *Lyon* faded out of history, her figure head lived on as the crest of the House of King.

The connection which Thomas King had established with Sydenham Teast, the head of the syndicate which owned the *Lyon*, was of value to him, for this gentleman was interested in sending ships to West Africa to exchange cloth, rum, iron rods, and other trade goods, for palm oil, ivory, and other African products. The King family tradition relates that Thomas sailed away to West Africa. Almost certainly he made his first voyages as a junior officer in Sydenham Teast's ships, for in 1787 he emerges as the captain of *African Queen*, the 150 tons (see plates 5 and 6), built at Folkestone in 1780 and owned by S. Teast and Company.[7]

---

[6] Brace, K., *Portrait of Bristol* (London: Hale, 1971), p. 83. On this voyage Rogers rescued Alexander Selkirk (Robinson Crusoe) from his exile on Juan Fernandez island, and he allowed Selkirk a share of £800 from the total of £170,000.

[7] Lloyds Register.

Sydenham Teast was a 'legitimate' trader who would have nothing to do with slaving. Thomas Clarkson, the organizer of the campaign against the slave trade, procured an interview with him, and wrote:[8] 'I had done this with a view to learning from him what were the different productions of the continent of Africa, as far as he had been able to ascertain from the imports by his own vessels. He was very open and communicative . . . Mr. Biggs, to whom I gained an introduction also, was in a similar trade with Mr. Teast; that is, he had one or two vessels which skimmed, as it were, the coast, and rivers for what they could get of the produce of Africa, without having any concern in the trade for slaves.' So Thomas King sailed to Africa in the employment of a man who, twenty years before the law forbade British ships to engage in the slave trade, would have nothing to do with it.

Clarkson made a collection of imports from Africa. He believed that by showing them to the committee which Parliament had appointed to examine the slave trade, he might influence them in his favour. 'I wished . . . that they might know what Africa was capable of affording instead of the slave trade, and that they might make a proper estimate of the genius and talent of the natives. The samples which I had collected had been obtained by great labour, and at no inconsiderable expense: for whenever I had notice that a vessel had arrived immediately from that continent, I never hesitated to go . . . even as far as Bristol.' He showed to the committee first of all a collection of African woods, tulipwood, satinwood, camwood, and barwood; one of them was a fine purple, and from two others, upon which the Privy Council had caused experiments to be made, dyes had been extracted. He then produced ivory, musk, four species of pepper, and three species of gum, followed by cinnamon, rice, tobacco, indigo, cotton, grains, and pulses. He concluded with an exhibition of articles manufactured by Africans, such as cloth, bags, ropes, soap, earthenware, golden ornaments, and metal instruments. After visiting a ship bringing such cargo back from Africa, he wrote 'My reflections on the better use which might be made of Africa by the substitution of another trade, and on the better use which might be made of her inhabitants, served greatly to animate, and to sustain me amidst the labour of my pursuits.'

Teast and Biggs had spoken to Clarkson of how their ships skimmed the coast and rivers for what they could get of the produce

[8] Clarkson, Thomas, *History of the Abolition of the African Slave Trade* (London: Longmans, 1808) pp. 302–4.

of Africa. A more detailed account of the way the trade was done comes from an American who also had some experience of privateering, though it was less fortunate than Thomas King's. Captain Carnes of Boston, Massachusetts, fitted out a privateer to prey upon British shipping, but upon setting out was almost immediately taken by a British frigate, and became a prisoner of war in England. Shortly after his release he fitted out an expedition to West Africa and after calling at Goree and Freetown proceeded to a village of the Kru tribe.

The Kru inhabit an area of the coast which now forms part of the Republic of Liberia. From the earliest times they welcomed European traders, with whom they engaged themselves as pilots, interpreters, guards, servants, and labourers. Their services were of great importance to the trading captains. Thomas King would cast anchor off Settra Kru or one of the neighbouring villages, and numerous candidates for employment would paddle out in canoes and present themselves, producing books in which the captains for whom they had previously worked had entered a record of their service.

Sailing along the coast eastwards, the trading ship would again cast anchor, on the advice of the Kru pilot, where the huts of a village could be seen on shore. Canoes would immediately come out to trade, bringing palm oil in calabashes and small 'elephants' teeth'. One gains the impression that there must have been a tremendous slaughter of small elephants. Fresh fruit and provisions were also available at each anchorage. Of course, all the trade was barter and what the Africans wanted were blue bafts (that is woven cotton with an indigo dye), muskets, powder, leaf tobacco, pipes, rum, second-hand clothing, and trinkets including beads.[9] This kind of trading could be done as far east as the Gold Coast forts, but beyond that everything was given over to slaving, and the legitimate traders did not venture. King avoided the places where the Company of Merchants Trading to Africa maintained castles, for that company was the organization of the slavers. In the period before 1807 the list of Bristol members of the Company of Merchants Trading to Africa did not include the name of King.[10] He would not be one of them since he was not engaged in the slave trade.

Having completed one voyage to Africa in the *African Queen*

[9] Carnes, J. A., *Journal of a Voyage from Boston to the West Coast of Africa* (London: Sampson Low, 1853).
[10] From the committee's election returns.

Thomas spent a year at home, for in 1789 he was one of the 'members of the society' of Lloyds, and was exhorted to furnish reports about shipping at Bristol. Early in 1790, however, he again sailed to the West Coast for Sydenham Teast in the *African Queen*.[11] In 1791 the *African Queen* passed into the ownership of Rogers & Company, and had another captain,[12] but Thomas must have been in love with her because he bought her and was favoured with letters of marque to sail in her against the French when war was renewed against the revolutionary government.[13] On one occasion, having taken a French ship, he only claimed the submission of the French captain to the English flag, took his sword and blunderbuss in token thereof, and allowed him to sail away home.[14]

A ship called *Ann and Susannah* was taken from the enemy by a British privateer, and having been 'condemned in prize' (as the phrase went) in the Court of Vice-Admiralty of Kingston, Jamaica, she passed into the ownership of a syndicate which included a certain Samuel Poole.[15] It is not known whether Thomas King had anything to do with this ship or with Samuel Poole, but it may have been so, for he married a lady whose name was Sarah Poole. She was the daughter of Thomas Poole, a tanner at Nether Stowey in Somerset. Her brother Thomas was the friend and benefactor of Southey, Coleridge, and Sir Humphrey Davy, and he undertook for the government the first census of England.

After getting married, Thomas spent less time at sea, but he engaged Captain Robert Buckle to command the *African Queen* and sent her off with a full cargo on his own account and a basket of apothecary ware for the Sierra Leone Company at Freetown.[16] However, he did not entirely sever his connection with privateering, for in December of the year of his marriage he took out letters of marque in respect of a new *Lion*, though he was not registered as her owner. The *African Queen* was sold in the following year,[17] and

---

[11] Bristol presentments. These are a valuable source for shipping information. They were compiled for the purpose of customs collection and they cover both imports to and exports from Bristol. They give the name of a ship, her captain and her destination, and the week or fortnight in which she set sail. They list the goods on board with the name of the merchant or merchants who owned them. Unfortunately the papers for the years 1780 to 1789 are missing.

[12] Lloyds Register.

[13] Powell, op. cit.

[14] Old printed pamphlet in possession of Mr. Edmund Poole King.

[15] Craig and Jarvis, *Liverpool Registry of Merchant Ships* (Chetham Society, 1967) p. 88.

[16] Bristol presentments.

[17] Lloyds Register.

her new owners used her as a whaler.[18] For his trade to Africa Thomas King replaced her by buying the *London*, in which Captain Buckle again set out, in 1799, carrying a cargo which on this occasion was mostly on behalf of the Sierra Leone Company, further evidence that the firm of King was free from the taint of slaving, for the Sierra Leone Company was sponsored by the abolitionists.

Their cargo consisted of East India goods, calicoes, linen, printed cottons, cotton, wool cards (wire brushes), pewter, brass, lead, earthenware, glass, wrought iron, iron pots, bars of iron, cutlery, tinware, grindstones, nails, paint, linseed oil, leather, tallow, pitch, tar, twine, cables, cordage, anchors, furniture, gunpowder, gun-flints, beef, mutton, tripe, pork, corks, rum, Spanish and Portuguese wine, salt, cheese, sugar, raisins, butter, tobacco, tobacco pipes, leaf tobacco, apparel, hats, and stationery.[19]

Buildings live longer than men, and create a sense of continuity. Walking through Bristol today, the sight of Lewins Mead Unitarian chapel, which Thomas King saw when it was under construction from 1787 to 1791, brings one into contact with him. Did Sarah ask him to explain to her why it was taking so many years to build? They must have taken an interest in Portland Square, laid out in 1790 with stone-faced houses dignified by Ionic columns; and, if Thomas King's choice of a crest gives any clue to his taste in design, he would have been well content with the neo-Gothic style of the church which was built to serve the spiritual needs of those who dwelt behind the Ionic columns. With his transatlantic trade interests Thomas no doubt welcomed the opening of the first American consulate in Britain, at number 37 Queen Street, Bristol, in 1792.[20]

The trade to Africa had now become a comparatively minor interest for Thomas, who was engaged with his father and friends in merchant voyages to many destinations. It was the custom of merchants in those days to make up syndicates to finance a voyage or a series of voyages, and an individual merchant might at the same time be a member of several syndicates. Thus Thomas traded under his own name, and also as J. King and Son, King and Poole (which shows that his wife's family, though principally tanners, could also put some money into merchant shipping), King, Son and Carter,

[18] *Records of Bristol Ships 1800–38* (Bristol Record Society publications, vol. XV).
[19] Bristol presentments.
[20] Brace, K., op. cit., pp. 39, 62, 73.

King, Son and company, King and Company, and T. King and Company.[21]

In 1797, besides sending the *African Queen* on her distant journey, Thomas was interested in three ships sailing to Dublin. The following year he had interests in eleven voyages, involving ten ships, but none of these went to Africa. The firm of King was prospering, for in 1799 he had interests in thirty-seven voyages, involving twenty-one ships, but only one of these, the *London*, went to Africa. The pattern is repeated in 1800; many voyages, but just one to Africa.

Thomas King had to learn that what was sauce for the goose was sauce for the gander, for in 1806 his *Gallant Schemer*, a brig of 197 tons, despite her armament of six twelve-pounder carronades, six six-pounder guns, three four-pounder guns and three swivels, was taken by a French privateer and carried to Guadaloupe.[22] The *Sally*, after making three Antigua voyages safely, was captured on the fourth and carried to Cuba. Then in 1813, the Americans being now at war against the British, his *Colin* was taken off Cork by the *Trueblooded Yankee*, privateer, but she was later recaptured and sent to Plymouth, whereupon Thomas set her to 'Guinea voyages'.[23] For Thomas this was a return to his early love, for in the first thirteen years of the century he had sent no more than two ships to Africa. In 1810 he sent the *Adventurer* to Africa under Captain Veysey, but that was a year in which he had interests in thirty-seven ships altogether.

In the last weeks of 1814 the long war seemed to be over. Peace had been made with the United States, and Napoleon was in Elba. Thomas decided to take a trip to the West Indies, and he bought the *Neptune*, a three-masted vessel of 366 tons, and entered himself as her master for the voyage to St. Croix.

It was Captain Veysey who took the *Colin* to Africa in 1816 and again in 1817. Then there was a pause, but in 1820 Thomas sent James Veysey out again in the *Pitt*. This ship was still on the Africa run in 1830, under Captain Crawford. By this time Thomas was doing more trade with Africa. He had ships running shuttle services to the Irish ports of Dublin, Waterford, and Cork, and, he sent the *Elizabeth* to Newfoundland, the *Arabian* and the *City of Edinburgh* to Calcutta, and the *Maria* to Grenada; but five voyages went to Africa. Besides the *Pitt* there was the *Tom Cod*, Captain Richards; the *Lisbon Packet*, Captain Ogg; the *Chesterfield*, Captain Bindon;

---

[21] Bristol presentments.   [22] as 18.   [23] as 18.

and at the end of the year a second voyage by the *Tom Cod*. There are strong reasons to suppose that at this period Thomas King's trade was confined to that part of the coast which is now known as the Ivory Coast and Ghana. The Ivory Coast was in fact so much frequented by Bristol ships that it was known as the Bristol coast.[24] He supplied African traders, generally on credit, and since he had no shore establishments, it was necessary to allow the debts to run from voyage to voyage; but such debts were fairly met.[25]

In 1829 there was an important development, namely the appearance as co-partners of Thomas's sons Richard and William, by whose names the firm was to become known. The firm bought the *John Cabot*, a two-master of 158 tons; she was bought by Thomas King, Richard King, and William King, merchants and co-partners, trading as T. King & Sons. Four years later Thomas sold his shares in the *John Cabot* to Richard and William, co-partners trading as R. & W. King; and this may be the year in which that name was first brought into use. The vessel was lost on the African coast in 1851, limping into Freetown in a leaking condition and being there condemned.[26]

Richard and William King specialized in the African trade. In 1840 they had eight vessels on this trade. The following year, 1841, was an outstanding date in the evolution of the firm. Thomas, who had led the family to Africa, died; and perhaps in tribute to his memory Richard and William built a second *African Queen*, the ship which Thomas had loved so dearly. She was of 166 tons, about the same size as her predecessor. Her first voyage took about a year and she returned with 361 elephants' tusks, 378 casks of palm oil, 3,000 coconuts, and eleven cases of African beads. She continued to ply between Bristol and West Africa until 1857, when she was sold to a firm at Newport.[27]

1841 was probably the year in which Kings went eastward to Cameroon. They were, however, not the first British palm-oil traders in that estuary. In 1832 the traders in the Cameroon River had received a visit from Macgregor Laird. Following the discovery of the course of the Niger by the Lander brothers in 1831, this gentleman fitted out an expedition with two small steamers to

[24] Kingsley, Mary, *Travels in West Africa* (London: Macmillan, 1897) p. 75.
[25] *Journal Society of Arts*, 17 April 1874, no. 1117 vol. XXII, p. 479.
[26] as 18.
[27] Index to ships, Bristol City Archives.

explore the river. Speaking to a House of Commons committee he said that he had seen the chiefs of Cameroon, men who annually did business with English ships to the extent of a quarter of a million pounds, wearing a gold or silver laced footman's hat, which the palm-oil captains had persuaded them was the distinguishing mark of a nobleman in Great Britain.

At this period Great Britain had a naval base on the island of Fernando Po for use in the suppression of the slave trade. The island was under Spanish sovereignty, but in 1827, with the permission of Spain, Great Britain took over the administration. A man named Beecroft was appointed as 'superintendent'. Beecroft was a remarkable person whose life was full of adventure. His experience of privateering had been less fortunate than Thomas King's, for in 1805, at the age of 15, being an apprentice in a coastal vessel, he was captured by a French privateer and kept prisoner in France until 1814.[28] In 1834 the British naval establishment at Fernando Po was discontinued, but Beecroft remained on the island, governing the freed slaves and other Africans, without authority but with their full consent.

In 1841 the Admiralty sent an expedition to explore the River Niger. It consisted of Her Majesty's steam vessels *Albert* and *Wilberforce*. The expedition suffered terrible casualties from malaria, but it may claim credit for discovering that quinine was an effective prophylactic.[29] The next expedition up the Niger was in 1854 and it was commanded by a medical doctor named Baikie, who used this knowledge to give his people 'quinine wine' each day.[30] He brought them all back hale and hearty, but unfortunately the value of quinine as a preventative against malaria was not generally understood until the twentieth century, and malaria continued to take toll of the trading community. The survivors of the expedition of 1841 spent the winter of 1841 to 1842 in the Bight of Biafra. They visited the Cameroon River and were much impressed by the size of its towns, the density of its population, and the cordial behaviour of its inhabitants. It would be nice to record that their narrative gave news of Richard and William King, but all their credits are handed out to the firm of Hamilton and Jackson, from whose agent they

[28] Burns, Alan, *History of Nigeria* (London: Allen and Unwin, 8th edition, 1972) p. 95 fn.

[29] Allen, W., and Thomson, T. R. H. *Expedition to the Niger* (London: Bentley, 1848), vol. II p. 167; and Thomson in *The Lancet*, February 28, 1846. For treatment of this subject by a medical writer *see* Schram, R., *A History of the Nigerian Health Service* (Ibadan: University Press, 1971) pp. 48–9.

[30] Baikie, *Exploring Voyage* (London: Murray, 1856) p. 34.

received much help and kindness.[31] However, they found other firms as active as well.[32] Their account of the trade suggested that it was highly competitive and not well regulated:

> the practice appears to be, on the arrival of a ship to trust the goods in advance to purchase a cargo . . . there is occasionally a regular scramble for the palm oil as it is brought down the river in canoes . . . sometimes the captain falls a sacrifice to the climate or to disappointment, when his death is considered by the natives to absolve them from all obligations. The mate not being able to procure his cargo, takes away an empty ship. This gives rise to arbitrary and summary proceedings on the part of the whites, and continual disputes—'bad bobs'.

This was the place into which Richard and William King decided to push as new competitors. Having already some experience of how things were done in Africa, they commissioned the firm of Rawle and Fisher of Union Street, Bristol, to make an umbrella of a diameter of twenty-one feet, as a present to the king of the area into which they were moving. The article was considered to be of sufficient interest to the citizens of Bristol to be exhibited in the Exchange before it went to Africa.[33]

In 1849 Beecroft was appointed consul for the Bights of Benin and Biafra, his jurisdiction extending from Dahomey to Cameroon. Now for the first time Kings, in the eastern extremity of their activities, came under some sort of hazy authority and protection of a British consul. In any case the consul's authority was less effective in the Cameroon River than in the Niger Delta. The Cameroon chiefs Bell and Akwa held authority over white and black people alike, though they were assisted in regulating the affairs of trade by a council of European merchants.[34] The first German factory in the Cameroon Estuary was established by Woermann of Hamburg in 1863, but no one could then foresee that this was a distant harbinger of the end of independence.

Richard King was Mayor of Bristol in 1845. In that year 245

[31] Allen, op. cit., p. 246.
[32] ibid., p. 244.
[33] *West Africa*, 28 April 1972, p. 509. It is of interest that the descendant of the Bell or Bonadoo clan chief, with whom R. and W. King entered into relations, was Prince Alexandre Douala Manga Bell, a deputy for Cameroon in Paris during the Fourth French republic. His funeral in 1966 was followed by 100,000 people and he was succeeded by his nephew René.
[34] Baikie, op. cit., p. 335.

British ships sailed to West Africa, and of these twelve belonged to Kings. Only one firm had a larger fleet in the trade, and that was Forster and Smith, of whom more will be heard in the next two chapters.[35]

In 1850 'a few gentlemen connected with or inhabiting the Gold Coast and others who see the yearly necessity and the great importance of procuring Cotton from other sources than the United States' formed an Association 'to produce Cotton on experimental plantations in the neighbourhood of the settlements on the Gold Coast'. The leader of those gentlemen was M. Forster M.P. of the firm of Forster and Smith, and among the others were 'Messrs. R., and W. King'.[36]

In 1853 Richard and William King purchased a dressing-case from a silversmith of Bristol for the King of Dahomey. It was made of rosewood massively mounted with silver and furnished with every conceivable convenience, including cold cream, cosmetics, agents for the hair, and brushes with silver backs.[37] In the museum at Abomey in Dahomey there is (1970) a nest of bottles in a silver basket inscribed—

Presented to
GEZO KING OF DAHOMEY
by Richard & William King
of Bristol.

King Gezo ruled from 1818 to 1858. Whether the Abomey exhibit formed part of the gift made in 1853, or whether it was a separate gift, is not clear; and the nature of the relationship between Richard and William King, and the King of Dahomey, remains a mystery.

In 1864 Consul Burton provided the Foreign Office with a list of all the British firms established in the Bight of Biafra. There were eleven settlements, and Richard and William King were at only one of these, namely the Cameroon River; but it would appear from the way in which the list is presented that at this place they were the most important of the six British firms.[38] The Foreign Office required Burton's statement in order to deal with a petition from a group of firms who had joined together to form the Company of

---

[35] Lloyds register.

[36] Original document in possession of the United Africa Company.

[37] Index to ships and shipowners, Bristol City Archives.

[38] P.R.O. Consul Burton to F.O., F.O.84/1221/1864. This was the famous Sir Richard Burton.

African Merchants. They sought a subsidy from the government in order that they might press on up the Niger. They also spoke of suppressing the slave trade. It sounds like a forerunner of the idea which inspired the Royal Niger Company. Merchants from London, Liverpool, and Bristol sent protests to the Foreign Office, saying that the subsidy applied for would give the Company of African Merchants an unfair advantage over the other traders, and that the remarks about the slave trade were not applicable since there was now no slave trade to suppress. On Bristol's copy of the protest the first signature was on behalf of R. and W. King.[39]

Although Kings were not listed by Consul Burton among the firms present in the Bight of Biafra in 1864, they must have pushed into that area soon after, braving the hostility which the established European traders reserved for interlopers. William Babington, one of R. & W. King's captains, was present in Bonny at the time when Ja-Ja, the leader of a faction in the politics of that town, led away his followers and set up a kingdom of his own in another place which he called Opobo, and that occurred in 1867. (Ja-Ja appears at more length in Chapter 5.) Babington was with Kings for many years, and he has left a description of much that went on in the trade, for instance how they floated the palm oil out from Grand Bassam and Assini in puncheons, which had to be pushed through the surf by swimmers before being loaded to canoes, each puncheon weighing over twelve hundredweight.[40]

Babington said that from the 1830s the English traders had used manillas as currency, and that they were made in Bristol. It appears, therefore, that when Richard and William King turned seriously to the West African trade in 1830 they shipped out manillas and stimulated a local manufacture in their home town. This interesting form of currency was introduced to West Africa by the Portuguese.[41] The word is derived from the Portuguese *manellio*, or from Low Latin *manilia*, meaning a bracelet. There were several types of manilla, but the commonest type, the *okpoho* manilla (see plate 13), consisted of a metal hoop or horseshoe, with lozenge-shaped ends, manufactured from bronze or from an alloy of copper, lead, and tin. It measured $2\frac{1}{4}$ inches across and weighed about three ounces. When Thomas King went to West Africa, manillas and iron bars were both used as currency in many parts of the coast, but it appears

[39] P.R.O. Liverpool merchants to Earl Russell, 3 May 1864, F.O.97/434/1862–4.
[40] *Journal Society of Arts*, 12 February 1875, no. 1160 vol. XXIII, William Babington.
[41] ibid., p. 249.

that iron bars gradually ousted manillas except in the area of Opobo. In that region the latter were in use as the principal currency for the purchase of palm oil until 1949, when the Nigerian government took steps to replace the manillas with West African currency.

By 1874, the iron bar was the standard measure of value in Benin, Brass, New Calabar, and Bonny, and each article represented a certain number of 'bars'. At Old Calabar, on the other hand, the things sold were set down at such a number of 'coppers'. In Cameroon there was a wider choice of units of value, for they used bars, coppers, crews, big tings, or little tings. The value of an iron bar was between six and twelve old pence, and a copper had the same value; crews were worth about thirty old pence. A big ting was worth about a pound sterling, and a little ting about twelve old pence.[42]

R. & W. King had grown accustomed to depend upon the local chief to help them recover their credit. This was traditional, going back to slaving days. It had been vital for the chiefs to ensure that European traders came to their ports, and they made it their business to see that their subjects who received credit paid it back. They would, however, only perform these services for traders who had paid the correct dues, which were described as comey. In the Benin River and the Brass River, comey was computed at a certain value of goods for each mast which a vessel carried, and that value was the goods required for the purchase of two puncheons of palm oil. Bonny and New Calabar were more sophisticated, because they took into account the registered tonnage of the ship and required a comey of five iron bars for every registered ton. At Old Calabar comey was twenty coppers for each registered ton. In Cameroon it was at the rate of ten crews for every 100 tons of the ship's register.[43]

John Harford, a young seaman, sailed from Bristol with seventeen others for the Cameroon River in 1872, in the *Burns*, a ship belonging to R. and W. King and commanded by Captain Harris. The day, he wrote, was one of the happiest of his life. They took three weeks to clear the Bristol Channel owing to contrary winds, but after that they had a quick trip. They took on Kru men at Beraby, and then called at the port of Half Jack, 'which ought to be called the Bristol port of Half Jack, for here we met some half-dozen Bristol ships, who gave our captain a regular good old Bristol wel-

[42] *Journal Society of Arts*, 6 March 1874, no. 1111 vol. XXII, Thos. J. Hutchinson.
[43] ibid.

come'. The area, at the time of Harford's visit, had just come again under French occupation. The French in this part of Africa had found it prudent, during the Franco-Prussian war, to lease their stations to an English mercantile firm.[44] By the time that Harford came there in 1872 the French were back. However, his main interest at Half Jack was not the tricolour, but 'that great produce palm oil'. This was sold by the forest dwellers to the African traders of Half Jack, who in turn sold it to the Bristol men and they shipped it 'to all parts of Europe'. Axim, he said, had recently come to the fore for the quantity of mahogany exported, and it was also the port for the gold mines. At Cape Coast the grey parrots formed a great article of barter. Hundreds of these birds were shipped to Liverpool each week. The ship anchored at Accra to engage mechanics, coopers, and carpenters, who had entirely replaced white men in these trades in 'the lower ports'. Cooks, stewards, and laundry men, were also recruited. The proficiency of the Accra men in these trades was attributed to the teaching of the Basel mission, a society which combined this type of education with evangelical work. Harford was much impressed by the Accra people: a fine race, he said, with superior women. Fernando Po [45] was a flourishing place, with half a dozen English merchants and a fairly good hotel.

At the mouth of the Cameroon River they had to anchor off the Dogs' Heads and wait for the tide to enable the ship to pass the bar. At King Bell's Town the ship moored with two anchors, and had to wait until the whole of her cargo was sold, or rather bartered, for palm oil, ivory, and coconuts. Top spars and yards were taken down, and put away with the rigging and the running gear. Spars were run from mast to mast, bow to stern, to form a ridge pole. Rafters were fastened to these, coming down each side, and roofed with split bamboo and palm leaf mats. All this took about a month. Some of the hands were then transferred to another ship to take her to England, but others were given duties to help the captain in carrying on trade.

Each ship had a cask house, a piece of land opposite to the ship's mooring. It was fenced with mangrove sticks, and inside the compound were warehouses and an open shed for cooperage, i.e. making shooks up into casks. These casks had to be filled with palm oil and stowed aboard for the homeward voyage. They landed their salt—over 200 tons—also their casks, which were broken down into

[44] ibid.
[45] Fernando Po was officially re-named Macias Nguema in 1973.

shooks. The earthenware and heavy loads were also landed. For trading they had about a hundred African customers on board each day, and from half-past five in the morning until after three o'clock in the afternoon the ship was a babel. The after end of the ship was partitioned off and made to resemble a shop as nearly as possible. The captain sat among the goods displayed. The mate was on the main deck to examine the oil, to see that it was clean, and having measured it he gave the supplier a receipt called a book. If the trader wished to shop both for the goods displayed on the ship, and for the heavy goods ashore, he got two books. This went on for more than fourteen months, during which malaria and dysentery killed three white men, and brought others down to a shadow. They were about to set sail for England when mail arrived from the owners, that they were sending out another ship and wished the mate to stay to take charge of her trading. But he was too ill, so the captain put him in charge of the homeward-bound vessel, and voluntarily stayed to trade off the next one; Harford stayed with him. 'We entered upon our work with cheerful hearts.'[46]

William King's son was Mervyn Kersteman King, who was born in 1844/5. He became the head of the firm, and was the Master of the Society of Merchant Venturers of Bristol in 1874. About this time King Bell (Mbeli) of Duala visited Bristol for the purpose of study.[47] Since the link between Duala and Bristol was the house of Richard and William King, it must be supposed that Mervyn King was concerned with the arrangements for King Bell's visit.

By the 1870s the trading ships which anchored off Gold Coast ports were no longer able to depend upon local chiefs to look after their credit risk. The sovereignty of the chiefs had been superseded by the sovereignty of the colonial government, and the law of the chiefs' will was now replaced by the law of the courts. The trading ships' captains found the new state of affairs much less convenient than the old. It was not possible for a ship's captain, on the occasion of his annual visit, to enter into legal proceedings for the recovery of debt. The courts went at their own pace and would not be hustled, but the captain had to heave anchor and sail away. Merchants complained that the colonial government was enacting laws for the protection of debtors which bore hardly on creditors. Richard and William King decided to avoid British colonies and settlements,

[46] Kingsley, Mary, *West African Studies* (London: Macmillan, 1899) p. 567.
[47] Cornevin, Robert, in Gann and Duignan (eds.) *Colonialism in Africa 1870–1960* (Cambridge University Press, 1969) vol. I, *History and Politics of Colonialism*, p. 398.

preferring to trade with independent African states,[48] so they gave up their trade in the Gold Coast and made arrangements with King Adam Archibong to trade from a hulk in the river at Old Calabar. To make the arrangement they sent Captain Harris, who had commanded the *Burns*, in which Harford sailed to Cameroon. He paid to King Adam goods to the value of seven puncheons of palm oil

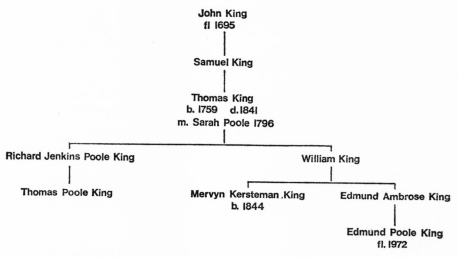

Fig. 2. The generations of the King family, compiled from information supplied by Edmund Poole King

'before I commenced trading his river, being the amount agreed upon for a partly made beach, and which will belong to the firm of R. & W. King as long as they continue to trade in this river'.[49] The hulk was the *Dawstone*, a barque of 496 tons, built in 1853 and employed in the West African trade, and acquired by Kings for the purpose of conversion to a hulk.

In the 1880s, Richard, and William King became associated with eight other British firms in opposition to King Ja-Ja of Opobo. The history of that remarkable struggle will come in a later chapter. The nine companies had become accustomed to acting together through the Ja-Ja affair, and while it was in progress they learned of the grant of a charter to the Royal Niger Company. The Niger Territories and the Oil Rivers jointly composed the Oil Rivers Protectorate, and while the former were administered by the Royal

[48] *Journal Society of Arts*, 17 April 1894, no. 1117, vol. XXII.
[49] United Africa Company of Nigeria property records, Lagos.

Niger Company, the latter were still without any proper administration, the Protectorate hardly existing except on paper. The nine firms hoped that, uniting as a single company just as the firms on the Niger had done, they would obtain a charter for the Oil Rivers.

In 1880 the African Association Limited was incorporated. It was a merger of the nine firms under the leadership of Thomas Harrison & Company, whose business was the most important of the nine firms in that area. By this merger the name of Richard & William King was extinguished in the Oil Rivers, and it did not subsequently appear in Nigeria, though it continued for many years in Cameroon and Ivory Coast. However, Kings retained an interest as shareholders in the African Association and in the African & Eastern Trading Corporation which subsequently evolved from it. Mervyn King was a director of the African Association for twenty-three years until 1912.

3

F. and A. Swanzy

Swanzy is the second name that provides continuity from the eighteenth century to the twentieth. Henry Swanzy, an Irish 'squireen' of Harrymount in County Monaghan, had seven sons, and four of them went to the Gold Coast in the service of the Company of Merchants Trading to Africa. This body, as noted in chapter 1, maintained a number of forts on the African coast and financed this work by collecting taxes from all British merchants, under powers conferred by the Act of Parliament of 1750.

Its functions included the provision of a medical service, and in this it enjoyed the co-operation of the College of Surgeons, who selected James Swanzy to go out as a surgeon in 1789. Since the treatment for malaria was bleeding, surgeons were essential for attending to the European community. Further than that, the slaves had to be kept in health pending shipment. Each slave ship normally carried a surgeon. Clarkson, the anti-slavery leader, in his studies of the slave trade at Bristol and at Liverpool, depended largely on the surgeons, for he found them more communicative than other people engaged in the trade. One surgeon, Alexander Falconbridge, shocked by what he had seen during his service in a slave ship, joined Clarkson in his work and became a leading advocate of Abolition. He and four other surgeons who had served in slave ships gave evidence in support of the suppression of the trade to a committee of the House of Commons.[1]

James Swanzy was born in 1767, so he was 22 when he sailed for Africa. A surgeon's pay was £100 a year plus a commission on the slaves exported. When the slave trade was suppressed and it became necessary to compensate the surgeons for the loss of their commission, the value of it was assessed at £100 a year.[2] The year after he arrived, James was followed by his elder brother, Adam.[3] A

---

[1] Abstract of evidence, 1791, James Philips.

[2] Lawrence, A. W., *Trade Castles and Forts of West Africa* (London: Cape, 1963) p. 310.

[3] Cape Coast Castle record book 1777 to 1803, in the possession of the United Africa Company.

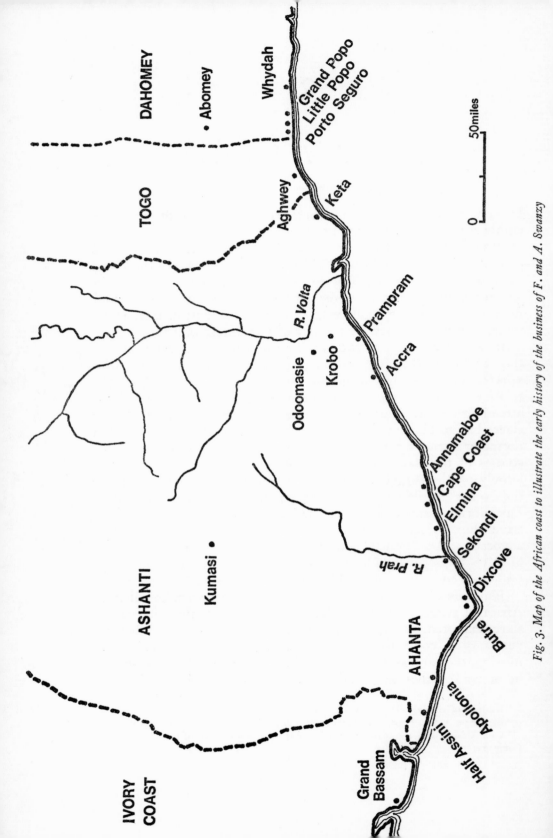

Fig. 3. Map of the African coast to illustrate the early history of the business of F. and A. Swanzy

younger brother, John, followed in 1796, and the sixth brother, Francis Lucas, went to the Coast in 1801.[4]

Recruits to the Company's service were normally graded as writers and received £200 a year, but Adam Swanzy was promoted to a position described as 'factor' within a few weeks of his arrival, with a salary rise of £40. In 1798 he was transferred as factor to Annamaboe, which ranked as the second castle after Cape Coast. He left the service in 1799 in order to devote his time to private trade, as the representative of his brother James who in that year set up at Austin Friars in London as a merchant. Adam died in Cape Coast Castle in 1803.

The death rate among Europeans was fantastic. It could be the recurring theme of this story, but, to spare the reader, the point will be made here, once and for all, with a few examples. Two companies of white soldiers arrived in Cape Coast in 1823 and all died in eighteen months, save one man. In 1824, 101 men landed from H.M.S. *Thetis* and 45 died within a week. The first five Wesleyan missionaries arrived in the Gold Coast in 1835–6 and all died within a few months.[5] In 1894 more than half the white population died.[6]

The Company had thirty or forty officials, working in eleven forts. They were paid in kind, that is to say with trade goods which were sent once a year in a special ship. The principal imports were cloth, canvas, linseed, tar, lead, brass, paints, and barrels. After the suppression of the British slave trade the principal exports were timber, gold, ivory, palm oil, and Indian corn.

James Swanzy started as a surgeon but he was soon appointed Governor of the fort at Dixcove (see plate 9), and after a short time in that position he became Governor of the British fort at Sekondi. He began trading on his own account, and he told a parliamentary commission in 1816 that he did 'more business than almost any other person'. He retired in 1799 at the age of 32, married and (as noted above) set up at Austin Friars as a merchant. In 1813 he became one of the London representatives on the committee which managed the Company of Merchants Trading to Africa.[7] Since the suppression of the slave trade, the committee had been trying to develop an alternative source of wealth by encouraging agriculture. They had sent out seeds of cotton, coffee, pepper, hemp, and wheat,

[4] Swanzy, Henry F., 'A Trading Family' in *Transactions of Gold Coast and Togoland Historical Society*, vol. II part II, 1956.

[5] Claridge, W. W., *History of Gold Coast* (London: Murray, 1915) pp. 381, 425.

[6] Kingsley, Mary, *Travels in West Africa* (London: Macmillan, 1897) p. 32.

[7] P.R.O., T.70/149 election returns, 3 July 1813.

with a hundred sheets of instructions. In the year following James Swanzy's appointment as a member of the committee, that body sent out a schoolmaster for Cape Coast. The total cost of the company in that year was about £27,000, of which £18,000 was met by a grant from the British Treasury. In 1816 total exports amounted to £127,000, of which about half was mahogany. During the decade to 1816 the total value of consignments to James Swanzy was about £12,560.

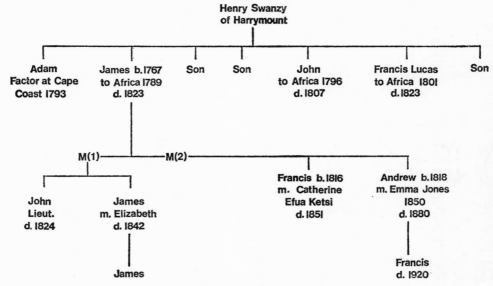

Fig. 4. The generations of the Swanzy family

Brother John arrived on the Coast early in 1796. He became factor at Prampram in 1797, was described as chief of Apollonia in 1800 and chief of Dixcove in 1801. In 1802 he was dismissed the service, but he remained in Africa in private trade and had a factory beside the gate of Cape Coast Castle. In 1803 he was weighing gold dust there with two Africans, when he accused one of them of cheating, and in the row which ensued the town broke into uproar so that all the Europeans took refuge in the castle until they were relieved by H.M.S. *Romney*. Four years later he was appointed Lieutenant-Governor in Accra.[8]

Francis Lucas Swanzy took service as a writer at Dixcove in 1801 and became the factor there before the end of the year. He was the factor at Cape Coast in 1802. Then for some years he was at Fort

[8] op. cit., p. 27, fn. 3; also op. cit., p. 29, fn. 4, pp. 91–2.

William, Annamaboe, with four other Europeans and twenty-four soldiers. During this period, the Fanti states of the Gold Coast were attacked and invaded by an army from Ashanti, a powerful kingdom situated inland, to the north of the Fanti country. The English company helped the Fanti people, and in retaliation an Ashanti army appeared at Annamaboe and laid Fort William under siege.

Reinforcements were hurried in from Cape Coast by sea, but Governor George Torrane thought it wise to secure peace by giving the Asantehene what he demanded, namely two refugee chiefs and a share of 2,000 Fanti refugees. John Swanzy was at Accra, sick in bed, when he heard this news, and it horrified him. He was a member of the council at Cape Coast, and he rose from his sick bed, proceeded thither by canoe, and expressed the strongest criticism of the governor's action. He died almost immediately after. Francis Lucas died in 1823.[9]

Meanwhile, James' business in London had not been doing well and he returned to the Coast in 1817. Before leaving England, he had given evidence at a parliamentary enquiry in 1816. Parliament was concerned as to what ought to be done with the settlements on the coast of Africa, now that the abolition of the slave trade had removed the prime reason for their existence, and the threat from Ashanti raised new problems in connection with their defence. James Swanzy, however, expressed a favourable opinion about the Ashanti, saying in his evidence, 'It is a singular thing that these people, the Ashantee, who had never seen a white man, nor the sea, were the most civil and well-bred people that I have seen in Africa'. Of the Asantehene he added, 'Of all the native sovereigns of Africa that I have either read or heard of, he is the man most likely to act with good faith'. Following this enquiry, Parliament passed an Act which abolished the Company of Merchants and transferred its settlements to the crown, to be placed under the government of Sierra Leone.

James died in 1823. He had two sons by a first marriage, and two by a second marriage which he contracted about the time of his return to the Gold Coast. The eldest, John, was a lieutenant in the African Colonial Corps, which was set up about 1823, and he was killed near Cape Coast in 1824 fighting the Ashanti, those people of whom his father had spoken so highly. This was the war in which the governor, Sir Charles McCarthy, lost his head. It was taken to Kumasi and kept there as a trophy. The war dragged on, and the

[9] Swanzy, op. cit., p. 92.

British government decided to abandon its possessions on the Gold Coast. However, the merchants successfully protested, and the forts were handed over to a committee of three merchants in London nominated by the government. The three were Barnes, Brown, and Forster. They made an outstanding contribution to Africa by selecting Captain George Maclean to be the president of the government of the settlements.

The second brother, another James, was a member of the council of merchants in Cape Coast which was set up to run the Gold Coast settlements following the withdrawal of the colonial government in 1828. With some intervals he continued to be a member of the council until his death in 1842. He was therefore closely associated with president George Maclean. For long periods the council consisted simply of Maclean and James Swanzy. The settlements had fallen on evil days, for the routes to the interior were closed by the Ashanti, the number of traders was less than half what it had been in 1807, and the grants from the British government had been reduced to £4,000.

This James Swanzy married a wife, Elizabeth, who was described as a creole. She was evidently a lady who was prepared to take part in public affairs, because with some other ladies she signed a petition to the Colonial Office in 1841; at any rate, she put her mark upon it. The Colonial Office in London wished to suppress the institution of domestic slavery in the settlements of the Gold Coast, but Elizabeth was in favour of keeping domestic slaves, together with her co-petitioners Fanny Smith, Mary Jackson, Mary Hutton, Sarah Cross, Catherine Bannerman, and Helen Coliver.[10] This Mary Jackson was the wife of a merchant named Jackson, who had been appointed governor by the committee of merchants in 1829. He occupied that position for the short period before Maclean took over. Mary Jackson was buried inside a building in Jackson Street, Cape Coast. This building subsequently belonged to the firm of Swanzy. It has an impressive colonnade in yellow stone, and within it the grave of Mary Jackson, described as wife of the governor, may still be seen.

Maclean succeeded in making peace with Ashanti, and to hold the boundary up to the Ashanti border he established military posts. This was a new policy for the British, who hitherto had remained in their castles by the sea. Maclean devoted a great deal of time to work as a magistrate, and he encouraged the governors in the other

10 Swanzy, op. cit., pp. 93–5.

forts to try cases for at least two hours a day. Two schools were started at Cape Coast, and one each at Accra, Annamaboe, and Dixcove, with the help of missionaries. With peace and good administration trade revived, the figures for imports and exports in 1840 being more than three times as high as they had been in 1830.

James Swanzy had close trading connections with the London firm of Forster & Smith. At the time of Clarkson's fight against the slave trade, T. F. Forster and B. M. Forster, both of London, had been members of the Anti-Slavery Committee, and William Smith M.P. had been a supporter of Wilberforce. In the 1830s, the head of the firm was Mathew Forster, M.P. for Berwick. Forster and Smith provided money to enable James Swanzy to make an attempt at growing cotton and coffee in the Gold Coast.[11]

The Admiralty expedition to the Niger of 1841, to which reference has been made in the previous chapter, called at Cape Coast on its outward voyage. The chronicle of the expedition tells that 'one of the spots near Cape Coast well worth a visit is the model garden and plantation under the superintendence of Mr. Schwansey (sic), an English merchant who has been endeavouring for some years to introduce a better system of culture'. Since the expedition's instructions laid upon it the duty of establishing a model farm at the confluence of the Niger and Benue rivers, they were interested in such a venture near Cape Coast. The chronicle continues, 'It is called Napoleon, and is about four or five miles from the town. The road thither is somewhat tortuous and bad, but the scenery is fine. Like everything else connected with Cape Coast, it suffered much during the Ashanti wars, and no one but an enterprising and zealous man would have made an attempt to support it. Almost every species of tropical fruit and vegetable grows well.'[12] The plantation employed pawn labour, which meant that when a man wanted a wife or other luxury he pawned himself for ten dollars, or some such sum, and worked till he paid it back. The government stepped in and stopped this, as it was considered to be too near to slave labour, and as Swanzy could not get workers on other terms,[13] the plantation was handed over to the Methodist missionaries;[14] but they could not get labour, any more than Swanzy, so the plantation was abandoned.

[11] ibid., p. 97.
[12] Allen, W., *Expedition to the Niger* (London: Bentley, 1848) vol. I p. 143.
[13] *Journal Society of Arts*, 6 March 1874, no. 1111 vol. XXII.
[14] Duncan, John, *Travels in Western Africa in 1845 & 1846* (London: Bentley, 1848) p. 67.

The wage offered was evidently not enough to attract a supply of labour. It appears that elsewhere in the Gold Coast at that period carpenters and bricklayers received a shilling for an eight-hour day, and canoemen, blacksmiths, carriers, and palanquin bearers received two shillings.[15] Such wages of course appear low by modern standards, but in the 1830s and 1840s they were on the high side compared with wages in England, where one shilling a day was more usual than two.[16]

It was in the house of Mathew Forster that Maclean, while he was on leave in 1836, met the poetess Letitia Landon, whose poetry had enjoyed 'an enthusiastic reception from the public'.[17] Letitia had written:

> Do anything but love,
> Or if thou lovest, and art a woman—hide thy love
> From him whom thou dost worship:
> Never let him know how dear he is;
> Flit like a bird before him,
> Lead him from tree to tree,
> From flower to flower—but be not won.

However, she did not follow her own counsel, but was won by George Maclean. In 1838 they were married and she went with him to Cape Coast Castle; but she only survived there two months, and died suddenly of heart disease.[18] James Swanzy, in his capacity as Justice of the Peace, conducted the inquest.

A visitor to Cape Coast Castle in 1862 read an inscription in Latin which commemorated Letitia Maclean, and he added, 'there was a sister tablet a few yards off, placed, I believe in honour of Mr. Swanzy, here a well-known colonial name. It was shivered by the shock of the huge mortar fired in front of it.'[19]

The council at Cape Coast was elected by the qualified resident merchants, and in 1835 James Swanzy was the successful candidate, mustering nine votes against seven for his rival, Barr. Barr was hostile towards Maclean and the election was bitterly contested. Following Swanzy's success his opponents alleged that some of his

---

[15] Swanzy, op. cit., p. 97.

[16] Hammond, J. L. and Barbara, *The Village Labourer* (London: Longmans, 1911) pp. 183, 259; and Bear, E. E. in Traill and Mann, *Social England* (London: Cassell, 1904) vol. VI p. 471.

[17] Allen, Marcus, *The Gold Coast* (London: Hodder and Stoughton, 1874) pp. 170–4.

[18] Gordon, C. A., *Life on the Gold Coast* (London: Baillière, Tindall and Cox, 1874) p. 56.

[19] Burton, R. F., *Wanderings in Africa* (London: Longmans, 1863) vol. II, p. 80.

supporters had secured their voting qualifications in an irregular manner. 'Mr. Swanzy . . . sells to Mr. Arkhurst five pieces of romals on the 13th July, which Mr. Arkhurst instantly sells to the secretary (Brodie Cruickshank) for a profit of 10/- to qualify him as a merchant on the 14th . . . Mr. Topp, the proposer of Mr. Arkhurst to buy for him from Captain Freebody a keg of tripe.'

James Swanzy died in 1842.

Francis and Andrew, the 'F, and A' of the firm of F. & A. Swanzy, were the children of the original James Swanzy by a second marriage. Francis was born in 1816, and at the age of eighteen he was the Commandant at Dixcove.

What a place for young Swanzy at the age of eighteen! The castle had undergone more sieges than any other on the African Coast. Its story is worth telling to give an idea of the tradition which came down to the Swanzys from the past. It stands on a bluff above the ocean, with a smooth beach below and the anchorage a mile-and-a-half at sea. Inland, a good path came down from the gold mines, only two or three days' walking. The town had in earlier times been divided between two states, each with its chief. The total population of the two states was estimated in 1737 at 2,000. They were not specially friendly to each other, and both were hostile towards the numerous Ahanta tribe by which they were surrounded. It was in 1684 that one of these states leased the site to the English, seeing the need for a European ally not only against their African neighbours, but also against the Dutch and the Brandenburgers, who were fighting each other for the control of that part of the coast, each using tribal allies. The Dutch fort was only three miles away at Butre, and the Brandenburgers tried to set up in Dixcove itself. In 1687 the Ahantas, allies of the Dutch, destroyed the Brandenburger fort at Takoradi. It was in a stormy political climate, therefore, that the Royal African Company of London began building the fort at Dixcove in 1692. It was not yet finished when the Ahantas attacked in 1696; but it withstood their assaults for four months, till they drew off to meet a threat from another quarter.[20]

At Dixcove timber and lime were available, and it was the only source open to the English of these commodities, both essential for the maintenance of the other castles: so a work-force of slaves was provided to develop these resources. As the decades went by they had to go further and further for suitable trees. To meet this situation, young slaves were brought in from other castles when a cutting

[20] Lawrence, A. W., op. cit., p. 292 ff.

party was required. Evidently the free men of Dixcove did not reckon to do that kind of work. The Brandenburgers interfered with the timber-cutting. They had a remarkable ally in an African chief named John Konny, and he attacked Dixcove fort in 1712. It may have been all the more disconcerting to the garrison, since Brandenburg and Britain were at that time allies in Europe in war against the French. During this action, a tower of the fort blew up, killing the commander and numerous Africans, both freemen and slaves. Nevertheless, John Konny was beaten off. The German interest did not long survive this setback. In 1716 the King of Prussia (as the Elector of Brandenburg had become) sold his African interests to the Dutch.

A survey of all the British forts was 'taken in ye years 1726 and 1727 by William Smith, Surveyor to the Royal African Company of England'.[21] The fort was reconstructed in 1750, and then had twenty-five cannon. In that same year it was attacked by the Ahantas, allies of the Dutch. Governor Roberts from Cape Coast gallantly hastened in a canoe to command the defence, but unfortunately he left behind the muskets which he had intended to bring! In repelling the first attack of the Ahantas the defenders nearly exhausted their ammunition, but a French ship called the *Providence Queen* (what a Providence!) entered the roads that day and supplied some warlike stores. The siege continued for nearly a year. Reinforcements of men and materials were put in by the Navy, rum was issued to the defenders after a good day's fighting, and the wounded were evacuated by sea to Cape Coast.

The domestic slaves were armed with muskets like the Europeans and the free men of Dixcove, and fought with the rest. It is an interesting indication of the standing of domestic slaves in those communities. As the war came to an end, the Committee of Merchants Trading to Africa took over the fort from the bankrupt Royal African Company, now in liquidation.

War broke out between Britain and the Netherlands in 1780 and the Dutch armed the free natives of Ahanta, who again attacked the fort at Dixcove.

In 1787 presents were given to the Dixcove chiefs in addition to their small stipends, because they did so much work in hauling timber through bad paths; so it appears that by this time the free Africans of Dixcove had been persuaded to undertake this work.

Although Holland was incorporated in the Napoleonic empire,

---

[21] Original in possession of the United Africa Company.

and was therefore at war with Britain in the early part of the nine-teenth century, the British and the Dutch on the Gold Coast agreed that they would not fight, so that there were no attacks on the fort during that period.

In 1816 Dixcove received American visitors, who were much impressed by an albino giant who guarded the gate of the fort, and fascinated by a pet gazelle.[22] It sounds like a scene from a Walt Disney film, complete with Bambi. By that time James and John Swanzy had served their terms as Governor of Dixcove: and now, in 1834, James's son Francis took over as commandant at the age of 18. He commanded a dozen soldiers. To the west across the Ancobra River there ruled a chief called Kweku Akka, who had set himself up in the old English fort at Apollonia, which had been abandoned. He terrorized the neighbourhood, and he executed a number of traders from Wassaw by tying them to stakes on the beach and leaving them to die of exposure. Maclean then decided to deal with him. With 150 men he crossed the river. Francis Swanzy, who at the age of 19 had been in his post for a year, did well in the fight and was presented with a sword by President Maclean. Four years later Swanzy was elected a member of the council. In 1842, there was an enquiry in London into the conduct of Maclean's government, and Francis Swanzy was the principal witness for Maclean. He spoke with great affection of the Dixcove country, 'dotted with pretty villages here and there', and he said that the climate was 'most beautiful'. He spoke Fanti fluently. He held a magistrate's court two hours every morning, had services on Sundays in the fort, and encouraged an American missionary to start a school. Dixcove, he said, consisted of seven divisions, of which one bore the name Swanzy Quacoe. The headland on the south of Dixcove Bay was called Swanzy Point, and six miles to the north was a hill 390 feet above high water, known as Mount Swanzy.[23]

The Committee of Inquiry exonerated Maclean from the accusations which had been brought against him, which were indeed preposterous ones. During the proceedings, Francis Swanzy was asked by Matthew Forster, who was on the committee, 'Do you think it desirable that our possessions on the Gold Coast should be transferred to the Crown?' He replied, 'I think it is'. And that in fact was the recommendation of the committee and the decision of

---

[22] Carnes, J. A., *Voyage from Boston to the West Coast of Africa* (London: Sampson Low, 1853) pp. 180–213.
[23] Admiralty, *African Pilot* (London, 1899) p. 396.

the government. One may wonder whether, in giving that reply, Francis Swanzy appreciated the implications of such a change for him and his brothers. In future the government service and trading personnel were to be separate, and it would be necessary for the Swanzys to decide in which direction they would move. Yet the choice was not one which had to be made immediately, for Francis Swanzy returned to Dixcove and in 1844 he negotiated the famous Bond with the local chiefs. One of the witnesses was his half-brother's son, James Swanzy.

This Bond of 1844 was a treaty by which the new British government authority (on taking over the functions of government from the committee of merchants) regulated its relationship with nine chiefs of African states in the neighbourhood of Cape Coast. The Bond was concluded in March 1844, but not until August of that year did Francis and James Swanzy secure the signatures of the chiefs of Dixcove to the document. The principal negotiator on the British side was none other than George Maclean, now serving as 'Justice of the Peace and Assessor' under the new government.

The committee of the House of Commons (to which reference has been made above) had been primarily concerned with the governance of the forts and settlements, which were under British sovereignty by virtue of purchase or conquest. But that was not the position in regard to the Fanti states, with which Maclean had established such cordial relationships. The committee recommended that the relationship of those states to the crown should not be 'the allegiance of subjects to which we have no right to pretend, and which it would entail an inconvenient responsibility to possess, but the deference of weaker powers to a stronger and more enlightened neighbour, whose protection and counsel they seek and to whom they are bound by certain definite obligations'. In the Bond the chiefs acknowledged 'the power and jurisdiction of the Crown', and they did not go so far as to cede sovereignty; indeed, by defining the extent of British jurisdiction the Bond gave the states ground for claiming that they were not in all matters subject to the government at Cape Coast.[24]

However, whatever may have been the meaning of the treaty or the intentions of those who negotiated it, the Cape Coast authorities did in fact from that time forth act as a sovereign government over the Fanti states. The British on their side, when challenged (as from

[24] Hailey, *Native Administration in the British African Territories* (London: H.M.S.O., 1951) part III p. 196.

time to time they were)[25] would claim that their legal powers rested upon Orders made under the Foreign Jurisdiction Act, and that the terms of the Bond were irrelevant. Be that as it may, it seemed, as time passed, that the chiefs had ceded their sovereign powers; and therein perhaps lies the importance of this transaction, for 'this treaty was the forerunner of many similar agreements'.[26] When the scramble for Africa took place, forty years later, representatives of the European colonial powers busied themselves in securing the assent of African chiefs to documents described as treaties, by virtue of which sovereignty was claimed by the colonial power. It will be necessary to describe in later chapters how two British companies, trading in Duala, were disconcerted when the Germans unexpectedly signed treaties of this character with the local chiefs, and also how the Royal Niger Company made use of this method in extending its authority.

Francis was offered a judicial post, but he refused it and returned to London. However, London was a disappointment, and in 1846 he applied for any job vacant under the government, but the Secretary of State for the Colonies, who at that time was Gladstone, did not find it possible to meet his wishes. In 1847 Francis was in Cape Coast where he married Catherine, daughter of Joseph Dawson, who had been Governor in Cape Coast. Her mother must have been a distinguished African lady because Catherine was chieftainess of Anona, in which capacity she bore the name of Efua Ketsi. She owned land in Cape Coast, and Francis set up the firm of F. & A. Swanzy and built an office on his wife's land.

In 1847 Francis received in Dixcove a cargo in *Emily*, a brig of 189 tons belonging to Forster.[27] He could not forget his Dixcove days. He still felt that the independent chief of Ahanta ought to be brought under the authority of Cape Coast, and he was a leading advocate of military action with this end in view. In 1848 the governor decided to move, and Francis accompanied the expedition. According to oral tradition he joined the fourth Asafo company of Cape Coast, who then adopted the war cry '*Swanzy abontua*', which being translated means 'Swanzy armed'. British sources describe him as leading a party of volunteers from Cape Coast. He and his men carried out far more operations than any other unit of

---

[25] Gold Coast Aborigines' Rights Protection Society, *Petition* (London: Matthews Drew, 1934) pp. 54 and 70.
[26] ibid., p. 71
[27] Gordon, op. cit., p. 2.

the force, and it was they who in the end brought in the chief as a prisoner. He had been given up by some of his own people in return for a substantial payment.[28] It appears that the expedition was equipped by the firm of Forster and Smith.

In 1849 Francis was in London, and together with Henry Smith he sent a memorial to the Colonial Office recommending that an advisory council should be set up to assist the Governor in Cape Coast. The following year he was again in London and with Forster (of Forster & Smith) and a man named Sewell he met the Secretary of State for the Colonies, Earl Grey. The purpose of the deputation was to seek support for the cultivation of cotton in the Gold Coast. They had been in correspondence with the president of the Commercial Association at Manchester, the owner of a mill where some samples of raw cotton from James Swanzy's plantation had been woven into cloth.

The subscribers were headed by Forster and included not only Swanzy but also Messrs. R. & W. King. Their Articles of Association included the following paragraph:

> The Natives are at first reluctant to take up any new branch of industry, until it is proved to them that they will profit by it. Many persons will recollect that Ground Nuts, now so largely imported into this country and into France, from the Coast of Africa, were comparatively unknown 20 years ago, and that the quantity of Palm Oil manufactured and exported from the coast of Africa, and the number of localities where it is procured have increased very much during the last 20 years. A similar result may be obtained in Cotton which does not require more cultivation than the Ground Nuts, or more labour than the manufacture of Palm Oil.[29]

Francis offered to get samples of wild cotton from Africa. A cotton expert from America was engaged, and a plantation of 25,000 cotton plants was made; but it was a failure.[30] During the talks Lord Grey suggested that a Chamber of Commerce should be created in the Gold Coast. Francis responded to this suggestion, and became the first President of the Chamber in 1851.

In the same year an executive council was set up and Francis

[28] ibid., p. 68: *see also* Newbury, C. W., *British Policy towards West Africa Select Documents 1786–1874* (Oxford: Clarendon Press, 1965) p. 299.
[29] Original in the possession of the United Africa Company.
[30] *Journal Society of Arts* as 13.

Swanzy was a nominated member of it. He proposed that the council should be elected, but that suggestion was not accepted. This same year he lost his life at sea in the schooner *Viper*: a full life, for he was only 37.

The 'A' of F. and A. Swanzy was Andrew, born in 1818. Francis had handed over the government of Dixcove to him when he went to London in 1845. Andrew, like Francis, was a bonny fighter, and he made an incursion into Dutch territory to release a Dixcove man who had been put in prison. He was itching to have another go at Ahanta, and the Acting Governor hurried to Dixcove with some troops to restrain him. He was moved to Annamaboe with the promise of a salary of £150, to be paid when arrangements had been completed to collect customs duties on certain imports. These arrangements depended on the consent of the Dutch, and the Dutch did not consent, so Andrew had no pay. Not unreasonably, he suggested that he might be allowed to trade within the fort: but times had changed, and the government would not have private trading in official premises.

From 1850 to 1853 Andrew was in London. It appears from his correspondence with his brother, that the main reason why he settled in London was his marriage to Miss Emma Jones: and 'Mrs. Jones said it was out of the question your leaving Emma'.[31] For Andrew it was also a chance to start trading in a new way. He took advantage of two elements which were new. Mission schools were beginning to provide literate Africans who could be employed as factors, and with their assistance Francis and Andrew set up establishments 'along the whole coast'. No longer were they obliged to depend upon the precarious health of European employees, or to limit activity to those places where the volume of business could support the cost of a European. Secondly, steamships were replacing sailing vessels.

In 1851 mail steamers from England to the Cape of Good Hope began calling at Freetown. Macgregor Laird, encouraged by Forster, secured a contract to provide a mail service to West Africa with a government subsidy. In 1852 steamers began to leave for West Africa every month from Plymouth, and in 1858 the terminus was changed to Liverpool.[32] Forster, in supporting Laird's enterprise, was acting contrary to the interests of his firm. Forster and

[31] Francis Swanzy to Andrew Swanzy, 26 December 1849, United Africa Company records.

[32] Fyfe, Christopher, *History of Sierra Leone* (Oxford: Clarendon Press, 1962) p. 266.

Smith had handled most of the imports to the Gold Coast and most of the exports from that country for more than half a century, acting as financiers, shipowners, suppliers, and customers, for independent traders in Africa. Faster communications now made it easier to operate a business with two ends, one in Britain and the other in Africa. Swanzy now gained the ascendancy and by 1863 was handling nearly all the trade.

After Francis Swanzy's death in 1851, Andrew paid a visit to the coast in 1853. No doubt he travelled in one of the new steamers. It must have made a difference to the possibility of visiting Africa even more dramatic than that which occurred when the air routes became available, ninety years later. During this visit Andrew Swanzy appointed William Cleaver as his principal agent. Swanzy was asked by the Governor to take command of an army which had been raised to face a new threat from Ashanti; but his fighting days were over (did he think what Mrs. Jones might say?) and he returned to London where he ran the firm with great success until his death in 1880.[33]

Meanwhile Swanzy and Forster had become involved in an unsavoury affair. There was in the eastern part of the Gold Coast, some thirty miles from the sea, a tribe called Krobo, and in 1857 they provided about half the total quantity of palm oil which was exported from the country. The government had not established control of their country, and in 1858 the attitude of the Krobo chiefs was unacceptable to the Cape Coast authorities, so a military expedition was sent against them. The government then charged the Krobos with the cost of the expedition, or to put the matter in another way, it imposed a fine. The only way in which the government could collect the fine was in accepting or seizing palm oil. Almost inevitably they turned to Swanzy, and in these arrangements F. & A. Swanzy were represented by an African named Hutchison. Swanzy undertook to pay to the government the amount of the fine in cash, and to recover it in oil from the Krobos. He proposed to credit the producers with ten pence a gallon. The current price of palm oil in the Gold Coast was a shilling a gallon, so it looked as though Swanzy was on to a good thing, and this provoked a vigorous protest from Forster and Smith; so Swanzy arranged to cut them in. But little joy came to either of the firms. The Krobos hated the fine, but being credited ten pence for oil that was worth a shilling was the last straw. They simply refused to deliver oil.

[33] Swanzy, op. cit., p. 112.

The Colonial Office does not appear to have become aware of all this until 1861, when a civil servant (in a minute on the file) described the government's action as handing over 'a luckless tribe of Africans to the tender mercies of irresponsible merchants'. The scarcity of oil, arising from the hold-up by the Krobos, caused the local price to rise to 1s. 3d. per gallon. The government now sent a second military expedition, which was to enforce the delivery of oil. But the Krobos continued their defiance and found an alternative outlet for their oil by sending it across the Volta to ports in independent Ewe country. However, they agreed to make certain payments in cowrie shells, and these, added to the value of oil seized by the troops, amounted to about half the sum required. At last in 1866 the British Treasury settled the firm's claims against the government.[34]

The decade 1863 to 1873 was a depressed period in the Gold Coast trade. Andrew Swanzy, with great knowledge of the country, kept going, but most other trading houses gave up.

The British and Dutch settlements were all mixed up together. Dutch Sekondi and British Sekondi were parts of the same town. As already mentioned, the Dutch fort Butre was only three miles from Dixcove. In 1867 the two governments sorted out their holdings into more manageable blocks by an exchange of territory. Dixcove became Dutch. But the Dixcove men were not willing subjects of Holland, and in 1869 the Dutch district officer turned the guns of Dixcove fort on Swanzy's store and allowed the Butre people to sack it.[35] Andrew was furious and wrote to the Governor-in-Chief at Freetown. The Governor, in reply, addressed Swanzy as 'you who have really done the lion's share in introducing civilisation at Dixcove'.[36] The Swanzy store at Sekondi was looted, but the gang was not caught.

Swanzy and Cleaver were angry with the government for failing to give them protection. They were hostile to certain taxes which had recently been imposed on ships visiting the ports of the Gold Coast, and in this they made common cause with the African merchants. Opposition to taxation involved criticism of government expenditure. But the hostility between the government and the

[34] Wolfson, Freda, 'A Price Agreement on the Gold Coast—the Krobo Oil Boycott 1858–1866' in *Economic History Review*, 1953, second series vol. VI no. 1 p. 68.

[35] Dyer, Hugh, *West Coast of Africa* (London: Griffin, 1876) p. 79; Horton, Africanus B., *Letters on the Political Condition of the Gold Coast*, ed. Ayandele, E. A. (London: Cass, 1970) pp. 94, 113, 171

[36] Kennedy to Swanzy, 27 September 1870, United Africa Company Records.

house of Swanzy extended further than that; while the government's relations with Ashanti were deteriorating, Swanzy was on good terms with the Asantehene, and supplied him with muskets and gunpowder. Most of this was landed at Half Assini, where Swanzy had a fleet of launches for the purpose. Possibly Swanzy had not fully appreciated the implications of his actions. In 1872 the Dutch sold their settlements to the British, and then for the first time the Ashanti kingdom faced a single power to the south. The Ashantis complained that the British did not provide them with the special facilities which they had enjoyed with the Dutch at Elmina. As this juncture Burton, the well-known consul and traveller mentioned in Chapter 2, proposed to Swanzy to organize a mission to Ashanti, and even after war had broken out he maintained that, with due prudence, and with some expenditure on presents, 'this ugly affair might have been settled'.[37]

In 1873 the Ashantis advanced across the River Prah and the British government decided to send an expedition against them under Sir Garnet Wolseley. Andrew Swanzy was the main source of information available to the War Office, and he did all he could to help the military expedition. This brought him into personal contact with Sir Garnet, and that eminent soldier's A.D.C. wrote back from Madeira, on the outward voyage.

Dear Mr. Swanzy,
You were good enough to express your willingness to help us in any way by sending out things to us in Cape Coast. Sir Garnet and the Head Quarter Staff are anxious if possible to live on good English mutton and I therefore write to you to ask if you could make some arrangement by which a sheep in prime condition would be put on board each steamer leaving Liverpool. We should then obtain a weekly supply of fresh mutton, which would be an immense thing. We thought you might possibly be able to arrange this for us without much trouble, and that being done through you, there would be less chance of the animal being killed and devoured before reaching us.[38]

The London daily paper *Pall Mall Gazette* attacked the firm for supplying arms to the enemy, and its criticism produced a letter to Andrew from the Secretary of State in which he said, 'So far as I can

[37] Burton, R. F., *Ocean Highways*, February 1874, no. 11 vol. I p. 452, cit. in *Journal Society of Arts* as 13.
[38] Charteris to Swanzy, 19 September 1873, United Africa Company records.

form an opinion from what I know about it, I believe that there are no grounds for the charge against you.'[39]

Swanzy spoke in his own defence at a meeting of the Society of Arts. He said that the French did a large trade in arms to Ashanti through the ports of Assini and Grand Bassam, where he was the only English merchant; if he had not participated in the trade it would merely have meant that the French would have done more.[40] He was speaking of the period before the outbreak of war between France and Prussia in 1870, for when that occurred the French found it prudent to lease their trading premises to Swanzy.[41] After the war was over, the French returned to the Ivory Coast and the Colonial Office then got in touch with Swanzy to establish the facts about the rents which he had paid to the French during their period of absence.[42]

Swanzy had extended not only to the west of the British settlements but also to the east, having factories at Keta, Porto Seguro, Aghwey, Little Popo, Grand Popo, and Whydah. Each of these was politically independent. The chiefs gave protection to Swanzy, and when in 1873 his premises at Keta burned down the chief recovered the safe which contained £200. There was however an embarrassing feature in trading on this part of the coast, because any ships which were wrecked were plundered, even to the extent of the sailors being stripped of their clothing—which happened when Swanzy's *Bentinck* went ashore at Grand Popo in 1872.[43] The people, having plundered the wreck, asked for a 'dash' for saving the crew. 'Swanzy,' wrote a naval officer, 'was too wise to ask for a man-of-war to punish the natives in the usual manner'. He could see that no bombardment would recover his loss, and it would be bad for trade.[44]

Swanzy had a supervising agent for the posts along this part of the coast, and his responsibilities extended as far east as Whydah, where in 1876 he became involved in an incident which led to naval action taking the form, not of bombardment, but of blockade. Whydah was different from the other places in that it belonged to the King of Dahomey whose dominions were extensive and whose

---

[39] Lord Grey to Swanzy, 2 April 1874, United Africa Company records.
[40] *Journal Society of Arts*, 12 February 1875, no. 1160 vol. XXIII.
[41] *Journal Society of Arts*, 6 March 1874, no. 1111 vol. XXII.
[42] Holland to Swanzy, 6 and 7 October 1873, United Africa Company Records.
[43] *Journal Society of Arts*, 17 April 1874, no. 1117 vol. XXII.
[44] Dyer, op. cit., p. 54.

capital, Abomey, was a considerable distance from the sea. The comey at Whydah was levied on visiting ships on a scale related to the number of masts of the vessel. The main customer of European traders was the royal house, and its members were in the habit of insisting that goods should be handed over to them, and then omitting to pay what they owed. One of the principal sufferers from this royal misbehaviour was an independent merchant named Dos Santos. In 1872 he gave up the unequal struggle and took service with F. and A. Swanzy as their agent. With Swanzy's backing he refused to deliver some cloth, ordered by a prince of the royal house, until outstanding debts were paid. For this defiance, Dos Santos was fined and his goods were seized, so Swanzy's agent Turnbull went to his rescue, and was arrested. At this point the Commodore who commanded the naval squadron in those waters ordered both traders to be set at liberty, and they were. He then deputed certain officers to investigate the situation, and they 'inflicted a fine' on the King of Dahomey of 500 puncheons of palm oil, worth about £6,000. The Commodore then threatened to blockade the Dahomey coast unless 'the fine' was paid. At this stage the affair was reported to London, where the Foreign Office took an unfavourable view of the Commodore's action. Pointing out that no British subject had been in danger of his life, they said that the Commodore would have done better to refer home. They were not prepared to adopt a suggestion, submitted by the Commodore, that a force should be sent to attack Dahomey by land. As for the blockade, the Foreign Office did not want to make the Royal Navy lose face, so they agreed that the Commodore might impose the blockade, but only on the condition that he was careful not to commit himself to continue the blockade until the fine was paid.[45] The Commodore had, however, instituted the blockade. There is no evidence that the King of Dahomey minded very much, but two French trading firms, Régis and Fabre, found it very irksome. Negotiations took place and they resulted in the signature of a treaty by the Dahomans, guaranteeing freedom of trade to the British, and in the payment of 200 puncheons towards the fine by the two French trading firms. The rest of the fine remained unpaid.[46]

By this time Andrew Swanzy was known for his interest in the

[45] Newbury, C. W., *British Policy towards West Africa Select Documents 1875–1914* (Oxford: Clarendon Press, 1971) p. 94.
[46] Newbury, C. W., *The Western Slave Coast and its Rulers* (Oxford: Clarendon Press, 1961) pp. 103–4.

insects of Africa and in prehistoric stone artifacts. He was also the patron of Winwood Reade, author of *The Martyrdom of Man*, a book which stirred the imagination of two generations and ran through twenty-six editions. Reade was born in 1838 and was the nephew of Charles Reade, author of *The Cloister and the Hearth*. He was educated at Henley Grammar School and Oxford.

In 1859 Charles Darwin published his *Origin of Species* and this aroused great public interest in gorillas, the 'missing link'. This inspired Reade to undertake a journey to Gabon to find out whether gorillas really existed. His experiences are described in *Savage Africa*, 1863. He found his gorillas. On returning to England he entered Saint Mary's Hospital as a medical student. In 1866 he was in charge of a cholera hospital at Southampton. He was invited to meet Andrew Swanzy by the Secretary of the Royal Geographical Society. He was apprehensive about Swanzy's attitude, because Reade was a Conservative and Swanzy was a Liberal. He stood as Liberal candidate for West Kent in 1874. However, despite their political differences the friendship ripened.

Swanzy sent Reade out to Cleaver in 1868, in the hope that he might open up new routes for trade between the Coast and the inland states of Ashanti and Dahomey, and at the same time engage in scientific work. Reade seems to have found Swanzy's enthusiasm for insects and stones something of a nuisance. 'With respect to collections,' he wrote on one occasion, 'I have done nothing or next to nothing . . . I was obliged to throw away everything at the last moment owing to the running off of two men . . . This time I shall take at all events a glass jar for beetles.' Nevertheless, he sent back boxes of specimens to Swanzy who handed them over to the British Museum.

Reade's relations with Cleaver, the Swanzy agent in Cape Coast, were not cordial. Cleaver may have written him off after his failure to get through from Half Assini to Ashanti in 1868, which was what he had been sent out to do. Instead of persisting, Reade went to Cape Coast where he made contact with the Governor-in-Chief, Sir Arthur Kennedy. As explained above, Kennedy may have had good reasons for turning a Swanzy agent away from Ashanti, and Reade may have felt disinclined to get mixed up with gun-running. Reade accepted a suggestion from Kennedy that he should transfer his activities to Sierra Leone, and Andrew Swanzy, to his surprise, learned that he was financing an expedition from Sherbro to the source of the Niger.[47] 'The success or failure of my present journey,'

[47] See Map p. 94.

wrote Reade to Swanzy, 'will not I feel sure influence you respecting money matters.'

Reade walked inland through Sierra Leone and reached the Niger near Farabana, but the country between that point and the source of the river was torn by war between tribes who were raiding for slaves: so Reade went down-river and then returned to Freetown and Cape Coast. Cleaver now tried to set him off on a trade mission to Dahomey, a task which Reade was not keen to undertake. He got as far as Odoomarie, near where the great dam now holds up the Volta, but turned back.

Reade published *African Sketch Book* in 1873, describing his journeys: it printed a letter to Reade from Swanzy, who wrote, 'I envy you, for I am not a man who can pursue the common track. I like striking out a course for myself; and if you ask for proof I have none, except perhaps the deep interest I take in you. I shall never pretend to any part of your merit; all I claim is the merit of starting you on your course. May that course lead you to a high place in the list of England's worthies.'[48]

Also in 1873, Reade published his *Martyrdom of Man*. The idea began as a history of Africa, but Reade decided that the history of Africa could only be presented as part of the history of the world. Africa, he said, had not existed in isolation. He was much impressed by the influence of the rest of the world on Africa, and of Africa on the rest of the world. It is fascinating to find this view propounded in 1873, a view which might appropriately form the theme of a conference of African historians in the 1970s. Reade went to Africa as *The Times* correspondent with Sir Garnet Wolseley's expedition. His book, *The Ashantee Campaign* cannot fail to fascinate anyone who is familiar with contemporary Ghana. His journeys in Africa had affected his health, and he died in 1875 at the age of 36.

Cleaver became a partner in the firm in 1870. He first went to Africa in 1859 in a brig which took sixty days at sea on the voyage. He left the Gold Coast in 1876 and joined Andrew Swanzy in London.[49] His successor in Africa was F. J. Crocker.

In 1873 Swanzys ceased to send their own sailing vessels from Britain to Africa. They made a public announcement attributing their decision to new charges which were being levied on ships by

[48] Shepperson, G., 'A West African Partnership' in *Progress*, no. 3, 1965.
[49] Rankin, p. 70.

the government; but no doubt the real reason was the competition of the steamships.[50]

Andrew Swanzy died in 1880, and here it is appropriate to interrupt the story of F. and A. Swanzy, for Andrew's death was indeed the end of a chapter. The Swanzys had always been personally involved with the Gold Coast, where they had lived and which they had loved; but Andrew on his death was succeeded by his son Francis, who never visited Africa.

---

[50] James Marshall to Swanzy, 29 July and 5 August 1873, United Africa Company records.

4

Forster and Smith and their Successors in Gambia

The English had had a fort in the estuary of the River Gambia, twenty miles from the sea, for a long time. It stood on a tiny island, and to this day the narrow beach which surrounds the ruined walls is littered with shards of ancient pottery, bearing designs familiar in eighteenth-century England. The English had been there as early as 1618[1] but on that occasion they did not maintain the position very long. In 1651 the island was bought from a local chief by some Baltic Germans, servants of a company founded by the Grand Duke of Courland, a country roughly coterminous with the present Soviet Republic of Latvia. They built a fort. A Dutch force captured this fort from the Courlanders, but in 1661 the English navy took it from the Dutch, and three years later the Grand Duke of Courland ceded his claims to the English by treaty.[2] It was named after the heir to the throne (afterwards James II) since when it has been known as Fort James or James Island.[3] The attempt to create a crown colony in these parts has been referred to in chapter 1. Fort James was blown up by the French in 1778 (the very year in which Thomas King volunteered for service against the French in the *Lion*) and was never rebuilt. In the Napoleonic wars, Saint Louis and the Isle of Goree were captured from the French, and English merchants established themselves in those places. After the wars they were restored to France, and the English traders transferred their business to the Gambia River and created Bathurst, naming it after the colonial minister of the day.[4] Like Saint Louis and Goree whence its founders had come, it was laid out as a town for people to live in.

At Bathurst some old premises were demolished in 1948, which

[1] Fage, J. D., *History of West Africa* (Cambridge University Press, 1955) p. 69.

[2] Anderson, Edgar, *Tur plivoja kurzemes karogi* (There waved the flags of Courland) (Riga: Gramatu Draugs, 1970) text Latvian, summary in English.

[3] Lawrence, A. W., *Trade Castles and Forts of West Africa* (London: Cape, 1963) p. 251.

[4] Bathurst was officially renamed Banjul in 1973.

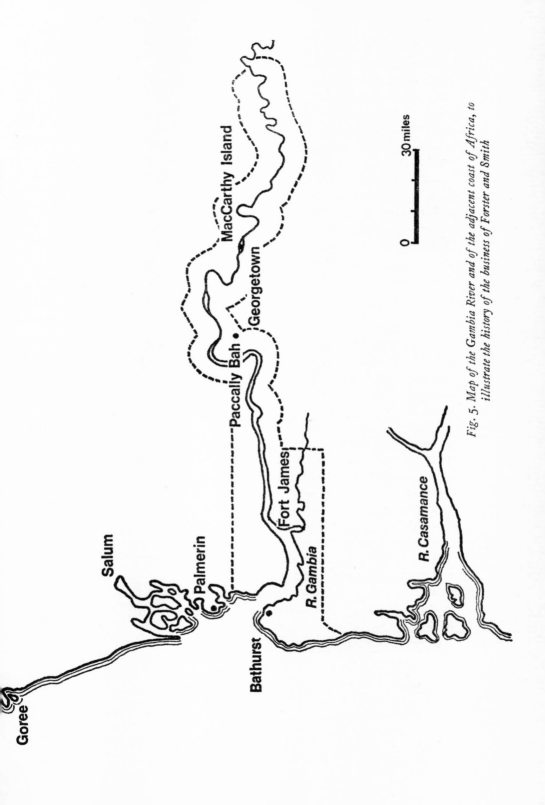

Fig. 5. Map of the Gambia River and of the adjacent coast of Africa, to illustrate the history of the business of Forster and Smith

had been the headquarters of the Bathurst Trading Company. In a pitched roof above the ceiling of the upper floor were found several tons of ancient paper. Much of this had been rendered illegible by time, mice, bats, and insects, but the papers which survived indicated that there was a continuous history from the time of the foundation of Bathurst, when the firm was connected with Forster and Smith. These names have already appeared in chapters 2 and 3. Forster and Smith financed the house of Swanzy, and provided London services for Swanzy in relation both to imports and exports during the period from 1817 to 1849. The Bathurst Trading Company's compound was, in 1948, referred to by the older citizens of Bathurst as Ker Forster, which in the Wollof language means Forster's yard.[5]

The firm Edward Forster and Sons, described as Russia Merchants, was active in the second half of the eighteenth century. The sons were T. F. Forster and B. M. Forster, both active members of the committee against the slave trade.[6] In this last activity they must have been acquainted with William Smith, Member of Parliament, also the son of a merchant shipowner of London.[7] When another Member of Parliament defended slavery on the grounds of its antiquity, Smith argued: 'Because a practice had existed, did it necessarily follow that it was just? By this argument every crime might be defended from the time of Cain!'[8] The business activities of the Forsters and Smiths must have been gravely embarrassed in 1806 when Napoleon imposed a blockade against British ships in all ports of the continent of Europe. In 1807 Russia agreed to co-operate in enforcing the blockade, and that winter underwriters ceased to quote for voyages between British ports and the Continent.[9] 'England relied on her ability to counter Napoleon's continental trade veto by opening fresh markets beyond the ocean.'[10] What more natural for the Forsters and the Smiths in such circumstances than to send their ships to West Africa? Their attention had been much engaged in that part of the world through their activities in the anti-slavery movement, and this year, 1807, was the very year in which an Act of Parliament made it illegal for British ships to engage in the slave trade. The abolitionists had hoped and believed

[5] Mallinson to Pedler, 18 August 1969.
[6] D.N.B.
[7] D.N.B.
[8] Fox, W., *History of Wesleyan Missions in West Africa* (London: Aylott, 1851) p. 65.
[9] Bryant, A., *Years of Victory* (London: Collins, 1944) p. 246.
[10] ibid., p. 232.

that the suppression of the slave trade would lead to a great increase of the legitimate trade, and to this trade the Forsters and the Smiths now turned their attention, in partnership. They started to trade in Goree.[11] They were not the only merchants with this idea. Indeed, so many British ships turned in that direction that the government provided convoys for merchant ships trading to Africa.[12]

When the move to Bathurst took place in 1816, a member of the Forster family, William, went to live there. He was not among those who had previously been at Goree[13] and it seems likely that he went to Africa after having been demobilized from service in the war which had ended in 1815. As early as 1818 Forster and Smith were in friendly rivalry with other British merchants 'in the elegant and convenient arrangement of their dwelling houses and stores, all of which are built with stone or brick, and roofed with slates or shingles'.[14] Forster and Smith acted on behalf of the merchants at Bathurst in representing their interests to the Colonial Office, transmitting petitions, memorials, and complaints. The issues which were important to the merchants were the need for a separate local government, proper arrangements for the defence of the settlement and the need for changes in customs tariffs and regulations to enable the British and African traders to compete more effectively with the French traders operating from Albreda. Forster and Smith's role as mercantile spokesmen was recognized, at least semiofficially, by the Colonial Office.

The accounts which survive from 1826 include a number of personal debits to William Forster, of which the following may serve as examples:

1826	16th February:	1 curry comb & 2 combs	£0.	3.	6.
	22nd May:	1 bottle gooseberries		2.	6.
	1st July:	9 loaves sugar @ 3. 9.	1.	13.	9.
	9th August:	1 halter		10.	0.
	10th October:	1 small paint brush		1.	3.
1827	24th September:	2 cross cut saw files @ 1. 3.		2.	6.
	18th October:	1 door lock		2.	6.

[11] Gray, J. M., *History of the Gambia* (Cambridge University Press, 1940) p. 309. For description of English settlements in Goree *see* Carnes, J. A., *Voyage from Boston to the West Coast of Africa* (London: Sampson Low, 1853) pp. 51–8.

[12] Dike, K. O., *Trade and politics in the Niger Delta* (Oxford: Clarendon Press, 1959) p. 108.

[13] P.R.O. CO 267/78 S.L. & African forts A to G 1826.

[14] Fox, op. cit., p. 262.

It is interesting to note that this was a horse-riding community. What a difference this must have made, compared with the Gold Coast and the Oil Rivers! (see plate 6)

For communications up the river they had a schooner *Regulator*, and she had a captain Demba whose wage was £1. 17. 6 a month. They maintained a pigeon post up the river. Pigeons were used to carry messages for a long time in the Gambia, for in 1914 a ship went aground up the river, and news of the progress of salvage operations was sent twice daily to Bathurst by pigeon.

In the early years the principal export was beeswax, and hides were a minor item. In 1823 the British occupied MacCarthy Island, 180 miles up the river, and built a fort on it, which was called Georgetown. The Wesleyan missionaries established there a settlement of West Indians. The traders came, seeking new products for commerce, and noted that groundnuts were being cultivated. The seed had been introduced by the Portuguese from Brazil many years before. The groundnut, *arachis hypogaea* (see plate 2), is also known as monkey-nut, peanut, and earthnut. It is, however, not really a nut but a legume. It comes from the pods of a small annual plant that grows to maturity in about four months. The yellow flowers of the plant change into small pods which turn downwards into the earth, where they swell and ripen. It likes between twenty-five and fifty inches of rain a year, concentrated in the months of the growing season. On the Gambia River, planting takes place from May to July, and harvesting from October to January. The oil content of the shelled nut is usually between forty-five per cent and fifty per cent. Groundnuts are used in Africa as a food, and the shells of the pods are burnt as fuel.

The export of groundnuts from the Gambia began in 1830 and rapidly increased. A market was found in France, where the oil was used for soap making. In France there was a heavy import duty on most kinds of oilseeds, but not on groundnuts. French trading houses established themselves in Bathurst, and they paid for their groundnuts with five-franc pieces locally known as dollars. These were being frequently exchanged for sterling by Forster and Smith in 1826. They were recognized in 1843 as legal currency in the Gambia and were not demonetized until 1922. It may well have been as a means of defending the English position in the colony that the government adopted English money as the official currency in 1844. Thus, the Gambia was more than half a century ahead of the Niger Delta region in the general use of money.

Forster and Smith had therefore to face, already in the 1830s, that most difficult feature in African trade, the annual crop. This involves heavy finance for a fairly short period. As with finance, everything else is highly seasonal. Staff, stores, and transport are frantically busy for a few months, and stand idle for the rest of the year. The crop all hits the market at the same time, and unless it is sold with skill it is likely that customers will hold off, so long as they know that merchants have large stocks in hand, thus causing the price to fall. As a protection against this merchants like to use the terminal markets for hedging their risks and to make forward sales before the harvest is reaped. However, this kind of thing may lead to an unseemly scramble for tonnage when the crop comes forward, especially if the weather has turned bad and the quantities available are not large. Competition inevitably takes the form of putting out advances to farmers, and when competition is aggressive these advances tend to go out earlier and earlier. The managers responsible are frantic to make sure they get the nuts to cover the advances, and this tends to push them towards accepting nuts which have been harvested too soon. All competitors have a common interest in avoiding these abuses, and so there is a tendency for the conclusion of agreements to regulate the methods of trade. In 1835 Forster and Smith began importing groundnuts from the Gambia into Britain, expressing oil from them.[15]

Although Forster and Smith had been associated as partners as early as 1816 for the conduct of their financial business, of their export/import business, and as proprietors of the branch in Bathurst, and although in the 1820s they were trading down the coast as far as Porto Novo in Dahomey under the name of Forster and Smith,[16] as ship-owners they continued to act separately, registering the vessels in the name either of Forster and Company or Smith and Company. In 1845 Forster and Company had fourteen ships plying between British ports and West Africa, and Smith and Company had two. The largest was the *Walmsley*, 266 tons, built at Sunderland in 1840. As mentioned in chapter 2, there were in that year 245 ships listed on the British register sailing to Africa, and even if we do not reckon in Smith's two ships, Forster with fourteen ships was the largest fleet owner in the trade. There was a West Coast flavour

---

[15] Fyfe, C., *History of Sierra Leone* (Oxford: Clarendon Press, 1962) p. 239.

[16] Newbury, C. W., *The Western Slave Coast and its Rulers* (Oxford: Clarendon Press, 1961) p. 38.

about the names of his ships, such as *Africanus*, *Gambia*, *Governor M'Lean*, and *John Forster*.[17]

Forster and Smith were Lloyds' agents. Their register shows that in the early 1850s the port of Bathurst was visited by about 170 merchant vessels annually. By types and nationalities, they were made up in 1852–1853 as follows:

French	86	Brigs	72
British	46	Schooners	39
American	29	Barques	24
Greek	1	Brigantines	17
Swedish	1	Steamers	8
German	1	Ships	6
Portuguese	1	Cutters	2
		Sloop	1
		Dandy	1

The commercial steamers were all British. The first to arrive was the *Emerald*; she came in from Madeira on 2 April 1852, and left six days later for the Leeward Coast, i.e. the African coast to the southward and eastward. By the end of that year regular monthly steamer services to and from England were established. In 1855 a steamer *Gambia* came into service. Her Majesty's Colonial Steamer *Dover* was on duty in the Gambia before the register opened. She was frequently called to rescue sailing craft which ran aground on the Red Bank, the bar at the entrance to the estuary. Visits of British, French, and American, naval vessels were frequent, and a 'Belgian War Schooner' made an appearance.

Dramatic incidents were recorded, of which the following, from 1851, may serve as an example:

May 8th—Capt. Gilbert Till, of the schooner *Despatch* with two Seamen arrived today in a Canoe from Salum, he states that, that vessel got into shoal water, 2 fathoms, off Palmerin on the 29th April, and he was attempting to heave her off when the Natives came off to her in great numbers, and cut the Hawser when the Vessel drifted nearer the shore the Natives then boarded her, threw the Captain and Crew overboard, who swam on Shore. Mr. Pierre Angrand in a small French sloop, at great risk to himself, saved the Captain and two men who swam off to him. He attempted to save the other three men but was fired upon by

17 Lloyds' Register.

the Natives. Her M.C.S. *Dover* and a small French Steamer of War, having arrived here last evening, will go there to render assistance.

June 3rd—Her M.C.S. *Dover* has since brought up the other three of the Crew of the *Dispatch*; the Cargo is plundered by the Natives, the vessel completely dismantled and breaking up.

In the 1850s there began a series of wars which became known as the Soninke–Marabout Wars, and continued intermittently for three decades. The antagonists were the supporters of militant Islam and the traditional rulers who refused to become Moslem.[18]

Winwood Reade visited the Gambia. He was not favourably impressed. The Governor told him 'that Africa must be the healthiest place in the world; for that men could nowhere else drink in such a manner'.[19] He noted that the civilians drank less than the military: at least they attended to the duties of the day after breakfast. He left Bathurst in the *Dover* to sail up the river on 10 January 1862. 'All along this river from Bathurst to Barraconda,' he wrote, 'there are trading-stations, the traders paying certain tribute or customs to the native owners of the soils. Every year the Governor or (as on this occasion) his deputy, ascends the river, encourages the Kings and Chieftains with words and presents to protect the traders, and attempts to settle any disputes that may have arisen between them. The Gambia trade consists almost entirely of groundnuts.' By this time, as Reade noted, groundnut oil was being used in France as a substitute for olive oil. It is extraordinary that Reade found that the 'strange farmers' were already established: 'the agriculture of the groundnuts is principally performed by a tribe called the Serawoullis, whose country lies towards Timbuctoo. They come down in hordes, as Irish reapers come to England in harvest time, and having sold a crop or two, pay the rent for their ground, and go home with their earnings.' But the Mahometans pressed the Sera woullis into their service, 'and from these crops of groundnuts sprang an army of fighting men'. The war had stopped all trade. The Deputy Governor could do nothing about it. The British garrison was withdrawn from Georgetown in 1866 and the community there might have been extinguished in the tumult of the war, but for the organization of a constabulary under the command of Africanus Horton, an African doctor of great character and distinction.[20]

[18] Gray, op. cit., pp. 437, 451.
[19] Reade, Winwood, *Savage Africa* (London: Smith Elder, 1863) p. 65.
[20] *West Africa*, 5 April 1969, p. 877.

Trade on the river being impossible, Forster and Smith had to find some other way of employing their resources, so they took to financing merchant captains to sail from Bathurst down the Leeward Coast. They supplied these merchants with trade goods, and took over from them in Bathurst the produce which they had purchased.[21] However, the steamship lines had just begun. The services which they provided between British and African ports left no profitable opportunity for those who would use Bathurst as a transit depot for the trade of the Leeward Coast. Further, the unique position which Forster and Smith had occupied in the West African trade by providing financial and commercial services for firms like F. and A. Swanzy was eroded when the quick and regular steamships placed Africa in easy communication with all the financial and commercial houses which offered such services in London and Liverpool. F. and A. Swanzy ceased to employ Forster and Smith, who retaliated by trying to open a branch in the Gold Coast. They became involved, with Swanzys, in the unfortunate Krobo incident (chapter 3). By 1863 Swanzys, at the peak of their prosperity, had to all intents displaced Forster and Smith from the Gold Coast trade. So Forster and Smith went out of business, and their assets in the Gambia were formally taken over by William Goddard and Company in 1869.

The Goddard family already had a long association with the firm of Forster and Smith in Gambia. William Goddard was the principal assistant under William Forster in Bathurst in 1826. Another William Goddard, probably the son of the first William, was the agent for Forster and Smith from 1858 to 1869, and it was he who took over the assets and gave his name to the business. Beginning in 1865, he had been carrying on business in his own name as well as in that of Forster and Smith. The most probable date for the ending of the Forster and Smith business is 1867, but William Goddard continued to use the rubber stamp which bore their name for a couple of years longer. Then, in 1869, he established himself in London, at Drapers Gardens, Throgmorton Street, and called his business William Goddard and Company, Merchants. The management in Bathurst was entrusted to George William Le Brun Corrie, who, in addition to the duties which he performed for William Goddard, held an appointment as consul of the United States.[22]

---

21 This information is derived from some of the documents referred to in the second paragraph of this chapter.

22 Correspondence copy book, 1880–6, p. 466: United Africa Company records.

The firm owned ships, for instance the schooner *Elizabeth*, 100 tons, the brigantine *Venture*, and the barque *Dora*. These last two fell into trouble and the owner, as Lloyds' agent, had to report on his own loss.

In the late 1860s there were negotiations between the British and French governments which envisaged the exchange of Gambia for positions in other parts of Africa. There was strong opposition from Britain's African subjects, and also from the firm of Goddard.

Despite the Soninke–Marabout wars, the export of groundnuts revived to 10,000 tons in 1880.[23] Perhaps this good round figure influenced Governor Rowe in Freetown in instructing the administrator to go up the river to obtain information concerning the commercial potentialities, and to open relations with the chiefs. It would appear that the administrator's visit, so well established in 1862, had not continued after the garrison was withdrawn from Georgetown in 1866. The administrator brought back a pessimistic report: it would be too costly to promote trade on the river.[24]

However, William Goddard and Company, Merchants, had not waited upon the government's decision. In the season 1879–1880 they made arrangements to buy groundnuts on the upper river, and were in that year the only firm which did so.[25] It was a bit rough sometimes: 'Young Evans (Edward) was flogged by the natives @ Paccally Bah the other day. Mr. E. reported the circumstance to the administrator who went up in the steamer St. Mary with some policemen and 2 field pieces. On his arrival he found that all had been settled between the people and Evans.'[26] Financially, too, the going was tough; Henry Goddard wrote to his father, 'we were in a state of impecuniosity like Mother Hubbard's cupboard. The safe was bare and we had not enough money to pay wages and salaries'.

William Goddard was under-capitalized for adventures such as opening up the river, so he looked around for associates who could provide funds. With the help of a firm trading under the name Staines Watson and Company he formed the River Gambia Trading Company Limited, which took over the Goddard business on 1 April 1882.[27] The London office continued to be in Drapers Gardens, and William Goddard was the chairman of the company;

---

[23] Gailey, H. A., *History of the Gambia* cit. Crowder, M., *West Africa under Colonial Rule*, (London: Hutchinson, 1968).

[24] Gray, op. cit.

[25] Correspondence copy book (as note 22) p. 12.

[26] ibid., p. 340.

[27] ibid., pp. 325, 357.

but the new partners were represented on the board and when William Goddard visited Bathurst (as he did every year) they expected him to keep them fully informed. In 1880 his son Henry C. Goddard, at the age of 23, had begun to reside in Bathurst and to work as Corrie's assistant.[28] They had bought 1,373 tons of groundnuts in the season 1879–1880[29] but believed that they would be able to secure 3,000 tons in 1880–1881. Hope springs eternal, but it turned out to be 2,000 tons.[30] In the following year again they bought 3,000 tons[31] and William Goddard expressed the view that if the new company had started sooner, they could have bought 4,000 tons—a figure which he aimed at exceeding in 1882–1883, in which event the River Gambia Trading Company would be the largest exporter.[32]

In 1882 the company suffered a sad loss. Le Brun Corrie, as Lloyds' agent, had to deal with the French barque *Ville de Bruxelles*: but he could not help her for twenty-eight days because she came from Goree where yellow fever was raging, and she was placed in quarantine. Alas, the quarantine may not have been effective, for a few weeks later Corrie[33] was described as 'the late agent'. However, he had not died; he had suffered a very severe illness and gone off as an invalid to the Cape of Good Hope.[34] He did not return. Henry C. Goddard, at the age of 25, now took charge as manager.[35]

The Goddards and Corrie were much concerned about competitors, all French firms, among which Maurel Frères of Bordeaux was the leader.[36] The others were Maurel et Prom, E. Pellegrin et Cie., Grenelle, Barrère, and Verminat. All the firms in Bathurst were acutely embarrassed in their operations by the physical shortage of cash. They frequently appealed to one another for help with ready money. Even when a firm held perfectly good bills it

---

[28] Correspondence copy book (as note 22) p. 29.

[29] ibid., p. 168.   [30] ibid., p. 29.   [31] ibid., p. 315.   [32] ibid., p. 379.

[33] Mrs. Corrie deserves to be mentioned, because she may have been the first European wife of a trading manager whose presence in West Africa was placed on record. But though she may be admired as a pioneer for joining her husband at his post, it was not a happy experience. Corrie wrote to a correspondent in Freetown in June 1880 that 'Mrs. Corrie goes home in a few days. Climate does not agree with her'. But in September, Henry Goddard wrote to his father, 'Mr. Corrie was very much put out @ not hearing from his wife seeing that she must have been @ home 9 days before the last mail left he particularly requests that not one penny piece more than the monthly money of £10 be given to her in fact if he does not hear from her by the next mail he will stop the allowance altogether'.

[34] Correspondence copy book (as note 22) p. 509.

[35] Henry C. Goddard to River Gambia T.C.L., London, 12 December 1882: United Africa Company records.

[36] Correspondence copy book (as note 22) p. 161.

might not be able to find anyone who had the money to encash them, and those who had cash naturally made hard terms, so that it was never possible to realize as much as ninety per cent of the face value of a bill.[37] These embarrassments forced the traders into complicated barter deals; for example, the River Gambia Trading Company exchanged rice for groundnuts on a barter basis.[38] They badly needed a bank.

Having formed his new company, William Goddard tried to persuade all his competitors to enter into an agreement. In July 1882 he wrote to his colleagues in London:

> I presided at a meeting of the merchants which was held at Mr. Barrère's the French consul. I spoke my mind pretty freely to them, showed them the folly of going on trading as they had been doing of late years, impressed upon them (the French houses in particular) how much more to their advantage it would be if they combined with the English merchants, had one uniform size Bushel, agreed to one price to be given for Groundnuts in the River, one price in town. Traders to be charged goods @ river prices and dealers @ town prices, suggested that each house should send round a list of Traders of bad character . . . All at the meeting coincided with my views and promised to adhere faithfully to the resolutions proposed by myself.[39]

The merchants appear to have continued to hold meetings, for five months later they all, except the River Gambia Trading Company Limited, decided to discontinue the trade in kola nuts; but that did not suit the River Gambia manager, who refused to be a party to the agreement.[40]

This agreement was a very early example of something that was to become a normal feature of the West African produce trades. In labour relations, too, the River Gambia Trading Company Limited had experiences which suggest that conditions in Gambia had already reached a point which would appear in other places later. In November 1882 the labourers went on strike, and held meetings. No man was allowed to work for less than two shillings a day.[41] A month later ships were still held up for lack of labour. The 'Jollaf women' had struck work, holding out for eighteen pence a day while the labourers were demanding two shillings plus rations.[42]

The firm imported cotton textiles, rice, and many other things

---

[37] ibid., p. 478. [38] ibid., pp. 43, 204, and 317. [39] ibid., p. 401.
[40] ibid., p. 490. [41] ibid., p. 475. [42] ibid., p. 490.

from Britain; but they found it convenient to use nearer sources of supply also. Thus from Goree they bought tobacco, kerosene,[43] nails,[44] and planks (*sic*),[45] and miscellaneous supplies such as a carboy of sulphuric acid for the ice machine.[46] Teneriffe was the supplier of salt[47] and haberdashery,[48] but Corrie turned down an offer of potatoes because he did not think that there would be any market for them in Bathurst.[49] An order went to Madeira for 'orange wood tooth-picks, same quantity as last'.[50] Another import, already mentioned, was kola-nuts; for some time supplies of this commodity were secured from Mrs. Sarah Richards at Freetown, who sometimes took some wine in part-exchange;[51] but she proved to be an unsatisfactory supplier, and the firm switched its orders to Mrs. Sarah Fany of 'Agra' (Accra).[52]

Goree was not only a source of supply but also a market for hides[53] and corn.[54] As a buyer of hides, Goree was acting as an entrepôt; but the corn was needed to feed the population of that crowded island, and the quantities involved were quite interesting from the point of view of the River Gambia Trading Company.

Palm kernels were beginning to be an article of trade, and supplies could be secured from the estuary of the Casamance River, that part of Senegal which comes to the sea south of the Gambia River. Corrie sent the firm's cutter *Willie* to the Casamance for palm kernels, but she capsized and was lost.[55] In the year 1882 the firm invested in a river steamer and a steam launch, and Corrie wrote to London full of confidence that with these advantages, 'we ought to take the lead and have our produce down early'.[56]

It was necessary to sell the groundnuts on the Continent, which may have been difficult and expensive for a small firm located in London. They usually travelled in sailing barques which carried 200 or 300 tons, to such ports as Marseilles, Genoa,[57] Trieste,[58] or

---

[43] Correspondence copy book (see note 22) p. 42.

[44] ibid., p. 210.   [45] ibid., p. 196.   [46] ibid., p. 42.   [47] ibid., p. 55.

[48] ibid., Goddard to Davidson and Company, Teneriffe, 5 February 1880.

[49] ibid., p. 192.   [50] ibid., p. 214.

[51] ibid., pp. 21 *et seq.* The kola or kola-nut is a fruit which naturally offers the same opportunity for chewing as chewing-gum. It is chewed by many people throughout the sub-Saharan savannahs of Africa. For a study of the trade in modern times, see my 'Study of income and expenditure in northern Zaria', in *Africa*, October 1948. I wrote then 'These are the African's indulgence which to many takes the place of the Englishman's cigarettes and the Englishwoman's tea'.

[52] ibid., p. 316.   [53] ibid., pp. 37 *et seq.*   [54] ibid., pp. 194 *et seq.*

[55] ibid., p. 52.   [56] ibid., p. 460.

[57] ibid., p. 443.   [58] ibid., p. 901.

Dunkirk 'as experiment'.[59] In 1882 the Bathurst manager was amazed to learn that the London office had made a contract with a Genoa importer to supply 600 tons, all to be loaded in one steamer; and their expressions of incredulity were justified, because it proved impossible to charter a steamer capable of lifting such a large quantity![60]

The new partners quickly became alarmed at the way the money disappeared up the river when the time came to give out advances for the groundnut season. In November 1882 they sent peremptory instructions to Bathurst that bills were not to be drawn for anything except what was required for duties and advances to ships. The manager at Bathurst replied with a brief lecture on the facts of life, pointing out that he had groundnuts to fetch down, cutters to pay, wages to sailors, and so on; his name was Dittling, and he went on to say, 'This business is an old-established one and has always stood A1, and it would be a pity for the Company just started should lose the prestige'.[61] This is of interest since it shows that in Bathurst Forster and Smith, William Goddard and Company Merchants, and the River Gambia Trading Company Limited, were all thought of as one continuing affair.

However, the tone of correspondence between London and Bathurst continued to deteriorate. London rebuked Bathurst for ordering goods direct from suppliers, and insisted that all orders should pass through head office.[62] Shortage of funds inhibited a policy of vigorous competition with the French rivals, and purchases of groundnuts fell off; in the season 1884–1885 they just topped 1,300 tons; and yet money was so short that a loan was raised on debenture terms.[63] Then arrangements were made for a London firm, J. Sherbrook and Company, to take over the management.[64] It may be assumed that they were put in by the debenture holders. Like most company doctors, they demanded drastic staff reductions, and all the clerks in Bathurst were discharged, save one.[65] At length in July 1886 the company went bankrupt.

William Goddard disappeared from the office in Drapers Gardens, and the Post Office, being unable to deliver mail from Bathurst, returned it.[66] In September the company was officially declared bankrupt, and J. Sherbrook and Company were appointed as receiver and official liquidator. Henry Goddard continued to correspond with J. Sherbrook and to report to him; they both seem

[59] ibid., p. 176.   [60] ibid., p. 451.   [61] ibid., pp. 468, 478.   [62] ibid., p. 490.
[63] ibid., pp. 925, 947.   [64] ibid., p. 953.   [65] ibid., p. 965.   [66] ibid., p. 968.

to have been anxious to keep the business going. In 1888 the assets of the River Gambia Trading Company Limited were acquired by a new company, the Bathurst Trading Company Limited. Evidently an investor had been discovered who was interested in putting money into this affair, and it seems probable that this was the firm of James Finlay and Company, East India Merchant.[67] Henry Goddard continued to manage the enterprise in Bathurst. In 1889 he went up the river to MacCarthy Island and took stock, for his new proprietor, of the assets. There were goods to the value of £4,000, produce worth £400, cattle £65, boats and canoes £50, cash and gold £15; debts were £4,878 of which, alas, £459 had to be classified as 'old'.

Henry C. Goddard, by this time, was a leading citizen, a member of the legislative council (1890) and vice-consul for the United States of America. He died in 1915, and a tablet in Saint Mary's cathedral at Bathurst records that he was 'a leading member of the commercial community of the Gambia colony, whose interests he always had at heart and whose prosperity he did much to advance'.

In 1896, Goddard proposed to ship a hippopotamus to England, and the collector of customs desired him to state its weight to enable export duty to be calculated.

Until 1914 nearly all the nuts went to France. But that part of France which the Germans occupied included many of the mills which crushed groundnuts, and so the French demand fell away. However, Britain came in as a strong buyer, and this naturally aroused the interest of Lever Brothers (see chapter 14). In 1917 they bought the firm of John Walkden, which at that time had an establishment in Bathurst. Influenced by a favourable report from Walkden's agent,[68] later in the same year Lever Brothers bought the Bathurst Trading Company Limited. The principal shareholder was James Finlay and Company, East India Merchant, and the price paid was £175,000 in fifteen per cent cumulative preferred ordinary shares of Lever Brothers.[69] This was a higher price than Lever paid for Richard & William King. The Walkden branch was absorbed by the Bathurst Trading Company.

In 1922 Lever Brothers bought a third company, called the Gambia Trading Company Limited. This had been started by Raul

---

[67] No contemporary evidence for this has come to light, but in 1917 James Finlay was the principal shareholder.

[68] Lever Brothers Limited policy committee minutes, 26 November 1917.

[69] ibid., 10 December 1917, p. 6.

Cirne, a native of Portugal, who had left that country when he was thirteen years of age and had spent the early years of his manhood in business in South America. He visited Bathurst in 1915 for the purpose of settling some affairs on behalf of the firm of R. L. Nicholson and Company of Liverpool. While so engaged, he stayed with a young employee of the Bank of British West Africa, R. W. Pullen. Cirne, realizing the possibilities that lay in the exploitation of piassava,[70] conceived the idea of establishing a company in connection therewith; and in its formation he was joined by Pullen and T. J. Gibbs, a government official who resigned his position because of his faith in the venture. This was the Gambia Trading Company Limited, which, besides dealing in piassava, imported goods of every kind and exported groundnuts and other products.[71] Lever Brothers continued to employ Raul Cirne after the acquisition. At the time when Lever Brothers bought the Gambia Trading Company, the firms engaged in the groundnut trade had recently entered into an agreement to regulate their shares, and since under these arrangements the Bathurst Trading Company had fourteen per cent and the Gambia Trading Company had five per cent, the total percentage of the groundnut crop bought by the Lever Group was nineteen per cent.[72]

[70] Piassava is a palm which grows in swamps but does not develop any stem, so that it looks like a large fern. The leaves, when dried and retted, are a commercial fibre used in making brooms and brushes, while other qualities of the material are used in industry in certain metal-smelting processes.

[71] MacMillan, A., *Red Book of West Africa* (London: Collingridge, 1920) p. 290.

[72] Leverhulme's African diary 1925, unpublished, p. 285.

5

Thomas Harrison

The trade and politics of the Niger Delta are the subject of a major historical study. It reveals what a troubled area this was in the nineteenth century. It was an area of city states, some kingdoms, some trading republics, and all for three hundred years had found their economic base in the slave trade. West of the Volta, the export of slaves quickly ceased to be significant after the British government decided to stop it. Not so in the Bights of Benin and Biafra. Here the attempt to stop the export of slaves gave rise to conflicts which lasted many years, for the traffic continued with great vigour into the sixth decade of the century.

The slave vessels were all armed, and engaged in a shooting war against the Royal Navy. The city states, too, were all armed, and had their alliance with European trading interests, whether slavers or palm-oilers. Bonny was the leading slave-trading kingdom. In the period 1827 to 1834 the export of slaves was running at the rate of 24,000 a year. Meanwhile the export of palm oil had become so well established that in 1828 over 5,000 tons were exported from places in the Bight of Biafra. The pioneers of the palm-oil trade in these parts, nearly all from Liverpool and several of them former slave-traders, did not include any names which identify them with the predecessors of the United Africa Company.

Until 1830 the white traders, slavers and oilers alike, made friends with the local governments, to which they paid great respect.[1] They traded through African middlemen and made no attempt to penetrate the interior. From 1830, however, a revolutionary factor had to be taken into account. In that year the brothers Richard and John Lander discovered that the Niger reached the sea through the Oil Rivers, and that it was navigable. This geographical discovery happened to coincide with a technological discovery, the steamship. The result was Macgregor Laird's expedition

---

[1] Dike, K. O., *Trade and Politics in the Niger Delta* (Oxford: Clarendon Press, 1959) pp. 5, 16, 31, 29, 50.

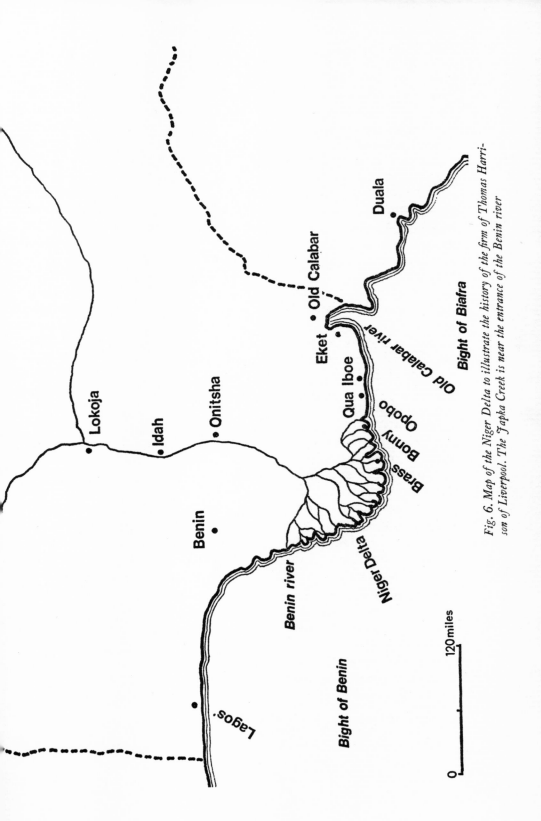

Fig. 6. Map of the Niger Delta to illustrate the history of the firm of Thomas Harrison of Liverpool. The Japka Creek is near the entrance of the Benin river

Lokoja

Idah

Onitsha

Benin

Old Calabar

Eket

Duala

Qua Iboe

Opobo

Bonny

Brass

Old Calabar river

Benin river

Niger Delta

Bight of Biafra

Bight of Benin

Lagos

120 miles

0

up the Niger, of 1832.[2] The era of 'penetration' had begun, and the idea stimulated much new interest in the Bights. In 1837 the Royal Navy initiated a new strategy against the slavers, the blockade system, in preference to the cruising system, and this was much more effective.[3]

Annual exports of oil in the 1840s were in the 18,000–25,000 tons range, and at a price around £34 it was worth some £700,000. The counterpart of this, manufactured goods of approximately equivalent value, was all handed over by the traders to African middlemen as 'trust', that is, on credit for six months at least and in some cases for as long as two years.[4] This was the state of affairs when Thomas Harrison first venture into the Oil Rivers.

Thomas Harrison and Company was formed in Liverpool in 1837.[5] In the course of time this firm took the leadership in forming the African Association, and extinguished its own name in the process. The African Association at a later date was amalgamated with other companies to form the African and Eastern Trade Corporation Limited, which in 1929 was one of the two main constituents of the United Africa Company. But all that belonged to the distant future. In 1837 Thomas Harrison was a new entrant to the trade, and had to contend with the tricks with which the old hands treated 'interlopers'. The new men had to fight hard for entry, for the old hands would not willingly agree that new traders should give goods on trust to the oil brokers who were already indebted to them, and, of course, still less could they agree to the new entrants' accepting oil from middlemen who had been financed by goods received on credit from traders long established in the place. To gain a footing the new men tempted the Africans with better terms, to which the old-established traders replied by 'chopping oil', which meant the forcible seizure of oil intended for the vessels of the 'interlopers'. This led to violence, and in this the interlopers had an advantage, for the middlemen invariably allied themselves with the interlopers to save their oil from being 'chopped'.[6] The resulting hostilities between rival British merchants became intolerable, and it was this situation which led to the establishment of the courts of equity, the first being at Bonny; courts consisting of equal numbers of Africans and Europeans. 'The merits of opponents are determined, and with the consent of the king, fines are levied on defaulters.'[7]

[2] see chapter 2.   [3] op. cit., p. 6.   [4] op. cit., p. 102.
[5] Rankin, p. 73.   [6] Dike, op. cit., p. 109.
[7] Baikie, W. B., Exploring Voyage (London: Murray, 1856) p. 356.

The interloper had either to fight the established firms in their entrenched positions, or to find a new place. The Benin River offered such an opportunity to Harrison. It had been a stronghold of the slave trade and had not in the early days of the palm-oil trade extended a welcome to the palm-oilers.[8] But times were changing. 'The inhabitants of a vast extent of coast have been led to give up the slave trade, and why? because they have been taught the immense increase of the value of the palm-oil trade over that in slaves.'[9] So Harrison went to the Benin River and became established there in the 1840s on the Japka Creek in the country of the Itsekiri people.[10] In 1845 Thomas Harrison of Liverpool had just two ships trading to Africa, *Hesperus* and *Nina*, barques of 408 tons, and 392 tons, but they were larger than anything owned by Forster, whose highest tonnage was 266, or by Kings, whose greatest vessel was 246 tons.[11]

In the 1850s the domestic slaves in the city states, discontented with their status, revolted against the traditional rulers. Again, European traders took sides. In the tumult, Pepple of Bonny, scion of a line of divine kings, was removed by the British into exile (1854) and then, when it was found that no one else could exercise authority, was brought back (1861). About this time Thomas Harrison was established among 'the banks and braes o' Bonny'.[12] It was a troubled time, for although King Pepple had returned, the spell of divinity, once broken, could not be conjured back. The quarrels between emancipated slaves continued, until one of them, Ja-Ja, led his party away and set up a kingdom of his own in another place, which he called Opobo (1869). Bonny and Opobo were henceforth hostile, and in this contest Harrison was for Bonny and the Miller Brothers were for Opobo. However, before their conflict is described there are certain other matters which may be mentioned.

In the early 1860s Harrison's relations with the Itsekiri seem to have deteriorated. He was the victim of piracy and some of his Krumen were murdered.[13] Then Harrison's agent, Hineson, was seized by an Itsekiri trader because the firm had refused to pay a debt claimed by the trader. Hineson was beaten and detained till he

[8] Fawckner, James, *Travels in Benin* (London: Schloss, 1837).
[9] Forbes, F. E., *Dahomey and the Dahomans* (London: Longmans, 1851) p. viii.
[10] Ikime, Obaro, *Merchant Prince of the Niger Delta* (London: Heinemann, 1968) p. 4.
[11] Lloyds Register.
[12] Burton, R. F., *Wanderings in West Africa* (London: Longmans, 1863) vol. 2 pp. 242, 245, 268.
[13] P.R.O. Consul Burton to FO, 15 April 1864, FO 84/1221/1864.

paid a ransom of three puncheons of palm oil. This news brought the British consul steaming to the Benin river in a gunboat, and he imposed a fine of twenty-five puncheons on the Itsekiri. Two years later (1886), Harrison was refusing to pay comey (the tax described in chapter 2) and the Itsekiri governor attempted to secure a settlement by 'placing armed canoes on the river and occupying the beach with an armed force' which stopped all trade. The Foreign Office informed Harrison, through the consul, that he could not expect support from the British government if he did not pay the comey, for which he was liable under agreements drawn up between the consul and the Itsekiri authorities.[14]

A seaman named Hartje (whose son, seventy years later, was supervising agent for the United Africa Company in Lagos) went to Old Calabar in 1862[15] in the *Golden Age*,[16] a four-master belonging to the firm of Tyson Richmond & Jones of Liverpool.[17] When he arrived, he was told he would have to work in the *Matilda*, a trading hulk (see plate 3). Her construction date was 1857,[18] from which perhaps it may be deduced that she was built to serve as a hulk. Hartje did not like the idea of working in her, but he was told he had signed articles to serve in any of the company's ships, so he was compelled to stay. After about twelve months he asked permission of his agent to go home, but the agent then put him to painting the side of the ship, which 'brought him to his senses'. He came to like it eventually, himself became the agent, and in 1868 he was responsible for arranging the sale of the *Matilda* hulk and the adjoining beach by Tyson Richmond & Jones to Thomas Harrison.[19]

In those days the chiefs exercised an important function in the control of credit. Their system of book-keeping was a row of enamel basins, into which they would break off pipe stems. If a man was owed ten puncheons, ten pipe stems would be thrown into the relevant basin, and the account was eventually squared up. Hartje belonged to the secret society called Ekpo; he would never divulge anything about it, but he said it was useful for squaring his books. When he was about to go on leave and had credit outstanding, he

[14] Ikime, op. cit., pp. 22–3.
[15] Solemn declaration, United Africa Company of Nigeria property department, Lagos, ER66/A101 R 843 1904.
[16] Hartje, H. G., oral to Pedler.
[17] Lloyds Register.
[18] ibid.
[19] Solemn declaration *cit. supra*.

would go to the king and explain the position; everything would be sorted out and paid by the King, who would settle with his chiefs later.

Hartje left Nigeria and started business in the United Kingdom but he eventually went back and was in Calabar in 1914, at which time his son was also there and would spend Sundays with his father. Thomas Harrison by then had ceased to exist, and Hartje senior worked for Thomas Welsh. This company owned the last trading hulk in Calabar, the *Parracca*, up to 1913, when they built ashore. Thomas Welsh and Company were acquired by the Niger Company, but as they had never dealt in gin they insisted, as part of the terms of sale, that the business should not be required to handle that line.[20]

The main part of the story of Thomas Harrison and Company, concerns their competition with the Millers, Glaswegian brothers whose story is given in chapter 8. They started with a partner, Archibald MacEachan, who had been a long time in the Oil Rivers. Under his guidance the Millers began operations by despatching a hulk, the *Lady Alice*, to the Brass river.[21] In the following year, 1870, they bought the *Hannah Salkeld*, barque, at public auction in Fernando Po for £121, and towed her to Opobo for use as a hulk. She had been condemned as unseaworthy.[22] Thus Millers entered into relations with Ja-Ja at Opobo; they were his friends through good times and bad. Their friendship with him alienated them from the rest of the British trading community and will have much influence in this story.

The hulk was almost an innovation. The trading sailing ship, housed in with a roofing of palm leaves and partially dismantled for a long stay, was the original mart for the exchange of European manufactures for African produce. The depot ship afterwards took its place. A firm possessing more sailing ships than one found it profitable to leave one vessel anchored at one place for longish spells as a store, emptying and replenishing it by means of another vessel, which was thus sure of a quick turn-round. The hulk succeeded the depot ship, and the shore factory succeeded the hulk. The last-mentioned transition did not take place on any large scale until the decade 1880–1890, and a few hulks survived that period. One survived at Burutu to 1926[23] as a coal depot.

Barter was the basis of trade in the late 1860s and for long afterwards. English silver coins came into general use only much later

---

[20] Lord Cole to Pedler, 25 September 1970.   [21] Rankin, p. 61.
[22] Holt, Cecil R., *The Diary of John Holt* (Liverpool: Young, 1948) p. 175.
[23] Dunnet, D. D. to Pedler, 30 December 1969.

and very slowly. Africans regarded such a measure of value and medium of exchange with suspicion and distrust, and preferred dealing on the basis of goods for goods; if money had to be used, to place their reliance on more solid and substantial tokens such as metal rods or manillas. 'Buying and selling for cash is "prosaic" whilst in barter, with its battle of wits, there is something indescribably attractive.'[24]

MacEachan's method for establishing the new company had something in common with that adopted by Harrison when he went to the Benin River, for MacEachan outflanked the established firms by setting up in a new place. It was the Middleton River, and Millers went there in 1872. This was strongly opposed by the people of Brass, because it diverted trade from them and they lost the comey. The Middleton area had supplied food to Brass, but as the Middleton people became more interested in cash crops, due to Miller's move, there was a shortage of food in Brass. Millers were determined to by-pass the coastal middlemen and to take part in the penetration up the Niger. This is described in chapter 9, and reference to that story will explain why Millers felt it necessary to provide themselves, for this purpose, with a well-armed steamship, with special iron screens for protection: she bore the name *Sultan of Sokoto*.[25] In 1876 John Hunter was in charge of Miller's affairs, and he took the *Sultan of Sokoto* up the Niger and sustained heavy bombardment from cannon on the banks. Casualties were one killed and twelve wounded, and the ship was seriously damaged. Millers considered that the attacks had been instigated by the people of Brass, aided by some of the Europeans in Brass.[26] At Agberi, near Onitsha, Hunter fought an action for three and a half hours, using rockets, ball, canister, and chain shot. A hawser, buoyed across the river with large pieces of wood, stopped the steamer, but Hunter managed to get the port paddle to work on the hawser until it was cut through, and manoeuvred the steamer to continue her way. This took place under heavy fire. However, eventually the *Sultan of Sokoto* became a wreck on a sandbank, and men came in canoes, and stripped her, even to the mast and steam winches. The consul organized a punitive expedition to avenge the *Sultan of Sokoto*, but it appears that Millers did not approve of this, for they gave the

---

[24] Cowan, A. A., 'Early Trading Conditions in the Bight of Biafra' in *Journal Royal African Society*, January 1936, p. 58.
[25] P.R.O. Consul Hartley to FO 27 March 1875, FO 84/1418/1875.
[26] P.R.O. Acting Consul McKellar to FO, 27 June 1876, FO 84/1455/1876.

expedition no assistance.[27] Up the river Millers established themselves at Yamaha, and although in 1877 the local chief set fire to their compound, and robbed the canteen, they persisted in maintaining their establishment.[28]

At that time four firms were trading up the Niger river, and in 1879 they all put their Niger river sections together, forming the United African Company, of which Alexander Miller was appointed a joint managing director. How this company went on to become first the National African Company, and then the Royal Niger Company, will be told in chapter 9.

Alexander and George Miller were both in their early thirties. They were already men of means, able to take a financial interest in the new company; but the invitation to Alexander Miller to accept appointment as joint managing director was due less to his financial interest than to his exceptional business ability. In accepting, he and his brother realized that he would have to live in London. Hitherto the head office of the Miller business had been in Glasgow, first in Waterloo Street and then in Saint Vincent Street. Now Alexander Miller took with him to London, and conducted thence, the Gold Coast branch of the business. Thus it was that for many years, first at other addresses and then at Surrey House, Victoria Embankment, the Gold Coast business of the Miller Brothers, and the business of the Niger Company under its four successive names, were carried on in the same building.

While Millers had been getting established, Thomas Harrison had been growing in strength. In 1876 he had seven sailing vessels plying between Liverpool and the Niger Delta, all of recent construction. Then there was the *Prince Will*, which was probably employed in local traffic in Africa, and three hulks, *Elizabeth*, *Matilda*, and *Montezuma*.[29]

The struggle over Ja-Ja draws near. The two principal contenders, Harrison and Miller, are in position. Before going further with their conflict, it may be useful to introduce a third element, whose experiences will help to explain the nature of Ja-Ja's activities. The third element is none other than Harford, who was seen at Duala in chapter 2. Harford joined the Liverpool firm of George Watts in 1880, and as this firm subsequently became a founder member of the African Association, that is an additional reason why Harford's experiences should be noted here.

[27] P.R.O. FO 84/1487/1877.   [28] P.R.O. FO 84/1541/12/1879.
[29] Lloyds Register.

Harford was employed on the Old Calabar river. His first job was to take an old ship, used as a trading hulk for many years, and now no longer safe to remain afloat, and beach her in such a way that she could be used as a trading establishment.

It was decided to open a branch at Qua Iboe, and Harford's chief went there in a small boat: but he had such a fright in crossing the bar that he preferred to walk back overland. Harford then fitted out 'a good large boat that would carry about ten tons'. He rigged it with mast and sails and loaded a house in sections, ready to be put up at whatever spot he should choose. With a crew of sixteen he anchored off a village on the Qua Iboe River, but was told by the inhabitants that King Ja-Ja of Opobo had threatened to burn down any place which permitted a white man to establish himself. Ja-Ja was determined to keep the middleman trade for himself. Harford moved on to the next village up the river, in the country of the Ibunos, built his house, and started trading. Sure enough, Ja-Ja came with a large force, burned seven villages, took away a hundred prisoners, and drove the rest of the population into the bush. Every plantation tree was cut down, and all growing crops destroyed. The prisoners, wrote Harford, were taken to Opobo, killed, and exhibited to the townspeople.[30]

This sort of thing naturally incensed British merchants against Ja-Ja, not only on commercial grounds, but on high moral principle. It is therefore important to appreciate how wholeheartedly the Miller men were prepared to defend Ja-Ja, not only commercially but morally. Alexander Cowan went to Opobo for Millers in 1887, and many years later he wrote:

There can be no doubt Ja-Ja was the most powerful potentate the Oil Rivers ever produced. He was just as shrewd and fore-seeing as he was powerful. His influence was great and extended far into the interior . . . He could be stern, and he was strict, but he was always just, and the form of government he set up was as near perfect as anything of its kind could be. Every man had the right of appeal, and, though in effect his own authority was never questioned, he conformed to his own rules, and governed through his council of chiefs.[31]

To return to Harford, he distributed rice and biscuits to the starving people, but Providence took a hand by supplying fish in

[30] Kingsley, Mary, *West African Studies* (London: Macmillan, 1899) pp. 583–611.
[31] Cowan, A. A., *Journal Royal African Society*, October 1935, p. 400.

unusual quantity, and the catching of these attracted large numbers of Ibunos to his trading post. Harford provided guns and drilled the able-bodied men in their use. Ja-Ja sent a force and there was a good deal of sniping. Ja-Ja set up a trading post at Okot, one of the market places in the Ibuno country, and built there a house with an iron roof, which was considered by the local people to be 'a great thing'. Harford also set up a store. There followed a period of strenuous competition, but after about a year Ja-Ja gave up and left the place to the firm of George Watts, which Harford represented.

Harford then built another post at Eket, where he put in charge an African named William Sawyer, 'one of the best men I ever had in the country'. Sawyer was set upon by some young men, and Harford threatened to move his post to another place: but the chief of the Ekets intervened and gave his protection to the enterprise, which became the centre of the whole trade of the river. Harford put a Gatling gun there for defence against attack. There it still stood in 1968 on the stoep of the house which is on a cliff over the creek, where in the cool of the evening the great forest trees and the last of the sunset are reflected in the dark waters below: a sight of inexpressible beauty.

At Opobo, about the middle of the 1880s, Alexander Miller, Brother & Company and several other local British firms quarrelled, and the consequences were far-reaching and enduring. Ja-Ja, as noted above, set up a kingdom for himself and called it Opobo. Of strong character, shrewd and gifted with organizing capacity, he rapidly drew trade with the British away from Bonny in his role of 'middleman' between the European merchant and the peoples of the interior. Commercial rivalry led to war, which went on until Consul Livingstone was appealed to by the King of Bonny to use his influence for peace. Consul Livingstone, who was a brother of the famous missionary, responded at once. A division of markets was made.

Consul Hewett in 1884 asked Ja-Ja to sign a treaty placing his territory under British protection. Ja-Ja agreed but only on the condition that the clause which stipulated free access to all parts of the territory and free trade for Europeans should be struck out. Consul Hewett was in a hurry and he had no option but to accede. The clause was eliminated.

A year or so later, trade being none too good, the merchants, thinking Ja-Ja was profiting unduly at their expense, came to an agreement among themselves to fix prices and divide produce; Ja-Ja retaliated by shipping his own produce to England; and the merchants countered by withholding payment of comey. Millers' agent, Farquhar, returning from leave and examining the agreement, did not think it sufficiently favourable to his firm and asked for some modifications. Farquhar was a young man. His influence was small. His neighbours thought to override his pretensions. He was told curtly that no alteration was possible. Thereupon Farquhar dissociated Millers from the agreement and resumed dealings with Ja-Ja. The effect was immediate and striking. Millers were getting all the produce they could take, and selling their merchandise as fast as they could supply it, while their competitors were doing little. British authority, represented by the vice-consul, favoured the competitors, the enemies of Ja-Ja. He, indignant at the consular endorsement of their refusal to pay comey and alarmed by the threatened invasion of his interior markets, sent emissaries to London to plead his cause at the Foreign Office. Lord Salisbury was both Prime Minister and Foreign Secretary. The question of deporting Ja-Ja was under discussion, and Salisbury was asked to receive a deputation from Thomas Harrison and the other Bonny merchants, who were expected to advocate that course; whereupon Salisbury wrote on the file, 'I should prefer to deport the deputation'.[32]

At that juncture, in 1887, there arrived in the Oil Rivers as acting vice-consul a young man named Johnston, who was later to become famous as Sir Harry Johnston. His view of Ja-Ja was succinctly stated in a telegram which he sent to the Foreign Office: 'Ask immediate permission remove Ja-Ja temporarily Gold Coast. Organizes armed attacks. Obstructs waterways, markets. Intrigues render this course imperative.'[33] Shortly after despatching that message Johnston received a telegram from the Foreign Office which said 'Your action re Ja-Ja approved'. It was in fact a belated reply to an earlier message, but Johnston took it as authority to proceed. He summoned Ja-Ja to a conference at the factory of Thomas Harrison on the Opobo beach, H.M.S. *Goshawk* being anchored in the river with her guns trained on the town. Fearing a design on his person, Ja-Ja hesitated about attending. Thereupon Johnston sent him a letter saying that if he did not come he would be treated as a rebel, and that if he did come he would be free to depart after hearing the proposal to be made to him. On this assurance Ja-Ja obeyed the summons. Johnston, flanked by several naval

[32] Oliver, Roland, *Sir Harry Johnston* (London: Chatto, 1957) p. 113.
[33] ibid., p. 114.

officers and merchants, informed Ja-Ja that he must constitute himself a prisoner and consent to be taken to Accra for trial. He was free to leave if he wished; but in that case, in one hour's time the warship would open fire. 'Ja-Ja was far sighted enough not to pit his strength against British power.'[34] He was taken to Accra, where he was tried. He was acquitted of one of the three charges brought against him, but found guilty of the other two: blocking the highway and not loyally endeavouring to carry out the treaty of 1884. The sentence was deportation for five years, during which time he was to receive a pension. Given the choice of several places of exile, he chose Saint Vincent in the West Indies. At Opobo Johnston set up a governing council consisting of merchants and chiefs.

Major Macdonald went to the Oil Rivers on a mission to enquire into charges against the Royal Niger Company. He formed the opinion that Ja-Ja had been unjustly treated, and though this was not the prime reason of his visit, on his return to London he intervened with Lord Salisbury on Ja-Ja's behalf. Ja-Ja's sentence was revoked and arrangements were made for Macdonald personally to accompany him back to Opobo; but the triumphal home-coming of the exiled king did not take place, for he died on the way.

By breaking away from the merchants' agreement which they considered unfair to themselves, and by resuming their dealings with Ja-Ja, Millers secured a preponderant share of the trade at Opobo. Now the gulf was widened between the other merchants and Millers. Millers were the champions of Ja-Ja; the others his antagonists, his undoers. This rivalry, material and sentimental, of interest and prestige, survived Ja-Ja's disappearance. It lasted for many years and had far-reaching consequences.

In 1886 Millers decided to establish themselves on shore at Old Calabar, and it was agreed between Ephraim IX, the ruler of that place,[35] and Alexander Henderson as agent for Millers that Horsfalls Beach should be given to the latter for trading purposes with the right to erect houses or stores. This did not constitute a sale of the ground. Millers had to pay beach comey as arranged by the court of equity in past years, and the deed provided that if Millers declared that they no longer desired the beach for trade, the ground should revert to the lessor.

The comey at Old Calabar was quantified in terms of a certain

---

[34] ibid., p. 117.
[35] The ruler Ephraim IX is referred to in contemporary documents as both duke and king; it is possible that Duke may have been a 'given name'.

number of cases of gin; thus, in 1894 Millers at Old Calabar secured an extension of their riverside frontage by twenty feet for a comey of 20 cases of gin a year, payable either in goods or cash. However, as early as 1891 an agreement had been made where the rent was specified in cash, and in 1911 agreements were made to convert the gin-case basis to a cash basis, the price being reckoned at twelve shillings per case of gin. No doubt at the time this was regarded as a progressive change, but how much better the African lessors would have done if they had stuck to the case of gin as a measure of value![36]

Alexander Miller, Brother & Company prospered not only in the Opobo district but in others. The support which it had given to Ja-Ja won the hearts of the Opobo people, and their gratitude, confidence, and goodwill, favoured the firm's trade in that quarter. The story of Ja-Ja passed from mouth to mouth over a wide area to the enhancement of Millers' esteem, and the promotion of good relations between every new branch of the firm and the inhabitants of the locality. By the end of the century Millers had stations throughout southern Nigeria. Almost the only important place where they were not established was Lagos. It was not until 1904 that a branch was opened there. Two years earlier the home office for the Nigerian section was moved from Glasgow to Liverpool.

The Ja-Ja affair was one of the two main factors which produced the amalgamation known as the African Association, because it brought together all the British firms except Millers. The other factor was the charter granted to the Royal Niger Company. It was the ambition, and the confident expectation, of the firms that, uniting into a single company just as the firms on the Niger had done, they would obtain a charter for the Oil Rivers similar in character to the charter which had been granted to the earlier amalgamation for the Niger Territories. They realized that their application would be more likely to succeed if it were unanimous. Therefore they endeavoured to persuade Millers to forget the recent quarrel over Ja-Ja and join the amalgamation. But Millers refused to come in without pledges from the other parties to protect the Opobo traders, adherents of Ja-Ja in the late troubles, against any discrimination in favour of their rivals of Bonny. These assurances were not forthcoming and so Millers held aloof. The formation of the African Association and the failure of its attempt to secure a charter will form the subject of chapter 10.

[36] Deeds in property department of United Africa Company of Nigeria, Lagos.

6

Hatton and Cookson

James Hatton was in the year 1800 carrying on in Liverpool the business of ironmonger and anchorsmith under the style of James Hatton, Son & Company. He seems to have been the only principal of the firm with this plural title. It occupied Nos. 1–3 in Mersey Street, Liverpool. The building, largely reconstructed in 1870, is of considerable age. In it are dungeons underground for the accommodation of recalcitrant seamen.

About 1830, James' son, Edward Hatton, and his son-in-law, Thomas Worthington Cookson, came into the business, and following the death of the founder in 1838 they changed the name of the firm to Hatton & Cookson in 1840. They also altered the character of the business and became active as an oversea merchant house. They bought ships and at first sent their cargoes to America and India as well as to West Africa; but before long they specialized in the palm-oil trade.[1] In 1845 they had seven sailing ships voyaging to Africa, of sizes ranging from 103 tons to 277 tons.[2] In 1854 they had twenty-four sailing ships, ranging from 218 tons to 1,339 tons. They were established in the Oil Rivers, at Calabar and Cameroon, the Gabon, the mouths of the Muni and Congo Rivers, and in Angola.

They were particularly attracted to Libreville on the Como River in what is now the Republic of Gabon. The inhabitants of this area belong to the Mpongwe tribe, and in 1839 and 1841 their kings Denis and Louis Dowe had signed treaties of co-operation with a French captain named Bouët-Willaumez under which France acquired rights to trade and to establish missions, and also to use the Como estuary as a base for operations against the slave trade. A few years later, the French felt the need for a town where they could accommodate liberated slaves who had been set free when French naval vessels captured slaving vessels. This was the purpose of the foundation of Libreville in 1849.[3]

---

[1] Rankin, p. 74.   [2] Lloyds Register.   [3] *West Africa*, 10 March 1972.

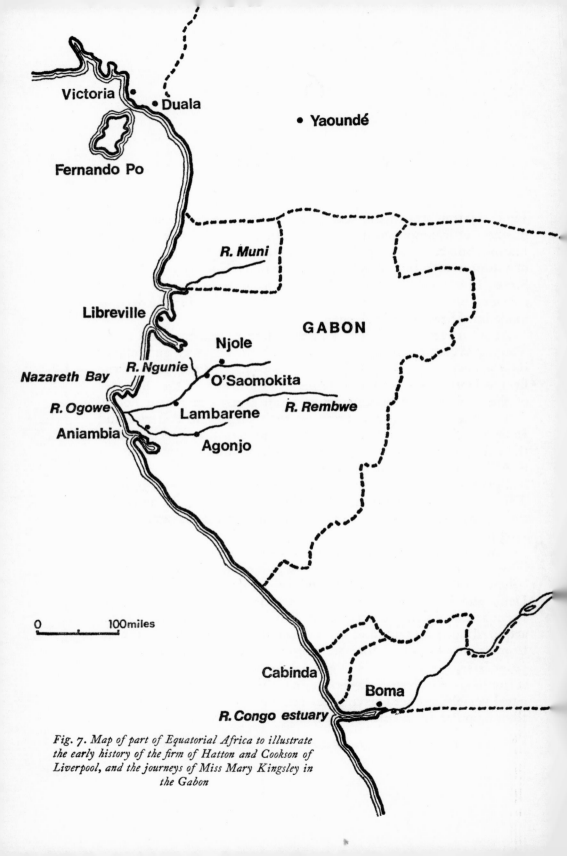

Fig. 7. Map of part of Equatorial Africa to illustrate the early history of the firm of Hatton and Cookson of Liverpool, and the journeys of Miss Mary Kingsley in the Gabon

In this area Hatton and Cookson were successful in getting ashore at a much earlier date than the traders in the Oil Rivers or in Cameroon. Their English flag floated to the breeze from a high pole at Aniambia by the Rembwe river in 1857.[4] They do not appear to have lacked competition, for in 1861 there was on the southern bank of the Gabon River a village of English factories, standing between the fort and comptoirs of the French, and an American mission with its houses, school, and church. The factory was a ground-floor house built of bamboo. The factor and his subordinates took their meals in a spacious piazza floored with deal. Their imports included bales of Manchester cloth, American tobacco in leaf, barrels of powder, barrels of rum, Birmingham trade guns (long as the ancient matchlocks, their stocks painted a bright red), beads, brass rods, and crockery. Trade with the interior was reserved by the African inhabitants at the coast, and was conducted upon the trust system. The exports included ebony, redwood, beeswax, wild rubber, and ivory.[5]

In that same year, 1861, Hatton and Cookson were established on the Cavalla river in Liberia,[6] but since no earlier or later record of their presence in that place has been traced, it must be concluded that they did not stay there very long.

By 1864 Hatton and Cookson were strongly established in several towns of the Niger Delta.[7] It is not surprising that in an area of such fierce competition they reduced their trading posts to one, which was on the Brass river.[8] While remaining at Cameroon in competition with R. and W. King, they concentrated their attention on the coasts to the south of that point.

Hatton and Cookson suffered a double disaster in 1864. At New Calabar the hulk *Merlin* caught fire, and as it was known to have gunpowder aboard the whole settlement fell into consternation. Ten ships and hulks were lying in a line to leeward of the burning one, and, as a strong harmattan wind was blowing, smoke and sparks were drifting across them. The hulks were covered by palm-mat roofs used as thatch, and, as the dry harmattan wind had been blowing for several days, everything had become as dry as tinder, so that a spark might create a conflagration. It was Saturday, and,

---

[4] Du Chaillu, Paul B., *Exploration and Adventures in Equatorial Africa* (London: Murray, 1861) p. 200.

[5] Reade, Winwood, *Savage Africa* (London: Smith Elder, 1893) chapter 11.

[6] Newbury, C. W., *British Policy towards West Africa Select Documents 1786–1874* (Oxford: Clarendon Press, 1965) pp. 177–80.

[7] P.R.O. Burton to F.O., 15 April 1864, F.O. 84/1221/1864.

[8] P.R.O. Craigie to Salmon, 31 July 1884, F.O. 403/32/1884.

following their usual custom, the agents had gone down in a party to Breaker Island, a small sandbar at the junction of the Bonny and New Calabar rivers, to take a rest while the weekly cleaning-up was done. The juniors, left in charge, slipped the moorings to get away from the burning ship by the aid of the ebbing tide, but after a while they met the up-coming tide, and drifted back into the vicinity of the *Merlin*. She exploded, and set fire to eight other ships. Every one of them had gunpowder on board, and all blew up in due course.

On the same day in Liverpool the *Lottie Sleigh*, belonging to Hatton and Cookson, took fire in the Mersey, and was destroyed, having on board a large quantity of powder. The explosion did immense damage in Liverpool and Cheshire.[9]

Cookson died in 1867, and Hatton retired in 1869. After that there was no Hatton in the business. It passed to Thomas Cookson's two sons, T. W. and E. H. Cookson.

It was their post at Boma which organized the relief of H. M. Stanley in the last stage of his journey across the continent in 1877. Stanley, the sole survivor of the four Europeans who had embarked upon the great exploration, having confirmed that the river which he had followed for a thousand miles was the Congo, struck overland for the last stage of his journey in order to shorten the way to the coast. Short of food, he sent men ahead to Boma with a letter requesting supplies. Hatton and Cookson responded generously, and Stanley wrote in his diary 'The long war against famine is over'.[10]

In the 1870s the Cookson brothers added steamers to their fleet,[11] both ocean steamers and smaller ones engaged in coastal trade; but in 1891 they decided to give up the role of shipowners and to devote their whole attention to their merchant business. They disposed of their ocean steamers and entered into an agreement with Elder Dempster to carry their cargoes.

During the decade 1880–1890 great changes took place in the political framework of the area in which the firm was established. In 1880 Hatton and Cookson still had their 'factory' at Brass: and that was, as it had long been, an independent trading community, although it was in an area which had come to be regarded as a British sphere of interest, and which was increasingly subject to the

[9] Cotterell, Harry, *Reminiscences* (Amsterdam: privately printed, 1968).
[10] Stanley, R. and Neame, A. (eds.), *The Exploration Diaries of H. M. Stanley* (London: Kimber, 1961) p. 203: Hird, Frank, *H. M. Stanley: the Authorised Life* (London: S. Paul, 1935) p. 164: Stanley, H. M., *Through the Dark Continent* (London: Low, 1878) vol. II pp. 455–6.
[11] Rankin, p. 75.

influence of British consuls supported by the Royal Navy. To the east, Hatton and Cookson were established at Duala, where their competitors were Richard and William King and two German companies.[12] The larger of these, C. Woermann, had come to Duala in 1863[13] and was to play a critical role in the history of the place. In Duala the firms traded from hulks under arrangements made with two African princely houses, the families of Mbeli and Akwa. Under those arrangements, the European traders remained on the coast and all inland trade was reserved for Duala merchants, who were financed by long credit from the Europeans under the system known as 'trust'. Following the coast to the south, Hatton and Cookson were again to be found at Libreville in the Gabon, where they had as competitors the English John Holt, the German Woermann, and a French firm. Here conditions were very different. The French had held the coastal area as a colony since 1843, and this had enabled European traders including Hatton and Cookson to build establishments ashore. South again, Hatton and Cookson had posts at Cabinda, an ancient Portuguese settlement, and at Boma on the northern shore of the Congo estuary, where they made their own arrangements with the local African political authority.

Ten years later, by 1890, the Brass 'factory' had been sold to the African Association. Duala had become part of a German colony, and to the south various international treaties had established the frontiers of Spanish Guinea, French Congo, Portuguese Cabinda, and the so-called Congo Free State. Thus, Hatton and Cookson were in the territories of five foreign powers, but not in any British colony.

In Cameroon it was not until 1884 that Hatton and Cookson had to deal with a European occupying power. In the previous year Bismarck, the German Chancellor, had held discussions with the Hamburg Chamber of Commerce and had promised to send Nachtigal, the German Consul-General at Tunis, down the west coast to raise the German flag in certain places. In July Nachtigal had already laid a claim to the Togo coast, and the agents of the Woermann company in Duala were daily expecting him. They appear to have had foreknowledge of his intentions. On 10 July they were horrified to see an English gunboat run into the Cameroon River.[14] They thought that all was lost, but on 11 July in the

---

[12] Meyer, Hans, *Das deutsche Kolonialreich* (Leipzig: Verlag des bibliographischen Instituts, 1909) p. 531.

[13] ibid., p. 419.   [14] ibid.

morning the gunboat sailed away and the same evening Nachtigal arrived. The very next morning three agents of the Woermann company, Eduard Woermann, J. Jantzen, and J. Thormählen, signed treaties with King Bell and King Akwa, by which those monarchs ceded their rights of sovereignty.[15] It seems, by later standards, a very remarkable thing to be undertaken by representatives of a trading company; but it was not without a recent precedent, for earlier in that same year David McIntosh, acting on behalf of the National African Company, had been making treaties with indigenous authorities on the banks of the Niger river.[16] Two days later, on 14 July, Nachtigal confirmed on behalf of the German government the treaties which the Woermann agents had signed[17] and he made a further treaty with a third African king named Deido.[18] Five days later the British consul arrived and protested; but he was too late.[19] Towards the end of the year some of the people and chiefs of Duala rose in arms against the Germans, but the movement was suppressed, and in 1885 the German claims were recognized internationally.

The seizure of Cameroon by the Germans cannot have been agreeable to the British companies which had long been established at Duala. Traders generally were not favourably disposed towards colonial governments, such as they had come to know in Sierra Leone, Gold Coast, and Lagos. They regarded them as expensive and interfering. Still, in the political atmosphere of 1884, when colonial rivalry seemed to be rising to boiling point, it was clearly preferable to be under a colonial government of one's own nationality than under a potentially hostile power. Fortunately for Hatton and Cookson, and for the other British firms established in that part of Africa, the treaties which were concluded at Berlin (1885) with a view to regulating the 'scramble for Africa' established a very liberal regime as regards trade. In fact, British traders were permitted to continue their activities.

During this period the senior partner of the firm was E. H. Cookson. In 1901 Hatton and Cookson were registered as a limited

[15] Cornevin, Robert, in Gann and Duignan (eds.) *Colonialism in Africa 1870–1960*, vol. I *History and Politics of Colonialism 1870–1914* (Cambridge University Press, 1969) p. 398.

[16] *see* chapter 9. Also in the early 1880s French agents signed many treaties with African rulers: *see* Brunschwig, Henri, as in note 15, pp. 145–58.

[17] Cornevin, op. cit., p. 398.

[18] Meyer, op. cit., p. 419.

[19] Robinson, R. and Gallagher, D., with Denny, A., *Africa and the Victorians* (London: Macmillan, 1961) p. 174.

liability company, and he became the chairman. He was an original director of the African Association (which took over Hatton and Cookson's interests in Brass) and was chairman of the African Association in 1892–1893. He was Mayor of Liverpool in 1889. He did not retire from business until 1920, by which time Hatton and Cookson had become part of the African and Eastern Trade Corporation; and he died two years later.[20]

In the French area extensive explorations extending inland from the coast were made under the leadership of de Brazza from 1875 to 1889. The penetration of the interior encouraged the commercial houses to invest in river steamers and to establish trading stores on the banks of the navigable waterways. Hatton and Cookson followed this policy.

Most of the information which is available regarding this phase of their business comes from the famous ichthyologist Mary Kingsley (see plate 8). She went to this part of Africa to study fish, and she declared that, among all the people who showed her kindness, she was chiefly indebted to C. G. Hudson, who was Hatton and Cookson's agent at Cabinda in 1893. Two years later she visited him again, realizing that her success would depend on the attitude which he 'might see fit to assume toward ichthyology'. She found that he had become 'a sort of commercial bishop', that is to say the agent-general for his firm in the French dependencies, and in this capacity he was able to arrange for her to go up the Ogowe river. On landing at Libreville in 1895 she was advised to run the gig on the beach, and not attempt the steps of Hatton and Cookson's wharf, which was said to be only fit for a hen. However, she preferred the steps, and was warmly welcomed. She accompanied Hudson up the Ogowe river in the steamship *Mové*. This was a fine little vessel; the food was excellent, and the society charming, including the captain and engineer. In Nazareth Bay at the mouth of the river they ran alongside the *Fallabar*, a steamship which Hatton and Cookson had been using on this coast before they acquired the *Mové*. Her hull had rusted through, so they had put concrete in it and used her as a depot hulk.

It took about twelve hours to get up the river from Nazareth Bay to Lambaréné, where the French Protestant mission was already established. Albert Schweitzer was to make it better known in the twentieth century. There were a French post and two trading establishments, one belonging to Woermann, and the other to

[20] Rankin, p. 75.

Hatton and Cookson. At Lambaréné Mary Kingsley left Hudson and went forward in the *Éclaireur*, a little stern-wheeler belonging to the Chargeurs Réunis. It took her a further ninety miles up the river to Njole. Cockshut, the Hatton and Cookson agent, went too, to inspect trading stores. They passed the point where the Ngunie River flowed into the Ogowe. This river was navigable during the rains, but now it was the dry season, so the trading posts on its banks were cut off until the following October. Shortly before Mary's visit, a section of the Akele tribe had sacked one of Hatton and Cookson's stores on the Ngunie River. The African trading agent in charge had been away on an expedition, and his wife had organized a gallant resistance, but she was seized and beaten. A French official had gone up to re-establish order, taking Cockshut with him; they had been engaged in 'a fine fight' before arresting the chief and his two principal lieutenants.

Half way to Njole, the ship spent a night at O'Saomokita. Woermann had a store there, and it was in the charge of a young Frenchman who had previously been employed by Hatton and Cookson, whom he had left to join Woermann. A few days later Mary heard that this young man had committed suicide, and this moved her to reflect upon the tragic isolation of a trader in such a place.

At Njole four companies were established, because besides Hatton and Cookson there were Dumas, a French firm, John Holt, and Woermann. There was a little avenue of cocoa trees in full bearing. Mary Kingsley wished to proceed up the Ogowe River beyond the rapids and then to leave that river and walk across the watershed to the upper reaches of the Rembwe River, down which she proposed to travel to the coast. It was difficult to find anyone who would take her above Njole, but again Hatton and Cookson came to the rescue and engaged two men of the Igalwa tribe. As she went up the river, the crew sang songs and there was one song in which they sang how they had been dissatisfied with the goods they got from Holt, and they had decided to take the next trade to Hatton and Cookson, or *vice versa*. Hatton and Cookson were known throughout the country by the nickname Ugumu. English seems to have been an acceptable *lingua franca* everywhere. It was thought to be very difficult for Africans to learn French. A Portuguese lady whom Mary met said she supposed they got on well with English because it was so similar to their own barbarous dialects.

Payments were made in goods. No coinage-equivalent was in use, 'not even the brass bars and cheetems [sic] that are used in Calabar, or cowries as in Lagos'. A written or printed piece of paper was employed, practically a cheque, and it was called a bon or book. These pieces of paper were in three amounts, fifty centimes, a franc, and a dollar, which was five francs. They could be cashed at any company's store, and no establishment of government, trade, or mission would hesitate to draw such cheques. Among the Africans, every article used in trade had a definite and acknowledged value. For example, six fish hooks and one pocket handkerchief had the same value, and either would be recognized as exchangeable against a determined number of matches, or quantity of pomade, etc. Now the traders' cost prices did not bear the same relation to each other as the valuation set on the articles by the Africans, and of course the cost prices tended to vary, so the traders were always bringing pressure on the Africans to accept certain items rather than others.

After her adventures in the interior, Mary Kingsley was engaged in complicated negotiations with some people of the Efoua tribe to take her down the Rembwe. She arranged to pay them off at Hatton and Cookson's store on the Rembwe and they said, 'Look my mouth and it be sweet, so palaver done set'. On the way down the river she stayed at a Fan village; and the chief complained to her that he could not trade direct with Hatton and Cookson owing to middlemen who asserted their interest. Mary Kingsley took some trouble to find out how these African middlemen traders managed to travel so far into the interior with large loads of valuable goods, which they were quite unable to defend against attack. She found that it all depended on these men having a wife in every village. It was the wife and her family interest that provided for the man's safety. One man whom she met had a chain of wives stretching over three hundred miles.

When at last they reached the Rembwe, she went to the Ugumu store, where she was greeted by a very black man who spoke perfect English. 'Where's the agent?' she said. 'I'm the agent,' he answered. This was a sub-branch under Agonjo, which was distant an hour's paddling. Here the agent was Sanga Glass, 'an exceedingly neat, well-educated M'Pongwe gentleman in irreproachable English garments'. Mary Kingsley and Sanga Glass proceeded to make the selections of merchandise for paying the three canoe men, whose names were Greyshirt, Silence, and Pagan; but when they saw what it was proposed that they should have, these three said that they would prefer to have cheques for payment in Hatton and Cookson's store at Lambaréné; and that is the way it was settled. Sanga Glass had worked for Hatton and Cookson for many years, and appeared to be very prosperous. Concluding her account of her visit to him, Mary wrote, 'Although I cite this factory as a typical factory of a black trader, it is a specimen of the highest class, for, being in connection with Messrs. Hatton and Cookson, it is well kept up and stocked. Firms differ much in this particular. Messrs. Hatton and Cookson, like Messrs. Miller Brothers in the Bight, take every care that lies in their power of the people who serve them, down to the krooboys working on their beaches, giving ample and good rations and providing good houses'.[21]

In Cameroon the trading houses remained at the seaboard for several years after the German occupation; they bought ivory, rubber, palm oil, and palm kernels (which had recently become an article of commercial interest); but the custom whereby only Africans were permitted to conduct the inland trade was respected, and the trust system remained the basis of commerce. However, the German government regarded this system as undesirable and set themselves to bring it to an end. According to the German government, African middlemen expected margins of seventy-five per cent, and it appears that the Germans thought that this was too much.[22] The attack on middlemen, both indigenous and expatriate, is a recurrent theme of colonial times; possibly in this instance too little recognition was given to the costs incurred and the services performed by middlemen who provided transport under most difficult circumstances. Be that as it may, in 1888 the Germans sent a military expedition inland with the object of 'opening up the country'.[23] Thereafter, the European trading houses established in Duala came under pressure from the government to open stores in the interior for the purpose of buying produce and holding stocks of imported merchandise for sale. Hatton and Cookson seem to have ignored this pressure for some years; at any rate, there is no record that in the period 1888 to 1905 they spread their organization as widely as their competitor Richard and William King. They may have taken the view that there was insufficient inducement for expansion, for in the first twenty years of German rule, the exports

21 Kingsley, Mary, *West African Studies* (London: Macmillan, 1899).
22 Kingsley, Mary, *Travels in West Africa* (London: Macmillan, 1897) p. 317.
23 Meyer, op. cit., p. 535.

of produce, while not exactly stagnant, showed only a gradual increase:

| | Million marks | |
	Exports	Imports
1890–1	4·1	4·7
1895–6	4·1	5·5
1896–7	3·7	5·9
1897–8	3·9	7·1
1898–9	5·2	11·1
1900	5·9	14·3
1903	7·1	9·4
1904	7·6	9·2
1905	9·3	13·5
1906	9·9	13·3
1907	15·8	17·3
1908	16·1	12·9[24]

However, from 1899 onwards the colony received considerable investments, as the excess of imports over exports indicates. By 1905 there was evidence of much greater buoyancy in the economy. Cocoa began to be important[25] and the construction of a railway to link Duala with the interior was begun.[26] It was intended to reach as far as Yaounde, and the Germans contemplated the establishment of an important administrative centre in that town. Hatton and Cookson appear to have decided on a policy of expansion, and they acted with speed and foresight. Between 1906 and 1911 they bought considerable areas of land in Yaounde, some of which they were subsequently able to sell to competitors at a profit.[27,28]

[24] ibid., pp. 531–2.
[25] ibid., p. 533.
[26] ibid., p. 541.
[27] United Africa Company property department records.
[28] I venture to comment on a statement by Robert Cornevin in the work cited at note 15 *above*, p. 398, that John Holt and the Ambas Bay Trading Company 'held their positions solidly in the face of German commercial and political programmes' and that the 'Ambas Bay Trading Company was absorbed in 1920 by the Unilever combine'. To deal with the second part first, Unilever did not come into existence until 1929 (*see* chapter 29). The first part of the quoted passage is unexceptionable, for it is true that John Holt and the Ambas Bay Trading Company held positions in German territory up to the outbreak of war in 1914. They were not however the only solid representatives of British commerce. At Duala Richard and William King, and Hatton and Cookson, had been established longer than John Holt, and in 1914 were probably no less important. The Ambas Bay Trading Company Limited was one of the smaller antecedent companies of the United Africa group. It was

While the Germans were active in developing Cameroon, the territories along the Atlantic coast to the south as far as the Congo River underwent little development during the period from 1884 to 1914. French Congo, an administrative unit which had been made by uniting the old settlements of the Gabon with the territories explored by de Brazza and others, and with areas far to the north conquered by French military expeditions, was not effectively administered, and had hardly any communications and no money. The population was very sparse, for there were no more than two million people in the whole of this vast area.[29] These circumstances did not favour the production of important crops for export, such as were becoming staples of trade in countries to the north and west. Spurred by a desire to stimulate development, but yet unwilling to incur heavy expenses, the French government in the 1890s embraced a policy of granting concessions of land to commercial companies, which were encouraged to believe that the area constituted a rich reserve of untapped wealth. No less than forty concessions were granted, and the land which was placed at the disposal of the concessionary companies amounted to 650,000 square kilometres, an area larger than France. The concession holders had to make an annual payment to the government and they were under contract to provide certain services such as communications and posts, but they received within their areas powers which placed them effectively in the position of a government. The concessions unfortunately provided opportunities for some very undesirable people, speculative

---

registered in England on 24 November 1888 with a capital of £10,000, for the purpose of adopting and carrying into effect an agreement made between Walter Dennis Woodin and Benjamin Bullock, to carry on a business lately carried on by Walter Dennis Woodin. The firm W. D. Woodin and Company was an important shareholder and several members of the Woodin family had shares, and W. D. Woodin himself was the manager of the Ambas Bay company, with a seat on the board. Its two principal centres of activity were Victoria (Cameroon) and Santa Isabel (on the Spanish Island of Fernando Po). The company acquired a plantation at Bwinga in Cameroon. The outbreak of war in 1914 interrupted business, and in 1915, when it became possible to start again, the property at Victoria and the branches which depended on Victoria were sold to W. D. Woodin and Company Limited. That company also provided management and finance for the plantation. In May 1920 all the shareholders of the Ambas Bay Company accepted an offer from the African and Eastern Trade Corporation Limited to purchase their shares. The Ambas Bay Trading Company Limited continued to trade under that name in Fernando Po until until 17 December 1970. (The source of the foregoing information is the company's minute book and other records in the possession of the United Africa Company.)

[29] Deschamps, Hubert, *Histoire générale de l'Afrique noire* (Paris: Presses universitaires, 1971) pp. 393 ff.

company-pushers in France and callous unprincipled rogues in the colony.

Hatton and Cookson did not become involved in those concessions. Whether or not they had wished to participate, the 1890s were a time of very acute rivalry between France and Britain in Africa, and no British company would have been welcome as a partner in the concession policy, whatever the Congo Basin treaties may have said about equal rights and open doors. There is every reason to suppose that the knowledge of what was going on must have caused distaste and embarrassment to the agents of Hatton and Cookson, for, as Mary Kingsley had noted, this firm employed men of quality whose standards of behaviour were good. R. E. Dennett, one of the trading agents, studied the African peoples of the area of the Congo estuary and wrote a book about them.[30] Another well-known agent was William Taylor, who arrived in those parts to work for Hatton and Cookson before 1900 and continued until 1931.[31]

The concession policy did, however, lead to a substantial increase in the production of logs for export from 1902 onwards.[32] Hatton and Cookson were active as buyers of logs from the producers for export to Europe. It is a trade which requires skill and expert knowledge, for while cocoa and palm oil are sold by the ton, subject to well-defined standards of quality, in the timber trade every log is different.

By 1910 it was recognized that the concession policy had failed: the area subject to concessions was reduced by half and the French government brought the behaviour of the agents under control by extending its administration throughout the whole country. These measures were associated with the establishment of the Federation of French Equatorial Africa, within which Gabon, Middle Congo, and Oubangui-Chari were colonies, and Tchad was a military territory.[33] Following this shake-out, one of the largest concessions was bought by Lever Brothers. That story will be taken up in chapter 14, but here it is appropriate to note that William Lever, a manufacturer, was regarded as a threat by the trading companies of which Hatton and Cookson was a typical representative. Lever was

[30] Dennett, R. E., *Folk-lore of the Fjort* (London: Folk-lore society, 1898).

[31] Taylor was the uncle of Winifred Brady, who herself made history with her work for the girl guides in Nigeria.

[32] Deschamps, Hubert, op. cit., p. 395, and Coquery-Vidrovitch, Catherine, in Gann and Duignan, op. cit., p. 190.

[33] Deschamps, op. cit., p. 394.

among those who entertained an unfavourable opinion of middle-men and of their margins. His philosophy was, to place the manu-facturer in direct contact with the Africans who produced his raw materials. Not only did he now appear in French Equatorial Africa, but he acquired important interests in the Belgian Congo, respond-ing to the invitation of the Belgian government which had replaced the Congo Free State in 1908. Here it might have been expected that Hatton and Cookson would have been the leading British company. They had been established for many years in Boma, which had been the capital of the Congo Free State.[34] But they had never moved up the Congo River or its tributaries. No doubt the menace of competition from Lever Brothers led the ageing Cookson to think of joining the large group which was being created by some of the leading trading companies. Liverpool circles were buzzing with rumours of amalgamations, when in 1914 war broke out between Britain and Germany and it became difficult for Hatton and Cookson to talk about putting their assets into a larger group, because for a year or two these were partly in the hands of the enemy.

On the outbreak of war in 1914 the British companies in Cameroon were in a difficult position. However, it appears that none of the staff of Hatton and Cookson were interned by the Germans. The reason may well be, that in order to secure staff who were able to speak German, Hatton and Cookson had already at that time followed a policy of recruiting Swiss, Germans, and Austrians. This is surmise; but it is supported by two facts, the first being that no Englishmen belonging to Hatton and Cookson were imprisoned, and the second, that after the war they had a Swiss national as the head of their business in Cameroon.[35]

Discussions were resumed at the end of the war with a view to amalgamation, and in 1919 all the shares of Hatton and Cookson were bought by the African and Eastern Trade Corporation. The supervising agent of that organization at Calabar had a general oversight of the Hatton and Cookson establishments farther down the coast. These continued to trade under the Hatton and Cookson name until 1929 at Duala and Boma, and thereafter for another forty years in Gabon, and in the Spanish mainland territory variously known as Rio Muni and Equatorial Guinea.

[34] ibid., p. 456.   [35] Barben to Pedler, April 1969.

7

G. B. Ollivant and Company Limited

George Bentworth Ollivant, an officer in the Indian army, was returning to the United Kingdom in a ship which called at Freetown. He was impressed by its trading possibilities, and in 1858 he set up a business in New Cannon Street, Manchester, which shipped cotton piece goods and other merchandise to West Africa and bought African produce for sale in Europe. He registered a trade mark (see plate 21) in 1858, the 'horseman' mark, which is said to represent Captain Ollivant, in his Indian army days, tiger hunting. The business soon required larger premises, and in 1860 a move was made to 20, Lever Street. By 1870 it was of a size to acquire commodious premises at 3 Albert Street, where a staff of buyers, clerks, and packers, was accommodated.

The principal business was, at first, the export of velvets, velveteens, cords, sateens, and croydons, but later business began to develop in every description of goods suitable for the West Coast of Africa.[1] The mode of operation seems to have been to appoint correspondents at places on the African coast. For example, in 1888 the firm was represented at Bonthe and Sherbro by Charles Benjamin Collier who mortgaged properties in those places to Alfred Ollivant as security for credit which had been extended to him.[2] This Alfred was the son of the founder. He was joined by his brother Charles and in 1894 they formed a partnership under the name, G. B. Ollivant and Company. The growth of the firm led to the establishment of 'factories' in Africa. The first was at Lagos, about 1880, and in 1887 the second Ollivant 'factory' opened in Freetown.

An employee named Thomas Chadwick (see plate 4) went out to take charge of the Freetown factory in 1891. He and his family were to become the mainstay of the business. His brother Leonard followed him to Africa three years later.[3] Thomas, finding that communication

[1] *Manchester of Today*, 1888, p. 150.
[2] From documents in the possession of G. B. Ollivant and Company Limited.
[3] *West Africa Review*, September 1937.

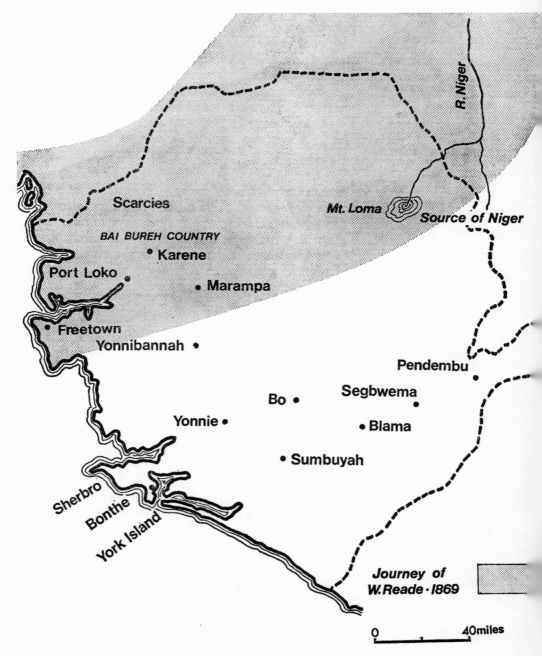

Fig. 8. Map of Sierra Leone to illustrate the early history of the business of G. B. Ollivant and Company

with the interior could be conducted only by runners, arranged for a loft of carrier pigeons to be sent to him from England. He used the pigeons to receive messages from the interior, and in this way he was always better informed than any of his competitors regarding the position of produce stocks and merchandise requirements, as a homing pigeon is capable of flying at a speed of about a mile a minute for several hundred miles.

On one occasion Chadwick placed his pigeons at the disposal of the Sierra Leone government, which at that time was experiencing hostility from a ruler named Bai Bureh in the interior. Governor Cardew ordered a detachment of troops to subdue Bai Bureh. Open hostility was not expected, but in fact serious resistance was encountered. The small supply of ammunition carried by the troops was used up and they were surrounded. Back to Freetown came a pigeon telling of their plight, and reinforcements were able to reach them in time. It was just as well that Chadwick had acquired the good opinion of the government by lending his pigeons, because he got into trouble for having sold gunpowder to Bai Bureh, and the Secretary of State, Joseph Chamberlain, wanted him to be prosecuted for supplying munitions to the enemy. While the law officers were considering how they could frame a charge under the complicated law of treason, Chadwick was paid and thanked for his pigeons, which made it hard to prosecute him, and the case was dropped.[4] How like Swanzy in the Ashanti war!

In 1899 Thomas Chadwick returned to Manchester and took control of the business as manager for the partners. Charles Ollivant disappeared from the firm about this time. Alfred was an old man, more interested in his home in the country than in trade: so in 1900 the business was converted into a limited liability company, G. B. Ollivant and Company Limited. Alfred Ollivant held nearly all the capital, but the management was in the hands of two directors, Thomas Chadwick and his friend Zeph William Brown, a member of a cotton business, Brown and Nephews, which owned the Golbourne mill: an interesting example of 'vertical integration' of manufacture with commerce, a phenomenon which thus appears for the first time in this story.

The company was not at first successful. After three years it was unable to meet its debts, and the creditors took over. Chief among them was Brown and Nephews. For eight years Thomas Chadwick, with the help of Zeph Brown, worked to pay off the debts. By 1910

[4] Fyfe, C., *History of Sierra Leone* (Oxford: Clarendon Press, 1962) p. 578.

he had succeeded and was able to acquire the controlling interest in the business. He was a great character, an expert in textiles who took trouble in communicating his skill to younger men.[5]

His brother Leonard remained in Freetown until 1902 and was then in charge of the activities in Nigeria until 1914. By this time Thomas's four sons, Leonard, William, George, and Victor, were working in the company in Africa.[6] The Chadwick family, with their personal activity at both the African and British ends of the business, are reminiscent of the Swanzys. Thomas Chadwick, on his frequent visits to Freetown, made a practice of interviewing school-boys who were candidates for employment, and in later years it was the proud boast of some long service pensioners that they had been engaged personally by Thomas Chadwick.[7]

G. B. Ollivant and Company entered into an agreement with Elder Dempster, the shipping company which operated the service to West Africa, under which that company undertook to lend money to Ollivant, and Ollivant promised to use only Elder Dempster ships. With this financial support, G. B. Ollivant was able to expand. Branches were opened at Kano and Zaria in Nigeria in 1912, that is to say, as soon as the railway was open to Kano, and at the very beginning of the great expansion of the groundnut trade. A branch was opened at Lomé in Togoland in 1916, taking advantage of the elimination of the German firms from the capital of the ex-German colony. The situation in Togoland presented an exceptional opportunity at that time, for this country had not been subject to the open-door treaties, and the Germans had taken advantage of this circumstance to eliminate all non-German firms save one, namely F. and A. Swanzy.[8] In 1919 Ollivant opened stores in Ivory Coast and in Dahomey. In spreading to new places, Ollivant acted in close consultation with Elder Dempster, and the expansion of Ollivant may be viewed as one of the measures which Elder Dempster took to safeguard the shipping line's position in face of the formidable combinations which were, at that time, being brought together by the African Association and by Lord Leverhulme.

[5] Shepherdson, Glen, to Pedler, 9 August 1969.

[6] For the information in the three preceding paragraphs I am indebted to Gordon A. Cowan, Alfred Nixon, William Sellars, Conrad Sheldon, Glen Shepherdson, and W. L. Stephens, members of the staff of Ollivant, serving or retired.

[7] From N. G. Cole, a pensioner of Ollivant who was recruited by Thomas Chadwick in Freetown in 1911 at the age of fifteen.

[8] Cornevin, Robert, *Histoire du Togo* (Paris: Berger-Levrault, 1959) pp. 194, 257.

In 1916 the British government offered for sale by auction the assets in Africa of several German trading companies which had been seized. It will be necessary to explain what happened in some detail in chapter 15; here it is sufficient to say that Ollivant was a member of a consortium of eight trading companies which bought most of the assets in Nigeria. The formation of such a consortium was facilitated by the general spirit of friendly co-operation which existed in 1916, but in the following year competition between the firms became more acute, and in 1918 it was very severe indeed. In these circumstances the consortium found it more convenient to divide up the ex-German assets, and Ollivant, with the financial support of Elder Dempster, was successful in securing the lion's share of the properties which had formerly belonged to the important German company, G. L. Gaiser.

Cecil Gilbert, demobilized from war service, took employment with Ollivant and was posted to Kano, where, owing to the illness of his superior, he found himself in charge within a few weeks. He had, during military service in Aden, made the acquaintance of Abou Zaid, an Arab who had previously been in Kano, buying hides and skins for the firm of Ambrosini. Gilbert invited Abou Zaid to join him in Kano, and subsequently recruited six more skin selectors from Aden. Gilbert made an extensive tour on horseback, taking in Kazauri, Daura, Hadeija, Gumel, and Ringum, and in all these places he made arrangements to buy groundnuts, and hides and skins. A branch was opened at Sokoto in the autumn of 1919. Camels carried the supplies of merchandise to that branch, and brought the produce back to the railway. Maidobi was developed through a European who was not an employee, but worked as a freelance trader on commission.[9]

For some years G. B. Ollivant and Company in Manchester had acted as an indent house for the firm of A. J. Tangalakis; that is to say, Ollivant provided Tangalakis with buying services and probably also with financial accommodation. In 1918 Ollivant bought the Tangalakis business. This gave Ollivant further expansion in northern Nigeria and a footing in the Gold Coast; but it presented a problem typical of mergers. The problem was resolved by putting the Ollivant name over the business in Gold Coast, but in Nigeria the Ollivant and Tangalakis branches were maintained separately in most centres, competing one with the other. There were two general managers, one for Ollivant and the other for Tangalakis, and they

[9] Gilbert, Cecil: letter, 14 February 1970.

had independent authority and were both responsible directly to Manchester. In the hides and skins business, however, the competition between the two sides of the group became ridiculous, and in 1924 the hides and skins activities were brought together under the Tangalakis name. In acquiring the Tangalakis business Ollivant took over another famous trade mark (see plate 21), which like their own contained a picture of a horse. The Tangalakis trade mark is very remarkable. It shows six British cavalry troopers crossing a river on a pontoon, with their horses swimming beside them.

Bernard Wilson and Company, brokers in Liverpool, handled West African produce for Ollivant, and they also bought oils and seeds for Bibby of Liverpool, soap manufacturer and seed-crusher. Through friendship with Wilson the broker, the Chadwicks and the Bibbys were brought together, and the families became connected by marriage. It was a period when the principal makers of soap were establishing positions in Africa with a view to protecting and developing their supplies of raw materials, and Bibby took this step in association with the Ollivant company. A joint enterprise was formed to operate in the Belgian Congo and in French Equatorial Africa. It was under the Ollivant name but the shares were held in equal parts by Bibby and Ollivant. It opened posts at Kinshasa, Stanleyville, and Bangui.

Thomas Chadwick died in the late 1920s and his son Leonard Chadwick became the head of the firm.

8

The Decline of Swanzy and the Rise of Millers

Andrew Swanzy, two years before his death in 1880, had extended the activities of his firm by engaging in gold mining.[1] F. and A. Swanzy bought concessions from the Wassaw chief north-east of Abosso, and the place was called Crockerville, after Crocker who had succeeded Cleaver as the manager in charge in Africa. Several companies invested in gold mining about that time in the Gold Coast, and F. and A. Swanzy were unique among them in employing Fanti miners, engaged locally. Their competitors brought in *krumen* from Liberia. Swanzys shared the proceeds with the workers, who were allowed to keep one-third.[2] These arrangements were such as might have been expected from Andrew Swanzy, with his great knowledge of the local people; but under the leadership of his son Francis (who never visited Africa), they did not provide a recipe for success. In any case, it seems that there was not much gold at Crockerville. The gold mining venture contributed to the undoing of the firm.

It is now necessary to come back to Alexander and George Miller, whose business became a major influence in the development of trade in West Africa. The Miller brothers beat F. and A. Swanzy at their own game in the Gold Coast. They were among the earliest firms to venture up the Niger Delta, where they opposed all the other British firms—nine of them—until those nine joined together to form the African Association, leaving the Millers' company independent and defiant.

James Miller was a soft goods merchant in Glasgow. His sons, Alexander and George, started a business with the West Indies, but it was not very successful and in 1868 the brothers turned their attention to West Africa, where they met with such good fortune

[1] *Journal Society of Arts*, 2 June 1882, no. 1541 vol. XXX.
[2] Claridge, W. W., *A History of the Gold Coast* (London: Murray, 1915) vol. II p. 246; McPhee, A., *Economic Revolution in British West Africa* (London: Routledge, 1926) p. 55.

that they decided to wind up their affairs in the Caribbean. They called their firm Alexander Miller Brother and Company. As will appear in a later chapter, this was one of the companies which went trading up the River Niger, and in 1879 formed the group which was first known as the United African Company and later as the Royal Niger Company. When the United African Company was formed, Alexander Miller became one of its joint managing directors. This made it necessary for him to move his office from Glasgow to London, and, as already mentioned, the Miller brothers decided that in London he should also deal with their activities in the Gold Coast, leaving Millers' Nigerian business under the direction of brother George Miller, who for the time being continued to live in Glasgow.

Alexander Miller became very busy with the affairs of the Royal Niger Company, and had little time for the business in the Gold Coast. A crisis occurred when death carried off all the Europeans employed by Millers in that country. Alexander Miller's immediate reaction to this catastrophe was, to give instructions to the African who had taken charge to liquidate the assets with a view to winding up. However, in the London office there was a young man named J. H. Batty, who subsequently had a remarkable career in Africa, and then became the chairman of the African and Eastern Trade Corporation in London. Though not yet twenty-one years old, he volunteered to go to the Gold Coast and to take charge there. Miller hesitated to agree, but Batty persuaded him although, being a minor, he could not hold a power of attorney. So Alexander Miller changed his mind about closing the business; but when young Batty arrived at Cape Coast there was no bungalow for him because it had already been sold in the process of liquidation. L. P. Coussey, the African agent of Lintott Spink and Company of Glasgow, took compassion on the young Englishman whom the surf-boat had deposited on the beach, and offered hospitality which Batty gratefully accepted. The juvenile appearance of the new chief caused surprise to the African staff but they rallied to him.[3] When after some years Batty relinquished the local direction to assume important duties in London, Alexander Miller Brother and Company in the Gold Coast was large and prosperous.

In 1883 Francis Swanzy presented to the Colonial Office a memorial of grievances about affairs in the Gold Coast. It bore his signature, together with those of William Cleaver his partner, the

[3] Rankin, p. 66.

Miller brothers, the Lintotts, and A. Hutton. They complained that taxes were too high and that the government wasted the money, doing nothing for roads, drainage, and lighting. They wanted the merchants to be represented on the legislative council. The memorial contained the interesting observation that many government officers were engaged for short terms, whereas commercial employees served for tours of three years.[4]

In 1887 F. and A. Swanzy opened a branch in Freetown. Their main trade there was in leaf tobacco from the United States. The importation of this commodity into Africa from America had been going on for a long time. The leaves were used by Africans for chewing, for smoking in pipes, and for making snuff. The leaves, bought by skilled selectors in Louisville, Kentucky, were treated with an oily fluid which earned for them in some parts of Africa the soubriquet 'black fat'. The trade needed special knowledge because there were several different ways of packing the tobacco, and the market women in each place insisted that every consignment should be packed in the way to which they were accustomed. The leaves had to be bound in bundles and each bundle was bound with a leaf which gathered the stalks together, but each market had its own idea as to how many leaves should be in a bundle. Woe betide the would-be seller if the market woman formed the view that the leaf used for binding was of inferior quality! In Freetown a number of local people were active in this trade and they complained about the new activities of Swanzys.

It seems to have been supposed in Freetown that Swanzys might be persuaded to build a railway to the River Niger (a distance of some two hundred miles), for an official of the Sierra Leone government named Major A. M. Festing visited the famous African king Samory, the ruler of the country into which the railway would have run, and secured his agreement in principle to the construction of a railway by F. and A. Swanzy.[5] However, it was an ephemeral idea, for in 1889, after no more than two years in Freetown, Swanzys packed up and sold their assets to Paterson Zochonis,[6] a company with its base at Manchester. Evidently it had been, for F. and A. Swanzy, a disappointing experience. They were probably frightened by Major Festing's activities, which might have embroiled them

[4] Newbury, C. W., *British Policy towards West Africa Select Documents 1875–1914* (Oxford: Clarendon Press, 1971).

[5] Hargreaves, John D. in Gann and Duignan (eds.) *Colonialism in Africa 1870–1960* (Cambridge University Press, 1969) vol. I p. 209.

[6] Fyfe, C., *History of Sierra Leone* (Oxford: Clarendon Press, 1962) p. 478.

with the French; for King Samory put up a spirited resistance to the French for no less than sixteen years, 1882 to 1898,[7] and Swanzys could not afford to come into conflict with the French government in view of their activities in the Ivory Coast and Dahomey.

In 1892 W. Waters was the chief agent of F. and A. Swanzy in the Gold Coast, and he was the first signatory among 517 petitioners who requested the Secretary of State for the Colonies to grant 'adequate representation of the general public on the legislative council. At the present time (they pointed out) there is only one un-official member.'[8] This followed the Swanzy tradition, for Swanzys had put forward proposals for more liberal representation on the legislature in 1849, in 1851, and in 1883.

When Batty ceased to reside in the Gold Coast and took up his appointment in London, his successor as the head of the Miller business was Percy Shaw, and after him came W. W. H. Grey. Grey was engaged by Millers in 1904 but he was no novice to Africa, having been in the service of the Lagos Stores (see chapter 20) and of Elder Dempster. Grey was alternating with a colleague as manager of the former firm at Lagos when he surprised his prin-cipals in Liverpool by seeking their permission to spend his leave in Nigeria. This was probably in 1900, but it may have been one or two years later. Accompanied by servants and porters he walked to Kano, a journey of several hundred miles. Kano was reached, but access to the interior of the great walled city was denied to this strange white man. Grey was aided by his fluent knowledge of the Hausa tongue. His career in the First World War was remarkable, for he joined up as a subaltern and rose to be a Major-General. Un-like most men of his generation, he never wore a topee.[9] In 1929 he became the first managing director of the United Africa Company.

When Batty started work for Millers, the business must have been insignificant in comparison with Swanzys. Yet twenty years later Millers took Swanzys over. These were years of exceptional growth in the Gold Coast, which offered splendid opportunities to a merchant house. Swanzys, with all their advantages, did not seize those chances, but young Batty took them on behalf of Millers. The rapid growth of the economy was due to the construction of rail-ways, which employed 10,000 people, to the development of gold

[7] Fage, J. D., *History of West Africa* (Cambridge University Press, 1955) p. 149.
[8] Newbury, C. W., op. cit., p. 265.
[9] Rankin, p. 67.

mines which employed 6,000, and to the creation of a civil service in which there were jobs for more than 4,000 Africans. Cocoa exports began in 1891, exceeded 800 tons in 1901, and rose to over 36,000 tons in 1911. The cocoa was packed in puncheons and rolled to the coast. The Public Works Department was building roads intended in the first place to enable puncheons to be rolled, but also used by traction engines and hand carts. The government received sub-ventions from Britain for creating a framework of control in Ashanti (newly annexed as a colony) and in the northern territories, which were being brought under administration as a protectorate. The growth of incomes caused a rapid increase in the private consump-tion of imported goods. Figures for 1891 and 1901 show an increase of more than a hundred per cent in the decade. Millers knew how to thrive in this situation. They must have concentrated on the merchandise trade, appreciated the potential of cocoa, and avoided commitment to the lines of produce which were declining. Mean-while, Swanzys missed their opportunities.

'The trading firms,' says the historian of this epoch,[10] 'were not in an expansionary mood,' by which he means that they did not open branches away from the coast. Was their attitude just a mood, or was it based on principle? The Swanzys had long propounded the opinion that European firms should stay on the seaboard, and depend on African traders for inland distribution. Millers in Nigeria had been pioneers in the establishment of trading stations inland, but in 1893 they had a humiliating experience, when they were compelled, by an alliance of European and African traders, to close their premises in interior markets and withdraw to the ports (chapter 10). This experience may have influenced the policy of the Miller Company in the Gold Coast. There were difficult transport problems in maintaining stocks of merchandise at inland points; transport by head load cost about £2 per ton mile, and it cost over £1 per ton mile to transport goods in hand carts.[11] For whatever reason, the firms stayed at the seaboard until well into the twentieth century. At length in 1905 European firms were established at Kumasi,[12] in 1907 at Tamale,[13] and in 1910 in the cocoa country.[14]

[10] Szereszewski, R., *Structural Changes in the Economy of Ghana* (London: Weidenfeld and Nicolson, 1965).

[11] Gould, P. R., *Development of Transportation Pattern in Ghana* (Evanston, Illinois: 1960) p. 25, cit. Szereszewski.

[12] Ashanti report, 1905, p. 29.

[13] *Gold Coast Government Gazette*, 6 June 1908.

[14] Eastern province report, *Government Gazette*, 19 August 1911.

The die had been cast, and a pattern of distribution through European-owned stores had been set, and was to last a long time.

In the early years of the twentieth century Swanzys ran into financial difficulty owing to their gold mining venture. They sold it for what it would fetch, but still a large sum of money was needed to get them out of trouble. They turned to Millers, their more successful competitors, and asked for help. Alexander and George Miller could have forced Swanzys into liquidation, but they decided to provide the money, and to take Swanzys over. Their action was not altruistic, but they carried it out in a large-minded way. Millers and Swanzys remained nominally distinct, but they worked in co-operation, and in the Gold Coast control was centred in a single supervising agent.

The question which Millers had to answer, whether to take Swanzys over on agreed terms, or to run them into bankruptcy, was a situation which occurred several times in West Africa. The decision was prompted by two main considerations: first, the purely defensive strategy of preventing the merchandise stocks of a distressed competitor from being 'flogged off' and thus breaking the price structure of the market: and second, the belief that by putting the two organizations together and sharing certain central services (such as, in this case, a single supervising agent) additional profits could be derived from the advantages of scale.

That much is obvious; but perhaps greater interest attaches to the decision of the Miller brothers that the firm of Swanzy should continue under its own name. This may well have been due to a sentimental regard for the ancient name, for sentiment accounts for more things in business than is usually supposed; and it certainly had more weight in those times when management was a very personal thing than it would be likely to have now, when management is usually a corporate exercise. But it would be difficult to distinguish the element of respect for the name from the element of commercial advantage which has to be secured from the goodwill attaching to that name. This goodwill could count for much, not only with African customers, but also with European and American manufacturers. When a firm, being the product of amalgamation, continues to trade under two or more names, it may hope to contain the goodwill of more than one supplier; indeed it may handle agencies (even so-called 'exclusive' agencies) of more than one supplier by entrusting one agency to one of its constituent parts and the other agency to the other. This practice is a special (and important) application of the broad policy of 'internal competition', of which a case was mentioned in the foregoing chapter. Every one of the amalgamations which became such a feature of West African trade led to a discussion, whether it would be more profitable to trade as one organization, eliminating such competition as had existed between the newly amalgamated units, or to continue to trade as separate units. In the latter case, there might be some administrative arrangements to modify competition (and this was the case in the Miller–Swanzy group) or the top management in Europe might prefer to encourage the fullest degree of competition between units in Africa; and experience indicated that there was no fiercer competition than the in-fighting which went on between 'cousins' in such circumstances.

In the first decade of the nineteenth century two private limited companies were formed, Millers Limited for the Gold Coast in 1904 and Miller Brothers (of Liverpool) Limited for Nigeria in 1907. The old name of Alexander Miller Brother and Company was then no longer used. One of the reasons which prompted the brothers to take these steps was the desire to create directorships for their sons and for the most senior managers who had helped to build up the business, of whom Batty was one.[15]

As already noted, F. and A. Swanzy had extended their activities eastwards from the Gold Coast into independent African territories before the colonial period. The Germans occupied Togoland in 1884, declaring it to be a colony, and Swanzys found themselves under German rule, just as Kings and Hatton and Cookson did in Cameroon. German policy in Togoland was hostile towards non-German companies. This was different from their attitude in Cameroon. No doubt the contrast is to be explained by the terms of the Berlin Treaties, which established the 'open-door' principle in a large part of Africa, a part which included Cameroon but did not extend so far west as Togoland. Gradually all the non-German companies gave up and withdrew except Swanzys, who after 1912 were the only non-German firm in the colony.[16] Their survival was to the credit of their agent Bolliger, a German-speaking Swiss. In the war of 1914–1918 the Germans had to leave the country, and after the war Togoland was divided into two parts, which were administered by France and Britain respectively under mandate from the League of Nations. The Swanzy organization, still under the command of

[15] Rankin, p. 66.
[16] Cornevin, Robert, *Histoire du Togo* (Paris: Berger-Levrault, 1959) pp. 194, 257.

Bolliger, became part of the African and Eastern Trade Corporation in 1919, and assured for that corporation the largest share of the trade. A pigeon post was maintained by Swanzys in this period to convey messages between Lome and Kpandu.[17] Bolliger took a great personal interest in educated young Africans whom he regarded as candidates for management posts. He was promoted to a position in London in the 1920s, and this enabled him to help some of his young friends who were studying in London. For instance, he would arrange for them to have a quiet room in the Corporation's office, where they could study without interruption.[18]

Trade between the United States and the Gold Coast was a speciality of F. and A. Swanzy. They carried it in sailing vessels, ranging from 500 to 1,000 tons. The ships carried rum, tobacco, sawn timber, patent medicines, and sewing machines, and returned to America with palm oil, rubber, gum copal, parrots, and monkeys. The round trip took six months. F. and A. Swanzy, with the help of their Boston agents, Pettingill and Everett, found a distiller of rum who was willing to grant them exclusivity; but his output fell short of their requirements so they financed him to produce on a larger scale (vertical integration again!). This profitable business came to an end in 1919 upon the enactment of the prohibition law in the United States.[19] The firms of Swanzy and Miller increased their employment of sailing vessels when the war of 1914–1918 made steamers scarce, and they set up a service of sailing ships between New York and Accra. Not a single voyage was attended by any mishap from raiders or submarines.

Swanzys and Millers became parts of the African and Eastern Trade Corporation in 1919, and that story will be told in a subsequent chapter. In the Gold Coast the two firms continued to trade as separate units.

Swanzys had for a long time operated small craft; on the Ivory Coast lagoons in 1870 and on the Volta River since 1891.[20] In the 1920s the government of the Gold Coast asked them to take over the operation of the ferries at Beposo near Sekondi, and on the Volta River. The enterprise will always be associated with the name of Cato. J. E. Cato senior joined F. and A. Swanzy in 1896. Promoted manager, in 1917 he experimented in crossing the Volta

---

[17] Stanbury, R. W. W., oral.

[18] The late William van Lare, Judge of the High Court of Ghana and High Commissioner for Ghana in Ottawa, oral.

[19] Rankin, p. 71.

[20] Szereszewski, op. cit., p. 25.

with his Ford car (see plate 15) by lashing canoes together and placing his car cross-wise over them. From 1924 the ferry across the Volta at Senchi was run by Cato's eldest son, J. E. Cato junior, but he was transferred to a petroleum prospecting venture which was being undertaken by the African and Eastern Trade Corporation, and the father moved to Senchi where he remained until his retirement on pension after serving Swanzys and their successors for fifty-four years. His wife, Mary Idun Cato, was a pass-book customer of the company from 1911 until the time of her death in 1965: this means that she ran a retail business, enjoying credit facilities and wholesale prices at the stores of Swanzys and their successors.

The ferry at Senchi was worked in one way when the river was in flood, and by a different method when the water was low. When the level of the river was low, the pontoon was moved by means of a chain stretching under water from one bank to the other, and passing round a wheel known as the gypsy wheel, situated in the engine house. In flood conditions, however, the speed of the current rendered the chain system impracticable, and the service was maintained by launches lashed to pontoons. Four of the old ferries are now drowned deep below the surface of the Volta lake. At one of these, Yeji, the ingenious device of a pendulum was used. It was on the main road from Kumasi to Tamale and the river was 500 yards wide in normal conditions. The principle of the pendulum was to allow the force of the stream to propel the pontoon across. An anchor in the river bed was connected by cable to a floating pontoon; between the anchor and the pontoon the cable was carried on a line of boats. By means of winches the boats and the pontoon were placed at such an angle to the current of the river that they were forced across from one bank to the other.[21]

Trade continued very much in the pattern that had been established by Francis and Andrew Swanzy in 1850. For instance at Elmina in 1912 there was a senior agent who was an African, W. Plange. He ordered goods direct from London and bought produce at prices cabled from London, without reference to Cape Coast. Most of the imports came by sailing ships, though the exports by this time were carried away in steamers. Elmina had four stores and six out-stations. The normal method of selling imported goods was to finance market women with a monthly credit, which was carried forward from month to month. This had gone on for sixty years and was to continue for sixty years more. The senior agent was on a

---

[21] United Africa Company, *Statistical and Economic Review* (London: 1954) no. 13.

monthly salary and a fifth share of the profits, and his total remuneration came to about £1,200 a year. In 1921 there was a Senior African Agents' Association in the Gold Coast with eighteen members.[22]

Among the many Africans who worked as managers for F. and A. Swanzy were several members of the families of Olympio, Amorin, and Baeta, who were interconnected by marriage. A family tree setting out the names of members of those families who worked for the company is shown on page 109.[23] The most distinguished member of those families was the late Sylvanus Olympio (see plate 19), first President of the independent Republic of Togo; though he took service with a competing firm, namely the Niger Company. The father of the late Sylvanus Olympio was Epiphano Elphidio Olympio. He was one of twelve children of Francisco Olympio and his wife Constancia Pereira Santos. E. E. Olympio worked for Millers and was stationed for many years at Kpandu, where Sylvanus was born. He was also posted to Peki whence he was transferred to Keta. He made a business trip to London in 1924 and retired on pension in the following year. His father Francisco Olympio (better known in his day as Favi Olympio) was never employed by any of the European firms. For some time he worked for his maternal uncle Cesar Cequiera de Lima as a slave dealer at Vodja near Keta until he had enough money to establish as an independent trader.

Sylvanus' uncle Octaviano was known in his day as a well-to-do coconut planter, businessman, and politician. He gave a great deal of help to the Roman Catholic mission to commence operations in 1897.[24] His son Christiano worked for John Walkden at Cotonou. Sylvanus' other uncle Cesar Francisco Olympio worked for F. and A. Swanzy. He retired on pension in 1935 and lived in Lomé growing roses and raising chickens. Joao Jeronimo Amorin was another uncle of Sylvanus. He was for many years the agent at Keta and was transferred to Lomé in 1920. He was taken ill on the boat while he was on his way back from a business trip to London and died a fortnight after his disembarkation. He had three sons who all became managers.

These particulars of the Olympio family are of special interest

[22] Swanzy, Henry, 'A Trading family', in *Transactions of the Gold Coast and Togoland Historical Society* (Achimota: 1956) vol. II part II p. 117.

[23] The late W. T. Baeta to Pedler, 24 August 1969.

[24] Cornevin, op. cit., p. 198.

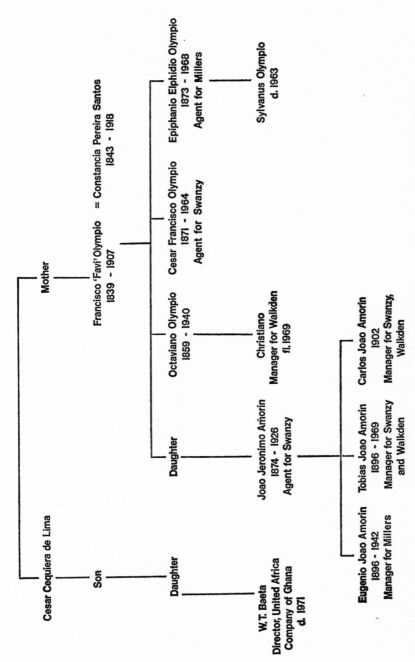

Fig. 9. *The generations of the families of Olympio, Amorin, and Baeta, compiled from information supplied by the late William T. Baeta, sometime Director of the United Africa Company of Ghana Limited*

because of the distinguished political career of Sylvanus Olympio, but F. and A. Swanzy had members of many other families working for them as agents. Bentsi-Enchill at Cape Coast became well known as a designer of textiles and paid several visits to Manchester. There were Centcil at Saltpond, Dennis at Nsawam, and Erskine Graham who became the Town Clerk of Cape Coast after retiring from trade. Korsah was at Winnebah and George Moore at Nsawam. Justino de Madeiros was manager at Keta.

Mention must be made of the brothers Taylor, James at Cape Coast and Samuel at Winnebah, the sons of Kurankyi, chief linguist at Winnebah and a manufacturer of salt. People still talk of a legal action in which James Taylor became involved: it is the historian's pleasant duty to record that the Privy Council found him innocent of the charges which had been raised against him. Space does not permit to mention all the Africans who worked as managers for F. and A. Swanzy.

In 1920 the Miller–Swanzy group opened in Accra a retail shop which they called Kingsway Stores. It was provided with a handsome building, which had excellent facilities for window display under the shade of arcades. Its standards of retailing, according to an account published at the time,[25] 'approximated to contemporary undertakings in Europe and America'.

The name Swanzy lives in the memory of the Ghana people, and there can be no better way of ending this chapter than by quoting from a study of the early Swanzys, from which this chapter has drawn much of its material. It was written in 1956 by Henry Swanzy, a distant connection of the trading branch, who was then acting as head of programmes in the Gold Coast broadcasting service, on secondment from the British Broadcasting Corporation:

> The firm of F. and A. Swanzy has vanished from the Gold Coast as an economic force, but it survives in the folk-memory with a certain social magic, and its symbol, the unicorn, which is the family crest, is still used in ways that make it more than a simple trade mark—on a block of offices, on a beach hut, encrusted in silver-gilt on top of an ebony palaver-stick. There are men still living who owe their education to Swanzy's, or the beginning of their careers to Swanzy's. A mammy lorry in Oda bears the slogan 'Swanzy Brothers' on its front, and the slogan 'Travel to See' at the back. As with the names of many early

[25] MacMillan, A., *Red Book of West Africa* (London: Collingridge, 1920) p. 173.

traders, the name is preserved in families in Cape Coast, in Christiansborg, Sekondi and Tarkwa. I had been told by one acquaintance that his car was damaged by a Swanzy in Sefwi Wiawso, by another that the electoral rolls of Christiansborg are largely made up of Swanzys. At Dixcove, there is a ruined villa among the trees of Swanzy Point. There is a Swanzy house on King Street in Cape Coast, a large baroque structure several stories high, backing onto the picturesque confusion of Dawson Hill in the quarter known as Nkotomase (you cannot say it). Another Swanzy house stands in Tarkwa, while the name was to be seen in plaster until 1955 at least on the U.A.C. premises in Lome. At Suhum a stream, the Swanse water, has been named to distinguish it from another watering point on the south of the town. A Swanzy rum, complete with the unicorn, is still retailed in places as far apart as Ashanti Mampong and Keta, while the cloth Swanzy *ayeyi*, 'In praise of Swanzy', is still to be seen on some ladies of the older generation, in brown, with alternating stripes of moiré and paisley. In short the name has accumulated a personality which is still redolent and alive, 25 years since the firm as such ceased to exist, 50 years since it existed in its own right, and 100 years since European traders bearing the name were personally active in the Gold Coast.[26]

[26] Swanzy, Henry, op. cit.

9

The Royal Niger Company

Trading vessels had for hundreds of years been entering the various channels of the Niger Delta, but their crews thought that each was a separate river and none realized that these waterways were in fact the mouths of a single great stream. The existence of the Niger had been known vaguely to Europeans for a long time, but there was uncertainty as to its direction and where it entered the sea, if indeed it did so. Some believed that it flowed in a westerly direction and that the Rivers Senegal and Gambia were its mouths. Others thought that it joined the Nile or the Congo, or that it lost itself in a great swamp or lake.

The British efforts to explore the Niger began with Mungo Park's journeys.[1] In 1821 Major Denham and Lieutenant Clapperton led an expedition from Tripoli across the Sahara to the country later known as northern Nigeria. They reached Bornu, and Clapperton then proceeded to Sokoto, the capital of the Fulani empire. Neither explorer was able to reach the Niger but both returned safely across the desert.

In 1825 Clapperton, with his servant Richard Lander, travelled from Badagri, on the Atlantic coast near Lagos, crossed the Niger close to the Bussa rapids where Mungo Park had lost his life, and went on to Sokoto, near which town Clapperton died. Lander got back safely to Badagri and to England, where he offered his services as an explorer to the British government. The offer was accepted and Lander, accompanied by his brother John, landed against Badagri in 1830, proceeded overland to Bussa and thence down the Niger by canoe to the delta and the sea, solving the mystery which had puzzled the outside world for so long.

It was now clear that the upper Niger was accessible through the Delta and that it provided a waterway to the Fulani empire. The Fulani were originally a pastoral people. Most of them continued to lead a pastoral life, tending their cattle, but some settled in the towns and mixed with the Hausa-speaking tribes. In 1804 Usuman

[1] *see* chapter 1.

112

Fig. 10. Map of those parts of Africa in which the Royal Niger Company operated

Dan Folio, a Fulani Muslim sheik, shocked by the lax habits of his co-religionists, preached a *jihad* and, with his Fulani followers and others, overthrew the indigenous rulers of the Hausa states, and replaced them by Fulani emirs. These emirs owed allegiance to Usuman's son Bello, who became Sultan of Sokoto and to his successors. Usuman's brother became Emir of Gando, and those who succeeded him, although theoretically independent, were in practice subordinate to Sokoto. The Fulani attempted to conquer Bornu, but were unsuccessful and Bornu continued to be an independent state.

Such was the state of affairs in northern Nigeria when the Landers' exploration opened the way to European influence and trade. The first attempt to develop trade on the Niger was made by

Macgregor Laird, a Liverpool merchant, in 1832.[2] In 1841 a naval expedition ascended the Niger in three steamers,[3] but disease took a heavy toll and the expedition was abandoned. The British government, however, still persevered. Between 1850 and 1855 Heinrich Barth, a German in the pay of Britain, travelled across the desert from Tripoli to Bornu and Sokoto (and to Timbuktu), reached the Rivers Niger and Benue, and got safely back to England with valuable information about the countries he had visited.

In 1854 another expedition under the command of Baikie[4] ascended the Niger in a steamer built and equipped by Laird under contract with the government. Careful surveys of the river were made and there was a certain amount of successful trading. Baikie established himself at Lokoja, under the protection of Nasaba, the Emir of Nupe, as the British representative on the Niger and maintained the settlement, to which many Africans flocked, out of trading profits. He died in 1864, and in 1866 the British government established a consulate at Lokoja, but this was closed in 1869.

Encouraged by the success of Baikie's voyage, Laird in 1857 entered into a contract with the government for a yearly visit of a trading steamer to the Niger and Benue at the time of high water, the enterprise to be assisted by a subsidy for five years, beginning with £8,000 and decreasing annually at the rate of £500. The annual steamer was to be escorted up the rivers by a ship of war on account of the danger of attack. With the exception of 1860, a man-of-war was therefore sent up the Niger each year until 1871. Hulks were moored at Onitsha, Abo, and Lokoja, where produce purchased by Laird's representatives could be stored pending the arrival of the annual steamer. These hulks were as a rule in the charge of educated Africans, generally from Sierra Leone, only a few Europeans being employed to supervise. Salt, beads, cotton goods, and, at stations near the coast, spirits, guns, and gunpowder, were the articles in chief demand by the people, and they brought in exchange palm oil, benniseed, and ivory.

Laird died in 1861 and his executors were unable to obtain from the government any extension of the subsidy which he had been receiving, but others were prepared to follow where he had led. Companies which had been trading in the coastal areas decided to seek business on the main river, sending small steamers and launches to trade with the people who lived on the banks of the Niger above

---

[2] *see* chapter 2. [3] *see* chapters 2 and 3. [4] *see* chapter 2.

the Delta. Among these was the West Africa Company Limited,[5] established on the Nun branch of the Delta in 1864, and renamed the West African Company Limited in 1877; and Holland Jacques and Company, which began trading on the Niger in 1869. Both these companies had their headquarters in Lagos. Other firms interested were Alexander Miller Brother and Company[6] and James Pinnock.[7]

Trading was by no means easy. Cargo steamers were attacked, trading stations were sometimes looted and Europeans and their assistants were frequently in danger. An example of the general disorder was the seizure of Bishop Crowther in 1867 by one of the rulers, who demanded the payment of a ransom; the bishop was rescued by Mr. Fell, the assistant consul at Lokoja, who was himself killed by a poisoned arrow in the fighting.

The violence and hostility of the riverain people were encouraged by the coastal states, and especially by the men of Brass, who resented the encroachment on their position as middlemen by the European firms in search of direct trade. The European companies long established on the coast were equally resentful of the intrusion of competitors, and encouraged the Brassmen and others in their hostility, selling them guns and ammunition. Cannon were mounted on the river banks, and fired on steamers passing. Although a ship of war occasionally bombarded a town in reprisal for such attacks or as punishment for the looting of a trading station, there was no permanent authority to maintain order and protect trade. The British consul on the coast seldom had time to visit the Niger.

The firms trading on the Niger were in fierce competition with one another. The smallest of them, Holland Jacques, lost a steamer (the *Lord Nelson*) and her cargo in 1871 from hostile attack, and was in serious financial difficulty in 1875. The secretary of the company, Captain Joseph Grove-Ross, appealed for help to his son-in-law,

[5] For five years from 1862 the Church Missionary Society had maintained an 'Industrial Institution' on the Niger. This was given up in 1867 after the West Africa Company began trading on the Niger, and the Society took shares in the Company in the hope of assisting the local people to improve their condition by cultivating marketable produce. This arrangement was made on the recommendation of the African missionary bishop, Dr. Samuel Crowther. Josiah Crowther, one of the bishop's sons, was for a time an agent of the Company.

[6] *see* chapters 3 and 5.

[7] James Pinnock joined the African Steamship Company as a purser in 1859 at the age of 21. For many years he was that company's agent in Sierra Leone and on the Gold Coast. Then he started to trade on his own account in the Oil Rivers and on the Niger. He traded and explored in a steamer of 200 tons which had been built according to his own specification. A qualified navigator accompanied him as captain of the vessel. He died at Colombo, Ceylon, in 1905 (Rankin, p. 15).

John Senhouse Goldie Taubman,[8] the head of a distinguished Manx family. As a result of this appeal the Taubman family formed a new company in 1876, the Central African Trading Company Limited, which bought all the shares of Holland Jacques; Grove-Ross and Taubman's younger brother George became the sole directors of the new company.

That remarkable man, George Dashwood Goldie Taubman[9] (better known as Sir George Goldie (see plate 17)) was born at Douglas in the Isle of Man in 1846, the fourth son of Lieutenant-Colonel John Goldie Taubman, Scots Guards, and Speaker of the House of Keys. George trained for two years at the Royal Military College, Woolwich, and was commissioned in the Royal Engineers in 1865. Shortly afterwards he inherited a small fortune and in 1867 resigned his commission. He went to Egypt, and to the Sudan where he lived with an Arab girl, learnt Arabic, and began to take an interest in Africa. He returned to the Isle of Man, and eloped with the family governess to Paris in 1870; he married her when they returned to England in 1871.[10] He had given up a military career and had a reputation for licentiousness which at that period was enough to bar him from any responsible position in Britain.

In these circumstances George Taubman was probably glad to take over responsibility for what was now the family business, and in 1876 he and his brother Alexander travelled to the Niger to examine the reasons why Holland Jacques and Company had failed to prosper.[11] There was more than one reason for this. In the first place the comparative smallness of the company made it unable to compete with the larger firms. One of the company's steamers, as mentioned above, had been sunk and looted, and the company had incurred the particular hostility of the Brass people by maintaining a trading station in their territory without permission, and without the payment of any comey.[12]

[8] He was Speaker of the House of Keys from 1867 to 1898.

[9] The best biography is that by John E. Flint, *Sir George Goldie and the making of Nigeria* (Oxford: Clarendon Press, 1960).

[10] Lady Goldie, as she afterwards became, died in 1898 after twenty-seven years of successful marriage. Mary Kingsley, an intimate friend, said that 'she was a sweet gentle woman' and 'from the first time I met her she fascinated me'. *West African Studies* (London: Macmillan, 1899) was dedicated by Mary Kingsley to her own brother 'and to my friend who is dead'—Lady Goldie.

[11] They intended also to travel overland to the Nile but Alexander became ill and the plan had to be abandoned.

[12] For comey, *see* chapter 2.

George Taubman quickly realized that the competition of rival firms on the Niger was ruining the trade prospects of all and that their disunity weakened them in their dealings with African rulers. In spite of his previous reputation and of his lack of business experience, he succeeded in persuading the heads of the other firms that amalgamation was the only practical answer to the problems that faced them all. In 1879 the United African Company Limited was formed, with a nominal capital of £250,000, each of the firms receiving an allotment of shares proportionate to the assets handed over to the new company. The allotments were as follows:

Alexander Miller Brother & Company	5,400 shares
Central African Trading Company Limited	4,400 shares
West African Company Limited	4,320 shares
James Pinnock	960 shares

Trading stations, ships, and staff, were pooled, and competition between the four constituent companies ceased.

The first directors of the United African Company were: for Miller—Alexander Miller, George Miller, James Croft, and A. MacEachan; for the Central African Company—John Senhouse Goldie Taubman, A. H. Goldie Taubman, and George Dashwood Goldie Taubman; for the West African Company—W. Dixon, John Edgar; and James Pinnock. The principal agent of the company on the Niger was David McIntosh, who had been the local manager of Holland Jacques.[13] The first headquarters of the company was at Akassa, on the Nun branch of the Delta; later Asaba became the headquarters. Throughout the existence of the United African Company, and of its successors until the end of the century, George Taubman, whatever his recognized position may have been, was the inspiration of his colleagues, and the most influential of the governing body.

The amalgamation of the British firms was designed to eliminate competition, but further competition came from French sources. In 1878 the Count de Semellé visited the Niger, and entered into a trade agreement with the Emir of Nupe, Umoru, who had succeeded the pro-British Emir Macaba. The Compagnie française de l'Afrique équatoriale was formed, with a capital of £600,000, to exploit this agreement, but in the meantime the United African Company had persuaded Umoru to cancel his agreement with the

---

[13] He died in 1888 at the age of 44.

French. This, and other matters, led to a revolt of some of Umoru's subjects, and he was only able to crush the revolt with the aid of an armed steamer of the United African Company, which scattered the canoes of the rebels, and made it possible for the emir's cavalry to cross the Niger. A French ship also joined in the attack on the canoes. The French company set up trading stations at Abo, Onitsha, Egga, and Loko, and two smaller French firms were established at other places on the river.

Resentful of this intrusion, and alarmed by the attempts of French agents to obtain political control by means of treaties with African rulers, George Taubman began to think of obtaining a charter from the British government. His first unofficial approaches met with no encouragement, partly on account of the small capital of his company, partly because of the reluctance of the government to accept responsibility for a protectorate (which would be implicit in the grant of a charter), and perhaps chiefly because of the presence of rival French firms on the Niger. George Taubman could therefore do no more than wage a commercial war to destroy the French companies,[14] but only the smaller firms were driven out of business, and the Compagnie française de l'Afrique équatoriale continued to be a serious commercial opponent, and a hindrance to George Taubman's political ideas.

To meet this difficulty he organized in 1882 the flotation of a new firm, the National African Company Limited, with a capital of £1,000,000 in 100,000 shares of £10 each, to take over the assets of the United African Company, and carry on its work.[15] Twenty-five thousand shares were allotted, credited as fully paid, to the United African Company for the acquisition of its business, and 66,675 shares (£1 paid up on each) were allotted on applications from the public.[16] Other shares were allotted later.

During the next two years the following served as directors of the National African Company: Lord Aberdare (chairman), John Senhouse Goldie Taubman (vice-chairman), James Croft, Clifford Edgar, John Edgar, J. F. Hutton, Sir James Marshall,[17] Alexander

---

[14] George Taubman lent some of his own money to the United African Company to allow it for a time to trade at a loss.

[15] The United African Company was liquidated in 1885.

[16] Of these, 2,816 shares were allotted to the Taubman family; 1,674 to John Edgar and his family; and 1,384 shares to the Miller family.

[17] Sir James Marshall had previously been Chief Justice of the Gold Coast and in 1888 was appointed Chief Justice of the Royal Niger Company's territories. He died in 1889.

Miller, George Miller, C. W. Mills, James Pinnock,[18] George Dashwood Goldie Taubman. George Taubman, John Edgar, and Alexander Miller were appointed managers of the company. In 1884 George Taubman succeeded his brother as vice-chairman. Henry Morley was appointed secretary in 1884.[19]

One of the first acts of the National African Company was to ask the Foreign Office to appoint David McIntosh, its head agent in Africa, to be a consular agent on the Niger, as assistant to the consul for the Bights of Benin and Biafra. Apart from the need for authoritative contacts to be maintained with the rulers of the hinterland, such an appointment was desirable as the French government had appointed the agent of the Compagnie française de l'Afrique équatoriale as their consul on the Niger.[20] McIntosh was appointed vice-consul with jurisdiction over the Niger and its tributaries.

Before he had been appointed vice-consul, McIntosh had begun making treaties, in the name of the National African Company, with the ruling authorities on both banks of the Niger up to Lokoja. He was authorized to do this by a resolution of the board, 'provided that such treaties as he may conclude with any people or potentate shall not make a condition of the special exclusion of others from trade'. Before the end of 1884 more than seventy of these treaties had been 'signed' by the rulers and by McIntosh, and they were submitted to the consul.[21] The treaties varied slightly in wording but the standard form generally started with a statement by the African parties that they, after some years' experience 'fully recognize the benefit accorded to our country, and people by our intercourse with the National African Company Limited, and in recognition of this we now cede the whole of our territory to the National African Company Limited, and their administrators, for ever'. They further agreed to refer disputes with other African states to the company, and to provide assistance for the protection of the company's property and people. For its part the company undertook not to interfere with any of the local laws, not to take land or other property without the owner's consent, and without paying for it, and to pay

---

[18] Pinnock resigned from the board in 1889 and was thereafter a violent opponent of the Company.

[19] He continued as secretary of the Niger Company after the revocation of the charter, and resigned in 1903.

[20] Letter to Foreign Office from National African Company, 28 February 1883.

[21] Lists of the treaties made and of the various forms used are given in Hertslet, Sir Edward, *The Map of Africa by Treaty*, 3rd ed. (London: HMSO, 1909, reprinted Cass, 1967) Vol. I, pp. 122–55.

an annual sum, in goods or money, to the rulers concerned. The company reserved to itself the right to exclude foreigners.

Some of the more powerful Fulani princes, such as the Emir of Nupe (to whom the company had previously paid comey in return for his protection) were, not unnaturally, unwilling to sign such treaties, but in 1885 the explorer Joseph Thomson was able, on behalf of the company, to secure agreements with the Sultan of Sokoto and the Emir of Gando, the overlords of these princes. The Sultan of Sokoto gave to the company 'my entire rights to the country on both sides of the river Benue, and rivers flowing into it, throughout my dominions for such distance from its and their banks as they may desire' in return for 'a yearly present of goods to the value of 3,000 bags of cowries'. In return for goods to the value of 2,000 bags of cowries the Emir of Gando gave his 'entire rights to the country on both sides of the rivers Benue, and Niger'. Both treaties provided that the company should have 'the sole right among foreigners to trade' in these territories.[22]

Major Macdonald,[23] the commissioner appointed by the British government in 1888 to enquire into the position of the Royal Niger Company,[24] reported that most of the rulers whom he had interviewed agreed that they had signed the treaties with the company, but in the opinion of Lord Lugard (and of others) the agreements were often misunderstood by the persons who signed them owing to faulty interpretation.[25] However, it was:

> agreed by all the Powers, and more specifically by Britain, the United States, and Belgium that 'treaties' with the natives, by which they were supposed at short notice to have voluntarily ceded all their sovereign rights, were to be accepted as valid titles to the acquisition of the African tropics by the European nations. . . . . It mattered not that tribal chiefs had no power to dispose of communal rights.[26]

In addition to the treaties entered into by the National African Company, Consul Hewett made a number of agreements in the

---

[22] English translations of these treaties are in Hertslet, op. cit., vol. I, pp. 122, 124.

[23] Afterwards Sir Claude Macdonald, Commissioner and Consul-General, Niger Coast Protectorate, 1891–1906, and later ambassador at Pekin and Tokio.

[24] see chapter 5, and page 130 below.

[25] Lugard considered that the annual payment by the company of 3,000 bags of cowries to the Sultan of Sokoto was regarded by that potentate as tribute from a vassal. Lugard, The Dual Mandate in British Tropical Africa, 2nd ed. (London: Blackwood, 1923) p. 15.

[26] ibid.

coastal area, and on the Niger. The treaty with Asaba (1884) includes the following as article VI:

> The subjects, and citizens of all countries may freely carry on trade in every part of the territories of the kings, queen, and chiefs parties hereto, and may have houses, and factories therein, subject to the agreement made on the 28th August 1884 between the kings, queen, and chiefs, and the National African Company (Limited) of London.[27]

However doubtful these documents might have been as against the African signatories, they provided Britain, under international law as then recognized, with a strong claim against other powers to political control over the territories concerned, and, as will be seen, this claim was successfully made at the Berlin Conference of 1885.

The presence of the Compagnie française de l'Afrique équatoriale on the Niger continued to be a threat to the trading prospects of the National African Company and an obstacle to the grant of a charter, which George Taubman thought to be essential, but in 1884 the Compagnie française handed over all its assets on the Niger in exchange for shares in the National African Company to the value of £60,000. The paid-up capital of the company was now £443,000. Two of the directors of the Compagnie française were added to the board of the National African Company.[28]

Since the formation in 1879 of the United African Company (and in 1882 of the National African Company) this commercial organization had assumed a practical though unofficial control of the Niger waterway, and the banks of the river. With the elimination of the separate French interests on the Niger it was easier for the British government to give favourable consideration to George Taubman's repeated requests for the grant of a charter to the company, but the delay in reaching a decision was frustrating and Taubman almost despaired. The delay was now caused by inter-departmental arguments. The Colonial Office was against the establishment of a colony, and while the Foreign Office favoured a protectorate under the general supervision of a consul, the Treasury stipulated that this should not involve any expenditure from Imperial funds, a typically stupid condition. Circumstances, however, forced the British government to take a decision.

[27] The treaty is given in Appendix F of Burns, *History of Nigeria*, 7th ed. (London: Allen and Unwin, 1969) pp. 328–30.

[28] They had to retire when the company received its charter in 1886, as by the terms of the charter all directors had to be British subjects.

Scarcely had the French presence on the Niger been eliminated when the international situation in West Africa was confused by the establishment of German colonies in Cameroon and Togoland. The 'scramble for Africa' had begun. However, in October 1884 Bismarck issued invitations to Britain and other powers to a conference in Berlin to discuss the setting up of an international commission to control freedom of commerce and navigation on the Congo and the Niger, and the conditions on which the occupation of Africa could be recognized. By this time the British government had come to regard the National African Company as, in practice, its representative on the Niger, and George Taubman as an important figure in this connection. He was therefore (with other unofficial persons representing companies operating in the coastal area) invited to accompany the British delegation to the Berlin Conference, and took an active part in the discussions. He was able to assert that British interests were supreme on the lower Niger, and, largely through his intervention, the proposal for an international commission was dropped and instead the conference adopted a Niger Navigation Act, which provided for the free navigation of the Niger and prohibited any discrimination against foreign nationals. In June 1885 notification was inserted in the *London Gazette* to the effect that a protectorate had been established over the Niger districts which included 'the territories on both banks of the Niger from its confluence with the river Benue at Lokoja to the sea, as well as the territories on both banks of the river Benue from the confluence up to and including Ibi'.[29]

International obstacles to the grant of a charter had now been removed, but arguments and delays still continued. The government was prepared to grant a charter which would provide for the formation of a council from the directors of the company, but this council would be required to act 'under the control and authority of Her Majesty's Government'. Taubman was not prepared to accept such a condition, and put forward an alternative proposal which, accepting political control by the government, would give the company monopoly of trade on the Niger in spirits, arms, and ammunition. If this could not be approved, he asked for financial compensation for the company's expenditure in connection with the treaties it had negotiated, and in buying out the French.

[29] A further notification in *The London Gazette* (18 October 1887) extended the British protectorate to include 'all territories in the basin of the Niger and its affluents, which are or may be for the time being subject to the government of the National African Company Limited (now called the Royal Niger Company)'.

As the argument dragged on Taubman lost patience and circulated to his fellow directors a draft resolution which, after recounting the efforts of the company 'with the patriotic motive of securing the whole territory to Great Britain' and deploring the procrastination of the government, proposed that negotiations be opened with 'a foreign power', which was understood to be France. The object of the negotiations should be:

(a) The transfer to the foreign power of the independent treaties of the company.
(b) The effective occupation of the countries thus transferred.
(c) The placing of the company under the flag of the foreign power.
(d) The obtaining of such conditions as shall be most advantageous to the shareholders.
(e) The restriction to a minimum of the capital risked among the tribes nominally protected by Great Britain, and a transfer of enterprise to the tribes to be placed under the effective protection of the foreign power.

The directors met to consider this draft resolution on 23 September 1885, but were then informed that further proposals had been received from the Foreign Office; in these circumstances Taubman proposed to his colleagues that discussion of the draft should be postponed, and this was agreed to.

It is unlikely that Taubman really intended to place the company under the protection of a foreign flag, but the threat was there, and although the British government probably did not take it too seriously the knowledge that there was such a proposal must have helped to accelerate action. The government finally agreed to the issue of a Royal Charter, which was signed on 10 July 1886.[30] In this charter some of the treaties negotiated by the company were mentioned, and the company was 'authorised, and empowered to hold, and retain the full benefit of the several cessions' made by the African rulers, and to exercise 'all rights, interests, authorities, and powers for the purposes of government [and the] preservation of public order'. The company was required 'as far as may be practicable' to abolish slavery, to administer justice to the inhabitants, and to respect their religion 'except so far as may be necessary in the interest of humanity'.

[30] For a complete copy of the charter *see* Appendix II of Flint, John E., op. cit.

Article 14 of the charter prohibited a monopoly of trade:

Nothing in this our charter shall be deemed to authorise the company to set up or grant any monopoly of trade; and subject only to customs restrictions on importation similar in character to those applicable in Our United Kingdom, trade with the company's territories under Our protection shall be free, and there shall be no differential treatment of the subjects of any power as to settlement or access to markets, but foreigners alike with British subjects will be subject to administrative dispositions in the interests of commerce, and order. The customs duties, and charges hereby authorised shall be levied, and applied solely for the purpose of defraying the necessary expenses of government . . .

It was stipulated that the company should remain British in character, that its directors and principal representative on the Niger should be British, and that the flag to be hoisted on the company's buildings and vessels should indicate the British character of the company. The flag chosen strongly resembled the white ensign flown on British naval vessels,[31] with the addition of a device of three arms symbolizing the main waterways of the territory; on each arm was a single short word. In a letter to the Foreign Office Taubman explained the significance of these words. 'ARS and JUS,' he wrote, 'supported by PAX are leading Europeans into the heart of Africa.' One wonders whether the device on the shield of the Isle of Man had any influence on Taubman's proposed three arms.

The government recognized that the company had incurred expenditure in securing the territory for Britain, and after negotiations the figure involved was agreed to be £250,000. With the sanction of the government the company made this amount 'the public debt of the Niger Territories 5 per cent inscribed stock', secured on the customs and taxes of the territories but not on the assets or commercial revenues of the company. £133,005 of this stock was distributed among shareholders, and £115,000 was applied to writing off an equivalent sum debited to 'goodwill' in the company's books.

In 1886 a general meeting of the company passed resolutions changing the name of the National African Company Limited to the Royal Niger Company Chartered and Limited. The titles of chair-

---

[31] *see* illustration at plate 18.

man and vice-chairman were changed to governor and deputy governor, while the board of directors became the council. Lord Aberdare was appointed governor, and George Goldie Taubman deputy governor. The other members of the council were the Honourable C. W. Mills,[32] J. F. Hutton,[33] Alexander Miller,[34] John Edgar,[35] and J. A. Croft.[36] In 1887 George Goldie Taubman was knighted. He then dropped the name of Taubman, and became known as Sir George Goldie, by which name he will now be described.[37]

Even before the grant of the charter the company had attempted to exercise control over the country on either bank of the rivers, and in 1885 had actually issued a proclamation forbidding other Europeans to trade on the Niger and the Benue. One British firm which tried to trade in defiance of this proclamation was prevented by force from doing so. The British government did not intervene in this case, but when an attempt was made to prevent a German, Flegel, from visiting the river with a view to establishing trading stations, the British government ordered that he should be allowed to proceed.

Regulations were quickly promulgated (and published in the company's *Niger Gazette*) for the administration of the territory now officially under its control. Sir George Goldie was appointed political administrator, and David McIntosh agent-general with his headquarters at Asaba.[38] A chief justice (Sir James Marshall) was appointed[39] and courts of law were set up. Dr. W. H. Crosse became medical officer. An armed constabulary of three European officers and about 150 Africans was raised.[40] Under the agent-general, at various river stations, were district agents, and executive

[32] Retired in 1898 and replaced by Lord Hillingdon.
[33] Retired in 1891 and replaced by the Earl of Scarborough.
[34] Retired in 1917 and died in 1922.
[35] Died in 1895 and replaced by C. B. Edgar.
[36] Died in 1898.
[37] Goldie was made a Privy Councillor in 1898.
[38] The headquarters of the company was moved in 1899 from Asaba to Burutu.
[39] Sir James was succeeded by W. V. Kane and S. Moore.
[40] It was reported in 1890 that the constabulary then consisted of five European and two African officers with 413 rank and file and a battery of mountain guns. There was then a detachment of 150 men at Lokoja, one of 50 men at Ibi, and smaller detachments at other places. Most of the Africans came from the Gold Coast, about a quarter of the force were Hausas, and there were a few Yorubas. There were, in addition to the constabulary, a few local police at stations on the lower Niger. By 1899 the establishment of the constabulary had been increased to eight officers and 1,076 other ranks. In 1900, after the revocation of the charter, most of the constabulary were incorporated in the West African Frontier Force.

officers with limited judicial powers and administrative responsibilities which they exercised in addition to their task of carrying
on the company's trade.

This trade was of course essential to the company if shareholders
were to receive a satisfactory return on their investment. The
dividends paid were not excessive, that for 1892 being $7\frac{1}{2}$ per cent,
and for each of the other years until the termination of the charter
no more than six per cent.

Great pains were taken to develop an export trade and to find new
products that might prove commercially valuable. Circulars were
sent from London to the company's agents urging them to send to
England samples of new products. Letters from agents on the Niger
and Benue refer to the samples sent,[41] and to the efforts made to
encourage people to bring in produce for sale. Steps were taken to
instruct the people how this produce should be prepared. A German
employee, J. Zweifel, was given a special commission to investigate
newly found products, and he seems to have been highly qualified
for this work. In a letter of 1887 Joseph Flint,[42] who succeeded
David McIntosh as agent-general when the latter died in 1888,
reported that 'the great drawback to our making headway with new
products is the fact that it is difficult to induce the natives where they
(the new products) occur to go into the bush, and gather them, for
they are in constant dread of the Mohammedan people who make
constant raids on them, and in many places the country is quite de-
populated by reason of this'. To meet the difficulty he proposed to
send some of the company's own employees, recruited from other
parts of Africa, as far away as the Congo and Sierra Leone, to
explore the inland areas in search of produce.

Trade was often held up by local wars, and other disturbances.
The company's stations were sometimes attacked by hostile forces,
and its stores looted or destroyed. In retaliation, and to stop slave
raids, the company's constabulary was often in action, and suffered

[41] The samples sent included annotto, bamboo nut oil ('which has a narcotic effect on
fish, alligators, etc.'), beeswax, benniseed, calabar beans, camwood, groundnut oil, gum,
hemp fibre, hides ('large quantities must be there; the natives attach no particular value to
them'), honey, indigo, ivory, jute ('probably too useful to the natives for them to sell it'),
oguru seed (stropanthus 'from which a poison is made used to tip arrows . . . it is more
deadly than the venom of two snakes'), pepper, rubber, shea nuts, tin, and turmeric.

[42] Joseph Flint's West African experiences dated from 1876 when he first went to the Oil
Rivers. He resigned his position as agent-general when the Company's charter was revoked
in 1900 and worked for some years after that in the London office of the Niger Company.
He died in 1925.

many casualties. At Ibi a headstone stands above the grave of an officer:

> Sacred to the memory of Captain Herbert Wykeham England Parker South Wales Borderers, who fell in action at Suntai, 18th March 1899, in the 27th year of his age. Erected by the Royal Niger Company as a tribute to a most gallant, and efficient officer who took an active part in numerous military expeditions during three years service in Nigeria.

W. P. Hewby[43] then the company's senior executive officer at Ibi, reported that Captain Parker had been wounded on three previous occasions by poisoned arrows, 'with no medical assistance beyond that of his Ijoh body-servant standing by attending to the casualties in the ranks with a razor, and a bottle of carbolic acid'.

On the whole, however, trade proceeded smoothly. In 1886 the agent at Abutshi reported, 'We are on the best of terms with the people, and they have great respect for the company.' In 1887 Zweifel reported from Idda that three of the principal minor chiefs had promised to help him in the collection of gum, and rubber. Of all the products the greatest attention was paid at that period to rubber and gum, and there are frequent references in the letters from agents to the difficulties experienced in getting the Africans to bring in produce free from dirt and other impurities. Tobacco was one of the imports chiefly prized by the people, and Zweifel advised that it should be bartered only for rubber and gum.[44]

In view of the great importance of tin to the company in later years it is interesting to find that William Wallace[45] in 1887 promised to make enquiries regarding the reported presence of tin in Bauchi, but doubted whether there was any. However, he reported that tin 'is found in the territory of Bauchi at the foot of a range of mountains', that it is obtained from rivers by washing, and removed by caravans which come 'from all parts'. By the following January he was able to report a little trade in tin and to send to England a forty-pound sample, but he added that the people were

---

[43] *see* note 45.

[44] At this period, and for many years later, trade on the rivers was by barter.

[45] Later Sir William Wallace, who joined the colonial service after the revocation of the company's charter and acted for a time as High Commissioner of Northern Nigeria. He died in 1916. Other employees of the Royal Niger Company who joined the colonial service included W. P. Hewby, who became Resident of Bornu Province, and Major (later Sir John) Burdon, formerly commander of the Royal Niger Constabulary, who became Resident of Sokoto Province and afterwards Governor of British Honduras.

dissatisfied with the prices, as the Nupes were paying more for tin than the company was offering.

There were considerable staff difficulties. European employees suffered much from tropical diseases, and there were never enough of them for the amount of work that had to be done. European agents were stationed at the main centres with African employees at the less important places. At least two Africans were appointed as officers of the constabulary (*see* note 40).

There were more serious difficulties facing the company. Even before the grant of the charter there had been opposition to the National African Company from various directions. The French companies had been bought off, but the British firms long established in the coastal regions were resentful of the company's attempt to keep for itself alone the newly found markets on the Niger and Benue. The people of Brass also suffered in their position as middlemen from the company's virtual monopoly of the interior markets.

When the Royal Niger Company's rule was established by the charter, the commercial regulations then enacted provoked even more hostility. They made it necessary for any firm or individual coming from outside the company's territories, and wishing to trade on the rivers to obtain a retail trade licence costing £100 (later reduced at the insistence of the British government in respect of a single trading station to £50, plus £10 for any additional station) with an additional £100 if trade in spirits were intended. Traders were only permitted to enter the territory at specified ports, of which Akassa on the Nun branch of the Niger Delta was the most important.

The tariff regulations imposed high duties on most of the principal articles of trade. Import duty of a hundred per cent *ad valorem* was charged on guns and ammunition, two shillings a gallon on spirits, a shilling a hundredweight on salt, and sixpence a pound on tobacco. Additional duty was levied on goods taken above Lokoja. Export duty was charged on ivory (one shilling a pound), palm oil, shea butter (a penny a gallon), palm kernels (twopence, afterwards raised to two shillings, a hundredweight), and twenty per cent *ad valorem* on all other produce.

The importation of spirits into the Benue territories was prohibited in 1887, except in reasonable amounts for the personal consumption of European residents or visitors. In 1890 the prohibition was extended to cover all the territory north of the seventh parallel of latitude and in 1893 the boundary of the prohibited area was brought further south to a point on the Niger near Asaba.

In 1887 the shipping companies, and the principal firms trading in the coastal area, who later formed the African Association,[46] protested by petition and through Members of Parliament against the tariff, and criticized the company's administration generally. Goldie met these attacks by initiating negotiations with the trading firms, but the shipping companies refused to negotiate. The conversations led to suggestions, first for the amalgamation of the company with the African Association, and the extension of the company's charter to cover the coastal areas (the Oil Rivers, and later the Niger Coast Protectorate), and secondly for setting up a second chartered company to administer the coastal areas.

While these negotiations were proceeding, an international incident occurred which led the British government to intervene. A German named Jacob Hoenigsberg entered the Niger, and began to trade at Nupe, paying the duties, and complying with the regulations. In 1887 a quarrel with the company's representatives over clearance papers for two canoe loads of salt led to Hoenigsberg's complaining to the Emir Maliki of Nupe, who reacted furiously to the company's pretensions, and insisted that he had never given his country to the company nor the right to impose taxes there. Pressure from the German government, based on the Nupe statement that it was independent of the company, led the Foreign Office to insist that the company should issue a regulation making transit trade on the rivers free for all vessels. While Goldie was obliged to obey this order he denied that Nupe was independent, and asserted that it lay within the company's territories in view of the treaty of 1885 with the Emir of Gando, who was the suzerain of Nupe.

Early in 1888 Hoenigsberg was arrested on a charge of illegal trading in Nupe, and was later convicted by the company's supreme court at Asaba on the more serious charge of promoting disorder. The court made an order for his deportation, and made him liable to imprisonment if he returned. The German government took little further interest in Hoenigsberg, but made a number of complaints against the company, mainly on its tariff, and particularly regarding the high import duty on spirits, which affected the Hamburg shippers of gin and rum, and the high export duty on palm kernels. To these and other complaints against the company the British government reacted in 1888 by the appointment of Major Claude

[46] *see* chapters 5 and 10.

Macdonald[47] as a commissioner to enquire into 'certain questions affecting imperial and colonial interests in the west coast of Africa, and into the position of the Royal Niger Company'.

Macdonald arrived in West Africa in March 1889, and visited first the coastal areas, where he was impressed by the bitter feeling of Europeans and Africans alike against the company, and their objections to any extension of chartered rule. In his first report[48] he advised that a separate administration for the coastal areas should be established, bounded on the west by the territories of the Royal Niger Company, and on the east by Cameroon. This was agreed to by the British government which set up the Oil Rivers (later named the Niger Coast) Protectorate.

Macdonald ascended the Niger, and visited most of the stations on that river and the Benue; he interviewed many of the African potentates but did not meet the Sultan of Sokoto or the Emirs of Gando and Yola. All the chiefs he met, except the one at Onitsha, agreed that they had signed the treaties with the company, and Macdonald's report generally supported the validity of the treaties and the company's claim to sovereignty over the territories concerned, including Nupe. For this reason Hoenigsberg's claim to compensation for the treatment he had received was rejected. Macdonald's report on the administration (and on the discipline of the constabulary) was generally favourable and did not support the view that the customs duties and licence fees were higher than was necessary to cover the costs of administration, or that they gave the company a monopoly of trade. He nevertheless recommended that the export duty on palm kernels should be reduced.

He criticized the judiciary,[49] and the treatment of the coastal Africans. He considered that the latter should not be treated as 'foreigners', and as such made liable to pay the licence fee before

[47] see note 23; also chapter 5.

[48] Neither this nor the later report on the Royal Niger Company was ever published, and neither was available to the public until 1952.

[49] Although the report does not refer to the notorious Zweifel case, Macdonald probably knew of it. In 1888 Zweifel (referred to at page 126 and Wallace (see page 127), then acting agent-general. took some Sierra Leone men up the river to collect rubber. At Lokoja the men refused to go further and in the dispute which followed Zweifel shot the ringleader dead. A fight started and Wallace ordered the soldiers of his escort to fire, six men being killed and a number wounded. Some of the survivors escaped and made their way to Lagos where they reported the incident to the colonial authorities. The company's Chief Justice, Sir James Marshall, conducted an enquiry and exonerated Zweifel and Wallace. In spite of demands from the governors of Lagos and Sierra Leone that Zweifel and Wallace should be tried for murder, Goldie succeeded in persuading the British government that the case should be dropped, and both men continued to be employed by the company.

they could trade on the Niger. Had this last recommendation been adopted the company's trading strength would have been seriously affected, and Goldie fought strenuously against it. A new international crisis, this time with the French, made the British government reluctant to weaken the company's position, and no action was taken to implement the report.

The company's competitors, however, did not wait upon the government's decision. Nine British firms came together to form the African Association (1889), and since their main object was to oppose the Royal Niger Company, they followed a vigorous policy of opening trading posts within the company's territory. Many smaller independent firms followed the Association's example. By 1892 the competition had reached such dimensions that the annual revenue accruing from the imports and exports of other traders was £91,000 as against £82,000 accruing from the company's trade.[50] It is proved by these figures that, however much competitors might protest against entering the region through the customs posts designated by the company, and against the charges which they were obliged to pay, the actions of the company in its capacity as the government did not prevent competitors from coming in; nor did it render the trade unattractive to them. However, the Royal Niger Company was not only a government but also a trading concern. It was not prepared to put up with competition of these dimensions without hitting back, and it did so in 1893, employing the usual methods by which commercial firms attempt to deal with competitors. It began by buying out the African Association, which transferred to the Royal Niger Company all its assets in the company's territory in exchange for 5,033 ordinary shares of £10 each of the Royal Niger Company. So the Association ceased to be a competitor, and became a partner. Strengthened by this deal, the Royal Niger Company hit hard at the independent traders by undercutting their barter rates, and drove them all away.

The French were now supreme on the upper Niger, which they had reached from Senegal, and desired to extend their empire eastward by acquisition of some of the territories which formed the hinterland of those under the control of the Royal Niger Company. In 1890 a French officer, Lieutenant Mizon, with a small armed party in a steam launch, entered the Niger Delta, and started upriver. Attacked by hostile Africans, he and several of his men were

[50] McPhee, A., *Economic Revolution in British West Africa* (London: Routledge, 1926) p. 83.

wounded. Their position was critical as they were without fuel, and had no means of obtaining it, but they were rescued by an official of the company, and brought to Akassa where the wounded received surgical aid. As the French government insisted that Mizon's mission was a scientific one, the British government directed, in spite of Goldie's protests, that he should be allowed to proceed to Yola. Mizon then returned to France where he was received as a national hero, and towards the end of 1892 was placed in command of a larger armed party which was to develop French political and commercial interests in Yola and its neighbourhood. Again Goldie protested, and again the British government accepted French assurances that Mizon's mission was essentially commercial and scientific. Turned away from Yola, where he failed to secure a treaty, Mizon signed a treaty with the Emir of Muri (with which emirate the company already had a treaty), and to please the emir agreed to join him in an attack on a pagan village. In this attack, which was preceded by a bombardment from the cannon of the French party, many of the inhabitants were killed. The women and children were enslaved by the emir, who presented two young women to Mizon as a reward for his services. Many of Mizon's French companions disapproved of his conduct, and he was discredited in France, and officially recalled.

Amidst all these international excitements it is interesting to record an enterprise which was less sensational and less ephemeral, namely the building up of Gana Gana. This was originally no more than a sandbank in the river. The Royal Niger Company beached a number of old vessels on the sand bank, and silt quickly gathered around them, and formed an island. In this way it was possible to find room for warehouses, and staff quarters. Gana Gana became a port of entry in 1892.[51]

Mizon's incursion did no damage to the company, and had the effect of improving Goldie's standing with the British government, but French aggression was by no means at an end. The French now disputed the company's claim to Borgu, a region on the western confines of the area claimed by the company. To assert its position, the company brought in Captain (later Sir Frederick, and afterwards Lord) Lugard. He was already well known for his work in Uganda, and the introduction of this powerful personality to the Nigerian scene was to have important consequences.

[51] The chief architect of Gana Gana was Murray Bruce, who was in West Africa about forty years.

Although the Niger Coast Protectorate had been established, with Sir Claude Macdonald as the High Commissioner, the boundary between the Protectorate and the company's territories had not been defined, and the company took the opportunity to advance its frontier in the Delta so as to close some of the waterways between the coastal regions and the Niger, and thus excluded the Brassmen from more of their markets, and further handicapped their trade. These were the citizens of that community, long famous for its commercial activity, to which reference was made in chapter 5 in connection with the sale of Hatton and Cookson's assets in Brass to the African Association. The Brassmen were driven to desperation. There were warnings that they intended to attack Akassa, but Joseph Flint, the agent-general, who was there, did not take them seriously, and took few precautions. Before dawn on 29 December 1895 the Brass canoes, containing over 1,500 men, suddenly attacked Akassa. Flint and the other Europeans defended themselves in a house, and later escaped in a launch, but many of the African employees of the company, mostly men from the Kru coast, were killed or carried off as prisoners; some of the latter were butchered and eaten, although the Christian chiefs of Brass refused to join in the cannibal feast, and released their own prisoners. Akassa was sacked, and what was not carried away was destroyed. Only the appearance of a steamer, which was mistaken for a ship of war, made the Brassmen withdraw. Although Sir Claude Macdonald sympathized with the Brassmen, and considered that they had acted under provocation from the company, he demanded the surrender of their arms, and when this was refused a British naval vessel attacked Nimbe, the chief town of Brass. The Brassmen put up a brave resistance but were forced to surrender, and later expressed their regret that they had fired on the 'queen's men'.

The British government sent Sir John Kirk[52] as a special commissioner to enquire into the causes of the raid. In his report he made it clear that the company had acted strictly within its legal rights in imposing the trade restrictions to which the Brassmen objected, but that the people of Brass had undoubtedly suffered as a result. He made various recommendations intended to benefit the Brass traders, the principal one being the setting up of a customs union with a common tariff between the Niger Coast Protectorate and the company's territories.

[52] A director of the Niger Company from 1900 to 1917. Died in 1922.

Goldie was willing to accept this solution, but the British government took no action, probably in the belief that the company's charter would have to be revoked at an early date. The Akassa raid and Kirk's report gave the opportunity for a fresh attack on the company by all its rivals and opponents in Britain, in Parliament and through the press, and it was obvious that for the charter the writing was on the wall. But for half a decade longer the company carried on. Lord Aberdare died in 1895, and Sir George Goldie was elected governor of the company to succeed him. The Earl of Scarborough, who had joined the council in 1891, was elected deputy governor. Goldie had been the driving force of the company since its beginning, and had in effect controlled its policy. He had now as governor to carry it through its final years, years of great danger and difficulty.

He was first faced with a military problem on the main river, in the Emirates of Nupe and Ilorin, and at the same time with pressure from the British government which was urging him to resist French encroachments on the western borders of the company's territories. The Fulani Emir of Ilorin had for some years been raiding the Yoruba country to the south of his emirate, and the governor of Lagos, who was responsible for the protectorate of the Yoruba states, was forbidden by the British government to take action against him on the ground that Ilorin was within the company's territories. For this reason the government wished the company to control the emir by force. At the same time friction was developing between the company and the Emir of Nupe, who was raiding for slaves in places nominally under the company's protection. In 1896 a patrol under the command of two British officers was captured by a party of Nupe slave-raiders; the officers and men of the patrol were released, but their weapons were retained.

The company's prestige was damaged by this incident, and war was inevitable. The company's forces were concentrated at Lokoja, and the British government sent a detachment of the West India Regiment to garrison Akassa while the company's troops were otherwise engaged. On 6 January 1897 the company's 'army' left Lokoja. It was accompanied by Sir George Goldie and commanded by Major Arnold, and consisted of twenty-five British officers and 500 African soldiers of the Royal Niger Constabulary, two guns, and over 800 carriers. William Wallace was in command of the company's river fleet which patrolled the Niger. Within a week the town of Kabba was occupied without opposition, and here Goldie proclaimed the abolition of slavery in southern Nupe. The Nupe troops in this area dispersed without fighting, and were prevented by Wallace's vessels from crossing the river to join their main army.

The company's troops then crossed to the north bank of the Niger, and formed a base camp. On 26 January an advance was made towards Bida, the chief town of Nupe, in front of which the Nupe army of some 30,000 men was drawn up. A charge by their cavalry forced the constabulary to retire. The discipline of the troops was admirable; they formed square, and drove back repeated cavalry charges by rifle fire until they reached their base camp in safety. During the night Bida was bombarded, and the following morning the town was once more approached by the constabulary in square formation, the Nupe cavalry again being repulsed by rifle and maxim gun fire. The town was bombarded at short range, the Nupe army scattered, and Bida was occupied. The casualties of the company's forces were one British officer and seven Africans killed, and nine Africans wounded. The Emir of Nupe had fled, and another Fulani was installed in his place on the understanding that Nupe was under the company's dominion, and was to be administered under the company's directions.[53]

The force then moved towards Ilorin. Attempts were made to avoid hostilities, but the war party refused all overtures, and the troops were attacked by about 8,000 men including 800 cavalry. The constabulary formed square, and drove off the enemy, and after a brief bombardment Ilorin was occupied. The emir surrendered, and was reinstated on his undertaking to obey the company's instructions, and to accept such a frontier with the Lagos protectorate as the company might decide. The constabulary then withdrew. On his return to headquarters Goldie issued a proclamation declaring that the legal status of slavery was abolished throughout the company's territories.

Fresh trouble with the French on the western borders was developing. Taking advantage of the company's preoccupation with the Akassa raid, and with military affairs in Nupe and Ilorin, the French moved troops into Borgu, and established garrisons in Bussa and other towns. Negotiations between the British and French governments in 1895 failed to achieve agreement, and the rivalry between the two nations, both on the borders of Nigeria, and in the Egyptian Sudan (the Fashoda incident occurred in 1898),

[53] This was the beginning in Nigeria of the system of indirect rule which was developed and improved upon by Sir Frederick (later Lord) Lugard when he became High Commissioner of Northern Nigeria in 1900.

seemed likely to lead to war. The company was not strong enough to resist French aggression and the British government accordingly decided in 1897 to raise and finance a locally recruited force, officered from the British army, and commanded by Lugard. For some months the West African Frontier Force, as it was named, faced the French troops in Borgu, but fighting was fortunately avoided and in 1898 an international agreement settled the western boundary of what is now the Republic of Nigeria.

Goldie was not at first in favour of government interference in the company's territories, but his personal regard for Lugard caused him to drop his opposition and to co-operate. The company's river fleet was used to transport Lugard's troops, and men of the company's constabulary were encouraged to join the imperial force.

It had now become obvious that the charter would have to be revoked. Throughout its existence the company's alleged monopoly of trade had been violently attacked; the Akassa incident had drawn attention to the hardship to the Brassmen which the existence of the company involved; while the maintenance of the West African Frontier Force gave the British taxpayer a direct interest. As Lady Lugard was to point out later,[54] 'it was undesirable that territories, of which the defence was provided at public expense, should be administered at private discretion'. Lord Salisbury, Secretary of State for Foreign Affairs, wrote that:

> the West African Frontier Force, now under imperial officers, calls for direct imperial control; the situation created towards other firms by the commercial position of the company, which, although strictly within the right devolving upon it by charter, has succeeded in establishing a practical monopoly of trade; the manner in which this commercial monopoly presses on the native traders, as exemplified by the rising in Brass, which called for the mission of inquiry entrusted to Sir John Kirk in 1895, are some of the arguments which have influenced the government's decision to revoke the charter.[55]

The government, however, felt that the company was entitled to recognition of its administrative work, and of the treaty rights which it had acquired, and agreed to pay £450,000 as compensation. The government also agreed to pay £115,000 for buildings and stores taken over, and assumed responsibility for the public debt of

[54] Shaw, Flora L. (Lady Lugard) *A Tropical Dependency* (London: Nisbet, 1905) p. 362.
[55] *Papers Relating to the Surrender of the Charter of the Royal Niger Company*, C9372 (1899).

£250,000.[56] It was later agreed that the correct figure for the public debt liability should be £300,000, and the total sum provided in the Bill for the Royal Niger Company Act of 1899 was £865,000. In addition the government undertook to impose royalties on minerals won from the lands between the Niger and a line drawn from Yola to Zinder, and to pay to the company, for a period of ninety-nine years, one-half of these royalties.[57]

When the Bill for the Royal Niger Company Act was brought before the House of Commons it met with strong opposition. In committee an amendment was moved to reduce the compensation to the company from £865,000 to £400,000. The mover of the amendment declared that 'the company are getting a monstrous price for their assets'. Another member, referring to the undertaking to give the company half of the mineral royalties for ninety-nine years, said that 'this was an arrangement that ought never to have been made', and another thought that 'of all the elements in this bad bargain, this is the worst of the lot'.[58] On the other hand, the Chancellor of the Exchequer, Sir Michael Hicks-Beach, defended the Bill, and the company:

> I do not mean to say that the founders of the company did not look to the profits to be made by their trading operations—but I do say that their main intention and purpose was to extend the British empire, British trade, and British commerce in territories which appeared to them to be of great value to the civilised world.

The amendment was defeated, and the Bill was passed in the House of Commons by 181 votes to 81.

In the House of Lords the Bill passed without a division. Lord Salisbury took the opportunity to pay tribute to the company:

> I think that no-one doubts for an instant that the main object of the Niger Company was philanthropic and political, and that it was not merely a monetary speculation. They risked their money enormously, a mere accident might have destroyed it, and it was

---

[56] *see* page 124.

[57] The total received by the Niger Company and its successors during the forty-three years from 1906 to 1949 was about £3,250,000. In 1949 the government of Nigeria purchased for £1,000,000 from the United Africa Company (as successors of the Royal Niger Company) the rights to this share of the royalties, rights which under the agreement had yet some fifty years to run.

[58] House of Commons, *Hansard*, 26 July 1899, cols. 282, 395, 417.

only fair that they should receive a handsome and sufficient price such as Parliament had given them. But I think that we cannot part with them without recognizing the enormous benefit which the civilising of those countries has received from their exertions.

He went on to refer to

the advance that we have made in stopping inter-tribal wars, in arresting the slave-raiding which is such a fearful curse in that country, and in diminishing the liquor traffic from which so many evils are derived.[59]

The Bill received the royal assent, and the charter was revoked as from 1 January 1900. On that day, at a parade at Lokoja, the company's flag was hauled down and the Union Flag hoisted in its stead. To replace the chartered company's administration the British Protectorate of Northern Nigeria was set up, with Lugard, now Sir Frederick Lugard, as High Commissioner, while the southern part of the company's territories was joined to the Niger Coast Protectorate to form the Protectorate of Southern Nigeria.

In its administration the chartered company had been as effective as its limited resources permitted. Its refusal to increase its profits by any traffic in spirits must stand to its credit. The tributes paid to it in Parliament were not excessive. It made profits ranging from £13,168 in 1892 to £43,183 in 1893. In the last year of the charter, due to exceptional receipts, the profits reached £123,898. In most years a dividend of six per cent, free of income tax, was paid to shareholders.

[59] House of Lords, *Hansard,* 1 August 1899, col. 1003.

10

The African Association

The African Association was incorporated in 1889. It was a merger of eight other firms of the Oil Rivers with Thomas Harrison and Company, whose business was the most important of all in that area, with the exception of Alexander Miller Brother and Company. The eight other firms, in alphabetical order, were:

British and Continental African Company Limited, of Liverpool; Couper, Johnstone and Company, of Glasgow; Hatton and Cookson, of Liverpool; Holt and Cotterell, of Liverpool; Richard and William King, of Bristol; Stuart and Douglas, Limited, of Liverpool; Taylor, Laughland and Company, of Glasgow; and George Watts, of Liverpool.

Richard and William King, and Hatton and Cookson, handed over to the African Association only those parts of their businesses which were in the Oil Rivers, and continued elsewhere in Africa under their existing names. Their stories are told in other chapters.

Thomas Harrison and Company nominated three directors of the African Association. One of them, Thomas Stanley Rogerson, was the first chairman. Two other firms were also each represented by three directors; one other firm supplied two; and one came from each of the remaining firms. The board therefore numbered sixteen members, three of whom were managers, Harry Cotterell, John Tunnicliffe, senior, and R. P. Gilbertson.[1] The board suffered, as was soon apparent, from a clash of temperaments.

[1] A photograph of the Directors of the African Association will be found at plate 16. Their names are shown on the plate. The following notes refer to some of them. Harry Cotterell, *see* chapters 10 and 20. George Watts, *see* chapter 5. Watts was at one time an individual trading captain, sailing his own ship. Edward Hatton Cookson, *see* chapter 6. John Tunnicliffe (senior), became chairman of the African Association Limited. His son became the joint managing director of that company. Mazzini Stuart and Hahnemann Stuart; their company was Stuart and Douglas, general merchants with large cooperage interests at Liverpool. They claimed descent from the Scottish royal family. The father of these two was a supporter of Garibaldi, and on that account baptized one son Mazzini, and the other Hahnemann after one of Garibaldi's generals. Because of the loss of a relative in a boating accident, Mazzini Stuart expressed a wish that all members of the staff of the members of the companies with which he was connected should learn to swim, and he spent much money in this cause. Thomas Harrison's son followed him in the African Association and was in charge of the

139

The head office of the African Association was in Liverpool. After having had two addresses in succession, each of short duration, the African Association occupied for many years two floors in the Royal Liver Building.

One of the constituent firms of the African Association claims special attention. It operated in the Oil Rivers alone. Yet it contributed three directors to the board, and two of these directors exercised a powerful influence, finally in opposite directions, over the African Association's affairs. The firm in question was Holt and Cotterell. It was founded in 1881 on the ruins of a small West African house named Irvine and Woodward, a firm whose scruples, like those of Thomas Welsh, forbade them to engage in the trade in spirits. They favoured Cotterell as their agent because he was a teetotaller. Irvine and Woodward were unable to continue, and Cotterell invited John Holt to join him in partnership, and carry on the business. The careers of the two partners deserve to be related, Cotterell's as that of the man who was chairman of the African Association for twenty years, and Holt's because he was the founder of one of the most important West African firms.

Poverty drove Cotterell to work at the age of ten. While filling a succession of small jobs in Liverpool, he increased his scanty education by study, and by reading in the public library. Next he became a ship's steward, and crossed the Atlantic several times. In 1863 he shipped as a steward in a 950-ton sailing vessel, the *Iphigenia*, belonging to a merchant firm of Liverpool, and bound for the Oil Rivers. He persuaded the firm's agent at Bonny to take him on, and for the next three years his life was spent in hulks there and elsewhere. It was a life of discomfort, privation, peril, and very hard work, but at the end of the three years Cotterell was earning £300 a year with a share in profits. His voice earned him many invitations to sing at parties, including African feasts, and he was called 'the singing white man'.[2]

---

produce department of that company in 1915. John Hampden Jackson, *see* chapter 10. Mervyn Kersteman King, *see* chapters 2, 11, and 14. John Holt, *see* chapter 10.

[2] Cotterell, Harry, *Reminiscences*, printed privately at Amsterdam 1969. The firm of Irvine and Woodward also traded on the northern shore of the Congo estuary, and here in 1871 they suffered the loss of a small boat. The value of the cargo was about £600, and this was described as 'a heavy loss'. The incident was reported to head office as a case of piracy, and following a complaint to the government the Admiralty instructed Commander Dyer, H.M.S. *Torch* 'to endeavour to bring offenders to justice'. H.M.S. *Torch* was a three-masted sailing vessel with an auxiliary steam engine, and she lit her fires if wind and current pre-

On his return voyage to England, made in a steamer, he met his future wife, also a returning passenger, the daughter of the bandmaster of the 3rd West India Regiment at Sierra Leone. Their married life was long and happy. Cotterell was a close friend of Crowther, the African Bishop of the Niger, who frequently stayed with Cotterell in his house in England.[3] Cotterell was at Bonny in 1873 during an epidemic of yellow fever which carried off seventeen out of twenty-three Europeans in responsible positions.[4]

John Holt and Harry Cotterell were both born in 1841. Holt's earliest years were spent at Garthorpe in Lincolnshire, and as a lad he made a voyage or two in a schooner belonging to his grandfather, which plied between English and French ports. His brother Jonathan, returning from voyages to West Africa, brought back such glowing accounts of its commercial potentialities that the imagination of John was fired, and he was no longer content to plod on in the unexciting business to which he had been apprenticed in Liverpool, that of coal merchant. During this period he worked in the same office as a young man named Alfred Jones, and these two lads who were mates at work were to be the leaders of rival forces in a great commercial battle forty years later. Their master was Laird, a brother of the famous MacGregor Laird. On completing his apprenticeship Holt secured a job in Fernando Po with a local trader named James Lynslager, who was the British consul. Laird advised young Holt that he would do much better to take service with Thomas Harrison.[5] Notwithstanding this advice, Holt went to Fernando Po. After a short time his employer died. Holt carried on the business for the widow for a little while but then bought her out.

Assisted by his brothers, he had greatly developed the business, and he had been directing it for some years from Liverpool when he came into contact with Cotterell, with the result that he entered the trade of the Oil Rivers as partner with Cotterell. Another partnership, contracted with George Watts, extended Holt's

---

vented progress under sail. Commander Dyer asked the merchants to prepare suggestions by which piracy in the river could be stopped without constant recourse to fire and sword. He went ashore unarmed at Banana to hold a friendly palaver with the chiefs, but he met with a hostile reception, and no progress was made. (Hugh Dyer, *West Coast of Africa* (London: Griffin, 1876; and a MS note by James Irvine in the United Africa Company's copy thereof.)

[3] ibid., p. 37.

[4] ibid., p. 38.

[5] Holt, Cecil R., *The diary of John Holt* (Liverpool: Young, 1948) p. x and xvi.

interests in the Oil Rivers. Watt's has already been mentioned as a founder of the African Association and one of its original directors. The third director nominated by Holt and Cotterell was Captain Jonathan Holt.

It was obviously of the first importance that the directorate of the African Association should know the value of the assets which the firms composing it were bringing into the common stock. The assessment could be made only on the spot. To make it, two managers of the company were in 1889 sent out to the Oil Rivers. One was John Tunnicliffe, junior, whose father had come from Thomas Harrison and Company, but who himself was new to Africa, having just arrived from India. The other was William Nicholl, a member of the firm of Couper, Johnstone and Company. He afterwards became known as Colonel Nicholl, the rank being that which he held in the Liverpool Scottish Territorials. The report which they brought back with them was far from pleasant reading. A good deal of the property taken over was in various stages of obsolescence. This disappointment was the forerunner of many which the African Association was to suffer in the next half-a-dozen years.

To obtain a charter was one of the purposes for which the firms amalgamated. A 'Preliminary Statement' with reference to the Oil Rivers charter was printed for circulation among the members of the House of Lords and the House of Commons, and the newspapers of the United Kingdom, and the arguments in favour of the charter were formulated. It is a lengthy paper, and a clumsy one.

A body seeking to be entrusted with the government of a large area in Africa under the crown should have been at pains to show itself animated by magnanimity, good will, love of peace, and the determination to discharge its high duties with justice and impartiality. These sentiments are far from conspicuous in the preliminary statement. On the contrary, it is strongly aggressive. It attacks Alexander Miller Brother and Company, Ja-Ja, and the Royal Niger Company.[6]

That Millers stood aloof from the application for the charter was an awkward fact, and it could not be passed over in silence. The African Association might have deplored the abstention of Millers, regretted the past differences which had occasioned it, pointed out that Millers had been invited to join the Association and that the

[6] Rankin, pp. 77–8.

invitation was still open. There might have been an assurance that fair treatment would be accorded to Millers even if they persisted in their aloofness. There is not a word of all this. Alexander Miller Brothers and Company are briefly and contemptuously referred to as 'the agents of Ja-Ja'. The statement contained a fierce attack on the Royal Niger Company's charter which could hardly fail to have the effect of a boomerang. If one charter had proved a mistake, was that a good reason why the government should grant another? The alternative, the preliminary statement declared, was to set up a system of colonial government in the Oil Rivers. It endeavoured to show this course to be impracticable. The African Association was denied a charter. What they alleged to be impracticable, the government put into practice. The Oil Rivers Protectorate, established in 1891, made colonial government a reality. Two years later the Oil Rivers Protectorate was enlarged into the Niger Coast Protectorate. In 1900, when the Royal Niger Company's territories became the Protectorate of Northern Nigeria, the Niger Coast Protectorate was renamed the Protectorate of Southern Nigeria.

The African Association invaded the markets of the interior. It will be remembered that by the arbitration of Consul Livingstone markets had been divided between Bonny and Opobo. Both sides had respected the arrangement, but rivalry between Millers and their neighbours was now intense and bitter. Having come to an understanding with the Opobo chiefs on the subject, Millers retaliated against the entry of the other firms into the Opobo markets by themselves entering the Bonny markets. This aroused the intense indignation of the Bonny chiefs. They protested to the consul. He told them he could do nothing to help them. He recognized the right of Millers to trade wherever they liked. The rival firms had no option but to follow Millers into the Bonny markets.

The stations opened in these interior markets gave disappointing results, though Millers fared better than their competitors. They had the good will of the Opobo people, and they managed to make some progress in the Bonny territories. But the general result of the sudden commercial penetration of the Oil Rivers district was to show that it was premature, and that the day of the 'middleman' was not over. It was found more advantageous to buy and sell through the 'middleman' at Opobo and Bonny than to go over his head. Having decided that a change of policy was imperative, the African

Association set about it in a bold and drastic way, giving Millers a disagreeable surprise.

In 1893, J. Hampden Jackson, secretary of the African Association, arrived in the Oil Rivers. He held conferences with the Bonny chiefs. He announced that the African Association was prepared to retire from the inland markets, and leave trade to the 'middleman' once more on two conditions. The first was that the chiefs should relieve the African Association of its premises in interior markets, paying a fair price for them, and the second was that Millers should retire too. It was useless, as those for whom Hampden Jackson was acting well knew, to approach Millers with a proposal of agreed retirement. They had determined on steps which would leave Millers with no choice. The chiefs of Opobo as well as of Bonny were naturally anxious to have their markets again to themselves. Hampden Jackson played upon their desire. He got them to promise that if Millers refused to follow the example of the African Association, withdrawing from the hinterland on the same terms and conditions, the firm should be subjected to a boycott in both Bonny and Opobo. When a cablegram from the Opobo agent of the firm brought the news to George Miller, he was indignant. His agent, Cowan, was home on leave, and was summoned to his chief for consultation. Cowan agreed to return to Opobo immediately. He felt confident of being able to break the boycott.

Sir Claude MacDonald, the High Commissioner for the Protectorate, had returned to Europe on leave. Miller got into communication with him. Sir Claude declared that, if the coercion with which Millers were threatened was a simple refusal on the part of the chiefs to trade with them, and if there was no intention to use violence of any kind, no official action was possible. That was the end of the matter. Millers abandoned the interior markets.[7] It is a remarkable example of harmonious agreement between African public opinion, all the trading houses except one, and the government, to act together in restraint of trade.

These were lean years, and in 1892 and 1895 losses were incurred by the African Association. The value of the shares on the stock exchange fell very low.

Bad times produced dissension on the board. John Holt and Harry Cotterell, originally partners and close friends, came into conflict. The board divided itself into two coteries, one the Holt, the other the Cotterell faction. They were otherwise known as 'the

[7] Rankin, quoting Cowan, p. 80.

55'

40'

30'

15'

0

Bunch of
Palm fruit

Cross-section of single fruit

Pericarp
Kernel
Shell

actual length 1½"

Thick shelled   Thin shelled

TYPICAL
WILD PALM
Uncertain age

15 year old
PLANTATION
PALM

1 *(above) The oil palm*,
elaesis guineensis

2 *(left) The groundnut*,
arachis hypogaea

3 *Two trading hulks anchored near the shore in one of the branches of the Niger Delta. In the left foreground a sailing ship, fitted with a temporary awning, is moored alongside the hulk. In the distance another sailing vessel, also with a temporary awning, lies at anchor near the shore. On the right are canoes carrying the insignia of a chief who is visiting one of the hulks to discuss business*

4 *Thomas Chadwick in his office at Manchester*

5 (*above*) *The barque,* Guiana,
256 tons, at Clarence Bay in the
Island of Fernando Po in 1883.
She was built in Sunderland in
1831. (Owned by Laing and
Company; Master, M. Tate.)

6 (*right*) *The* brig, Sarah, *118*
tons, in the harbour at
Bathurst. She was built in
Denmark in 1806. Acquired by
Forster in 1824, she sailed to
Africa in that year. Note the
horses on the beach; also the
trading premises equipped with
warehouses below and with
offices and living quarters
upstairs. Thomas King's
African Queen *would be larger*
than Sarah *but smaller than*
Guiana

7 *Thomas King 1759–1841*

8 *Miss Mary Kingsley*

9 *The Fort at Dixcove*

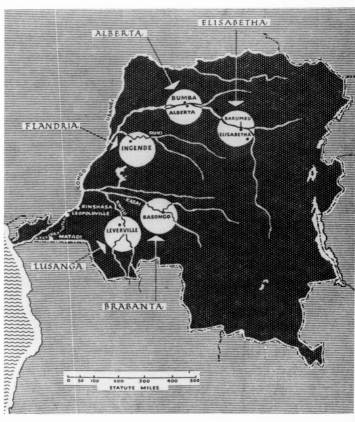

10 *Diagram indicating the position of the concessions granted to Lever Brothers Limited (Huileries du Congo Belge) by the Government of the Belgian Congo under the Convention of 1911*

11 *The quarter-wheeler river steamer* Sir John Kirk *at Burutu*

12 *(above) Kano; groundnuts stored in pyramids and camels transporting hides and skins*

13 *(left) An* okpoho *manilla*

A New & Accurate Map of
NEGROLAND
and the Adjacent Countries; also
UPPER GUINEA,
shewing the principal
European Settlements,
distinguishing wch. belong to
England, Denmark, Holland &c.
The Sea Coast & some of the Rivers being Drawn from Surveys & the best modern Maps and Charts
Regulated by Astron. Observ.
By Eman. Bowen
English & French Leagues 20 to a Degree
CANARY ISLANDS
Palma
Tenerif
Gomera
Ferro
Canary
Lancerota
Forteventura
THE ATLANTIC OCEAN
Tropic of Cancer
CAPE VERD ISLANDS
St. Nicholas
Sal
Buenavista
St. Jago
Mayo
Brava
C. Bojador
Hilil Arabs
Country of the Ludayes
The Duleim Arabs
KINGD. OF
SAARR
The Derveches
SANHAGA
C. Blanco
KINGD. OF GUALATA
Inhabited by the BENAYS
Azagar
SAHRA
I. St. Louis
Sanaga Bar
KINGD. OF FULI
Cape Verd
The JALOFS
Lambaya
Mouth of the Gambra
MANDINGOS Inhabited by the SOUSOS
Cachao
Km of Bitouin
Km OF MELLI
SIERA LEONA
GRAIN
UPPER
COAST
Malagueta
Sunken Rocks
C. Palmas
Equinoctial
Longitude West from London
Kingd. of Sus
Prov.
Burbus
Gamel
Makanna
Barrakunda
Songo the Capital of Mandinga
Conde Quojas or Upper Quojas
K. of Quojas
The Letters E.F.D. &c. annexed to the Names of places on ye Coast of Guinea &c. denote those places to be Factories belonging to the English, French Dutch, or Danes

14 *This map could have been available to Thomas King and James Swanzy when they first went to Africa in the 1780s. Note how the River Niger is shown*

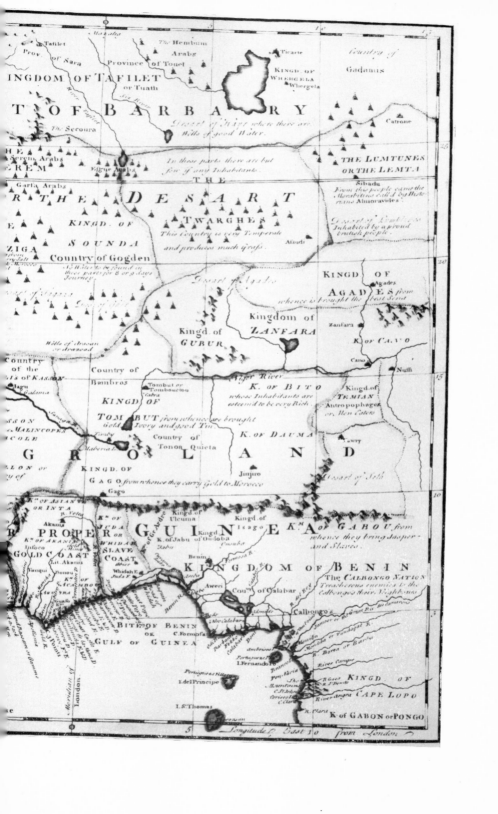

15 *J. E. Cato, Senior, seated in his Model T Ford immediately after his pioneer crossing of the River Volta at Senchi in 1917*

16 *The Directors of The African Association*

(*back, left to right*) *H. Cotterell, G. Watts, E. H. Cookson, J. Moore, J. Tunnicliffe Senr., A. S. Graves, R. C. McKinnon, M. K. King, H. Stuart*
(*front, left to right*) *R. P. Gilbertson, W. Cooper, M. Stuart, T. Harrison, J. Holt, T. S. Rogerson, J. C. Holt, J. H. Jackson*

17 *Sir George Dashwood Taubman Goldie, 1846-1925*

18 *The flag of the Royal Niger Company*

19 *Sylvanus Olympio, merchant and statesman*

20 *The Rt. Hon. Viscount Leverhulme, 1851–1925*

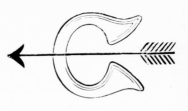

21 *(from left to right)* (i) *The Anta: trade mark of Jurgens Colonial Products* (ii) *The Lion's Head; the crest of Richard and William King* (iii) *The Manilla and Arrow: trade mark of the African Association and of the African and Eastern Trade Corporation* (iv) *The principal trade mark of A. Tangalakis and Company* (v) *The elaborate ticket registered by F. and A. Swanzy in 1921* (vi) *The principal trade mark of G. B. Ollivant and Company* (vii) *The Gottschalck trade mark* (viii) *The Berewa (gazelle): trade mark of the Niger*

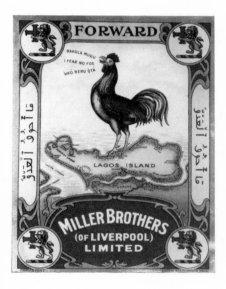

Company (from left to right) (ix) The Slate: a trade mark of the Lagos Stores (x) The Comb and Crescent: a trade mark of the Lagos Stores (xi) The Boar's Head: trade mark of W. B. MacIver in the south of Nigeria (xii) A most defiant sign; adopted by Miller Brothers when they opened a branch in Lagos (xiii) A Pod of Peas and Two Bees; trade mark of Pickering and Berthoud (xiv) The Link, or Northern Knot; trade mark of W. B. MacIver in the north of Nigeria (xv) The Demi-lion of Hatton and Cookson (xvi) The Demi-lion with the Mill-rind; trade mark of Alexander Miller Brother and Company

22 *Jasper Knight*   23 *Rowland Muir*

24 *Frank Samuel*

war party', and 'the peace party'. Holt was a fighter. He believed the African Association could defeat its rivals, and was in favour of maintaining the struggle. Cotterell was disappointed by the poor trading results, and alarmed about his personal situation. His entire capital was sunk in the African Association, whereas Holt had a business of his own, and an increasing one. Cotterell came to the conclusion that intransigence had been carried far enough.

It was evident by this time to Cotterell that competition with the Royal Niger Company in the chartered territory was an injudicious policy. After a good deal of discussion on the board it was decided to dispose of the properties on the Niger River. In 1893 the African Association sold those stations to the Royal Niger Company for 5,033 of the latter's £10 shares.

Nothing would have pleased Cotterell better than to make terms of peace at the same time with Millers. This came to be desired by every member of the board as the lean years dragged on. T. Stanley Rogerson and George Miller were friends outside business. More than once Rogerson went to Glasgow for a talk with Miller in the hope of inducing him to throw in his lot with the African Association. He was always well received, but Miller remained obdurate.

Even Holt would have been glad to see Miller inside the African Association. The two could hardly be described as friendly, but when circumstances brought them together they met on terms of rather more than courtesy. On one such occasion Holt attempted the task which had defeated Rogerson. Holt, Miller, and Cowan, travelled north from Euston in the same railway carriage. The train stopped at Crewe on its way to Glasgow, and Holt got out to take the connection for Liverpool. Miller alighted to stretch his legs, and bid goodbye to Holt. During the journey not a word had been said on the subject of Miller's joining the Association. Oddly, Holt raised it at the last moment. The sands were running out, he said, and Miller had better decide without further delay whether he was coming into the Association voluntarily or not. He would be made to in the end, Holt declared, even if the speaker had to spend the Association's last sixpence, and his own last sixpence in the process. Miller was not in the least ruffled. He answered with a smile, and a few calm words. He hoped, he said, that Holt, and his friends would reflect before they tackled a job which they would not find very easy. They shook hands; Miller returned to the carriage; and the journey to Glasgow was resumed. He had bought a Scottish newspaper on the platform, and he glanced up from it soon after

145

the train started, to remark reflectively to his companion that Holt was a peculiar man.[8]

Holt became chairman of the African Association in 1894. Friction between him and Cotterell increased, and Cotterell resigned his managership, retaining, however, his seat on the board. Cotterell had to find other employment, and A. L. Jones (of Elder Dempster) appointed him manager in Liverpool of the Sierra Leone Coaling Company. It was a trading enterprise established by Jones as a personal venture.[9]

Several sailing vessels were among the assets brought into the African Association by constituent firms. Some foundered on treacherous West African bars, and the rest were sold. The Association therefore depended for its communications upon the steamship companies. Alfred L. Jones had achieved control of Elder Dempster in 1884, and after 1890 this firm managed both the British lines plying to West Africa, the British & African, and the African Steamship Company. The General Steam Navigation Company came in as an interloper, but Jones was able to eliminate it in 1895. In that same year he made an agreement with the Woermann Line of Hamburg to establish the West African Conference. The conference granted a deferred rebate of ten per cent of the freights to its customers, but only to merchants who signed a declaration that all their shipments would be made in conference ships for the succeeding six months. Then the claim for deferred rebate could be made, but it was not payable until a further period of six months' exclusive shipment had taken place. Thus the merchants, having once entered into agreement, were unable to leave the conference without a heavy financial sacrifice, and, as they put it, they were forced to lend money to the conference firms. This was not the sort of situation that Holt found congenial, and under his chairmanship the African Association in 1896 bought the steamers *Erasmus* and *Eboe*, and built another, the *Ebani*. A number of sailing craft were also bought. Jones was anxious to come to terms, and accordingly began negotiations with John Holt. The negotiations led to the sale of the Association's ships to Elder Dempster, but Holt maintained that Jones deceived him, and failed to carry out his part of the bargain. This was the occasion of John Holt's resignation from the chairmanship and from the board of the African Association.[10] The precise reasons for actions such as this are rarely

[8] Rankin, p. 82. [9] Cotterell, op. cit., p. 28.
[10] Davies, P. N., Master of Arts thesis (Liverpool University) by courtesy of the author.

placed on record for the benefit of posterity, and when such actions are taken under great stress of emotion, as this one was, it is probable that the reasons for the action are confused even in the mind of the person concerned. It may be that John Holt felt so humiliated that he was ashamed to face his colleagues and the share-holders, or it may be that he felt that he could not be responsible for leading a company which had become too dependent on the goodwill of the shipping lines. Anyway, he resigned, and the command of the sea was left to the conference.

After Holt left the African Association, he devoted his powerful qualities to the development of the family's business. He was succeeded in the chair by John Tunnicliffe, senior, who died in 1900. Cotterell was reappointed as a manager in the African Association after Holt left, and he followed Tunnicliffe as chairman.

The victory of the 'peace party', led by Cotterell, resulted in the establishment of friendly relations with George Miller, who was the executive head of the Nigerian activities of the firm of Alexander Miller Brother and Company. At the same time, Alexander Miller himself was a director of the Royal Niger Company. This organization was about to lose its charter, and to take on a more normal commercial shape as the Niger Company Limited. The African Association had been a substantial shareholder in this company, since 1893 when it had accepted shares of the Royal Niger Company in payment for the trading posts on the Niger River which it handed over to the Royal Niger Company in that year. In these circumstances it is perhaps hardly surprising that an agreement was made between the three firms, the African Association, the Niger Company, and Alexander Miller Brother and Company. A fourth firm also joined the agreement, a smaller concern known as the Company of African Merchants (see chapter 14). The agreement, which was negotiated in 1899, and entered into effect in 1900, was intended to restrain competition between the contracting parties, and included arrangements for pooling profits, and dividing them up between the participating companies in predetermined percentages.[11] This was an important development in West African trading affairs, and will receive further attention in chapter 25.

The 'peace policy' brought the dawn of prosperity. In 1897 £2 per share was refunded on both the founders' shares and the ordinary shares, reducing the shares of each denomination from £10 to £8, and the issued capital to £342,792. In any year when profit

[11] Rankin, p. 86.

was available for distribution, the ordinary shares were entitled to all of it until their dividend was twelve per cent. Any profit beyond that point was divisible equally between the founders' shares (of which there were only 1,500), and the ordinary shares (the number of which exceeded 41,000). The founders' shares received no dividends until 1898, but after that they did very well, except for one year, 1908. In 1917 the founders' shares ceased to exist, being converted into ordinary shares. The ordinary dividend for 1917 was twenty per cent, and for 1918 twenty per cent, plus a bonus of ten per cent. The carry-forward from 1918, £46,225, entered the first year's balance sheet of the African & Eastern Trade Corporation, formed in 1919. The financial policy of the African Association has been criticized as improvident. For the first ten years nothing was placed to a general reserve account, and as late as 1916 that account had to its credit only the insignificant sum of £8,000.

Some businesses in the Oil Rivers were purchased by the African Association, those of D. Jones and Company and Hutton and Osborne very soon after incorporation, and Pinnock Limited [12] in 1906. Operations were extended to the Gold Coast in 1896, when the business there of Taylor, Laughland and Company, one of the African Association's constituents, was purchased. However, this acquisition was not the prelude to energetic development in the Gold Coast, and it seems likely that it was made for the convenience of Taylor, Laughland, rather than for the fulfilment of any basic purpose of the African Association. On the other hand, it did lead on to another acquisition in 1899, when the African Association bought a business at Las Palmas in the Canary Islands. The main purpose of this was to buy *corbinas*, dried fish which might be sold in the Gold Coast by Taylor, Laughland. (At that time, the importation of dried fish into Nigeria and the Gold Coast was an important trade, and while the Nigerians preferred stockfish from Norway, the Gold Coasters insisted on *corbinas* from the Canary Islands).

A number of stations were opened throughout Nigeria in the first two decades of the present century. The Nigerian Cold Storage Limited was established in 1906, but the African Association was not alone in this enterprise; three other firms were its partners. Another subsidiary, the African Association (Congo) Limited, opened at Kinshasa in 1912.

[12] Purchased jointly by the African Association, and by Alexander Miller Brother and Company. Rankin, p. 84.

Two factors contributed to the decision of the African Association to extend its activities to Sierra Leone in 1913. One was the fact that Lever Brothers bought a company in Sierra Leone in 1912, and by this time the African Association was becoming concerned at Lever Brothers' activities in West Africa, and was in a mood to face up to the new competitors wherever they appeared. The other factor was the death of Sir Alfred Jones.

Sir Alfred Jones, the chairman of Elder Dempster, the shipping company, had a business called the Sierra Leone Coaling Company. The Coaling Company's prime activity was the supply of coal to ships and railways up and down the African coast, but it also engaged in various kinds of inland trade in Sierra Leone. It will be remembered that when Cotterell quarrelled with Holt, Jones engaged him to manage the Sierra Leone Coaling Company. Cotterell returned to the African Association, and became its chairman in 1900, but he remained on terms of the closest personal friendship with Jones.[13] As long as Jones was alive, the African Association confined its interest in Sierra Leone to the placing of advertisements in the Freetown Press offering its services to supply importers from its premises in Liverpool.[14] Sir Alfred Jones died in 1909, and his successor, Sir Owen Philipps, reconstructed the Sierra Leone Coaling Company by confining its activities to the coal trade, and hiving off the general merchandise activities under the name of the Sierra Leone Old Company Limited, which built separate premises, and opened them at Christmas 1913.[15] As chairman of the shipping conference Philipps was engaged in difficult negotiations with the principal trading companies, and when he tried to prevent them from running their own ships, they were apt to say to him, 'If you want us to keep off the sea, you had better get off the land.' As a gesture of friendship towards the trading companies he therefore sold the Sierra Leone Old Company to the African Association. The Association constructed in Wilberforce Street imposing premises which were described as the largest and finest commercial establishment in Freetown.[16] They rapidly opened branches at Port Loko, Bo, Blama, Segbwema, Pendembu, York Island, Yonnie, and

---

[13] Cotterell, op. cit.

[14] S. L. Weekly News, 1890–1912.

[15] MacMillan A., Red Book of West Africa (London: Collingridge, 1920) pp. 252–3. The merchandise business of the S. L. Coaling Co. had been known locally as 'The Old Company' since 1891 at any rate. See Davies, P. N., The Trade Makers (London: Allen and Unwin, 1973) p. 433.

[16] ibid., p. 251.

Sumbuyah. At stations on the railway line they opened bank agencies on behalf of the Bank of British West Africa.

Also about 1913 the Gambia was added to the African Association's trading territory by the purchase of a business at Bathurst, the Société Commerciale de Sénégambie.

The outbreak of war in 1914 brought personal grief to the chairman in Liverpool, 'dear old' Cotterell. His son, working in the African Association's Hamburg office, was taken by the Germans, and interned. Cotterell, cut off from his own boy, made each lad on the staff promise him that he would always write regularly to his father.[17]

In the early part of the war of 1914–1918 there were protracted discussions between the four partners in the Nigerian pool (the Association, Millers, the Niger Company, and the Company of African Merchants) with a view to amalgamation; but it proved impossible to reach agreement. After the failure of these negotiations, the Association and Millers, acting together, broke the pool, which came to an end in 1917. It is of interest that the reason which they gave for their action was that the Niger Company was not sufficiently competitive in dealing with new firms which had recently established themselves in northern Nigeria. Of those firms the most menacing were those controlled by the soap manufacturers, Lever Brothers. The extension of Lever Brothers' activities, and the breakup of the pool, created an entirely new situation for the African Association. How the Association dealt with that situation will be the subject of chapter 20.

[17] R. H. Fox, oral.

I I

Richard and William King in Cameroon and Ivory Coast

The house of Richard and William King allowed its name to be extinguished in the Niger Delta, putting its assets into the African Association in exchange for shares of that company, as was described in chapter 2; but Richard and William King continued to trade in Cameroon and Ivory Coast under their own name. It is appropriate at this point to take up their story again, for like the African Association which formed the subject of chapter 10, and like the Niger Company (chapters 12 and 13) and the Lever group (chapter 14), Kings became involved in the amalgamations which took place in 1917–1920.

In 1884 Richard and William King at Duala were trading partly from 'factories' on shore but still partly from moored hulks. The treaties of that era safeguarded the open-door principle of trade, and the establishment of German power encouraged Kings to acquire property on shore. In 1884 they bought, for 400 marks, the island of Kobolla in the mouth of the River Sanaga. In 1885 they bought, for 600 marks, 415 square metres of land in the Bonaku-Akwa quarter of Duala, land which subsequently became the corner site of Avenue Poincaré and Rue Pau.[1]

The political events of the next few years have been explained in chapter 5. It will be recalled that for some years the European trading houses remained at the seaboard and the coastal people maintained the custom whereby only Africans were permitted to conduct the inland trade. In 1888 the Germans sent a military expedition into the country and for the first time it became possible for Europeans to establish trading posts inland. Immediately, in 1888, Kings bought for 1,000 marks 240 square metres of land at Bona-Musadi, on the bank of the Wuri river about five kilometres above Deido (which is now part of Duala). In 1893 they bought 600 square yards (sic) at Bonendale on the Wuri river. Also

[1] United Africa Company property records, London.

151

in 1893 Kings registered their title to a second island, Kobolt, in the mouth of the Sanaga River, which they had bought for 1,200 marks.

In spite of the establishment of European trading posts away from the coast, to the disappointment of the German authorities the methods adopted in the inland posts were exactly the same as those which had formed the basis of trade at the coast: that is to say, African middlemen brought in produce, and distributed merchandise, and they were financed by the European firms with long credit under the well-established trust system. The Germans described this system as 'Sperrhandel' a word which has no equivalent in English, but which indicated that they regarded this type of trade as an obstacle to be overcome. They even sent out government expeditions with supplies of merchandise to trade with people in distant villages, and bring back produce; but they complained that this type of trade was too expensive![2]

In 1898 the Germans undertook a rapid extension of their effective administration. It was associated with the development of the trade in wild rubber. Again Kings followed with purchases of property,[3] and by 1902 they had European managers at Victoria, Kribi, Nchumba, Edea, and Yabassi. The farthest from the coast was Nchumba, 225 kilometres inland. The Germans were anxious that a Duala house should set up trading at Garua, which was left entirely to the Niger Company: but that was four times as far from Duala as Nchumba, and the communications to Garua were controlled by the Niger Company which operated the river fleet on the Benue. All Kings' early establishments inland were on the banks of rivers, which were the arteries of trade; but it was a short epoch. In 1909 the railway from Duala to Eseka was under construction,[4] and soon after that, motor transport became available. Several riverside sites were abandoned. The two islands washed away and ceased to exist; the asset was liquid! Kings bought land at Dibombari (Mungo district) in 1904, at Edea in 1911, and at N'Dokobele and N'Kongsamba in 1912. When the Germans set up their administrative headquarters at Yaoundé, Kings seem to have been behindhand, for Hatton and Cookson invested in land at Yaoundé between 1906 and 1911, and Kings bought nearly 7,000 square metres from them.

---

[2] Meyer, Hans, *Das deutsche Kolonialreich* (Leipzig: Verlag des bibliographischen Instituts, 1909) p. 535.
[3] United Africa Company property records, London.   [4] Meyer, op. cit., p. 634.

On the outbreak of war between Britain and Germany in 1914 Kings at Duala were in trouble. The port was bombarded by the British navy, and surrendered in September 1914. It was, however, not until February 1916 that the last German force surrendered in the interior.[5] Two of Kings' managers, Lord and Brayshaw, were interned by the Germans. Their companions included another commercial manager named Francis, who worked for the firm of Heywood and Robins, and a professional hunter named Merfield. They spent two dreary months in the *Hans Woermann*, a ship moored in the Wuri river.[6] Then Francis was released on parole not to take up arms, and made his way to freedom through Spanish territory. Heywood and Robins were required to walk with their captors from Duala to Yaoundé. When that town was taken by the British in January 1916 the German armed forces made off towards the frontier of the neighbouring Spanish colony, taking the prisoners with them. A British force followed in chase, and there was a rearguard action at Kolmaka on the Nyong River, where the release of the prisoners was secured.[7]

Thus for three decades Kings had been active in two areas, widely separated, namely Cameroon and the Ivory Coast. The Ivory Coast had already been in the French sphere of influence when Harford was there in the 1870s (chapter 2) but it was not until 1893 that the French organized it as a colony. In that very year Mary Kingsley saw the Bristol ships on what she called the Half Jack coast. They were floating depots, using the regular lines of steamers to ship their cargoes to and from Africa.[8]

The capital was established at Grand Bassam, where Richard and William King held property: but recurrent epidemics of yellow fever in that town drove the colonial government, about the turn of the century, to new headquarters at Bingerville. Kings remained at Grand Bassam. Trade was dull; only a little palm oil and timber; until after the First World War when at last cocoa, coffee, and bananas began to be exported.[9] Before the First World War the French had announced that a new town would be created at Abidjan, destined to become the capital, and in the 1920s the shape of the town was laid out in the forest. Kings did not repeat

[5] Burns, Sir Alan, *History of Nigeria* (London: Allen and Unwin, 8th edition, 1972) p. 227.

[6] Merfield, F. G., *Gorillas were my Neighbours* (London: Longmans, 1956).

[7] Gorges, E. H., *The Great War in West Africa* (London: Hutchinson, 1930) p. 258.

[8] Kingsley, M., *Travels in West Africa* (London: Macmillan, 1897) p. 632.

[9] Deschamps, Hubert, *Histoire générale de l'Afrique noire* (Paris: Presses universitaires, 1971) p. 391.

the error which they had made at Yaoundé. On the contrary, they took every precaution to acquire good trading sites at an early date. Being a respected trading house, they were able to secure good property at Abidjan in 1914 and in 1922. In the main street of the new city Kings started a shop which remains to this day a favourite shopping centre for the ladies of Abidjan.

After the war of 1914–1918 Cameroon ceased to be a German colony, and the League of Nations mandated France and Britain as administrators of the territory. The larger part, including Duala, was placed under French rule, while Britain had a smaller area, adjoining the Nigerian frontier, and including the port of Victoria. Richard and William King were established in both parts.

However, for Kings as a business the political changes were less dramatic than a change of ownership. In 1918 Mervyn King sold the business to Lever Brothers, a British firm of soap-makers which at that time was still under the personal leadership of its remarkable founder, Lord Leverhulme. The entry of Lever Brothers into the African trade will form the subject of a later chapter. The purchase of Kings' business was by no means their first venture into West Africa.[10] Nevertheless the transaction surprised the West African trade, and shocked some members of it, because the African Association had been negotiating with Mervyn King with a view to a merger. When he received Leverhulme's offer, Mervyn King did not give the African Association any opportunity of improving on it. The total price paid by Lever Brothers was £111,300.[11]

That price appears to be low in relation to some of Lever Brothers' other transactions. They had just bought the Bathurst Trading Company for £175,000 (chapter 4) and were shortly to pay more than £8,000,000 for the Niger Company. But the larger part of Kings' business was in Cameroon, and was suffering the effects of the war. The future of that country still had to be discussed at a peace conference before anyone could know what was to happen to it. Mervyn King was 74 years of age. He had no son, and no other member of the family wished to carry on. In the African trade many mergers or take-overs had recently occurred or were being discussed, and it was therefore to be expected that, after the war, conditions would be much affected by the policies of a few large companies. Mervyn King felt that competition would be too severe for a unit of the size which he commanded, and did

[10] Wilson, Charles, *History of Unilever* (London: Cassell, 1954) vol. I, pp. 168, 181.
[11] Lever Brothers Limited policy committee minutes, 10 June 1918, p. 3.

not wish to commit Kings, as an independent firm, to the large capital expenditure which would inevitably arise in reconstructing the business in Cameroon.

Furthermore, it would have been necessary to move the firm's headquarters from Bristol to Liverpool, the latter city having become the headquarters of the West African trade. The members of a dozen firms sharpened their wits against one another in companionable competition. They saw the ships from Africa come and go every day. They had active markets in the town for buying and selling everything. But Bristol had become a backwater.

So Mervyn King sold out for a price which, now, looks low compared with the sums which Lever Brothers paid for the Bathurst Trading Company in the previous year, and for the Niger Company two years later. Lord Leverhulme took a great personal interest in these transactions: his sparkling eye could envisage the high stacks of groundnuts which Bathurst and Niger had under their hands, and he was determined to have them: but Kings' little trickle of palm oil did not really interest him.[12]

Lever Brothers already had a West African section in their head office in Liverpool, and the responsibility for Kings' business was now entrusted to that section, so that the traditional headquarters in Bristol ceased to exist. In Cameroon, however, the name was retained and the business was enlarged by bringing into it the local branches of the firm of MacIver. This business was active mainly in Nigeria. It had been bought by Lever Brothers some years before their acquisition of Kings, and they now placed the MacIver branches in Cameroon with the local organization of Kings. A couple of years later Lever Brothers bought the Niger Company, and its affairs also were entrusted to the West African section. However, from that date the group which Lever Brothers had created was generally spoken of as the Niger Company or as the Niger group, and Richard and William King were thought of as a branch or subsidiary of that group.

It was characteristic of Lord Leverhulme that he soon paid a personal visit to his new acquisition. Early in 1925 his yacht cast anchor in the harbour of Duala in Cameroon, and again at Port Bouet in Ivory Coast.

Returning to Cameroon, it is appropriate to conclude with a review of Kings' situation and activities in 1928. They had six substantial competitors. The most troublesome was the African

[12] Beaumont, L. C. to Pedler, 3 February 1973.

155

Association, which was established in Cameroon under three different names, trading under a nebulous central control. The other large competitors, in order of importance, were Paterson Zochonis of Manchester, John Holt of Liverpool, the Compagnie Française de L'Afrique Occidentale, the Societé Commerciale de l'ouest Africain, and the Deutsche Kolonialgesellschaft. Kings sold goods to the value of £115,000 at a gross profit of £16,000. They bought 1,805 tons of palm oil, 9,922 tons of palm kernels, and 1,602 tons of cocoa, representing respectively thirty-one per cent, seven per cent, thirty-four, and thirty per cent of the trade. For palm kernels Kings, with their six principal competitors, operated a pool agreement, and for palm oil and cocoa there was a price agreement between the same firms. Advances of cash or goods for the purchase of produce had been suppressed by agreement between the firms. The sale of goods, on the other hand, was normally on a credit basis. Eighteen Europeans were employed by Richard and William King.[13]

In 1929 the Niger group amalgamated with the African and Eastern Trade Corporation, and the merged companies were thereafter generally known as the United Africa Company; but not in the French mandated territory of Cameroon. In that country the standing of Richard and William King was such that it was decided to retain that name for the whole of the enlarged group.

[13] United Africa Company Limited, *Report on the Merging Firms in the Cameroons* (1929, unpublished).

I2

The Niger River Fleet

Although it is sometimes said that the Royal Niger Company was the government of a large inland area, it never built any stations away from the rivers nor established any physical presence in the great cities of Kano, Sokoto, or Katsina. One African ruler referred to the English as a species of fish that would die if taken from the river. The company depended so completely on its fleet that it is no exaggeration to say that the fleet was the principal part of its enterprise.

The Niger and the Benue are not easily navigable at all seasons. They are fed by seasonal rains, and the depth of water fluctuates. The heavy seasonal rainfall carries down a great quantity of silt, and many sandbanks are formed in the rivers which make navigation difficult and render charts out of date from year to year. At Bussa, just over 600 miles from the sea, the Niger is unnavigable owing to rapids. There is a bar to be negotiated on the Benue at its confluence with the Niger, and at low water there are only two feet of water on this bar. The depth at this point determines the date when ships can first enter the Benue each season, and the last date for the descent. Any vessel which does not escape from the Benue at the end of the season while there is yet sufficient water on the bar is imprisoned in that river until the next season.

The lower Niger reach is open throughout the year, but operations between Onitsha (196 miles from Burutu) and Lokoja (332 miles) are restricted to the smaller vessels during April and May. Between Lokoja and Baro on the Niger the river is open from July to March, and the reach from Baro to Jebba (532 miles) is accessible from August to February. On the Benue, operations are restricted between Lokoja and Makurdi to the months of June to November; between Makurdi and Yola to the period July to early October; while the full voyage to Garua (986 miles) can only be carried out in the months of August and September.

The seasonal nature of the river used to set a difficult problem in organization. In August and September the fleet had to be

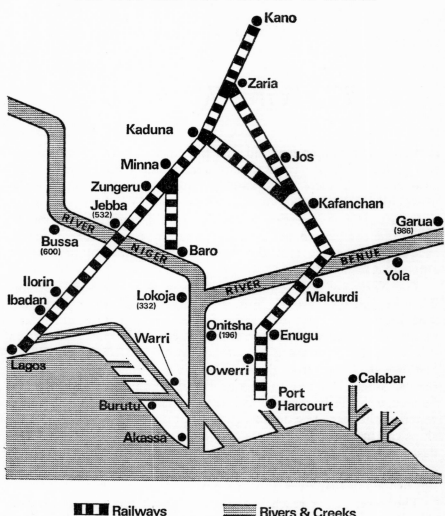

Railways | **Rivers & Creeks**

*Fig. 11. Communications in Nigeria: rivers and railways, 1931. Mileages indicated
in brackets are distances by river from Burutu*

concentrated as far as possible for the Garua traffic. Immediately
afterwards it had to be concentrated on the Baro and Jebba reaches
in order to make the best possible use of that part of the Niger up
to February. On the other hand, the needs of the lower Niger from
Lokoja to the sea could be met throughout the year. In fact, it was
necessary to starve the lower Niger during the autumn and winter
months, concentrating the fleet on the lower reaches of the Niger
in the period from February to August.

The Royal Niger Company established its terminal for ships from Europe at Akassa (the scene of the destructive raid by the men of Brass in 1894) which is situated on the Nun, one of the rivers of the Niger delta, a few miles from the sea. The Nun began to silt up, and crossing the Akassa bar became difficult. The Royal Niger Company was therefore obliged to look for another site, and its fleet manager, H. E. Ratsey[1] chose Burutu, a small island about twelve miles up the river. To approach Burutu from the sea it was necessary for ships to cross the Forcados bar, which in 1899 had twenty-one feet of water. It was impossible at that time to foresee that the Forcados bar, like the Akassa bar, would silt up. By 1929 the depth of the channel had decreased by five feet, an average of two inches a year. The loss of one inch of water meant that ships had to reduce the weight of cargo by 43 tons.[2]

Reclamation and filling at Burutu was a heavy task, and continued for some years until the port consisted of wharves, warehouses, a shipyard, and engineering works, with bungalows and gardens for Europeans and well-built dwellings for Africans. In 1918 the port was destroyed by fire, and the amount of the insurance claim, £1,250,000, gives an indication of its size at that time. The port was reconstructed so that it could accommodate three ocean-going vessels simultaneously. Its sheds were sufficient to store 33,000 tons of produce and merchandise. There were also bulk storage tanks for palm oil. The dockyard had three slipways, and the largest of these was nearly 600 feet long.

Before the advent of Colonel Ratsey, the river vessels had side paddles and towed their barges. They were difficult to control in narrow and tortuous channels. Control was found to be easier with the barges alongside, but this method was inclined to cause damage to the paddles. Full sternwheelers were tried and they were an improvement, but the answer was found by Ratsey, who introduced quarter-stern wheels. A full-stern wheel involves an overhanging weight at the stern of the ship without compensating buoyancy, a poor flow of water to the floats, a heavy thrust deduction unless the vessel is trimmed by the head, and outboard rudders which virtually

---

[1] H. E. Ratsey joined the Royal Niger Company in 1893, and served that company and its successors for forty-seven years. He was a member of a family well known at Cowes as sail-makers. He had a distinguished record of service in the Middle East during the war of 1914–1918. The War Office made a special request for his services, and with the rank of Colonel he employed on the Rivers Euphrates and Tigris the methods, including quarter-wheelers, which he had worked out on the Niger and Benue. (Lord Cole to Pedler, June 1970.)

[2] United Africa Company, *Statistical and Economic Review*, no. 4, September 1949.

increase the length of the vessel and may act erratically when the engines are put astern. With quarter-wheelers (see plate 11), water could flow to the paddles from the sides as well as from below and some buoyancy could be provided between the wheels. These could be worked independently and thus assist in the control of the vessel. The first ship of this design was named *Lander*, and from this the design became known in Nigeria and elsewhere as the Lander type.[3]

The commonest operating unit was one power craft with two barges lashed alongside. Barges were not towed in line astern because when sailing up river it would be difficult to manoeuvre a line of barges round the sharp bends, and when sailing down river, if the power unit were to run aground, barges towed in line would bear down on the grounded vessel, and dangerous collisions would occur. The journey from Burutu to Garua, nearly a thousand miles away, took on the average seventeen days, while returning with the current the distance could be completed in eleven days.

The position of the port was selected in the time of the Royal Niger Company, at a period when the responsible managers may have seen advantages in isolating themselves from the local communities, both expatriate and indigenous. They would be safer from attacks such as Akassa had suffered (chapter 9). It was before the agreement of 1899 with the African Association and Millers (chapter 10), and the hostility of those competitors may have been another reason for getting away from any point through which access might have been gained to local markets. So they built their port in a place where it could only serve as an entrepôt between the ocean and the rivers. Being on an island, it had no landward communications in any direction, and the width of water surrounding it put the construction of a bridge out of the question. From the point of view of developing the Delta region, it was irrelevant.

In the course of time it became apparent that the choice of this remote situation was unfortunate. It imposed limits on the growth and versatility of the port. It meant that the Burutu community would be for ever denied the advantages of wider social contacts. The dockyard and port employed more than 1,500 people, there were more than 700 men in the crews of the ships, and the clerical staff numbered about a hundred. The cost of amenities such as water, sanitation, hospital, electricity, school, and sports, were charges on the port and fleet, and could not be shared with the other

[3] 'Ratsey of the Niger 1861–1953', printed in *Syren & Shipping*, 11 May 1953, p. 501.

economic enterprises which would have come to a port on the mainland, as in fact they did come to Burutu's closest rival, the port of Warri. It was all the greater pity since from the point of view of working cargo Burutu was such a good port. The line of warehouses behind the quay was exactly parallel and co-extensive with the line of ships along the quay, and there were no bottlenecks nor awkward traffic crossings. Although Burutu was a private port, it was open to all ships wishing to use it.

The economic disadvantages of the remote situation were more keenly felt when a competitive fleet was established by John Holt. The competitors naturally chose Warri as their headquarters, a convenience which had been left wide open for them by the Niger Company's decision.

In the beginning power for raising steam was provided by burning wood, but when the Nigerian government developed the coal mine at Udi the fleet changed over to coal for fuel. The first boats to cross the Benue bar discharged their upward cargo at Makurdi, then loaded coal for the refuelling dumps, and continued with this work until the dumps were fully established. When the water was deep enough, usually about the turn of the month from June to July, the medium-sized vessels next came up the river and started the real business of transport, taking merchandise up and carrying groundnuts and other produce down. During this period the smaller vessels of the advance guard would go up the shallower tributaries of the Benue, and bring down produce for loading into the medium-sized vessels. As soon as the bar at Lokoja had a sufficient depth of water, the largest vessels steamed up. The retreat from the Benue had, of course, to be conducted in the reverse order. Grounding on sandbanks was not uncommon. Each unit towed a dinghy, which carried a heavy anchor. When the craft went aground, this dinghy was rowed out to a suitable point, the anchor was dropped, and the vessel, hauling the anchor on its windlass, warped itself clear.

When the Royal Niger Company's charter came to an end, on 31 December 1899, the company owned two river steamers which were specially suitable for maintaining mail and passenger services. One of these bore the name *Empire*, and the other was called *Liberty*. Arrangements were made to transfer the *Empire* to the Protectorate Government. The symbolism of the transaction was not allowed to escape without notice; someone despatched a telegram saying, 'We give up our Empire but retain our Liberty'.

The Niger Company, like other major trading concerns, stood in uneasy relationship with Elder Dempster, who controlled all the British liner services to West Africa, and who combined with the German Woermann Line to form the West African Shipping Conference. There was an informal understanding between the Niger Company and Elder Dempster that the former would not own sea-going vessels nor charter sea-going vessels save a small number at the height of the produce season, and that Elder Dempster would not run ships on the inland waterways in competition with the Niger Company. In 1907, however, the Nigerian government wished to ship a very large tonnage of railway construction equipment up the Niger to Jebba, and, since this order clearly required special arrangements, the head of the Niger Company, Lord Scarborough, met the head of Elder Dempster, Sir Alfred Jones, to discuss how the business should be handled. In principle, Elder Dempster should have lifted the cargo as far as ports in the Niger Delta, where the Niger Company's fleet should have picked it up for onward transport to Jebba. The Niger Company, however, did not have enough ships, so Elder Dempster helped by chartering nine of their steamers (of a size suitable for the river) to the Niger Company. Jones and Scarborough took the opportunity to place the relationship between the two companies on a more definite footing. Elder Dempster undertook to keep off the river while the Niger Company in return undertook to restrict its chartering of ocean vessels to two in any one year; it also undertook to buy its coal from Elder Dempster (the Nigerian colliery at Udi was not at that time in existence) who granted a special price. It was also arranged that in future freight services between British ports and ports on the Niger and Benue Rivers would be provided by Elder Dempster and the Niger Company in consultation.[4]

The river fleet carried supplies for the German garrison stationed at Garua, which stands on the Benue river in Cameroon, and also for the Niger Company station there. Major Festing was appointed as agent at Garua by the Niger Company. He was much liked by the German officers, and one day in 1914 he was just about to leave the Niger Company's bungalow to dine at their mess when he received news from Yola that war had been declared. He turned up at the mess, trusting to luck that they had not received the news, and with his usual gaiety carried on through a late night. Returning to the bungalow, he at once embarked in a canoe, and arrived safely at

4 Davies, P. N., *The Trade Makers* (London: Allen and Unwin, 1973) p. 136.

Yola. He rejoined his regiment, the Royal Irish Rifles, and was killed in France later in the same year.[5]

When the Niger Company made special arrangements to deliver railway construction material at points inland, it was helping to create a serious competitor. As the map shows, after the railway between Lagos and Kano was built, traffic between northern Nigeria and the sea coast had a choice of routes. It could go all the way by rail to Lagos, or it could travel by rail to Baro on the Niger river and thence in a boat to Burutu. A third route became available in 1926 when the government railway opened the eastern line which connected the north with Port Harcourt. These two (or three) routes might be considered as complementary parts of one system of transport; or they might be regarded as two systems in competition. The railway, if it chose to adopt a hostile attitude, was in a position to stop freight from using the river route by reducing services, or raising charges, on the railway section which terminated on the river at Baro. During the period of the Niger Company, however, relations with the railway authorities were sufficiently cordial to avoid friction.

Twenty-three African captains were employed, of whom the senior was Commodore Howudulai. When the commodore retired from the service of the Niger Company's successor, he had been with the fleet for forty-eight years. Captain Yakubu had even longer service. He joined the fleet in the time of the National African Company and served for fifty-nine years. Second engineer Conteh Sori Morgan completed thirty-nine years' service, and Shadow Gaba, master pilot, threaded his way along the shifting channels between the sandbanks for thirty-six years.

[5] Lenthall, Robert, Note for the United Africa Company, 13 December 1947.

13

The Niger Company 1900-1920

After the revocation of the charter the company's name was changed to The Niger Company Limited, and it continued in business on the same legal basis as other trading concerns. Sir George Goldie retired from the board and ceased to take any further direct interest in the company or in Nigeria. During the First World War, however, he agreed to act as honorary adviser while the chairman, Lord Scarborough, was on war service; and in 1921 he offered £20,000 to the company, being under the impression (it appears) that the directors did not then wish to sell the company to Lever Brothers, and that such a sum of money might assist them in avoiding that eventuality.[1]

The council of the chartered company was replaced by the board of the Niger Company, which at first consisted of

The Earl of Scarborough	Chairman
Lord Hillingdon	Vice-chairman
Lord Aberdare	Director
Sir Henry Howarth	Director
Sir John Kirk	Director
C. B. Edgar	Director
Alexander Miller	Director
J. L. Goldie Taubman	Director

Joseph Flint resigned from his post as agent-general on the revocation of the charter and H. J. Drew was appointed agent-general of the Niger Company, but died within a few months. He was succeeded by W. Watts, who held the office until 1914, in conjunction with R. Lenthall from 1906. Lenthall continued in the post until 1915, when he was succeeded by the company's last agent-general, N. D. Maidman.

The capital of the company was £493,680, but this was reduced to £319,760 by the distribution to shareholders of part of the money

[1] Flint, J. E., *Sir George Goldie and the Making of Nigeria* (Oxford: Clarendon Press, 1960) p. 318. The sale of the Niger Company to Lever Brothers had, however, already taken place.

received under the compensation arrangements (chapter 8). The capital so reduced was then divided into 319,760 shares of one pound each. In 1901 the authorized capital was increased to £500,000, of which £350,000 was issued and £250,000 of five per cent debenture bonds were created. Additional shares and debenture stock were issued in 1908, 1912, and 1913, bringing the total issued capital to £500,000. This was increased in 1914 to £3,000,000 by the creation of 1,500,000 new ordinary shares and 1,000,000 six per cent preference shares. (Financing the ground-nut crop, which, as will be seen, underwent enormous expansion in 1912–1914, demanded a large amount of new money.)

During the nineteen years 1900 to 1918 inclusive, the company paid regular dividends of ten per cent on its ordinary shares except in the one year 1914, when there was no dividend because a small loss had been sustained on the year's trading. In addition to the dividends, shareholders received special bonuses in respect of receipts from tin mining royalties.

The government of the Protectorate of Northern Nigeria, which was created to take over the administrative responsibilities of the Royal Niger Company, was placed under Sir Frederick Lugard as High Commissioner. He pursued an energetic policy, extending effective occupation and close administration. As the government established posts far away from the rivers, it was Lugard's expectation that the Niger Company and other firms would seize the opportunity of opening branches in new places. However, the traders showed little inclination to follow the flag. There was already a note of disappointment in Lugard's first annual report, that for 1900–1901:

in spite of all the clamour that the Niger should be thrown open to trade competition, I am unable, after enquiry, to discover any British firms who are willing to enter the field under the principles of free trade without bias or discrimination. The country is now open to them to reap the supposed benefits for which they have so long agitated, but none have come forward to introduce capital or competition, and, so far as I can ascertain, those traders who desired to enter Northern Nigeria have coalesced with the Niger Company, or are debarred either by lack of capital or by pre-existing contracts, from becoming their rivals.[2]

[2] *Colonial reports, annual*, no. 346.

'Coalescing with the Niger Company' was Lugard's description of the pool agreement between the Niger Company and three other firms, which was described in chapter 10. This agreement lasted until 1917 when, as a result of friction between the parties, it was cancelled. In the same report Lugard expressed:

> regret that the Niger Company, who by their enterprise, and the experience gained by years of successful effort, have secured an unrivalled position in the protectorate, have not seen their way so far to utilise that position to the enormous good of the country and their own ultimate benefit, by encouraging local natives to become small traders, and by making advances against their stock or utilising their agency.[3]

There is something illogical in Lugard's two criticisms, one that the firms did not advance into the newly occupied areas, and the other that the Niger Company did not encourage African traders. In remaining on the rivers the Niger Company was depending on African traders for all distribution on dry land, a function which the Hausa merchants were well qualified to perform.

The company continued to maintain the largest proportion of the trade of northern Nigeria, so much so that in the annual report for 1902[4] the trade returns of the Niger Company are given, in the absence of any complete record of the trade of the protectorate. In 1902 the principal imports by the company were cotton goods (valued at £28,891) and salt (£7,965). The principal export was shea nuts, valued at £15,204. The total imports by the company were valued at £81,684 and the total exports at £68,442. Since in that year the company paid out £47,500 in dividends and debenture interest, the conclusion must be drawn that the greater proportion of the company's trade was carried out in the southern area which did not form part of the Protectorate of Northern Nigeria, to which the figures in the report related.

Barter was still the principal form of trade, but the annual report on Northern Nigeria for 1904 stated that the Niger Company had 'agreed to purchase produce with cash if demanded by the natives, and this will greatly promote the circulation of the coinage'.[5] This

---

[3] It appears from the context that by 'local natives' Lugard meant natives of northern Nigeria and not Africans from southern Nigeria, who, he thought, would give trouble in their dealings with the local people and by their fondness for litigation.

[4] *Colonial reports, annual*, no. 409.

[5] ibid., no. 476, para. 242.

policy of promoting a more modern financial framework for trade, to replace the old system of barter, was consistent with an initiative which the company had taken in partnership with two of its friends in the pool agreement, the African Association and Alexander Miller Brother and Company. In 1900 these three firms provided the capital needed for the establishment of a bank in Nigeria. First called the Anglo-African Bank, the name was changed in 1905 to the Bank of Nigeria Limited, and in 1907 a branch of the bank was opened in Lagos. The Bank of Nigeria was bought in 1912 by the Bank of British West Africa, in which the Niger Company continued for many years to have an investment. The Niger Company acted as agent for the Bank of British West Africa in some places in northern Nigeria.

The company continued its successful trading on the waterways[6] but it was slow in developing trade away from the rivers. For some years much of the country was still not under the effective control of the protectorate government, and trading in many areas was unsafe. In 1906, for example, the company's store at Abinsi was destroyed by the Munchis (later called Tivs) with a loss of several thousand pounds in buildings and stocks. In these early years also, the company could afford to be complacent and satisfied with its trade on the rivers, since there was as yet little competition. It is possible that the first trading post established at a distance from the river banks was at Gombe, where in 1909 considerable business was done in skins and ostrich feathers.[7] Although the protectorate government informed the company in 1903 that Zaria was then a government station and suggested that trading premises should be opened there, it was not until 1910, after the railway from Lagos had reached Zaria, that the company opened a store in that town. A similar suggestion regarding Katsina, made in 1905, was not acted on for several years, and the company did not establish themselves in Kano until 1912. The policy of these years, 1900 to 1912, seems to reflect a resolution not to become involved in camel transport. Until the railway was opened, the company preferred to stay where it could use its river fleet for moving its goods.

The company at this time took considerable interest in the purchase of shea nuts and of cotton, acting as agents for the British Cotton Growing Association for some years from 1906; but they

---

[6] *Colonial reports, annual,* no. 476, para. 213.

[7] Falconer, J. D., *On Horseback through Nigeria* (London: Fisher Unwin, 1911) p. 147.

practically ignored groundnuts until the great 'groundnut rush' of 1912, which inaugurated the modern development of Kano, which had, of course, for hundreds of years been a great trading metropolis of the sub-Saharan region.

The first firm to open a branch in that city was the London and Kano Trading Company, which set up in Kano in 1905. Shortly after the railway from Lagos was completed in 1911, the Lagos Stores also opened in Kano (see chapter 16). The Niger Company followed shortly after. Its local manager at that time was A. J. Langley, and he received a great deal of help from a Kano citizen named Adamu Jakanda, who had been known to officers of the Royal Niger Company before 1900, and who as a merchant enjoyed a great reputation for honest dealing. Groundnuts were first bought for export in Kano in 1912. It appears that in order to stimulate production the Niger Company and other firms sent in some seed for distribution, but in the main the farmers were able to provide their own seed, having long practised the cultivation of groundnuts for local consumption. In 1912–1913 no less than eighteen firms (three of them being African) bought groundnuts in Kano. Middlemen were employed, advances were issued, and it became the practice for middlemen to secure the loyalty of farmers, before the harvest, by giving them a 'dash'. During the first year this usually consisted of a double handful of refined salt, one six-yard piece of baft, or a piece of shirting worth about four shillings. Nobody realized how much the Hausas were extending production. At the end of the year 1912, heavy deliveries began to come into the mud and grass stalls in Kano market where the Hausa merchants had their premises. Trading sites beside the railway were demarcated by the government and auctioned to firms in 1913. Farmers brought their own nuts to firms' canteens on the new plots, where prices were marginally better than in the Hausa market. There was a frenzy of competitive buying. When a farmer appeared with a donkey-load of nuts crowds of touts rushed up and grabbed his animal, and the firms sent out touts along the trade routes. The trading quarter was 'buried in groundnuts'. The railway could not handle the traffic. At the opening of the season 1912–1913 the price had been £5 a ton in Kano, but it rose to £10. The farmers were surfeited with cash. Sales of merchandise in the Niger Company's store in Kano rose from £935 in January 1913 to £4,100 in December that year. The Niger Company emerged from this tumult with a share which exceeded fifty per cent. Their slowness in penetrating the country away from the rivers did not seem to have dulled their competitive edge when it came to a scramble.[8]

The quantity of groundnuts vastly exceeded the covered storage capacity. The railway seemed unlikely to clear the crop before the onset of the rainy season. What could the merchant-stockholders do to preserve their asset from the weather? It was Langley of the Niger Company who invented the groundnut pyramids (see plate 12), to deal with this problem. It was necessary to level a base sixty feet square, and to pack it with stones, ashes, and earth. The site was then surrounded by a mud wall eighteen inches high which had to be finished off with local plaster so as to protect it against the rush of the waters of tropical rainstorms. The base was then covered three feet deep in groundnut shells as a deterrent against white ants. Nine thousand bags, containing 750 tons, were then stacked to a height of forty-five feet. The pyramid was covered with tarpaulins which had to be lashed down and weighted with heavy stones as a precaution against losing them to the wind when a hurricane blew up. Lord Leverhulme was interested to see pyramids in Kano when he visited that place in 1925.[9]

After the first frantic outburst of competition, during which firms saw good reasons for paying very high prices in order to establish positions and shares of the market, the groundnut trade was carried on by several of the principal merchant houses (including the Niger Company) in accordance with the terms of an agreement; but they continued to experience competition from other firms which were not parties to the agreement. The reason given by the Niger Company's erstwhile friends in the Nigerian pool for breaking up that pool in 1917 (chapter 10) was, that the Niger Company was not sufficiently competitive in the north to secure for the pool firms a sufficient share of the trade in that area.[10]

The Niger Company continued to employ Africans in positions of responsibility, as the Royal Niger Company had done. Its personnel records classified people as (a) white, (b) coloured, and (c) natives. The so-called coloured men were educated Africans, with or without some European ancestry, and most of them came from Sierra Leone. Any Nigerian whose education enabled him to secure the same kind of employment as the immigrants from Sierra Leone

[8] Hogendorn, J. S., *The Origins of the Groundnut Trade in Northern Nigeria* (Ph.D. thesis, London University, 1966).

[9] A groundnut pyramid was adopted as the principal feature of the armorial bearings of Kano State, one of the twelve states of the Federation of Nigeria.

[10] Rankin, p. 92.

was listed among the 'coloured'. The most senior of the African managers in the later years of the Niger Company was Frazer Davies, who ran one of the larger stations on the river Niger and had several white men working under him.[11]

The company's contribution to the development of the mining in Nigeria was considerable. A great deal of exploration and prospecting was done and the quality and quantity of tin in various areas was verified. The company obtained its first concession for tin mining in 1902, and tin was first exported by the company in 1906. Investments were made in a number of other companies mining tin, which had the benefit of the Niger Company's experience and advice.

In 1912 the company took a large interest in the Belgian nut-cracking firm of De Bruyn, with which it had an important standing contract, and a British company of De Bruyn was formed. This was considered valuable not merely as an investment but as securing a useful outlet in Europe for the company's purchases in Africa. This measure betokened the adoption, in reverse, of the policy of vertical integration which Lever Brothers, Jurgens, and Van den Bergh, the European manufacturers, had adopted. If the industrial company could reach out to Africa to take over the merchant's function, the merchant could equally well reach out to Europe, to take over the manufacturer's function.

In 1913 the Niger Company set up the Compagnie du Niger Français in Paris as a subsidiary, to operate in Senegal and the French Sudan (now the Republic of Mali). It was the year following the 'groundnut rush' to Kano, when manufacturers and merchants acquired a new awareness of the importance of groundnuts; and Senegal and the Sudan were groundnut country. Dakar, where the business set up its African headquarters, was already important as an international port and fuelling station, as a naval and military headquarters, and as the capital of the government of the Federation of French West Africa.

During the First World War, as several steamers of the West African services were lost through enemy action, the company (like some of its competitors—see chapter 8) bought some sailing vessels which were used to transport produce to American ports.

In 1916, acting again in concert with other firms, the Niger Company made an investment in the West African Publishing Company which produced the periodical journal *West Africa*. In

[11] Beaumont to Pedler, 23 July 1972.

the same year, the firm R. Hassan and Company Limited, dealing mainly in hides and skins, was taken over. In the following year the Niger Company acquired a controlling interest in the Company of African Merchants, that fourth party in the pool agreement of 1900 which had just been discontinued. In the disputes which led to the break-up of the pool, the Company of African Merchants had sided with the African Association and Millers, against the Niger Company. The chairman and largest shareholder of the Company of African Merchants was G. A. Moore. After seventeen years of comfortable existence within the pool, he did not like the bleak prospect of free and open competition! He was only a small fish! So he invited the African Association to take over his company, but he stipulated that he should have a seat on the board of the Association. His proposal was not accepted, however, so he approached the Niger Company with the same suggestion and the Niger Company accepted it.[12] In 1918 the general merchant firm of G. W. Christian and Company was taken over.

The two acquisitions, African Merchants and G. W. Christian, might be described (in terms of swallowing up opposition) as nibbles rather than bites. In terms of geographical expansion, the Compagnie du Niger Français was an intelligent and timely venture which was amply justified in the sequel. But for a great company these few measures of expansion, spread over a period of eighteen years, are not sufficient to leave an impression of ambition or energy. In Nigeria, suitable properties were built in the new trading stations of northern Nigeria but the main additions to investment were in debts and stocks, primarily to finance the groundnut trade. In retrospect, this looks like a company which was well content to maintain its dividend of ten per cent, and just jog along. Its friends in the pool had complained that it was not sufficiently competitive. Such companies are very likely to be taken over by a more vigorous competitor. The directors of the Niger Company appear to have decided to anticipate that likely event.

The year 1919, the year of the post-war boom, brought great prosperity to the Niger Company, and the directors decided that it would be wise to explore the possibility of selling the company to one of its principal competitors.[13] The buyer was Lever Brothers, and that story will be taken up in chapter 14.

[12] Rankin, p. 91.
[13] Wilson, Charles, *History of Unilever* (London: Cassell, 1954) Vol. I, p. 250.

14

Lever Brothers Limited in West Africa

For the next act of the drama it is necessary to introduce two new characters, the manufacturer and the palm kernel. Both of them were to have an important influence on the West African trade.

The manufacturer was William Hesketh Lever (see plate 20), born in 1851, created a baronet in 1911 (whereby he became Sir William Lever), raised to the peerage in 1917 (from which time he was Lord Leverhulme), and promoted to be a viscount in 1922. His father owned a retail grocery business, which William Lever joined at the age of sixteen. They lived in Bolton in Lancashire, attended the Congregational church, and were teetotallers. William Lever was already 34 years of age when he began to manufacture soap in a small factory at Warrington, under the registered name, 'Sunlight'. In 1894 he formed a public company under the name Lever Brothers Limited.[1]

William was a man of astounding vision, seeing great undertakings as possible of early realization, even when he had little to work with except his own indomitable resolution to make the dreams come true. He created Lever Brothers, a very large company manufacturing soap and allied products in many countries. He was convinced that his work conferred great benefits upon the human race, and as an employer he was a leader in enlightened practice, creating garden cities for his workers and making provision for their retirement long before these ideas had been widely adopted.

It has been suggested[2] that one of the driving motives which inspired his enterprise was the desire to make fructify what was barren. This was why he selected an area of heath and marsh as the site for his garden city of Port Sunlight and why he started a vast enterprise in the poverty-stricken islands of Lewis and Harris.

[1] Wilson, Charles, *History of Unilever* (London: Cassell, 1954) gives the full story of Lever and his business.
[2] Sir Malcolm Knox, oral.

This, it has been suggested, was the basic reason for his enduring interest in Africa.

Lever's business philosophy was based on making soap of high quality, and as early as the 1880s he discovered that the ideal formula required a high proportion of lauric oils. The main lauric oils are coconut (copra) and palm kernel oil. The oil palm and its fruit were described in chapter 1, and it was mentioned there that each fruit contains a nut, the kernel of which is the commercial palm kernel. The use of palm kernel oil by Africans as a cooking oil had been noted by travellers long before there was any international trade in kernels; but the local people cannot have used[3] more than a tiny percentage of the quantity of kernels that were available. It was a long time before manufacturers began to be aware of the value of this product as a raw material, but in 1870 there was already an export trade in palm kernels from Lagos, amounting to 16,000 tons in that year. The revolution in soap-making of which Lever was the pioneer greatly increased the demand, and the Lagos figures illustrate how the trade grew, for in 1911 exports from Lagos amounted to 176,000 tons.[4] To sustain such levels of exports involved the cracking of many thousands of millions of kernels a year; and each one of these was cracked out of its nutshell by women and children, one at a time. They used a large stone as an anvil, and a smaller stone as a hammer. The development of this vast activity made a great difference in African villages. It was a very social activity. The nut-crackers, mothers and children, sat together in happy groups, laughing and chattering; and of course they acquired a dexterity which made it appear as though they accomplished the work without effort or thought. It may be said that the opportunity cost of all this manual labour was zero. If the women and children had not done this, they would not have done anything.

The manufacturing process, by which the kernels were converted into oil in Europe, yielded a residue which could be made up as cake for feeding cattle or pigs. At first this was regarded as a by-product, but the market for it improved progressively until in the seed-crushing industry the manufacture of cake became as important as the extraction of oil.

[3] Duncan, John, *Travels in West Africa 1845 and 1846* (London: Richard Bentley, 1847) p. 296; Cowan, A. A., 'Early Trading Conditions in the Bight of Biafra' in *Journal Royal African Society*, October 1935.

[4] Newbury, C. W., *Western Slave Coast and its Rulers* (Oxford: Clarendon Press, 1961) pp. 88 and 148.

Lever's soap business depended on imported vegetable oils, and the fear of being 'squeezed' for these materials by the merchants and brokers became almost an obsession with him.[5] He therefore sought to safeguard his position by becoming a partner in a company which in 1896 was about to enter the trade in Nigeria. He was associated with a man named Charles Napoleon De Cardi. The name of their enterprise was the Oil Rivers Trading and Exploration Company Limited and they began by purchasing trading premises at Abonnema and Buguma from a merchant of Hamburg named H. C. Nolting, who received payment in shares. It does not appear that Lever had any part in managing the company. The firm very soon amalgamated with the Company of African Merchants which had been engaged in trade in Nigeria (apparently in quite a small way) since the 1860s.[6] As has been related in chapter 10, in 1899 this company entered into an agreement with the Royal Niger Company, the African Association, and Alexander Miller. These were the very people against whom Lever had sought protection. Evidently the Company of African Merchants was not the tool he was seeking, so he sold his shares in 1904.

In any case, by then he had found another method of reaching out for raw materials. It took the form of an investment in coconut plantations in the Pacific. He sent his friend Harold Greenhalgh to the South Seas to study further possibilities, and this experience appears to have established Greenhalgh as Lever's principal assistant on this side of the business, for the following year Greenhalgh visited West Africa, where he tried to negotiate concessions with the British colonial governments. Lever's plan was to establish plantations of oil palms of moderate size, and to install a large mill at each plantation, which would process not only the fruit grown in the plantation, but also the fruit brought in by Africans from the forests all around. But Lever and Greenhalgh made no progress with the Colonial Office nor with the colonial governments, whose policy was generally opposed to the alienation of land. Lever thought that this policy was unintelligent, and simply held back progress. He had visions of happy communities of Africans, bringing in their produce to Lever Brothers' mills, making better incomes by learning how to improve their palms and how to process their produce to secure a higher price. It is curious that though Lever and Greenhalgh were unsuccessful in trying to persuade the governments to grant them facilities for oil palms, for the govern-

[5] Wilson, op. cit., p. 159.   [6] Newbury, op. cit., p. 87.

ment of Southern Nigeria actually made land available for rubber plantations to Miller and to other companies, as will be recounted in chapter 22.

However, in 1911 opportunity came knocking at the door. Dr. Max Horn, an emissary from the King of the Belgians, visited Lever and invited him to put his ideas into operation in the Congo. Lever sent a reconnaissance party to the Congo, consisting of L. H. Moseley, a banker, and H. Beckwith, an engineer. It was necessary to go a long way inland, depending on the rivers as arteries of traffic. However, Lever at the age of 60 decided to go ahead, and in 1911 he made a 'convention' with the colony of the Belgian Congo, which was of such importance that it was ratified by the Belgian Parliament in Brussels. Lever undertook that within six years he would set up five oil mills, at Bumba, Barumbu, Lusanga, Basongo, and near Ingende (see plate 10). Each was to process not less than 6,000 tons of fruit per annum, bought from the local people who would gather the fruit from the wild palms in the forests. In each of the five areas, when the mill had been erected the *concessionnaires* were to have the right to choose up to 75,000 hectares of land for the development of plantations. If by the tenth year they had installed in any area sufficient equipment to treat 15,000 tons of fruit, they might take up to 200,000 hectares, provided that the total of land taken up in all areas did not exceed 750,000 hectares. The land was to be leased from the colony until 1945, and if on that date all obligations had been fulfilled, it was then to become the freehold property of the *concessionnaires*, subject however to the payment of an annual rent. The obligations included a guaranteed minimum daily rate of pay for the workers, and the provision of services for health, education, and social amenities, in the communities which it was intended to create in each of the milling centres. There were also clauses designed to ensure that Belgium's trade and industry would benefit, and that Belgian citizens would secure employment. To undertake this gigantic task Lever created a special company, La Société Anonyme des Huileries du Congo Belge, usually referred to as H.C.B.[7]

While the negotiations were in progress, Lever had taken another step into Africa. In 1910 he bought W. B. MacIver and Company Limited, a Liverpool firm trading in Nigeria, mainly in timber. The business of W. B. MacIver and Co. was founded in 1875 by two brothers who were born in Dumfries. The younger, whose

[7] Wilson, op. cit., p. 168 *et seq.*

name was Charles, had previously been interested in a firm in Sierra Leone, but it did not thrive and came to an end shortly after the brothers entered into partnership. The death of his brother in 1883 left Charles the sole owner and he was very successful for some years. The firm started in the Gold Coast, but soon found greater scope in Lagos. The British headquarters, originally in Glasgow, were moved to Liverpool. The business in Lagos was known to Africans as the Iron House, from the fact that in the early days of British influence the British government's representative had lived in a house with a corrugated iron roof, and that house was taken over by MacIver.[8] Trouble came with the aftermath of the boom in forest rubber of the 1890s and Charles MacIver was in 1900 forced into bankruptcy. He was granted unconditional discharge in 1901. The public trustee sold the business and the new owners maintained the old name. Branches were opened at twenty-two places in Nigeria and also at Duala.[9] With the support of Lever Brothers, W. B. MacIver and Company very quickly enlarged their activities in the palm-oil trade. They overtook the Niger Company and the African Association, and Miller Brothers (of Liverpool) Limited, and by 1920 they were thought to be the largest operators in the trade. This was in no small measure due to the expert leadership of W. K. Findlay. He had been the chairman of MacIver before Lever bought that business, and Lever had the wisdom not only to keep him on, but also to make him the head of a new department, the West Africa department of Lever Brothers, set up in 1910 to be responsible for the conduct of all Lever Brothers' West African trading interests.[10]

Also in 1910, Lever Brothers formed a company called West African Oils Limited. It set up mills for crushing palm kernels at Opobo and Apapa (Lagos) in Nigeria and at Yonnibannah in Sierra Leone. This move was inspired by the idea of taking the process of manufacture near to the source of raw material. There are some obvious arguments in support of this, but in this instance there were also difficulties, which were not appreciated before the

[8] MacMillan, A., *Red Book of West Africa* (London: Collingridge, 1920) p. 72. The Lagos branch was mentioned in a government dispatch of 1886 as C. McIver & Co. (Newbury, op. cit., p. 87).

[9] Rankin, p. 56.

[10] Findlay secured, under the terms by which Lever Brothers acquired MacIver, an employment contract for ten years at a salary plus twenty per cent of net profits. In the last year of the 1914–18 war the profits were so high that Findlay drew three times as much as a director of Lever Brothers (Interview with Timberlake, recorded at Port Sunlight, 13 July 1948: Unilever secretarial department.)

investment was made, though they soon revealed themselves. It was found that the shipment of the oil to Britain in wooden casks and barrels was very expensive and terribly inefficient in regard to leakage. It was seen that the business could not be profitable unless better transport facilities were created, so they chartered a tank steamer. In the different tanks different systems of heating were installed, with a view to finding out by experiment which was the most suitable. However, this brought Lever Brothers into serious trouble with Elder Dempster and Company, who threatened (on behalf of the shipping conference) to withhold the repayment of deferred rebates to companies in the Lever group unless the chartering of tankers was discontinued.[11]

The outbreak of war in 1914 caused the price of kernels to rise very high, far higher than the mills could afford to pay, so they were shut.[12] However, after two years Lever personally insisted that they should be started again[13] although he was warned by Greenhalgh that it would be cheaper to bring the kernels to Britain than to pay freight for the oil and the cattle cake.

These mills depended on kernels collected by local people. They were not slow to exploit their position, and local kernels turned out to be expensive raw material. The oil, when pressed out, had to be carried to Europe, which was costly compared with the freight on palm kernels. The by-product, cattle-cake, had no sale in Africa. It may be asked, why these disadvantages could not have been foreseen. The short answer is, that Lever made his decisions impulsively and did not brook the delays which must be involved in preliminary study. As explained, he feared that he might be squeezed for raw materials by the merchants, and there may have been an idea in his mind that these merchants were making large profits, so that there would be plenty of margin to play with if he could dispense with their role and establish direct contact with the African suppliers. If so, it betokened a failure to appreciate the competitive character of the trade, of which he was soon to learn more. Lever was not only concerned about the price of raw materials, but he also wanted to increase the quantity of raw materials available; an increase in quantity available would, of course, be the surest way of putting a curb on prices. Clearly it was assumed that in buying kernels from

[11] Parliamentary Committee, *Edible and Oil-producing Nuts and Seeds* (London: H.M.S.O., 1915) Question 2646.
[12] Lever Brothers policy committee minutes, 25 August 1914, p. 7.
[13] ibid., 28 February 1916, pp. 3–4.

a limited area for local processing, the establishment of an increased local demand would evoke the response of an increase in local supply, without causing the local price to go up much, if at all. This was tantamount to a belief that the ordinary principles of supply and demand would not operate in Africa.

Following the theory through, it might be argued that if the local factory were able and willing to pay a comparatively high price during an initial period of some years, supplies would eventually increase as desired, after which it would cease to be necessary to pay a premium price. However, that argument assumes, first that the additional fruit could be found in the limited area of forest, and secondly that the investor would be patient. In fact the mills were all so unprofitable that they had to be closed and abandoned. Whether more co-operative support from the shipping companies might have saved them must remain an open question, but it seems doubtful whether it would have had that effect. There were sound economic reasons why the processing of palm kernels and groundnuts should take place in Europe. The groundnut and the palm kernel are good travellers. They are easy to handle and make convenient freight, whereas oil and cattle-cake require expensive packaging and very careful handling. These raw materials, when scientifically processed, provide oil and valuable by-products to the extent of about ninety per cent of their original weight, which means that the nut and the kernel are the best available containers for the oil in transit.

The purchase of MacIver and the inauguration of the kernel-crushing venture did not complete Lever's African initiatives in that year 1910. A company holding a land concession in French Equatorial Africa was up for sale. Lever pressed his managers to act with speed 'as the door would be closed to secure such concessions sooner than any of us thought'.[14] Acting in this spirit, he sent a manager named J. T. Irvine to Paris and bought the concern for £70,000, without any prior inspection of the properties.[15] This was the Compagnie Propriétaire du Kouilou Niari, usually known as C.P.K.N. Its concessions were derived from a series of con-

[14] Lever Brothers Policy Committee minutes, 7 November 1912, p. 9. This was Lever's personal comment after the completion of the purchase of C.P.K.N.

[15] Irvine, J. T., record of interview at Unilever House, 10 October 1949. The date of the acquisition of the C.P.K.N. by Lever Brothers is given as 1899 by Catherine Coquery-Vidrovitch at p. 187 of *Colonialism in Africa*, edited by Gann and Duignan (Cambridge: University Press, 1969). Papers in the possession of Unilever Limited support 1910 as the date.

ventions concluded in 1893, 1894, and 1897 between the colony of the French Congo on the one hand, and on the other hand, first the Société Anonyme Le Châtelier, and then the Société d'Etudes et d'Exploitation du Congo Français. The latter company was at the time responsible for the transport of passengers and goods between the sea coast and Brazzaville in the interior, and the land concession in question was granted by way of remuneration for the company's work in the discharge of those responsibilities.[16] There was a good deal of criticism about the treatment of the local population, but that was long before Lever became associated with the region. In 1899 the concessions passed to the C.P.K.N., in which the principal shareholders were industrialists of northern France. Having bought the concern, Lever sent out a reconnoitring mission, and in 1912 an oil mill was erected. Owing to the scarcity of labour, however, and the insufficiency of palm fruit it was found impossible to feed the mill regularly, and the company had to abandon the hope of creating a palm-oil industry on the lines which the H.C.B. were following in the neighbouring Belgian colony.

Another difficulty in developing the property lay in the mountain range which, running parallel to the sea, isolated the inland plateau. With a view to surmounting this obstacle, an eminent civil engineer went out in 1912 with a party of three to survey a railway lay-out. Numerous trading stores, established throughout the concession, proved unremunerative, and trade had to be limited to the coastal ports. In 1913 the company resolved to test the mineral possibilities of the concession, but failed to discover mineral wealth in quantities sufficient to warrant investment. After the war of 1914–1918 the climate of opinion regarding the concessions in French Equatorial Africa became generally hostile, and official attitudes reflected that hostility. A policy of taxing the land was adopted, which was intended to force the concession-owners either to develop their areas or to release them. The French government decided to build a railway from Pointe Noire to Brazzaville, and this was the occasion for the conclusion of a new convention between the government and the company, whereby the company abandoned all the land granted to the original *concessionnaires*, which was south of a line selected for the railway. A further convention, made in 1925, gave the company the option of exchanging certain parts of the estate for smaller blocks situated along the railway or elsewhere in

[16] Rankin, p. 54, quoting Léon Genon, a manager of the Lever group from 1911 to 1928.

the colony. An extensive survey failed to bring to light any blocks of land which could be selected as lending themselves to agricultural development, and the whole thing turned out to be a great disappointment.[17]

In 1912, however, Lever was still full of optimism. In that year, with Findlay's assistance, he bought two more trading companies, and then at the end of the year set out, accompanied by Lady Lever, on a very remarkable journey to the Congo.

As already mentioned, Lever Brothers' company, West African Oils, made an agreement with the government of Sierra Leone to open a mill at Yonnibannah. This took place in 1912, and in the same year Lever Brothers bought the small business of Peter Ratcliffe & Company Limited, with a view to their acting as shipping agents. Peter Ratcliffe had been established in Freetown since 1899, at the time of its acquisition by Lever Brothers it consisted of nothing more than an old and dilapidated shop, where it handled a general import trade and occasional exports of ginger. The arrival of Lever Brothers was naturally regarded with some apprehension by other merchants who were active in the export trade of palm oil and palm kernels, and they readily accepted the suggestion that a working agreement should be made under which Peter Ratcliffe would limit his exports to ten per cent of the total available. Under Lever Brothers' direction the firm opened branches at Segbwema, Pendembu, Blama, and, of course, at Yonnibannah. It made its first profit in 1916.[18]

The second purchase of 1912 was the Cavalla River Company, trading in Liberia. Here, as in Sierra Leone, Lever hoped to buy raw materials, and he also had dreams of securing plantations in a country which was outside the orbit of British colonial policy. His experience in Liberia must be told in another chapter.

As already mentioned, Lever himself started out on his first visit to Africa in 1912, when he was already sixty-one years of age. At that time his vast affairs in other parts of the world were facing critical problems which might well have claimed his attention. Nevertheless, he left his associates to deal with those matters, and devoted four months to his new enterprise in the Congo. Rising at five o'clock each day, he visited all five areas of the concession.[19] He was much concerned over the difficulty of attracting workers,

[17] Léon Genon, in a letter to Rankin.
[18] Lever Brothers policy committee minutes, 13 November 1916, report on West Africa.
[19] see Wilson, op. cit., for fuller treatment.

and he was 'continually getting rude shocks', to use his own words, about extravagance in capital expenditure and about errors in engineering. Summing up, he wrote, '. . . the difficulties are greater than I judged. We have got hold of something we can employ all our talents and energy upon for the next quarter century and still find plenty to do . . .' His forecast proved to be strangely right, for it did take about twenty-five years to get the Congo palm oil enterprise on the right lines. His personal contact with Africa did not discourage him from further investments; on the contrary, it seemed to stimulate his enthusiasm. He expressed his intention of paying a second visit to Africa in the near future, but this intention was frustrated by the outbreak of war between Britain and Germany in 1914.

The British government foresaw that under war conditions Britain's supplies of butter, drawn largely from the Netherlands and Denmark, would be placed in danger. They therefore asked Lever to undertake the manufacture of margarine as a substitute for butter, and he threw himself into the task with characteristic energy. Finding that the flow of raw materials from West Africa was interrupted through the scarcity of shipping, Lever Brothers decided to run their own ships and for this undertaking they adopted the name, Bromport Steamship Company Limited. There was now no opposition from the conference, which had ceased to exist (*see* chapter 24). Lever Brothers already owned a ship in the Pacific, and this was transferred to the West African trade. They then purchased six vessels. Three of this fleet of seven were sunk by the German navy.

The manufacture of margarine increased Lever's need for groundnuts, and this was probably a major reason for his purchase in 1917 of John Walkden and the Bathurst Trading Company. Those transactions have been mentioned in chapter 4, and the origins of the Bathurst Trading Company were described in that chapter. The history of John Walkden provides several points of interest.

In the year 1865 John Walkden from his residence in Manchester began to trade with West Africa on the mail order system.[20] He made money, and opened offices in Africa at Rurisque, Bathurst, Conakry, Freetown, in Dahomey, and in Nigeria. It was in Dahomey that he found the design for his principal trade-mark. He adopted the emblem of King Gezo, a pot with several holes, meaning that

[20] Rankin, p. 57.

Dahomey cannot live unless all its children work together, each one stopping up a hole.[21]

The Walkden children followed the Dahoman precept, for John had four sons with him in the business. In 1900 it was converted into a private limited company, the founder being chairman and the four sons directors. The business was maintained on a sound footing by means of a practice which, so far as is known, was unique in the trade; agents in Africa had to send money home before any goods were shipped out to them![22] This may have been a practice continued from the firm's mail order days. At Lagos a handsome building was erected 'after the design of the residence at Prestwich, Manchester, of the managing director, Arthur Walkden'.[23] Close relations were established with Lever Brothers in 1912 with regard to the supply of palm products, and in 1917 Lever Brothers became the owners of the business, which was afterwards extended to northern Nigeria, Togoland, and the Gold Coast.[24]

The purchase by Lever of Richard and William King (1918) has been described in chapter 2. Here it may be well to pause, to consider what a large business Lever had put together in West Africa before he made his most spectacular acquisition. The Congo business had its own separate management, but under the direction of Findlay and his department there were now grouped no less than seven trading companies: MacIver, the trading activities of C.P.K.N., Peter Ratcliffe, Cavalla River, Bathurst Trading, King, and Walkden. The first six of these were looked after by an administrative section in the Royal Liver Building at Liverpool, while Walkden continued to be administrated from its own traditional headquarters in Manchester. It was in any case convenient for the group to have an office in Manchester to maintain contact with the cotton printing trade.[25] The department was strengthened with men demobilized from the forces, and they worked out (for MacIver in the first instance) an accounting system which was to become very important in the ensuing decade. It was a system of double entry and it included such features as profit-and-loss accounts by stations, and a detailed control of the movement of produce from point of purchase to on-board-ship.[26]

[21] Ménard to Wallerston, 7 September 1970.   [22] Beaumont, L. C., oral.
[23] Macmillan, op. cit., p. 80.
[24] Lever Brothers policy committee minutes, 11 December 1916.
[25] Beaumont, L. C. to Pedler, 25 June 1971.
[26] ibid. Luke Cyril Beaumont entered the service of Lever Brothers Limited on leaving school in 1912. He was born in Yorkshire in 1896 and was the son of a Congregational

In 1919 Lever received a suggestion that he might be able to purchase the Niger Company, and it appears that the suggestion emanated from the Niger Company itself.[27] That company had made a profit of £597,022 in the previous year and had exported from Africa nearly 100,000 tons of oilseeds. As would-be sellers they did not neglect to dress their shop-window: for example, about this time the Niger Company took plots at the stations along the new railway line leading north from Port Harcourt in order to be able to say that they were established in those places. They had applied for plots after all the other companies in that region and were consequently given the plots furthest away from the African markets; but at Umuahia just after this was done the government moved the market to the other end of the line, so the last became first.[28]

In January 1920, at a time when Lever himself was in America, the Niger Company directors pressed Lever Brothers for an urgent decision, and it appears that after no more than five days of negotiation, Lever Brothers agreed to pay a price exceeding £8,000,000. Lever cabled from America, 'Price high but suicidal if we had let opportunity lapse'.[29]

Lord Scarborough and his colleagues on the board of the Niger Company had shown remarkable business acumen. Between February and July the price of palm kernel oil fell from £115 a ton to £55 a ton, and other African produce suffered comparable falls in value. Lever Brothers had been holding stocks which had cost them £18,000,000 so they had to write off a loss of more than half of that figure on raw materials alone. Lever was under contract to pay the purchase price to the Niger Company's shareholders on or before 1 July. But no examination had been made of the Niger Company's books before the contract was concluded, and it now transpired that the Niger Company owed £2,000,000 to its bankers, which increased Lever's liability to £10,000,000. Lever's bankers refused to give him any help in raising this sum; but Lever asked

minister who was a personal friend of William Lever. Educated at Birkenhead Institute and Taunton School, he joined Lever Brothers as stated, volunteered for the army in 1914, was commissioned and twice wounded. On demobilization he was posted to the West African department of Lever Brothers under Findlay. He is referred to several times in this chapter, in the preparation of which he has given much assistance. He became a director of the United Africa Company and was decorated by the Belgian government with the Order of Leopold. He died in 1973.

[27] Wilson, op. cit., p. 250.
[28] Beaumont, L. C., to Pedler, 25 June 1971, p. 8.
[29] Wilson, op. cit., p. 253.

the public to subscribe for new shares in Lever Brothers Limited, making the offer without the support of any underwriters; and to the surprise of the professional financiers the offer was fully taken up.[30]

Lever paid the Niger Company's shareholders, but he did not pay off the Niger Company's debt to the bank. In September he extended his financial commitments by making an offer to buy the other very large trading group in Africa, the African and Eastern Trade Corporation (for details see chapter 20). Fortunately for Lever, he was able to withdraw that offer. But in February 1921, the Niger Company's bankers threatened to issue a writ unless they received prompt payment. Lever now stood under the threat of financial ruin. He called upon his friend D'Arcy Cooper to rescue him, and Cooper was able to negotiate a loan from Barclays Bank, but on terms which included the stipulation that the management of the Niger Company should be strengthened to their satisfaction. From this moment, D'Arcy Cooper was the effective controller of Lever Brothers. Lever 'had surrendered control of the policy of his business to another.'[31]

When the purchase of the Niger Company was completed, Lord Scarborough (the chairman) and four of his colleagues retired from the board, and a number of Lever men joined it. Lord Leverhulme took the title of governor. Findlay, as head of the West Africa department, was naturally chairman. Moseley (who had visited the Congo on Lever's behalf in 1909) was managing director. Lever's son, the Honourable W. Hulme Lever, was a director. Moseley and Hulme Lever, accompanied by a third director named McNalty and by an accountant named L. C. Beaumont from the West African department, visited Nigeria to see what had been bought.[32]

The Niger Company's system, as it existed at the time of the take-over, responded to the needs of a period when correspondence between northern Nigeria and Britain took a very long time, and when there were no local clerks. These factors induced a policy of relying on agents to do their best with the capital entrusted to them, and of not insisting on detailed accounts. Trigge, a holder of high office in the Salvation Army as well as a director of the Niger Company, used to tell his agents when they called on him before leaving for Africa, that he wanted a reasonable profit and that if he

---

[30] Wilson, op. cit., p. 255. [31] ibid., p. 258.
[32] Beaumont, L. C., to Pedler, 25 June 1971, p. 42.

got it no queries would be sent from head office. He expressed the view that 'policing' would cost more than it saved.[33] The Niger Company in England kept a 'Nigeria working account', to which it debited the cost of the merchandise which was sent to Africa and credited the produce which came out of Africa. What happened in Africa was the responsibility of the agent-general, and local accounting arrangements were left to his discretion. There was no double entry system. Each trading post made a statement of value of its assets at the end of each month, and sent a copy to England on a sheet of foolscap, with a narrative explanation of differences between the month's opening and closing figures.

Moseley, Hulme Lever, McNalty, and Beaumont, were disturbed by what they saw. The system did not permit effective control, and there was much laxity and inefficiency. Bad habits were encouraged by the very low salaries of the European staff, salaries which were frankly based upon the supposition that the men would engage in private trading. A newly appointed European started at £80 a year, and more senior men were on salaries much smaller than those paid by the African and Eastern Trade Corporation and by W. B. MacIver. The new management of the Niger Company immediately increased these salaries. The new recruit's starting point became £300, and at more senior levels the new salaries were generally about three times what had been paid before. At the same time it was made clear that agents and assistants would no longer be permitted to supplement their incomes by private trading or other means.[34]

While the party was still in Nigeria, Greenhalgh arrived in Lagos. He, too, was one of the new directors of the Niger Company. He brought with him an architect named Lomax Simpson. Their purpose was to make plans for the construction of a head office in Lagos for all the Lever interests. They chose a fine site, but it belonged to the Trading Association of Nigeria, so Lever Brothers bought that company in order to secure the site.[35] Upon it was built Niger House, a worthy edifice, the dignified proportions of which look particularly fine when seen from the lagoon.

Shortly after the return of the inspecting party, Beaumont was sent back to Nigeria and he spent fifteen months reorganizing the accounting system of the Niger Company along the lines which,

[33] Sir Arthur Smith, oral, and Beaumont, L. C. to Pedler, 25 June 1971, p. 7.
[34] Beaumont, L. C. to Pedler, 25 June 1971, p. 7.
[35] ibid., 12 June 1970, p. 8.

under Findlay's guidance, he had previously worked out for Mac-Iver.[36]

In 1922 the Niger Company's interests were carried further afield by the establishment of an American subsidiary, the Niger Company Incorporated, which took an initiative which turned out to be of great value to the trade of West Africa, in providing facilities for handling palm oil in bulk at New York, to be supplied to the steel industry in America.

In the same year the Company took a financial interest in a business in the Seychelles Islands, in the Indian Ocean. The Company became involved in this because of unsatisfactory transactions with another firm over purchases of copra, and in the hope of recovering losses it formed the Seychelles Guano Company Limited, which took over the leases of some islands in the Seychelles from which copra and guano were exported. Difficulties in management and the loss of an uninsured schooner led to further losses which had to be written off.

In 1923 the Niger Minerals Development Company Limited was formed to administer the mining companies which the Niger Company controlled, but this arrangement was soon terminated and in 1925 the Niger group sold most of its mining properties to the Nigerian Base Metals Corporation in exchange for shares in that Corporation.[37] These shares were sold in 1927. For several years, until 1927, Messrs. Laws, Rumbold, and Company acted as the Niger Company's mining engineers.

The Niger Company established a tannery at Jebba in Nigeria. All chemicals and other tanning materials had to be imported and were therefore expensive, and for this and other reasons the tannery was a failure and involved the group in a loss of nearly £80,000. Like the kernel-crushing enterprise, it was before its time. Yet the group continued trying to establish local industries.

Lever Brothers started manufacturing soap in 1923 at Leopoldville (Kinshasa) and in 1924 at Lagos. They thus became the pioneers of modern industrial manufacturing in both the Congo and Nigeria. The manager appointed to Nigeria to inaugurate the manufacturing business received a very strange assignment shortly after his arrival. It happened in the following manner.

One day about the year 1912 Lever took Findlay to look at a

[36] Beaumont, L. C. to Pedler, 25 June 1971, p. 10.

[37] This Corporation was amalgamated in 1929 with the Anglo-Nigerian Corporation, which was liquidated in 1934.

Woolworth store in Liverpool and asked him whether it would be a good idea to put up stores like Woolworth in Africa. Findlay told him that Africa was not yet ready for anything like that.[38] However, ten years later Lever was no longer to be restrained. On his written instruction the enterprise was launched in Lagos, and it was also by his instruction that it was called 'Lever Stores'.[39] None of the merchant firms of the Lever group was willing to undertake the management, so it was given to the man who had recently arrived to take charge of the West African Soap Company. The lease of a plot in Broad Street was obtained, and a building was put up on plans prepared by Lomax Simpson, the architect of Niger House.[40] The merchandise was displayed in open trays on the counter tops and was all priced at threepence, sixpence, or ninepence. There was a cashier at the exit to take the customers' money, but many of the customers proved unco-operative and the pilferage was enormous. The merchant companies in the group considered the project ill-conceived as a competitor of the African market stall-holders. Its life was short.

Yet Lever became more and more interested in Africa. In 1924 and 1925 at the age of 73 he made a most extensive tour. It began in the Congo and then, travelling in his yacht *Albion*, he visited the ports of Equatorial Africa and Cameroon and spent some time in the harbour at Lagos. He toured extensively in Nigeria, visiting the trading posts of the Niger Company and its associates. Again in the Gold Coast he made a tour on shore. He called at Grand Bassam, and at Monrovia had a most interesting exchange of visits with the President of the Republic. Freetown, Conakry, and Dakar, were visited, but by this time *Albion* had so many barnacles on her bottom that she could not go fast enough for her impatient owner, so he left her at Lisbon.[41] His visit to Lagos was the occasion of an altercation with the Governor, Sir Hugh Clifford. They had already engaged in public controversy. In 1923 Lord Leverhulme included in his speech to the shareholders of Lever Brothers certain criticisms of the government of Nigeria. Clifford took this up with him in a personal letter, saying that Leverhulme had compared the best pre-war years with the worst post-war years and had drawn erroneous conclusions from this comparison. Leverhulme sent a reply, but

[38] Wilson, Charles, *Unilever 1945–1965* (London: Cassell, 1968) p. 219.
[39] Leverhulme to Greenhalgh, 16 February 1925, Lever correspondence 8104.
[40] Beaumont, L. C. to Pedler, 25 March 1970, pp. 2–3.
[41] Knox, Sir Malcolm, oral.

Clifford did not consider that it was satisfactory. Three months later, at the annual general meeting of the Niger Company, Leverhulme returned to the subject, unrepentant, and said among other things that 'The colonial system of administration was founded on the recognition of the principles that the encouragement of trade and commerce and the development of the colonies were of first consideration.' Clifford referred to this in his address to the Legislative Council in Lagos in February 1924.[42] He described it as 'The most monstrous and mischievous heresy'. He went on to say that these so-called principles died finally and for ever when Warren Hastings was impeached, and he declared his adhesion to the principle of the paramountcy of African interests.[43]

He expressed the hope that the people of Nigeria would retain their independence, and would 'not fall into the temptation of producing any crop which is valueless to them unless they can dispose of it for export'. Leverhulme's rejoinder to this was delivered at the annual meeting of Lever Brothers in April 1924 when he said that there was not one word which he would withdraw, but that he did not intend his remarks to be taken personally. Three months later the Liverpool Chamber of Commerce secured the attendance of both these gentlemen at a dinner, which must have been considered quite an achievement. Leverhulme made a speech in which he paid a compliment to Clifford as 'A man who has the highest ideals of the British Empire' and then continued at length to expound his well-known views on plantations.[44] This was the background of their relationship when Leverhulme's yacht cast anchor in Lagos Harbour, and the Governor promptly invited him to dinner. It was, according to Leverhulme and those who were with him, a pleasant social occasion, and Leverhulme invited Clifford to dine with him aboard the yacht *Albion* two days later. Clifford declined, saying that it had surprised him to receive an invitation to dine, and that he could not accept it until such time as an apology had been made with as much publicity as the original unsustainable charges. Leverhulme replied that he had never intended to make a personal attack on Clifford, but that as he was representative of the system it was necessary to make use of his name. Clifford in a further letter said

[42] Opening speech of Sir Hugh Clifford at the second session of the legislative council, 11 February 1924 (Lagos: Government printer, 1924).

[43] A phrase derived from the Devonshire White Paper on Kenya, Cmd. 1922 of 1923.

[44] Leverhulme, *The West African Trade*, speech delivered at a dinner of the West African Trade Section of the Liverpool Chamber of Commerce, 9 July 1924 (Port Sunlight: Lever Brothers, 1924).

that the sentence was meaningless; Leverhulme had made definite, reckless, damaging, and unsustainable, charges against the administration, for which Clifford and he alone was responsible to the Secretary of State.

The idea that it was possible to have a high regard for Clifford as a person, while maintaining damaging criticisms of Clifford as Governor, was no doubt derived from contemporary political attitudes at Westminster, but clearly it had been strained too far. On the other hand, inviting a man to dinner and then declining to accept an invitation in return, seems strange social behaviour. The real issue in dispute was, whether the interests of African producers, and the interests of European manufacturers, could be regarded as complementary; or at any rate, whether they could be reconciled. But that debate could not be continued between these protagonists, because within a few weeks Lord Leverhulme was dead.

The activities of such a man and their total impact on Africa call for some words of assessment, but it will be better to leave that until the final chapter, for various matters remain to be related which will need to be taken into account when striking the balance.

Hulme Lever followed Findlay as chairman, and occupied that position until 1925 when, at D'Arcy Cooper's suggestion, it passed to E. Hyslop Bell, who had held senior responsibilities in Barclays Bank. It will be recalled that the financial crisis of 1921 was overcome by D'Arcy Cooper with the assistance of Barclays Bank, and that the bank made it a condition that the management of the Niger Company should be strengthened to their satisfaction. It seems possible that the introduction of Hyslop Bell by D'Arcy Cooper may have been a compliance, albeit somewhat belated, with that stipulation. By this time the West African department of Lever Brothers had taken the name 'Niger Company' and the whole of the trading activities of the concern in West Africa were generally referred to as the Niger group. Of this concern, the managing director under Hyslop Bell was Snelling, a man of brilliant intellect and impish character. He had been an expert on taxation, about which he had written authoritatively. He was employed by Lever to pursue a claim for the repayment of £800,000 excess profits duty; he refused to allow Lever to accompany him to the critical interview and, without Lever's assistance, was completely successful.[45] Lever liked a man who behaved like that, and did not resent the rebuff. Snelling acquired a Hollerith punch-card machine.

[45] Beaumont L. C. to Pedler, 12 June 1970, p. 6.

It was of course much less than a computer, but it gave him powers of analysing data which at that time were new and exciting. By this means a great deal was found out about the African trade, about what made profits and what made losses. These investigations made it clear that the most important factor determining profits and losses was the quality of the man in charge of a post. The necessary conclusions were drawn. The investigation showed that to win profits it was necessary to specialize.[46] So with Beaumont's help, Snelling classified the whole of the merchandise which the group imported into Africa under ninety-nine heads.[47] This opened the way to a more intelligent control of sales, stocks, and indents. It facilitated a degree of specialization and enabled the results of the various branches of activity to be reported in the accounts. To discourage agents from being hasty and superficial when they went on tours of inspection, Snelling provided them with questionnaires which had to be completed.

Snelling would not be told what to do by Lever Brothers and he did not keep them informed. In fact he established a position of arm's-length operation which was strangely different from Lever's original idea of having a merchant organization under his control. It was clear to Snelling that a merchant company could not hope to be successful if it took orders from a manufacturer-customer-supplier. Lever Brothers were able to accept the position without difficulty, because by now it had become obvious that Lever's anxieties about being squeezed by merchants and brokers were unfounded. There were many eager sellers of oils and oilseeds who were delighted to supply Lever Brothers at competitive prices.

The Niger group's activities in the Gold Coast were limited to the small establishment in that colony of John Walkden, until the purchase in 1926 of the firm of Pickering and Berthoud. This company was engaged in buying any kind of produce that could be exported from Africa at a profit, and in selling in Africa the usual range of trade goods. It had been established in Manchester in 1868 under the name of Roebuck Pickering and Company. H. L. Berthoud joined in 1878 and the name was then altered to Pickering and Berthoud. In 1910 the firm became a private limited company. George E. Pickering, who had entered the business in 1882, was the chairman, and his colleagues on the board were two Pickerings and two Berthouds. The business was established at

[46] Beaumont, L. C. to Pedler, 19 May 1971.
[47] Ibid., 25 June 1971, p. 14.

Accra, Sekondi, and Kumasi in the Gold Coast, at Freetown on
Sierra Leone, at Lagos in Nigeria, and at Hamburg in Germany.
It was a continuously thriving one.[48]

Although the Niger group was well represented in the Ivory
Coast by Richard and William King, it extended its investment in
that colony in 1928 by buying the Continental Overseas Trading
Company, which owned the Compagnie française de la Côte
d'Ivoire. The Continental Overseas Trading Company was
established in 1915 with headquarters in the Rue de Paradis in
Paris and it was managed by a man named Ino Jabriel. In the
following year a Danish bank, the Landmansbanken of Copen-
hagen, purchased the business and appointed Aage Dessau to take
charge of it. The company engaged in imports and exports with
South America, India, China, Japan, Guadaloupe, Martinique,
Madagascar, and Réunion. In 1921 a merger was arranged by
which the C.O.T.C. acquired the Compagnie française de la Côte
d'Ivoire, and trade then began with the Ivory Coast, Senegal and
Guinea. In 1928, when the Niger Company bought this concern,
it was still under the management of Aage Dessau, while the produce side of the business was run by another Dane named Frorup.[49]

The Compagnie française de la Côte d'Ivoire was strongly
established at Bamako in the French Sudan (now the Republic of
Mali) where its manager Annette had built a great house which
was known as *Palais Annette.*

Activities in the Gold Coast and in the Ivory Coast gave the
Niger group an important interest in the cocoa trade. As merchants
they were very conscious of their weak position *vis-à-vis* the manu-
facturer-customers, and this led the Niger group in 1925 to enter
into an agreement with their principal competitors, the African
and Eastern Trade Corporation, to form a pool for dealing in cocoa.
This agreement proved, however, impossible to operate. The two
parties were too hostile and suspicious of one another. After many
disputes and several arbitration proceedings, the agreement was
terminated early in 1929, just a few weeks before the two contracting parties both lost their independent existence.

After the Niger Company was taken over by Lever Brothers, the
Niger group made losses for five years. At last Hyslop Bell was
able to announce that a profit had been earned in 1925. Thus encouraged, Lever Brothers made financial arrangements to give the
Niger group a fresh start. They made a free gift of £1,023,250

[48] Rankin, p. 103.   [49] Note by Madame Frorup, January 1971.

to the Niger Company and also funded £1,500,000 of debt by converting it into seven per cent second debenture stock. These measures wiped out the accumulated losses and provided the Niger group with the working capital which it required. Profits continued to be earned: £201,000 in 1926, £205,000 in 1927, £140,000 in 1928, and £212,000 in 1929. In this last year, for the first time since Lever Brothers bought the Niger Company, a dividend was paid: a modest dividend of five per cent, but it made all the more impression because in that very year the great competitor of the Niger Company, the African and Eastern Trade Corporation, incurred a loss.[50]

[50] Rankin, p. 103.

15

The Dutch Companies

This book is not, of course, concerned with all the Dutch companies which traded into Africa, but only with those which subsequently became part of the United Africa Company; and this means, in practice, those which were associated with the margarine manufacturers, Jurgens and Van den Bergh. It is appropriate to deal with this group immediately after the chapter about Lever Brothers, for the theme is basically the same; the reaching-out by European manufacturers for raw materials in Africa.

The brothers Jurgens began to manufacture margarine at Oss in the Netherlands in 1871.[1] In the following year the four brothers Van den Bergh started a factory in the same industry in the same town.[2] Both firms achieved tremendous growth and became established in many countries. The competition between them was mitigated for a period, 1907–1914, by what has been called 'an uneasy partnership',[3] taking the form of a pooling agreement. After that, competition again became very bitter, and by 1927 it was being conducted in such a hostile manner that both firms were wasting their substance. At this juncture better sense prevailed, and the two firms came together in an amalgamation under the name Margarine Union.

Anton Jurgens was a managing director of the Jurgens group from 1902, and as the group had important interests in Germany, he conceived the idea of using those interests as a base for developing the production of palm oil in the German colony of Cameroon. A company called the Syndikat für Ölpalmenkultur G.m.b.H. (known as S.O.K. for short) was registered at Berlin in 1907 by a group of seventeen German investors. Within a few months Anton Jurgens had bought the shares of all save two of the founders. At this moment, as mentioned above, Jurgens concluded a pooling agreement with his competitor Van den Bergh, and in accordance

[1] Wilson, Charles, *History of Unilever* (London: Cassell, 1954) vol. II, p. 29.
[2] ibid.
[3] ibid.

with the terms of that agreement half the Jurgens shares in S.O.K. were transferred to Van den Bergh.[4]

Between 1908 and 1911 S.O.K. acquired areas of land at various places in Cameroon, but these activities appear to have provoked in the German government much the same doubts as Lever's overtures provoked in the British colonies, for in 1910 the German government declared large tracts to be inalienable native land, which had the effect of withdrawing from the possibility of development eighty per cent of the area which S.O.K. had hoped to use. They built a crushing factory for palm kernels near Duala and managed to buy some more land which was not subject to the ban on development. They created a plantation at Dibombari, but since palm trees must grow for some years before they yield a crop, the war of 1914 broke out before any results were seen, and the plantation was abandoned and ran wild.

During the war the Dutch firms felt that the pool of British merchant companies in West Africa (*see* chapter 25) charged them excessive prices for their raw materials, and they determined to create their own buying organizations in West Africa. An opportunity seemed to present itself to the Dutch in 1916 when the British government decided to offer for sale by auction the Nigerian assets of several German companies which had been seized. The most important were G. L. Gaiser, and Witt and Busch. Jurgens enquired of the British government whether there would be any objection to the British subsidiary of Jurgens putting in a bid for one or more of these firms. The government was willing, but the pool firms (including Niger Company, African Association, and Miller-Swanzy) were determined to keep the Dutch out. In this they were supported by another British group headed by the Maypole Dairy Company. Parliamentary support was organized and much was made of the interests which the Dutchmen possessed in Germany. Under pressure, the government announced that bidding would be restricted to firms who could prove that at least ninety per cent of their shares were either in allied or in neutral ownership. Jurgens could have proved this, but they did not have time to prepare the documentation, and so they could not bid. The properties of Gaiser and of Witt and Busch were purchased for about £150,000 by the newly formed 'British Nigerian Company', of which the shareholders were the leading British and French firms established

[4] From original documents supplied by Margarine Union, Hamburg, now in United Africa Company records.

in Nigeria, that is to say, the Lagos Stores, John Holt, Miller Brothers, MacIver (= Lever Brothers), G. B. Ollivant, H. B. W. Russell, the Compagnie française de l'Afrique occidentale, and Paterson Zochonis.

This result was disappointing to Jurgens but he was still determined to acquire his own buying organization so he formed a new British subsidiary, Jurgens Colonial Products. As manager he appointed C. A. Birtwistle, an Englishman with great experience of Nigeria, where he had been employed both in commerce and in the government service. Birtwistle bought a small business named Fairley in Kano and also set up buying arrangements in Lagos, Gambia, Sierra Leone, Gold Coast, and certain places in French West Africa.

The pool firms were no longer so friendly with each other as they had been, and Birtwistle tried to woo Millers[5] but could not bring them to terms. The Niger Company invited all its competitors to pay the same price for groundnuts in Kano, but Birtwistle bluntly refused. As a result there was frenzied bidding for groundnuts in 1918; the Niger Company, MacIvers (= Lever Brothers) and Ollivant were mainly responsible for forcing up the price. Jurgens took no part in the scramble, and his share of trade was small. What he hoped for was that the larger buyers would form a pool and leave Jurgens as an independent buyer to operate at a level slightly higher than the pool's limit. In 1923 he was gleefully anticipating this situation.

Van den Bergh did not enter the Nigerian trade until after the War, but in December 1918 he took shares in the Standard Company of Nigeria. This belonged to a Manchester Greek named Pappadimitrion. It made no profit, and in 1924 'a very bad epidemic of plague in Lagos' was mentioned as one of the reasons for the disappointing results. Van den Bergh took over Pappadimitron's interest in settlement of debts outstanding.[8]

A company called Palmine Limited began to operate in the Gambia in 1915. The story how Jurgens acquired the Palmine name is of interest, because he approached it along two roads which eventually converged. The German version of the name was Palmin, and it was registered by the firm Schlinck of Hamburg in

---

[5] Anton Jurgens to Gerard Jurgens, 8 November 1917.
[6] C. A. Birtwistle to Gerard Jurgens, 13 August 1919.
[7] Unilever N.V. records, M.D.M.J., 15 July 1923.
[8] Corrrespondence and balance sheets supplied by Unilever N.V.

1902. The mark registered at that time was a simple design, in which the name was placed on a patterned background.[9] In 1907 a British firm, the Vegetable Butter Company, registered a label with the name Palmine, ornamented with an exotic scene of 'palms, a lagoon, and happy Africans'.[10] The Vegetable Butter Company transferred its business to a company called Palmine Limited which belonged to the Maypole Dairy Company (at that time the largest firm in the margarine industry in Britain). Schlinck in Germany had by then been using the ornate trade mark with the palms.[11] The Maypole, wishing like Lever to buy groundnuts in Africa, set up in Gambia in 1915, using the name Palmine Limited.[11] By 1920 Palmine had no less than sixty branches on the Gambia river. Meanwhile Jurgens acquired control of Schlinck in Germany.[13] Thus he already owned the Palmin mark before 1924 when the Maypole Dairy Company fell into trouble and sold out to Jurgens, who thus acquired Palmine Limited.[14]

The Margarine Union, shortly after its formation in 1927, bought a French company, the Société des huileries Calvé-Delft, which had an ancient connection with Africa. As long ago as 1816 Victor Calvé, a surgeon in the French navy, was shipwrecked in Senegal, and in 1825 he returned there to set up a trading company. In 1866 this company began crushing groundnuts for oil, and in 1895 it opened a groundnut oil mill near Bordeaux. In 1897 the four brothers Calvé of Bordeaux combined with the Oliefabrik of Delft in the Netherlands, and founded the Société des huileries Calvé-Delft, S.A., with its head office in Nantes. From 1901 the Société des huileries Calvé-Delft was a partner in the Bordeaux firm of Pascal Buhan & Cie., which had branches in Senegal and was a large exporter of groundnuts. In 1912 Calvé-Delft bought out the other partners in that Bordeaux concern and became sole owner. In that same year Calvé-Delft absorbed a German firm, Soller of Hamburg, who operated in the Casamance (the southern district of Senegal) and Portuguese Guinea. A new subsidiary was then formed under the title of Nouvelle Société Commerciale Africaine, S.A., embracing the Bordeaux and Hamburg firms, with its head office at Nantes. A Frenchman and a

9 Howarth, W. C. to Pedler, 1 December 1970.
10 ibid., 3 November 1970.
11 Wilson, op. cit., p. 177.
12 MacMillan, A., Red book of West Africa (London: Collingridge, 1920) p. 287.
13 Wilson, op. cit., p. 177.
14 ibid., p. 256.

German were appointed joint managers.[15] The German fled from France to avoid internment and never returned. The war over, the NOSOCO, as the subsidiary was commonly called, operating at many places in Senegal and Portuguese Guinea, continued to yield profit to the Société Calvé-Delft, besides fulfilling its mission in supplying groundnuts to the parent company.[16]

[15] The Frenchman was Amedée Thubé, who became the head of the United Africa Company's organization in Paris (chapter 29).

[16] Rankin, p. 123.

16

The Cavalla River Company

Lever Brothers' second purchase in 1912 was (as noted in chapter 14) the Cavalla River Company, which was established in the extreme eastern district of the Republic of Liberia.

The Cavalla river rises in the beautiful Nimba mountains on the confines of Guinea and Ivory Coast. It flows for about 300 miles to reach the sea at Cape Palmas, a town of Liberia. For more than half its course the river constitutes the boundary between Liberia and Ivory Coast, and it is navigable by small craft for fifty miles from the sea. Unfortunately there are reefs off shore in front of Cape Palmas, so that ocean ships have to anchor some way out, and work their cargo in small boats.

In the early years of the present century a business was conducted in those parts by John Harold Dickinson Fredericks. Fredericks described himself as being 'of the republic of Liberia and of Taunton in the county of Somerset in England, merchant'. The records of the Cavalla River Company refer to his 'participation in the administrative affairs of the republic of Liberia'. However, he did not devote the whole of his time to the service of the government, for he had set up an enterprise described as the Liberian Timber and Trading Company, of which he was the sole member. In January 1911 the legislature of the Republic of Liberia granted a concession to this company 'to cut, prepare, despatch, and export timber and wood goods and to form and carry on trading stations in Liberia and carry on the business of African merchants, traders, brokers and agents'.

Fredericks evidently felt the need of financial assistance to enable him to discharge the responsibilities which he had assumed, and he secured the interest of a Liverpool business man named Alfred S. Collard. Collard persuaded four other investors to join with him in forming a company, the Cavalla River Company Limited, which came into existence in August 1911. The total number of shares issued for cash seems to have been 5,253, of the nominal value of £1 each; but Collard, in recognition of his services as the connecting link between Fredericks and the other investors, was registered as the owner of 15,000 shares credited as fully paid. Of these shares, 8,350 were subsequently assigned to some of the other directors and members of the staff.[1]

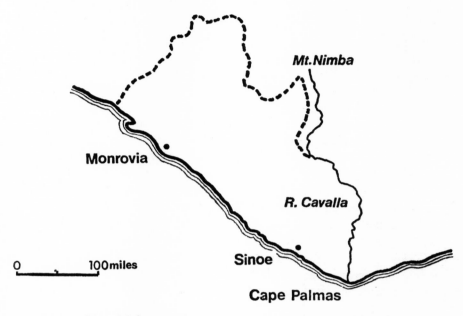

Fig. 12. Map of Liberia to illustrate the history of the Cavalla River Company Limited

The new proprietors wished to arrange for their property in Liberia to be inspected by an independent person, but the chairman reported that this was not immediately possible 'owing to the present critical position respecting the concessions'. It seems probable that this critical position arose by reason of a revolt against the Liberian government by the Grebo tribe, who lived around Cape Palmas. They beleaguered the town.[2] It could not have been good for trade. A branch was opened at Sinoe, another small port. Fredericks made over his concession to the company on condition that he should be employed as general manager in Liberia. However, after about a year the company felt dissatisfied with the way he was running the business and dismissed him. Proceedings of arbitration and litigation ensued.

[1] Original documents in possession of United Africa Company.
[2] Taylor, H. R., *Jungle Trader* (London: Jarrolds, 1939) chapter IX.

199

It was in the mind of Collard that he should find a more powerful financial backer for the development of the concession, and after attempts had been made on both sides of the Atlantic to find a buyer, the deal was made with William Lever in 1912. Lever Brothers paid Collard £3,300 for 7,500 of his shares, and they also put in £7,500 of new capital, for which they received 7,500 shares. This gave them three-quarters of the voting equity, and Lever Brothers' control of the company was made effective by the appointment to the board of Greenhalgh and Findlay. Collard continued to act as chairman for another year, and then retired. From that date the board of the company consisted entirely of persons nominated by Lever Brothers, and the administration of the company was entrusted to their West African department.

There was no inspection of accounts before the takeover. The chairman regretfully reported at the second annual general meeting that 'owing to unsatisfactory returns from the coast, the accounts of the company were not yet ready for audit'. It was, in fact, like the acquisition of the C.P.K.N., an example of rushing into an investment without any precautionary checks, in the belief that 'the door would soon be closed'. When Lever Brothers succeeded in sorting the figures out, it was established that in the first year-and-a-half of its existence the company had made a loss of £18,000.

In acquiring this company, Lever hoped to proceed with development in Liberia along the same lines as those he had recently arranged in the Belgian Congo. Under the terms of the agreement of sale, Collard undertook that he would use his best endeavours to obtain from the Liberian government a concession, direct to Lever Brothers, as far as possible on the lines of the concession granted by the colony of the Belgian Congo with the approval of the Belgian government to Lever Brothers.[3] The intention was no doubt irreproachable, and the phraseology was a tribute to Lord Leverhulme's great pride in the Congo arrangements, but the words chosen betrayed a curious insensitivity to the feelings of those with whom Lever Brothers had to deal. Any form of words more likely to alarm and alienate the sovereign government of Liberia could hardly have been imagined. The concession was not secured.

The company therefore had to depend on trading, and this was difficult. There were losses of £2,000 in 1914 and of £1,000 in 1915. Then the branch at Sinoe was closed and branches were

[3] as note 1.

opened in those parts of the interior which could be closely supervised from Cape Palmas.[4] Thereafter the company did better, making profits of £5,000 in 1916, £4,000 in 1917, £2,000 in 1918, and £3,000 in 1919.[5] The products available for export were palm oil, palm kernels, piassava, coffee, and cocoa.[6] In return the company supplied gin, tobacco, salt, rum, stockfish, pickled herrings in barrels, gum, printed cottons, beads, enamelware, and a selection of other trade goods.[7] As competitors, they had the English firm of Woodin[8] (*see* chapter 20) and a German company.

The government now had another war on hand, for the Kru tribe had risen in revolt. The Cavalla River Company supplied the government with military stores; but it was difficult to secure payment from the government for the stores which had been supplied. This was arranged, with the assistance of the British Foreign Office, by the company's accepting settlement in the form of a fifty per cent reduction of import and export duties, by which means the company recovered what was owing to it.[9] The company was fortunate in having an agent who stayed a long time and became well liked in Liberia: A. J. Barrow was appointed as agent in 1920 and retained the post for eleven years. He had gone out to the Ivory Coast in 1898 for Richard and William King, and is remembered for his great knowledge of African folk-lore.[10] His appointment as agent of the Cavalla River Company is an early example of the advantages which Lever Brothers derived from being able to deploy managers within their increasing African businesses. The company carried out banking functions as agents of the Bank of British West Africa. In the years 1920 to 1923 heavy losses were made, but by the end of 1925 the accumulated losses had been cleared off. In that year Viscount Leverhulme visited Monrovia in his yacht and exchanged visits with the President of the Republic. Soon after the visit the headquarters of the Cavalla River Company were moved from Cape Palmas to Monrovia.

[4] Lever Brothers policy committee minutes, 13 November 1916.

[5] as note 1.

[6] as note 4.

[7] Taylor, op. cit.

[8] The Woodin property in Cape Palmas was written off in October 1933; United Africa Company board minutes.

[9] Beaumont, L. C. to Pedler, 24 August 1969.

[10] For these particulars I am indebted to A. C. Orris-Bird, who, like Barrow, exemplified the facility which the Lever group had in deploying staff between African businesses; Orris-Bird joined Peter Ratcliffe (Sierra Leone) in 1925, and the following year was transferred to Cavalla River Company at Cape Palmas.

17

The Life of European Trading
Staff 1885-1929

In 1885 a young man entering the service of Thomas Harrison and Company had to sign an agreement in which he undertook to proceed to the coast of Africa to act as clerk and general assistant. The company undertook to pay him a salary 'at and after' the rate of £6 per month for the first year and £7 per month for the second year, subject to deductions to cover any shortages for which the employee was unable to render account.[1]

A visitor to the Oil Rivers in 1893 was Mary Kingsley, who went ashore at Bonny to have tea with Captain Boler, whom she described as 'the old coaster who then had charge of my education'. He told her that Bonny was a nice place when you got used to it, and went on to discourse on the last epidemic, when nine white men out of the resident eleven died from yellow fever. She liked the traders and defended them against charges of drunkenness, which, she alleged, were exaggerations spread by missionaries. The trading community, she believed, was 'a very excellent substratum for English pioneer work', for 'everywhere the English trader and his goods stand high in Western African esteem'. These were men who went to death with a joke in their teeth.[2]

Alexander Alexander Cowan was recruited in 1887 by Alexander Miller Brother and Company for service in the Niger delta. He subsequently had a very successful career in commerce, served on a government commission of enquiry, and became known for his lectures and writings on African subjects. He considered that Mary Kingsley was 'perhaps too indulgent'. In his opinion the white traders of that epoch were a mixed crowd. He describes how the European staff in a trading post were housed in one large estab-

---

[1] From an original agreement in the possession of F. G. Frost, lately general manager of G. Gottschalck and Company, and a member of the Nigerian legislative council. The agreement was entered into by his father.

[2] Kingsley, Mary, *Travels in West Africa* (London: Macmillan, 1897).

lishment *en famille*. As terms were all-found, there was no question of separate messing. At mealtimes the agent sat at the head of the table. The system had many advantages, and not the least was that the senior was kept in close touch with his assistants. He could study his younger men and watch them develop. Cowan lived under the system, both as assistant and agent, and liked it. The breakfast table on a trading day was an institution and an entertainment, for leading Africans were invited to join the table. The firms established on each river joined together to employ a private doctor. Local labour was not procurable, so the carpenters, coopers, cooks, and washermen were brought from the Gold Coast, while the unskilled men came from the Kru coast.[3]

Another contemporary observer took a less favourable view. He found that the agents and assistants were gaunt and sickly, some of them wearing the stamp of alcohol, and the faces of the rest the impress of many fevers. No amusements were available to them, and they worked with feverish energy, trying to make enough money to begin again in some more favoured region. They looked forward to the arrival of the quarterly liquor supply, for firms often sent out an assortment of spirituous comforts every three months. Then they had a carnival for a week.[4]

'The impress of many fevers' was inevitably the fate of white men in malarious country until they began to take quinine regularly as a prophylactic. Although the Royal Navy's expedition to the Niger had established the value of quinine in the 1840s, and though Baikie had used it successfully in the 1850s, quinine does not appear to have been generally adopted by the trading community until after the turn of the century. This may seem surprising, but it must be remembered that Baikie's success with quinine was purely empirical; no one knew why quinine protected the human body against malaria until Ross's discoveries in the last years of the century. Furthermore quinine (at any rate in the form in which it was available at that time) did not give complete protection. By 1906 quinine was taken regularly by European trading staffs; yet still, all suffered a good deal from malaria, and blackwater fever (from which few recovered) was not infrequent. Topees were always worn out of doors.

A description of life in Nigeria with the African Association comes from H. G. Hartje, son of the Hartje who worked for

[3] Cowan, A. A., *Journal Royal African Society*, January 1936, pp. 59–62.
[4] Bindloss, Harold, *In the Niger Country* (London: Blackwood, 1898) p. 153.

Thomas Harrison.[5] Young Hartje took this job in 1906 on the advice of his godfather George Watts, a director of the African Association. He was attracted to Africa because he would not have to work in an office, and it held out the prospect of early retirement. He went to Calabar and found it a pleasant place: it seemed a very happy family. With the agent and three other assistants, he was accommodated in *Matilda*, which preserved the name of the old hulk from which trade had previously been conducted; but by this time *Matilda* had become a 'beach', and was built out over the river on piles, occupying the actual position of the old hulk. In fact this pier had been built by Hartje's father in the 1880s. The nautical tradition persisted. The agent was addressed as 'captain', and the kitchen was a 'galley'. Travelling was by gig with four oarsmen. When the 'captain' went out the junior assistant had to meet him on his return and welcome him 'aboard'. When son Hartje arrived, a steward who had worked for father Hartje for forty years presented his son to son Hartje 'as dash-o', and the son worked for Hartje junior for twenty-six years. In Hartje's opinion there was not so much drinking in the Bights in his day as in 1969. The young men could drink only what the agent allowed them, the amount depending on the individual agent. Most would allow one whisky and soda per day, and some would add a gin before supper. This was free, as part of the remuneration. The salary was £80 in Hartje's first year of service and £120 in the second year. All food and lodging was found, and servants were paid for. The men fed in a mess; in Calabar this consisted of the agent and four assistants. They wore white coats, buttoned up like stewards' coats. This was not a uniform, but merely the fashion at the time. Normally the junior European assistant looked after the mess, arranging the marketing and cooking. Apart from chickens the food was nearly all tinned, but a mail boat came in about once a month bringing veal, mutton, and beef, as well as some blocks of ice which were kept in a barrel covered with sawdust. The chickens came from Lagos in large baskets. A hundred or two would be bought, and the junior assistant had to look after them and count them daily to make sure that none were being stolen.

In 1906 there was a golf course in Calabar, but the juniors were not allowed to use it. This rule also applied in the European clubs at Lagos and Port Harcourt up to 1925.[6] If juniors were seen playing it was assumed that they had no work to do. There was

5 Hartje, H. G., oral.   6 Dunnet, D. D., to Pedler, 30 December 1969.

little in the way of recreation, and assistants spent their evenings reading by the light of hurricane lamps. The day began at six o'clock; breakfast was eaten 'below' at eight; the lunch interval was two hours, and work was then resumed until six or half-past six in the evening. The only recreation in *Matilda* was billiards, which the juniors were allowed to play.

For water the trading community was dependent on the supplies of rain which they collected in their own tanks. At times when they ran short they would fetch water, for use in baths, from the upper reaches of the river where the danger of pollution was not so serious as in the surroundings of Calabar.

Palm oil, palm kernels, a little rubber, a very little cocoa, and ebony, were being bought in 1906. The palm oil came in puncheons. Each puncheon was tested with a try-rod and samples were taken; these samples were cooked and tested for water and excess fat. Free fatty acid was not measured until seven or eight years later. Produce was bought by barter, and the unit of exchange was a 'piece'. This may sound like a material object, but in fact it was a concept of value. It was worth four shillings (one-fifth of a pound sterling): so that if the buyer was prepared to pay £10 for a puncheon of oil, he quoted to the seller 'fifty pieces'. The trader who had delivered the oil could then select goods: a bag of salt rated one 'piece', a roll of printed cotton worth about twelve shillings would be three 'pieces', sixteen heads of tobacco at three (old) pence each would be one 'piece', and so on.

The adulteration of produce was a serious problem. Water was mixed with palm oil, and banana stems were placed in the oil to make it ferment and so fill up the cask; palm kernels were soaked in the river to make them swell and so increase their volume (for all kernels were bought by cubic measure). All the rubber had to be cut open, stones and other material being often found inside. There were some special balls of rubber made by winding strips of latex into the shape of a sphere, and these could be tested only by bouncing them off the deck.

The main imports were textiles, salt, gin, rum, iron bars, flint-lock guns, gunpowder, rice, biscuits, barrels of beef and of pork.

When Hartje first arrived in 1906, produce was bought only from a limited number of important individuals in the African community who were known to the Europeans as 'chiefs'; but a few years later, as the Cross River became used as an artery of trade, many new traders and even some individual producers began to bring produce to market. The quietening down and protection of the country by troops allowed people to travel on the waterway without the fear of being robbed or murdered, or of being taken into slavery. The young men from Arochuku in particular were good traders, even though they earned a reputation for turbulence. They insisted on receiving cash for their produce, and would not be content with being credited with a certain number of 'pieces', for barter. Having cash in hand, they were able to visit all the stores in the town and to hunt around for bargains. It was British money, for at that time Nigeria had no currency of her own, and the West African Currency Board had not yet come into existence. The firms had to make special arrangements to get British money for trading with the Arochukus, because in general there was very little money in Calabar at that time. Any market woman who happened to have a coin would carry it in her mouth. Market goods were purchased for brass rods, and in order to provide small change there were little wire rods worth one-tenth of a brass rod. The little ones were called cheathams (also spelt cheetem, but the thing was named after a Captain Cheatham). The Arochukus had a good opinion of the African Association, and many of them would ask that their bags of money might be locked up in the Association's safe for the night, and then camp under the stars on *Matilda* beach.

No credit was given to traders for produce in 1906, although before that time it had been given out extensively. This was, presumably, a result of an agreement between the firms; such agreements will be discussed in chapter 25.

The labour position was as it had been ten years earlier. No local labour was employed, apart from interpreters. The labour was brought from the Kru coast. This was done as a form of protection; the Kru were the white men's servants, sharing their compound, each group looking after the other. In contrast to the position in the Gold Coast, no local Africans were employed in senior positions. There were African book-keepers, but these were nearly all Gold Coast men, as were the carpenters and coopers.

In Calabar in 1906 there were no horses and no motor cars. There was one solitary rickshaw, but generally people went about on foot. On trek a hammock was used. Merchandise was head-loaded whenever it was necessary to leave the banks of the water-ways. A porter would carry 60 lbs. or even 80 lbs. weight on his head.

European staff were not allowed to have their wives with them in Africa. The only European women were nursing sisters and missionaries.

Hartje was a Mason and took his mark in a Lodge in Calabar of which most of the members were Africans. Relations with the 'chiefs' were very friendly. Most of the produce trading was done with them, and they would invariably lunch with the agent when they came to sell. In return, the agent would be invited to the 'chief's' house for a meal, probably a palm-oil chop on Sunday.

As a second tour assistant, Hartje was on a salary rising from £350 to £500. He was at Opobo in 1912, and here he became the agent in charge. On promotion he had to exercise a serious option: whether to take his remuneration in the form of a straight salary, or in the form of a lower salary with a commission on profits. Hartje chose the second of these options, and reckoned that it turned out to be the wrong choice.

At Opobo in 1912 staff were authorized to give out credit up to a limit of about £5,000. In fact about £25,000 worth of goods were entrusted to middlemen on credit, and all knew of this although it was not officially recognized. The creditors would wave to their goods and say '*au revoir*' as they went up the river, knowing that it was a risky business. The only security for such advances was manillas: during the slack season, when little produce was moving, the principal customers would take merchandise and bring back manillas, which would be stored for them. These were the only goods (that is to say, the only currency) with which produce could be bought. The storage of manillas was a tiresome job. During the off-season the firm accumulated over four millions of them. Sometimes they were counted into bags containing a thousand, but an alternative method of 'counting' was by measurement. An area of known dimensions was chalked on the floor of the store. Into this area, in one layer flat on the floor were put the maximum number of manillas possible, and this area of manillas was taken as a certain number. The business was not unremunerative, for the manillas were counted in at the rate of seven for one shilling, and were issued at the rate of five for one shilling (see plate 13).

Kernels continued to be bought by measure at Opobo long after they were bought by units of weight in other places. The measure was a bucket, but the unit of payment was a bag, and a bucket contained a little more than two bags of kernels. Payment for the bucketful was always made as though the bucket contained exactly two bags. The buyer therefore always secured a little surplus. The value of this surplus was carefully brought to account, and the fund was used to give presents to the middlemen who delivered kernels, especially at Christmas.[7] (This is an early form of the commercial device of giving presents in return for coupons or stamps.)

In purchasing produce at Opobo in 1912, certain companies maintained an agreement by which they attempted to regulate the shares of trade between themselves. Monthly meetings were held, when purchases, amounts shipped, and stocks were reported, and if purchases above the agreed quota had been made they had to be handed over at the current price to someone who had under-bought. This was intended to restrain competition between the agreed firms. The meetings were sometimes held at Gana Gana, where McCormick of the Niger Company acted as host. To receive his colleagues, he sat in a hip-bath of water, and wore an opera hat! Some firms refused to join the agreement—Pinnock, MacNeil Scott, and the German Kaiser, who was strong around this area.

As supervising agent in Benin, Opobo, and Calabar, Hartje was responsible for ordering merchandise. The head office in Liverpool usually sent out what was ordered, except in regard to printed cottons. For these, buyers in Lancashire frequently took their own initiatives. Design was important, and sometimes an agent would send a design-pattern to Lancashire, to be printed. The African Association agents, in addition to all their other duties, acted as Lloyds' agents.

H. C. Crookenden[8] had his first impressions of Bonny and Opobo in 1913. His first year was the last of an epoch, for things were to be different after the war. Engaged at the age of 21 for Millers after an interview with Cowan, he was recruited for a tour of two years, at a salary of £100 a year with all found except alcoholic drink, but for that he had a wine allowance of £2 a month. Any part of this which was not used could be drawn in cash. He and his mates drank mineral water on weekdays, and beer with palm-oil chop on Sundays. He went to Bonny in the mail boat, and it appears that co-operation between Miller Brothers and the African Association was close, for when he arrived at Bonny he was looked after by the manager of the African Association. He set out for Opobo in the government mail launch, but it stuck on the Bonny River flats for many hours, and the mosquitoes made a meal of the new boy.

[7] Crookenden, H. C., a written statement to Pedler, 1969.   [8] ibid.

The 'chiefs' of Opobo were known as heads of houses, and each of them could trade with one company only. A house-chief would not attend at a trading store in person, but appointed as his representative a headman, who delivered palm oil and palm kernels and was responsible for the canoes and canoemen, being all the time in close touch with the house head. At the end of every six-month period, 'chiefs' and agents met to settle their accounts and arrange terms for a further period. This meeting was termed 'squaring the book'. The house-heads arrived, sumptuously clad, in huge canoes (see plate 3), some of which had as many as sixty paddlers, with house flags and several instrumentalists with bells, tom-toms, and bugles. The heads of houses received a commission on every cask of palm oil and every measure of kernels supplied by their headmen.

As before, the beach staff were Krus, and the cook, the carpenter, and the head cooper, were always from Accra.

Each fortnight the agent and the chief clerk decided what goods to order, and whether by mail or by cable. In addition to the imports mentioned by Hartje, Crookenden remembers stockfish, hogsheads of tobacco, lead sheets, fish nets, fish cord, salmon, corned beef, sardines, matchets, paving stones (used for sharpening matchets), axe heads, Scotch whisky, Geneva gin, and matches. His main textiles were real India Madras, imitation Madras, low Madras, shirting, khaki and white drill, and dhooties (mosquito nets). In addition to these, his company had just started to import block prints from Ankersmit in Holland, and claimed to be the first importer to bring wax block prints (*see* chapter 21) into Nigeria.

As competitors at Opobo Millers had six British companies and one German.

About 1913 the West African Currency Board coins were introduced, and the new shilling became known as the palm tree shilling, by reason of the design upon it. Its introduction caused trouble. The Ibibios and the Ibos became restless because it was said that the palm tree which was impressed on the coins indicated that the government was going to take over the palm trees. The new shillings were currently exchanged for two British shillings, bearing the heads of Queen Victoria or King Edward. The market value of the manilla became very difficult to determine under these conditions, and market prices of foodstuffs were upset. Popular discontent was so acute that there were rumours that the companies' premises might be attacked, and all European staff were asked to perform guard duty at night, two hours on and four hours off.

In 1906 an event occurred which inaugurated the era of refrigeration, which was to make a very great difference to the feeding habits of people in the tropics, and especially to those of the European residents. The Nigerian Cold Storage Limited was set up by the African Association in partnership with three other firms, all established in Lagos.[9] The main business of the company was the manufacture and sale of ice. To this was added meat, which was imported by mail boat. Supplies were consequently spasmodic, and when a boat came in there was a great rush to the store. It was the practice to open early in the morning and to close at 9 a.m. A branch was opened in Calabar before 1914. In 1920 it was held that 'to describe in detail the intricate system, scientific ingenuity and achievement, that render possible the daily output of the Nigerian Cold Storage company would involve an effort too technical for ordinary presentations';[10] the motive force was supplied by a suction gas plant, and there were two engines of eighty horsepower each.

The enterprise went to Port Harcourt when that place was founded. It was necessary to secure from the government a lease of land on which premises might be built, and the Resident used this circumstance to impose price control in an unusual way. In granting the lease he made it a condition that ice and meat should be sold to members of the public at the prices shown on a list attached to the lease.[11]

Domestic refrigerators, operated by kerosene lamps, were first used in West Africa in 1928. The Nigerian Cold Storage was not at first inclined to promote the sale and use of refrigerators, believing that its business depended on the sale of ice.[12]

Hartje left Africa to volunteer for military service. He came back from the war to Warri with a Military Cross but very little money. Chief Onitchima, a famous trading woman, had expected that the returning hero would be better provided, and when she realized how poor he was she offered to lend him £500. She had done well during the war.

Levantines had established themselves as a new element in the trading community. Everybody spoke of them in those days and for many years to come as Syrians. They were subjects of the Ottoman

[9] Rankin, p. 84.
[10] MacMillan, A., *Red Book of West Africa* (London: Collingridge, 1920) p. 85.
[11] Dunnet, as cited.
[12] ibid.

Empire. It was not until some decades had elapsed, and when independent states had come into existence in the Levant, that it was generally appreciated that many of these people were Lebanese, while others were Syrians, Druses, Tripolitans, Iraqis, Adenese, and Bulgarians. Before the war they had been few in numbers, itinerant traders dealing in such items as coral beads, and generally considered to be poor people. Now, however, they were established as a prosperous middle-class trading community. No government had helped them, and any credits which they secured from bankers were only accorded on stringent commercial terms. Their success was attributable solely to their qualities: hard work, thrift, credit-worthiness, and a flair for trade.

There was a general impression of progress. Africans seemed to be more prosperous and there were more educated Africans. One African in Calabar had managerial status, a Gold Coaster. But social contacts between Africans and Europeans seemed to be less frequent than they had been before the war. Perhaps it was due in part to the fact that many of the senior Europeans now had their wives with them. The juniors were still not allowed to belong to the Calabar social club in 1924.

For the first-time assistant the 'all-found' agreement was not used after 1919 but the African and Eastern Trade Corporation provided him with first-class passages, furnished accommodation, one steward, a share of a cook, and medical attention. His pay was £300 a year with half salary on leave. Leave was three months including voyage time after eighteen months' service. Juniors were not allowed to have their wives with them. Senior agents received £650 plus £200 guaranteed commission. Nothing more than guaranteed commission was paid from 1920 to 1929 by the African and Eastern group.

Millers' produce manager in Lagos lived over a store and went to work in a rickshaw drawn by a Kruman. However, the rickshaw was doomed, and by 1922 the young men had all provided themselves with motor bicycles.[13, 14]

In 1925 Lord Leverhulme paid his second visit to Africa, and a diary written by his secretary sheds some light on the social conditions of the European staff.[15] 'The managers of Huileries du

---

[13] Dunnet, as cited.

[14] For a fuller treatment of the life of the trading community in the Niger Delta in the nineteen-twenties *see* Gore-Clough, Raymund, *Oil Rivers Trader* (London: Hurst, 1972) with a foreword by Professor J. D. Fage.

[15] Sir Malcolm Knox, diary.

Congo Belge and SEDEC,' he wrote, 'have most lovely houses: if they *have* to live in Kinshasa, there are compensations. After dinner we went in a car to Leopoldville, which is about six miles from Kinshasa. The drive was delightful, cool, and refreshing. Mr. Irvine says that he would supply all tropical managers with cars, if he were allowed, so that they could have drives after dinner like this that I had, simply as a health preservative.' Returning from the Congo in his private yacht, Lord Leverhulme visited many places, and among these was Duala, as mentioned in chapter 11. In the years between the end of the War and Lord Leverhulme's visit a great change had taken place in the social life of the trading community, for the principal agents of the various companies now had their wives with them. Lord Leverhulme was therefore received by Kings' agent Morten and Mrs. Morten. All the managers were invited to meet Lord Leverhulme in the yacht. The guests went out to the vessel in surf boats, every man wearing a helmet, and the ladies in double terais and thigh-high buckskin mosquito boots.

A young trading assistant watched these goings-on from a distance, and without enthusiasm. He had served as a subaltern in the Royal West African Frontier Force in northern Nigeria, on secondment from a British regiment, and he so greatly enjoyed the Hausa and the polo, that when his period of secondment came to an end he resigned from the army and took employment with the African and Eastern Trade Corporation, who promptly sent him to work for Hatton and Cookson at Duala, where there were no Hausa and no horses. Furthermore, there was nothing for a young man to do except work and drink. After a couple of years, to his joy, he secured a transfer to Zaria.

By this time motor cars were becoming more common, and several roads had been built, but transport still took a long time. In 1928 staff at Zaria reckoned to take eight hours to get to Funtua (fifty-four miles) in a model T Ford.

Up in those latitudes, however, the life of the trading staff was very different from what it was in Lagos and the delta. Though the younger men, like their colleagues on the coast, might share a bedroom over a trading store, they had far more opportunities for enjoying open-air activities. They played polo, and there were plenty of geese, duck, guinea-fowl, and partridge, for the shot-guns. The senior agents built themselves large mansions of mud in the Hausa style, with a wall a yard thick at the foot, and beams of mud bricks curving inwards to make a vaulted roof. Though the trading community had little time for sport from November until May, when the crops were being bought and railed, the extremely seasonal nature of the trade ensured that leisure was in plentiful supply from June till October. The excitement of buying ground-nuts was much enhanced by the employment of camels (see plate 12) as transport. A camel's burden is three hundredweight[16] so thirty-four camels were required to carry the weight which subsequently would travel in a five-ton truck. In most parts of the north the vast trains of camels were a familiar sight. Everybody spoke Hausa and some of the managers in the African and Eastern Trade Corporation amused themselves by corresponding in that language, using the old Ajemi version of Arabic script.[17]

[16] Doughty, C. M., *Arabia Deserta* (London: Cape, 1936) vol. I, p. 560.
[17] Ruston, Clifford, and Watson, Geoffrey, oral.

18

G. Gottschalck and Company

The business of G. Gottschalck and Company was never one of the largest firms in Africa, nor was it among the oldest, but it is of interest because it was always successful and because it was always different from the others. It was managed by ingenious men who did not wish to join in the competitive scramble for buying palm oil and selling the usual range of trade goods. They present an early example of market research, consistently carried on through many years with the object of identifying sections of trade in which specialization could earn profits.

The Gottschalck family came from Hamburg and migrated to England in 1847 because of the unsettled state of Germany at that time. In 1848 G. Gottschalck entered into partnership with Max Robinow, also from Hamburg, and they started an export business to South America, India, and China. Their head office was in Manchester to handle the textile trade, and an office was opened in Birmingham to buy hardware. Later Ernest Frank, another native of Hamburg, joined the partnership. After the passing of the first generation Ernest Frank's son Norman took charge, but the business fell to a low ebb and they sent to Hamburg for a man named Max E. Cohen to join them. At that time Max was in his early twenties.[1] He directed the attention of the business towards Africa. In 1896 an agent was sent to Cotonou in the French colony of Dahomey. It was soon realized that there was more trade in Lagos, so a branch was opened in that city in 1897 and the store in Cotonou was closed.

Gottschalck established a reputation for textiles, and some of the designs which the partnership introduced in 1898 were still in active demand sixty years later. Such for instance was the white brocade with the design of a head, cloven with a deep V, as though by the stroke of an axe. It was always immensely expensive, and a roll of it was therefore appropriate as a present for a high personality.

Gottschalck concentrated on quality, both in textiles and in hard-

[1] Drew, D. E. to Pedler, 13 and 17 June 1970.

ware. In the first forty years of the twentieth century, high quality was synonymous with the label 'Made in England', and so it was that Gottschalck's supplies were drawn almost exclusively from Britain. In textiles they handled the best quality prints, but in brocades (as already mentioned) and in woven domestics[2] they bought with such skill that they were ahead of all competitors. Their trade mark was the 'hand and globe' (see plate 21), translated by southerners as *sapu olowo* and by the Hausa as *hannun duniya*, the hand of the world. The textile trade was conducted with market retailers on a three months' credit basis. The long credit no doubt went with high margins, but it is of interest that Gottschalck found this a satisfactory method of trade when most merchant houses were trying to insist on monthly settlement of credit advances.

When the typewriter began to replace the copperplate handwriting of clerks, Gottschalck identified it as an article for specialization, and in due course duplicating machines and other office specialities were added.

Perhaps the most unusual feature of Gottschalck was not what was done, but what was not done. Apparently alone among the trading companies, this firm did not buy and export produce. Thus there was no barter trade for Gottschalck. There is little doubt that this enabled the staff to become more expert in the merchandise business than their competitors.[3]

In 1904 the company acquired a site in Lagos which was to become closely associated with its name. It was on one of the highest points in the town, that is to say, it rose nineteen feet above water level. It had historic interest, containing the grave of chief Mabinuori, who had been the head of one of the old families in Lagos. It was a condition of the lease that the grave should always be accessible to members of the Mabinuori family, and that it should be kept clean and in good condition. Standing in a corner of the compound beneath a bougainvillea, it was marked by a

[2] 'Domestics' were a variety of cotton cloth in which a pattern, usually red on white, was woven into the fabric.

[3] There was one temporary exception to this general policy. Shortly after Gottschalck established a branch at Kano (1914) the British Cotton Growing Association asked that branch to buy cotton on its behalf. The B.C.G. Association was formed in 1902 by private enterprise as a non-profit-earning corporation, providing facilities in several colonies (of which Nigeria was one) to promote the cultivation of cotton. Gottschalck bought cotton both from farmers and from middlemen. They gave out no advances and paid cash. They checked that the cotton was clean, but were not concerned with grading. This activity was discontinued in 1923. (Drew, D. E., to Pedler, 16 February 1973.)

marble headstone imported and set up at Gottschalck's expense. The premises included staff quarters above, and in 1920 these were provided with baths and wash-basins with running water. These created interest in Lagos, for they were innovations in that city. Again, Gottschalck had found something that the other firms had not yet thought of.

In hardware the policy was to leave the other firms to scramble for large contracts, to take little interest in the trade with market retailers, and to concentrate on giving personal service to small contractors. At first these were all Africans, but from about 1915 Syrians began to establish themselves in this sector of activity. Gottschalck tried to make it possible for the small contractor to buy all the supplies that he needed out of stock. Agencies were held for a number of manufacturers, all firms of first class reputation. Gottschalck did not hesitate to take high margins, and was able to do so because of the quality of the goods and the personal service which was offered to customers.

Another special sector which was identified was trade with the tin mines. This involved an establishment at Jos, and the posting there of a manager who, by virtue of his personality and knowledge, could always be sure of a welcome when he visited one of the mines.

A further field of specialization was the trade with the native authorities. The present-day reader may not be well acquainted with this term. In the 1920s the colonial government in Nigeria was engaged in a policy of using traditional rulers and tribal councils as its agents in the government of the country. These agents were gazetted as native authorities. They collected the hut tax and the cattle tax on behalf of the government, and retained a proportion of the sums collected in their own local treasuries. They then became responsible for the expenditure of those moneys on local services, and here Gottschalck came in as supplier. The general manager in person made it his business to keep close contact with the government officers who advised the native authorities. Special stocks were held of uniform cloth for the employees of the native authorities. The supply of tools and materials for their road gangs linked up nicely with the business of supplying small contractors. Stationery for native authority schools was conveniently handled in association with the department devoted to office supplies.

Before 1914 branches were opened at Abeokuta, sixty-five miles north of Lagos, and at Ibadan, another sixty miles east-north-east.

The building in the latter city was on the site of the old Iddo gate through which travellers from Lagos formerly entered the old walled city. The branch at Kano was opened in the month of the outbreak of the First World War. Gottschalck at that time was under the dynamic leadership of Harry Scott Taylor. He had married the daughter of Max E. Cohen, who became senior partner in 1908 on the death of the last member of the Gottschalck family. When the First World War was over, Taylor pushed out to Sokoto, Katsina, Gusau, Bukuru, Gombe, Birnin Kebbi, and many smaller places.

When a site had been chosen, a fleet of three or four lorries would leave one of the main centres, and bump away on the inadequate roads. The loads consisted of a selection of goods for the new station, and all the essential materials for building a temporary store on arrival. The coming of such a convoy was sufficient to arouse the inquisitive interest of the inhabitants, and within half an hour of pulling in to the selected spot, willing labour had been engaged, the lorries unloaded, and the temporary building begun. This took the form of a wooden frame clothed with galvanized iron sheeting which could be ready for occupation on the second day. It served until the erection of a more permanent structure of mud block, stone, or brick. Such was the tempo in those days.[4]

During the whole of the time that the Gottschalck partners were trading in Nigeria, not one of them ever visited that country.[5]

[4] *West African Review*, June 1948, pp. 733–60 (Gottschalck centenary section).
[5] Frost, F. G. to Pedler, 29 June 1970.

19

The Lion and the Unicorn

When the lion's head with a crown was chosen by the King family as the sign of their business (*see* chapters 1 and 2) they adapted for commerce a crest which had been widely used in heraldry.[1] The symbols of heraldry were the means by which important individuals identified themselves, their servants, and their property, to people who could not read. That is exactly what a merchant in Africa in the nineteenth century needed to do.

The adoption of a stylized animal as a symbol showed a deep appreciation of the Africans' propensity for exactly that kind of insignia. On the Gold Coast for example every *omanhene* had his linguist, and each linguist bore a staff ornamented with carvings of stylized beasts or familiar objects, exactly comparable with the designs of European heraldry. In many parts of Africa clans or tribes were known by the symbol of an animal. African kings too had their signs—the golden stool for Ashanti, and for Dahomey the calabash with holes which John Walkden took as a trade mark, as mentioned in chapter 14. Since party politics came to Africa it has become normal for political parties to identify themselves by the sign of an animal or bird. To enable people who do not read or write to exercise the franchise, votes have been cast by dropping a ticket into the box bearing the party's sign, which in several cases has been the lion or the cock—both signs which were used by old trading companies as their marks.

The symbol, when successfully identified with the merchant firm in the eyes of the public, became very valuable. The firm would be known as 'the house of the lion' (Kings) or 'the house of the horse' (Ollivant—*see* chapter 7) and these were better names (because they translated easily) for earning goodwill than the cumbersome official English family names. The symbol, painted on a board or enamelled on a metal plate, was exhibited over the trading premises. It was embroidered or printed on a flag and flown as an ensign over the

[1] Illustrations of most of the trade marks mentioned in this chapter will be found on plate 2.

craft owned by the firm. Finally it was used to mark goods. Since, in the days before packaging, rolls of cloth were much easier to mark than hardware or provisions, up to the end of the nineteenth century most of the trade marks placed on merchandise were on cloth. The mark was either stamped on the cloth with a blue dye, or to avoid defacing the design it might be fixed on the cloth by means of adhesive paper; but some market retailers preferred to have the merchant's mark actually stamped on the cloth. Marks could of course be put on the labels of bottles, and the other item of merchandise on which marks could easily be placed, with great advantage, was bags of salt. Different markets took their salt in bags of different weights and different colours, but the standard unit for northern Nigeria was a white bag of forty pounds, and on such bags the Niger Company's *berewa* (the red-fronted or dorcas gazelle) was a very popular mark. Every bag, after it had ceased to contain salt, was converted into a singlet, so that generations of young men in Hausaland have worn the gazelle on their chests.

Since the firm of King had chosen a lion's head as its mark, it seems possible that the house of Swanzy may have taken the unicorn's head as an act of defiance. The lion and the unicorn have since 1603 been the two supporters of the royal arms of England; traditionally, according to an old song, they were 'fighting for the crown'. The unicorn's head is a family crest for the family of Swanzy.[2]

F. and A. Swanzy did not have the unicorn all to themselves. The unicorn's head symbol was widely used by G. B. Ollivant from about 1859 onwards and was included in most of Ollivant's early marks, including the 'horseman' which eventually became the house-mark of G. B. Ollivant (*see* chapter 7). Under the rules of heraldry the unicorn's head was recognized as belonging to the family of Oliphant, and it may be that the original G. B. Ollivant regarded himself as a scion of that line. Over the years there was a great deal of controversy between Swanzy and Ollivant, as each

[2] The source of this information and of all subsequent information concerning heraldic crests is Fairbairn's *Crests of the Families of Great Britain and Ireland,* revised by Laurence Butters. The 4th edition of this work was published in 1905 by T. C. and E. C. Jack of London and Edinburgh. Earlier editions, published by Fullarton, have in general been used for the purpose of this chapter, on the ground that they would be the books which the nineteenth-century traders would actually consult. However, there is a very important difference between the third edition and the fourth edition. In the third edition the name Swanzy is not listed. Among the fairly numerous families wearing unicorn-head crests, there was listed Swanly of Middlesex. But in the 1905 edition, Swanzy is listed as the owner of a crest, namely a unicorn's head *or,* collared with a bar gemel gules, and motto *Per Deum et ferrum obtinui.*

company expanded territorially, as to who should be entitled to the unicorn. The issue was finally settled by an agreement in 1922 whereby Swanzy retained the unicorn in the Gold Coast, Togoland, Liberia, East Africa and certain non-African territories, while Ollivant had the mark in other West African countries except Dahomey, and in Dahomey the agreement provided that both parties might use the unicorn.[3]

While Swanzy was quarrelling with Ollivant about the unicorn, Richard and William King appear to have made no formal protest against the use of 'demi-lions' by Alexander Miller Brother and Company, and by Hatton and Cookson. The Scottish family of Miller was entitled, under the rules of heraldry, to 'a lion rampant sable, between the paws a cross moline gules', with the motto 'Forward'. That is an exact description of the design which Millers used in Africa. The cross moline had particular reference to the name Miller, for it was in the shape of the mill-rind, the iron in the centre of a mill-stone, through which the power of the wind in the mill-sails, or of the water in the mill-wheel, was transmitted to the mill-stone for turning it round.

Similarly, Hatton and Cookson used a lion as the principal feature of their house symbol. It was a demi-lion rampant, wearing a ducal crown and a collar, between the paws a shield bearing the design of a leg in armour, and underneath the motto *Nil desperandum* (do not despair). This design was based on heraldic crests to which several families of the name Cookson were entitled. All the Cookson families (of which there were five in the heralds' list) wore the demi-lion rampant. One of them, the Lincolnshire branch, had that lion ducally crowned. Three such families, those of Cumberland, Durham, and Northumberland, bore the motto *Nil desperandum*. So much for Cookson. The leg in armour was the traditional heraldic crest of a family named Haddon, with which evidently Cookson's partner felt he could identify himself, at any rate for this purpose.

The first law providing for the registration and protection of trade marks was an Act of Parliament which came into force in Britain (and indirectly in British territories overseas) in 1875. At that time about four-fifths of all trade marks in use were placed on

[3] My authority for this information and for all subsequent particulars relating to trade marks is W. C. Howarth, of the United Africa Company's Secretary's trade marks department, sometime member of the firm of Leeming Ray and Whittle. I am most grateful to him for his generous help.

cotton goods and so there was a flood of applications from weavers, spinners, bleachers, printers, converters, and cotton exporters or merchants. Almost all of them claimed simple device marks such as lions, tigers, and elephants, because these were marks capable of being identified by the mainly illiterate communities in India, Africa, and South America, to whom the textiles were sold. The British Registry of Trade Marks found it impossible to decide who had the first and best claim to such marks and quickly gave up trying to do so. Apart from the earliest starters the majority of applications were refused and a long list of animal and bird devices were declared to be common to the cotton trade and thus incapable of being registered for the exclusive use of any company. This common list included lions and unicorns and from about 1877 the only way to get either device registered was to use it in a distinctive setting.

Richard and William King never registered their lion crest, or any other trade mark. They seem not to have been interested in registration. Technically they might have been able to register the crest in Britain between 1875 and 1883 as an old mark, in use before the first Registration Act, but they did not apply and so the opportunity was lost. Other British companies trading into Africa were slow to take advantage of the facilities provided by the Act of 1875. Swanzy did nothing until 1890, and then applied to register both the unicorn crest and a device which consisted of a ticket with a unicorn's head. The crest was registered, but not in a way which secured its exclusive use for Swanzy, and the registration of the device was refused on the ground that the unicorn was common to the trade.

Experience proved that the registration of trade marks was both in the interests of the business community and a simple means by which the governments could collect some revenue, and so about the turn of the century the registration system was extended to a number of colonies and protectorates, including the Gold Coast and Southern Nigeria. However, the cotton manufacturers of Lancashire argued, both on grounds of protectionism and also on grounds related to the effective administration of the law, that cotton marks should not be registrable in the colonies unless they had previously been registered in Britain. In effect this made the Manchester Registry the arbiter of what could be registered for cotton anywhere in the Empire. The Gold Coast legislation of 1900 contained a provision of this type, but, strangely, the Southern Nigeria ordinance of 1900 did not. This presented a golden opportunity to merchants established in

Nigeria to register marks such as lions, unicorns, and eagles, but with the exception of John Holt and Lagos Stores, the British merchants let slip the chance. On the other hand several German firms, among which the leaders were Gaiser and Witt and Busch, jumped in quickly and registered many marks, including (in the case of Gaiser) an eagle and a 'lion and flag'. The Lancashire community were quick to react and within a short time the Southern Nigerian law was amended and registration in Britain became a prerequisite for registration in respect of cotton goods; but this was shutting the stable door after the horse had bolted.

Millers registered their 'lion-forward' mark in 1905 for a wide range of non-cotton goods. Pickering and Berthoud (bought by the Niger Company in 1926—*see* chapter 14) registered a lion device in Sierra Leone in 1915. The African and Eastern Trade Corporation had a device of three demi-lions with globes (similar to Millers' demi-lion with cross) which they used extensively from 1921 onwards, and the Niger Company introduced a three-lions mark in 1924.

All the companies with which this book is concerned, and many others, employed a firm in Stockport called Leeming Ray and Whittle to register their trade marks and textile designs and to protect them. This firm's first trade-mark customer was the Compagnie française de l'Afrique occidentale, but very soon many other companies found it necessary to use the services of Leeming Ray and Whittle. The firm was the Whittle family, father, mother, and daughter, and was accommodated in a Victorian house in a residential street, except in the summer months when business, files, and family, moved to more picturesque places such as Harrogate or Anglesea. Joshua Lyon Whittle was a scholarly man, and his parlour walls were lined with files. Ask him about any mark, and away he would go; when it was first registered and in what class; the origin of the design; what the motto meant; what attempts had been made to infringe it, and how he had defended it. Meanwhile Mrs. Whittle would brew tea. His opinions were charged by the written line, and he made them very long.[4]

Joshua Whittle had retainer agreements to act for nearly all the leading merchants. The terms of his retainers had special provisions concerning disputes between his clients. These provided for Whittle to judge the issue and pronounce his findings, and if either party disagreed he would be free to act for the other in any litigation which then took place.

[4] Lord Cole and Raymund Gore-Clough, M.B.E., to Pedler.

When war broke out between Britain and Germany in 1914 German assets were seized and among these was a number of valuable trade marks. The custodian of enemy property offered these trade marks for sale at public auction. Joshua Whittle advised his many clients that it would be unethical to buy the marks, and most of them stayed away from the sale, but Arthur Walkden was there and also Thomas Chadwick (*see* chapter 7) for Ollivant. They evidently felt more inclined to accept the British government's view on the propriety of the transaction, than Joshua Whittle's. In view of the general boycott of the sale, these two people were the only serious bidders, and it did not take them long to realize that there was no point in bidding one against the other; so while the sale was in progress an arrangement was made whereby the two firms divided the German marks between them. The Gaiser cotton marks of the eagle and the lion-and-flag became the property of John Walkden. The ownership of these marks gave to that firm the benefit of Gaiser's goodwill in some of the best-selling textile lines in Nigeria.

Shortly after the end of the war in 1918, a merchant who imported textiles for sale at Kano made a close copy of Ollivant's horse-and-rider mark, and had it stamped on his cloth. Ollivant lodged an objection and the offender was obliged to remove the pirated mark. He did this by cutting a circular hole in the cloth, which was offered for sale in that condition. It sold like wildfire. The circular hole provided positive identification of a unique variety, and for some years that importer continued to place his cloth on sale with a circular hole, and his lines were best sellers in the Kano market.

In 1921 the British act was amended to make it possible to register in a new 'part B' of the register (with restricted rights) many marks used on cotton or other goods which until then had been unregistrable because they were common to the cotton trade, or for other reasons. This awakened the interest of the West African trade community. Many applications were made, and these were not confined to cotton marks because the need for protected trade marks was now felt in other branches of the trade. Millers registered a version of their 'lion-forward' mark (but without the cross moline) for virtually all classes of merchandise. Swanzy registered a unicorn device in the same way. On cotton goods Swanzy now began to use an elaborate ticket which contained no less than five unicorns' heads. Four of them occupied the four quarters of a shield, while over the shield was the old crest; the whole was in a light blue square, at the four corners of which was the manilla-and-arrow, the mark of the African and Eastern Trade Corporation, of which F. and A. Swanzy now formed a constituent part.

This manilla-and-arrow mark was adopted by the African Association on its formation (chapter 10) and it naturally passed on to the African and Eastern Trade Corporation (chapter 20) which succeeded the Association.

The Lagos Stores (chapter 20) had three major marks, all of which went back to 1893 or earlier, namely the slate, the turtle, and the comb-and-crescent. The so-called slate is the traditional reading-board used in the Koranic schools, which every Moslem child in northern Nigeria attended. The Arabic writing on the Lagos Stores' slate mark means, 'Patience conquers the world'. This mark was the subject of the first trade mark action head in Nigeria, in the court of Southern Nigeria in 1901.

W. B. MacIver (bought by Lever Brothers in 1910—*see* chapter 14) had two major marks, the boar's head and the 'link, or northern knot', which was a conventional pattern which one might regard as a design of indigenous heraldry. The boar's head was a heraldic crest to which the MacIver family was fully entitled, but having put it to use in the south of Nigeria, where the firm was first established, they felt the need for a different sign when they went north into Moslem country, considering the offence which Moslems might take from a boar's head.

As mentioned in chapter 5, Millers did not establish a branch at Lagos until 1904; but when at last they went to that city they adopted a most defiant design. In addition to four lions with the cross-moline, they had a cock standing on a map of Lagos island and crowing, in four languages, 'I fear no foe'.

Jurgens Colonial Products (chapter 15) used an indigenous African symbol, the *anta* or charm. This was sometimes used alone, and at other times in the form of two, three, or four *antas*, suitably arranged. At the point of the *anta* is the monogram JCP, ingeniously contrived so that an elephant's trunk provides the J.

Pickering and Berthoud have already been mentioned in connection with their lion device. This company was, naturally enough, known as 'peanbees', and they registered a bold design consisting of a pod of peas and two bees. Another of their emblems developed a theme which was the inspiration of several trade marks, namely the idea of friendship between Africans and Europeans; the mark in question showed a black hand and a white hand, clasped in friendship.

20

The African and Eastern Trade Corporation Limited

This chapter resumes the story of the African Association and of their friends in the Miller–Swanzy group from the point at which it was left in chapter 10. These companies had enjoyed a prosperous decade in the first ten years of the century, and a major element in their prosperity had been the agreements and understandings which existed between them and the Niger Company, to which numerous references have already been made. But the purchase of MacIver by Lever Brothers in 1910 meant that those comfortable arrangements would have to come to an end. It was all very well accepting voluntary restraints on competitive practices when the competitors who were outside the agreement were smaller, weaker, firms: and even when powerful opponents had to be met, such as the leading French and German firms, it was reassuring to know that they, too, had to make their livelihood by taking a merchant's profit. But when a large, powerful, aggressive, and efficient, manufacturer such as Lever Brothers moved into the area, it was obvious that every competitive method would have to be employed unless the older companies were prepared to see their trade seriously eroded. Might they dispense with the merchant's profit altogether in the interest of their manufacturing activity?

This was the situation which led the African Association to establish itself in Sierra Leone as soon as Lever Brothers acquired a company in that colony and also the underlying reason which caused the Association, with Millers, to seek amalgamation with the Niger Company. They wanted to create a more powerful unit, with larger borrowing powers, so that a united front might oppose the Lever attack. But the Niger Company were less disturbed; perhaps they already had ideas of another solution, which in due course was the one which they adopted. Anyway, they were not prepared to amalgamate except on terms which would give the Niger Company a predominant voice in the direction of the merged group, and neither the Association nor Millers would agree to that. So the Association and Millers denounced the pool and resumed their freedom of action.[1]

As mentioned in chapter 8, two private companies were formed, Millers Limited for the Gold Coast in 1904 and Miller Brothers (of Liverpool) Limited for Nigeria in 1907, and the old firm of Alexander Miller Brother and Company then disappeared. Neither of the Miller brothers ever saw Africa. They were fortunate in the succession of able and loyal servants whom they found to look after their interests. Both possessed qualities not often found in combination. They were adventurous yet shrewd and cautious; regardful of trifles yet of broad outlook and disposed to plan on large lines; hard and dogged fighters yet magnanimous in victory. Alexander was chairman of Millers Limited, and George of Miller Brothers (of Liverpool) Limited. Each was on the board presided over by the other. Both continued to hold their positions almost to the end of their long lives. Alexander died in 1922 at the age of 85, and George in the following year at the age of 84.[2]

The closest friendship now united the African Association and Miller Brothers (of Liverpool) Limited, one-time enemies, and from it arose the idea of a complete fusion of interests to include not only the two companies mentioned but also Millers Limited and F. and A. Swanzy. By the middle of the year 1918 the idea had been accepted in principle but the war was still raging and the general disorganization was held to preclude action. Then came the sudden purchase by Lord Leverhulme of the business of Richard and William King, which was noted in chapters 11 and 14. It was rumoured that he had his eye on the African Association as well. If he made an attractive offer to the general body of the Association's shareholders, he might succeed in acquiring control. Alarmed by this possibility, the directors of the African Association hurriedly completed arrangements for merging with Millers. The agreement was signed on 20 May 1919.[3]

The African and Eastern Trade Corporation and the African Association are commonly regarded as identical and the former as the continuation of the other in amplified form. That is true in the technical sense. Nominally the other companies were absorbed by

---

[1] Minute book of the Nigerian pool agreement, United Africa Company records; and Rankin, p. 91.

[2] Rankin, p. 68.

[3] Verbatim record of extraordinary general meeting of 16 June 1919: United Africa Company records.

the African Association because the Association was a public company and the others were private companies. Moreover, the African Association was financially the most important unit of the four companies, but the combined assets of the three constituting what might be called the Miller group exceeded the assets of the African Association.

Cotterell of the African Association became the first chairman of the African and Eastern Trade Corporation. With him to the new board he brought five colleagues from the Association. Miller Brothers (of Liverpool) Limited were represented by Robert B. Miller, A. A. Cowan, and M. H. McNeill. The directors nominated by the London partners, Millers Limited and F. and A. Swanzy, were J. H. Batty, G. Munro Miller, Hutchinson, and W. W. H. Grey. G. Munro Miller joined the board just after its constitution, and so did J. Pickering Jones, chairman of the Lagos Stores Limited, which was bought by the Corporation.

At the time of the amalgamation the African Association was housed in the Royal Liver Building, Liverpool, Miller Brothers (of Liverpool) Limited not far away in Water Street, and the London companies, Millers Limited and F. and A. Swanzy, at West Africa House in Kingsway. It was intended that the head office of the Corporation should be in London, and land was acquired on the east side of Kingsway, near Holborn, for the purpose of erecting new offices which were to be called Africa House.

Cotterell very soon retired and was succeeded by Batty. However, before he went Cotterell told the shareholders of the Association, at an extraordinary general meeting,[4] of the programme which he and his colleagues had in view. He spoke of plans to open businesses in East Africa, in the Near East and in the Far East, and of important investments in Britain. Under the leadership of Batty those plans were now pursued with vigour, and even more important was the massive invasion of northern Nigeria which the Corporation made, now that it was free from any agreement to moderate competition with the Niger Company. In 1919 and 1920 several West African businesses were acquired. The most ancient was Hatton and Cookson, of which the story has been told in chapter 6. It was a valuable acquisition from the point of view of facing up to the Lever group, for Hatton and Cookson were strongly represented in Cameroon, where Lever Brothers had just acquired Richard and William King, and their activities extended down the

[4] ibid.

227

Gabon coast as far as the Belgian Congo, so that the Corporation acquired by this means a toe-hold in the Congo, where the Lever interest was strong. The others were the Ambas Bay Trading Company Limited,[5] the Lagos Stores Limited, the African Traders Company Limited, the Standard Mahogany Company Limited, Crombie Steedman and Company Limited, the Gold Coast Machinery and Trading Company Limited (which had been incorporated in England in 1901), the Mano Company Limited, and McNeill Scott and Company Limited.[6] Amalgamation on such a scale could not fail to make a sensational impression. There is no reason to suppose that any of the companies which were taken over was reluctant to join the group.

The antecedents of the Lagos Stores are of special interest. In the penultimate decade of the last century there was in the office of Elder Dempster in Liverpool a clerk named T. E. Tomlinson. He was ambitious and wished to make his way in the world. Making friends with captains and pursers of the steamers, he established contact through them with several African merchants at Lagos. There were in those days many such merchants who were in a fair way of business. In 1884 the opportunity offered of taking over one of these African businesses, and Tomlinson seized the chance. He resigned from Elder Dempster, opened an office in Liverpool, and appointed a European agent in Lagos. He was doing well, when in 1889 two more African merchants, seeing greater advantage in selling their businesses than in carrying them on, approached Tomlinson's agent with the proposal that he should buy them out. Tomlinson found the offer attractive but had not enough money to take advantage of it. Therefore he had recourse to some friends, whom he induced to subscribe capital. To regularize the arrangement he formed the Lagos Ready Money Store Company Limited, with an authorized capital of £30,000, about half of which was issued. Tomlinson was the chairman, and the secretary was J. Pickering Jones. The Lagos Ready Money Store Company Limited made £2,200 in the first year, paying a dividend of 7½ per cent. In 1891 it paid ten per cent on a larger issued capital. Meanwhile,

---

[5] see note 28 to chapter 6.

[6] At this time the Corporation also became the proprietor of the British Nigerian Company. This was the consortium of eight firms which had been formed to acquire certain ex-German assets (see chapter 15). The Corporation already owned two of the eight parts, through Millers and Lagos Stores. It now took over the company, but not with all its assets, some of which went to other members of the consortium (see chapter 7).

Tomlinson had been running his original business side by side with the limited company, and in 1892 the two were united as the Lagos Stores and Tomlinson Limited. Tomlinson retired in 1897 and the name was changed to the Lagos Stores Limited. By this time the authorized capital had been increased to £100,000 and the issued capital to nearly half that sum.[7] Tomlinson's place was taken by C. A. Birtwistle, who had joined the firm in 1890 and had for a time been employed at Lagos. In 1907 he 'trekked by road from Ibadan to Kano and Sokoto before the railway had been extended beyond Oshogbo'.[8]

A little while before they became part of the African and Eastern Trade Corporation, the Miller group had acquired the firm of W. D. Woodin and Company Limited, together with its subsidiary, the Bai Rubber and Cocoa Estates Limited: so that these two companies also came into the Corporation with the Miller group. The history of Woodin is of interest. In the year 1880 Walter D. Woodin was a purser in the Elder Dempster line. In those days captains and pursers of the steamers used to supplement their official emoluments by private trading. The practice was of course irregular. A. L. Jones, the chairman of Elder Dempster, winked at it and was incurious about the ownership of cargo, provided it had paid freight. Complaints about this form of competition were from time to time made to him by established merchants. Jones could not ignore the complaints, for he had to retain the favour of his customers. Each complaint was investigated but there was little evidence of disciplinary action.

Woodin was one of the trading pursers and he did so well that in a few years he was able to give up the sea. In 1888 he opened an office at 18, James Street, Liverpool, as an African merchant. In that same year he secured outside finance for part of his business by forming the Ambas Bay Trading Company Limited, which he continued to manage.[9] However, he did not put all his activities into the Ambas Bay Company. Those which he retained personally formed the subject of another company formation in 1898, when W. D.

[7] Rankin, p. 96.

[8] Memorandum presented by Birtwistle to parliamentary committee, *Edible and oil-producing nuts and seeds* (London: H.M.S.O., 1915). After leaving the Lagos Stores Birtwistle acted as commercial intelligence officer to the government of Southern Nigeria. He was managing director of Jurgens Colonial Products at the time of his death (*see* chapter 15).

[9] *see* note 28 to chapter 6.

Woodin and Company Limited was registered.[10] He registered the
Bai Rubber and Cocoa Estates Limited as a subsidiary in 1910, and
he acquired the African Mahogany Association Limited. Woodin
was established at Cape Palmas in Liberia before Lever Brothers'
Cavalla River Company (chapter 16). When the African and
Eastern Trade Corporation was formed, the Woodin companies
had recently been acquired by Miller Brothers, and their inclusion
in the Corporation followed.[11]

In addition to all these acquisitions in Africa, the Corporation
acted with speed and boldness in extending its business to many
other parts of the world. The extension to East Africa will be
described in chapter 27. As mentioned above, one of the directors
of the Corporation was W. W. H. Grey, that same Grey who had
walked from Lagos to Kano, and subsequently taken charge of the
Miller business in the Gold Coast (chapter 8). He had volunteered
for military service during the war, and had risen to the rank of
Major-General. His service with the army had made him acquainted
with the countries of the Levant, and it seems to have been due
mainly to his initiative and enthusiasm that the business of the
Corporation was extended to Morocco, Palestine, Persia, and
Singapore. Through personal contacts which he had made during
the war he negotiated the purchase of a controlling interest in the
firm of G. and A. Baker of Constantinople, and with his support
that company extended its activities beyond the borders of Turkey
to Rumania, Bulgaria, and even the Crimea. The story of G. and
A. Baker will be told in chapter 26. In 1920 the Corporation purchased a substantial interest in T. T. Robinson and Company
(Export) Limited, a substantial concern trading in the Mediterranean, the Near East, and the West Indies. Trading posts were
opened in Basra, Beirut, and Aleppo. The need was felt for a framework into which all these activities might be fitted, and for this
purpose a subsidiary company was formed in 1923 under the name
African and Eastern (Near East) Limited.

Millers Limited had set up a branch at Casablanca in Morocco in
1919 just before they became part of the Corporation, and the Corporation took this over. The business was accommodated in a

[10] W. D. Woodin and Company Limited was incorporated on 24 February 1898 under the
Companies Acts 1862 to 1893 to adopt and carry into effect an agreement between Walter
Dennis Woodin and Frank Beever Pownall dated 10 February 1898. The certificate of in-
corporation and memorandum of association are in the United Africa Company records.

[11] Minute book of the board of W. D. Woodin and Co. Ltd., in United Africa Company
records.

building known as the Café Alhambra, opposite the main gate which gave access to the old town. The business grew, and in 1925 it moved to premises in the Rue de Strasbourg. It developed as a specialist in building materials.

Such rapid and ambitious expansion overseas might have been enough to occupy the whole time and energy of the directors, but on the contrary they also acquired a large number of companies in Britain, most of them engaged in the manufacture of products which either used raw materials which could be derived from Africa, or made goods which were (or might be) suitable for export to Africa. Between May 1919 and July 1920 the following sixteen companies were brought into the group. The Corporation became the sole owner of some of them, and acquired a controlling interest in the others.

T. H. Harris and Sons Limited	Soap works.
Poulton and Noel Limited	Preserved foods.
E. H. Perrin and Company Limited	Produce brokers.
Nicholl and Knight Limited	Produce dealers.
Loder and Nucoline Limited	Oil crushers.
T. Middleton and Company Limited	Cotton mills.
Thomas Welsh and Company Limited	Cotton mills.
S. F. Armitage and Sons Limited	Cotton mills.
Joseph Holt and Sons Limited	Cotton mills.
Rice and Company Limited	Cotton mills.
Ribbleton Mills Limited	Cotton mills.
George Kay and Company Limited	Dye works.
Joseph Dunkerly and Sons Limited	Garment makers.
Forster, Moone and Company Limited	Jacquard weavers.
A. J. Seward and Company Limited	Cosmetics.
Ellesmere Port Estates Limited	

To this long list must be added the name of A. J. Caley and Sons Limited, a Norwich company manufacturing chocolate, mineral waters, and Christmas crackers, in which the African Association had acquired a substantial interest in 1917.

All this showed that the Corporation had adopted Lord Leverhulme's idea of building up an integrated group which would combine the manufacturing process with the merchanting process. Of all this programme, the most audacious item from the point of view of competing with Lever Brothers was the acquisition of T. H.

Harris and Sons Limited, soap-makers. Harris had two subsidiary concerns, the Jolly Boy Company and the Sanagen Soap Company. The African and Eastern Trade Corporation used the products of Harris and Jolly Boy to undersell Levers' soaps in African markets, and embarrassed Levers by securing more than half of the market, even though Levers were manufacturing locally in Nigeria and Congo.[12]

This great organization began its career in the boom year of 1919, and the results of the first year's trading were very good. There had been a turnover of some £22,000,000, and the net profits were £1,721,618. A dividend of thirty per cent was declared, and bonus shares were distributed in the proportion of one new share for every twenty held.

Relations between the Niger Company and the African and Eastern Trade Corporation were very unfriendly, and everything pointed to a bitter commercial war between them; yet in October 1920 they nearly joined together under the banner of Lever Brothers. In July the purchase of the Niger Company by Lever Brothers had been completed, and in October it became known that Lever Brothers intended to bring all their other West African businesses into the Niger Company, and that Lord Leverhulme wished to acquire the African and Eastern Trade Corporation also. He offered terms which were breathtakingly attractive,[13] and they were naturally accepted. Following the formal acceptance of the offer (November 1920) the next step should have been for both

---

[12] Leverhulme's African diary, 1924/5 p. 178: minutes of Lever Brothers' export council meeting, 12 July 1924, LC 3686, 1/AC, 13 January 1925.

[13] Each £1 ordinary share of the Corporation already issued was to be exchanged for two-and-a-half fifteen per cent cumulative preferred ordinary shares of the Corporation. These would be created by the capitalization of the Corporation's reserves to the extent of about £5,000,000. Thus, each £1 ordinary share so converted would earn a dividend of thirty-seven-and-a-half per cent. There would be a fresh issue of four million £1 ordinary shares, constituting the equity of the Corporation and carrying all the voting power, and these would be handed over to Lever Brothers in exchange for four million £1 twenty per cent 'A' preferred ordinary shares of Lever Brothers. The Corporation's holding in Lever Brothers should then yield it an annual income of £800,000. In order to pay the dividend on the new fifteen per cent cumulative preferred ordinary shares the Corporation would have to make an annual net trading profit (over and above corporation tax and excess profits tax) of £1,400,000, with which to supplement its income of £800,000 from Lever Brothers. Unless and until that level of profit was exceeded, Lever Brothers would not receive any return at all from the Corporation. It was intended that five directors of the Corporation should join the board of the Niger Company, but there was to be no reciprocal transfer of directors from the Niger Company to the Corporation. (A. and E.T.C. circular to shareholders 24 September 1920, and verbatim reports of shareholders' meetings of 5 and 26 November 1920, in United Africa Company records).

parties to apply to a court for legal approval of the reconstruction of the Corporation's capital which was a condition of the offer. However, weeks went by and no such application was made.[14] The delay caused surprise and it was rumoured that the deal was off. Batty told the shareholders (14 April 1921) that the scheme had been abandoned by mutual consent chiefly because of the deterioration of world economic conditions which the last few months had witnessed. The true reason for the change of mind was that Leverhulme's accountants had at last discovered the truth about the financial straits of the Niger Company.[15] He was not in a position to go forward with his offer to the shareholders of the African and Eastern Trade Corporation. The offer had been preposterous. In being able to withdraw it in time, Leverhulme had a very lucky escape.

The sentiments with which the parties mutually agreed to remain independent seem to have been friendlier than those which animated them before the negotiations began. At the meeting just mentioned, Batty made the significant declaration that the abandonment of the merger proposals did not preclude the possibility of a working agreement being negotiated when stable conditions returned. Lord Leverhulme went further. Addressing the shareholders of Lever Brothers, he said that the affair had strengthened the friendly relations of Lever Brothers with Batty and his colleagues. However, these generous sentiments at the top were not widely held by the management. The two concerns engaged in vigorous competition.

During the early months of 1920 the boom of the previous year continued, but towards the end of the year adverse influences asserted themselves. Supply overtook demand. People began to realize how much damage the war had caused, and to recognize that it could not be made good by squeezing reparations out of the defeated foe. Currencies began to depreciate, and all kinds of restrictions were imposed in the effort to protect them. For the African and Eastern Trade Corporation 1920 was about half as good as 1919. Then came the plunge. There was a loss of £1,794,000 in 1921; but 1922 showed a remarkable recovery and a dividend of eight per cent was paid. Moderate prosperity continued

---

[14] The situation was explained to shareholders in the Corporation's circular of 4 April 1921. The verbatim report of the extraordinary general meeting of 14 April 1921 also refers: both in United Africa Company records.

[15] Wilson, Charles, *History of Unilever* (London: Cassell, 1954) vol. I, p. 257.

over the next few years. The dividend of eight per cent was maintained. Here are the tax-paid profits:

1923	£382,353
1924	£403,549
1925	£410,815
1926 (nine months)	£264,698 (dividend was six per cent)
1927	£382,612.

In 1923 Africa House was formally opened by the Mayor of Holborn. It was generally expected that it would be made the head office of the Corporation, but this did not happen. Only the London subsidiaries occupied it. The chairman and some of the directors were there, but the head office remained in Liverpool, and in that city most of the directors continued to reside. Board meetings were held sometimes in London and sometimes in Liverpool.

There was nothing abnormal in the accounts relating to 1926. Batty, chairman since 1919, who presided, was one of the three directors retiring by rotation and offering themselves for re-election. All three were re-elected unanimously. There was nothing to suggest that there were divided counsels on the board, and the first revelation of the fact came to the knowledge of the public in the announcement which appeared in the press just three weeks later, that Batty had resigned. He was succeeded by Robert B. Miller, who had been vice-chairman of the Corporation since 1919.

Sic transit J. H. Batty. It was forty-four years since he had gone out to the Gold Coast to rescue the Miller business. What caused his removal is not known.[16] Like most board-room rows, this one was not well documented. But if an explanation is required, it might be found in the subject of the cocoa pool agreement which the Corporation under Batty's chairmanship had concluded with the Niger Company in 1925, as already noted in chapter 14. This agreement never worked well and it can hardly have failed to form a subject of controversy on the board of the Corporation.

A new director joined the board in 1927, Major Cecil R. Bates, D.S.O., M.C. He had been in the regular army and had served in India. After his retirement from military life he had acquired some experience of African trade through a connection with the London and Kano Trading Company—one of the comparatively few British

16 The minutes of the board of the Corporation of this period have not been preserved. *West Africa*, 30 April 1927, commented, 'those who know how great a part of his life Mr. Balty has put into hard, constant work, will not be surprised at his deciding to take a little ease'.

companies in West Africa which had retained its independence through the flurry of amalgamations in 1919 and 1920.

To the businesses purchased or founded by the Corporation during the first eighteen months of its existence others were added, twenty in all between 1923 and 1929.[17] These included the Pesquerias de San Cristobal, supplying dried fish from the Canaries to Gold Coast. In 1928 Kingsway Chemists was registered, using the name which had become identified with Millers' retail store in Accra (chapter 8).

A mining department was set up—again showing a proclivity for imitating the Niger group. It mined a little platinum in Sierra Leone. It investigated traces of iron ore which had been located by a government geologist at Marampa in Sierra Leone, and proved an ore body which appeared to be capable of development; this subsequently turned out to be important.

In 1928 misfortune came. A circular was issued to the shareholders saying that, in the absence of any improvement, the directors would not consider it prudent to distribute any interim dividend. It was evident from this announcement that the year which had just closed had been a bad one. How bad they would not know until the accounts were issued, which would not be for a few months. No serious alarm was felt. But in the following month the storm burst with devastating force.

Like almost every other trading organization, the Corporation depended on the banks and credit houses for the financial accommodation needed to carry on its purchases. It was in debt to both and they now refused to continue granting the facilities hitherto accorded. Without them the Corporation's activities would be at a standstill and the Corporation would not be able to meet its contracted obligations. The withdrawal of credit, if persisted in, spelt

[17] The twenty companies were as follows:
Registered to accommodate various activities: African and Eastern (Malaya) Limited 1928; African and Eastern (Near East) Limited 1923; African and Eastern (Spain) Limited 1923; African and Eastern Trading Company (Hamburg) G.m.b.H. 1925; African and Eastern Trading Company (Holland) Limited 1921; African and Eastern Trading Company Incorporated 1921; Angola Land Company Limited 1922; Gold Coast Petroleum Company Limited 1926; Kingsway Chemists Limited 1928; Takoradi Coaling and Lighterage Company Limited 1926; West Africa Publicity Limited 1928.
Acquisitions: Bullows and Roy Limited 1927 *see* chapter 27; Hunt and Son Limited 1922; Martinet Slate and Sheet Company Limited 1922; McLaren Brothers (Manchester) Limited 1926; Pesquerias de San Cristobal S.A. 1926; Povson Limited 1927; Talbot and Company Limited 1924; Wenol Limited 1921; Rosenblum Bullows and Roy, registered in 1929, was an amalgamation of Bullows and Roy with Rosenblum, which had been acquired: *see* chapter 27.

liquidation. What was the amount of the loss in the year 1927–8 which produced this grave embarrassment for the Corporation? The precise figure was not known until several months had elapsed, months during which important events to be related took place. Then it was found to be the comparatively insignificant sum of £96,953, barely a quarter of the profit realized in the previous year.

Though the banks and credit-houses were nervous about the situation of the Corporation and unwilling to continue financing it, nevertheless they had no wish to force it into liquidation. Indeed they were anxious for their own sakes, because of the large sums owing to them, to see that catastrophe averted. The banks would continue to lend the Corporation their assistance on the condition that a nominee of theirs became the Corporation's chairman.

One of the credit houses suggested to D'Arcy Cooper, the chairman of Lever Brothers, that he should make a proposal for taking over the Corporation. D'Arcy Cooper was not prepared to accept the suggestion. Then he was asked if he could think of a suitable chairman for the Corporation to be nominated by the financial interests. He mentioned Sir Robert Waley Cohen, K.B.E. who earlier in the year had resigned, at the age of 51, from the position of joint managing director of the Royal Dutch–Shell group of companies in the petroleum industry.[18] Among the many businesses which Leverhulme had acquired for Lever Brothers was Price's Patent Candle Company. This firm manufactured soap as well as candles. The candle department was afterwards merged with the petroleum interests with which Waley Cohen was connected, the soap department being retained by Lever Brothers, and as a consequence D'Arcy Cooper and Waley Cohen sat as co-directors on the board of the organization called Candles Limited.

The Westminster Bank, acting as intermediary between the financial interests and the Corporation, proposed to the directors of the latter that the appointment should be offered to Sir Robert and they agreed. The chairman of the Westminster Bank invited the directors of the Corporation and Sir Robert to lunch at the offices of the Bank. Two of the principals of Messrs. Samuels were also guests. After the lunch Sir Robert was formally asked if he would accept the chairmanship of the Corporation. His appointment was announced in December 1928.

One of the first things that Waley Cohen did was to send Major Bates to Africa to investigate what was going on. Bates' report be-

[18] Rankin, p. 110.

236

came available in March 1929. It told a story of wasteful competition between the constituent firms of the Corporation, trading under their ancient names. They were mostly trying to cover the whole field of trade and thus failing to secure any advantages of specialization. In Nigeria there was no pattern of administration. Different arrangements obtained in different parts of the country; and while they might have originally been well adapted to local circumstances, their diversity had become a source of confusion, and made it difficult for anyone to understand what was going on.

The Corporation never solved its basic problem of organization, nor put itself in a position to use its strength. It did succeed in putting all its shipping interests together, and was rewarded by securing valuable concessions from the conference shipping lines (chapter 24); but it took no comparable action in regard to its relations with banks and suppliers. The African Association, Millers, Swanzy, Hatton and Cookson, Woodin, Ambas Bay, and so on, all had their headquarters in Britain and their establishments in Africa. Supervising agents at points in Africa held vague overlordship, and there was the board in Britain, but whatever measure of co-ordination there may have been, it fell far short of central direction. It was hindered by old rivalries which went right up to the board, rivalries between companies and between families. They never even established a pool of cash in Africa. One unit might be borrowing at interest while another unit in the same town had a credit balance, and money was transferred between Britain and Africa at unnecessary expense. It is therefore hardly surprising that they did not establish a proper system of financial control. Hence their failure to know what their position was when the creditors turned upon them. They fell into panic.

The Miller companies at the time of their merger with the African and Eastern Trade Corporation kept their accounts on a single entry system. In one foolscap book it recorded transactions with the head offices in Britain; accounts for merchandise, casks, and bags, cash transactions, produce purchases, and produce shipments. The more elaborate system which the Corporation had established in the Gold Coast was introduced into its Nigerian businesses about 1924. Managers were horrified to discover that books for a branch cost £60, and that it was necessary to recruit a book-keeper from the Gold Coast in order to maintain the system.[19]

[19] Dunnet, D. D. to Pedler, 17 August 1970.

237

The splintered structure of the group in Africa was a bar to proper management. In such circumstances, the standards of commercial practice are inevitably set by the weakest management: by the management that cannot resist pressure to extend over-risky advances, by the management that liquidates its merchandise in panic as the season draws towards its end. The policy of 'internal competition' may have been rationalized by the argument that it enabled the Corporation to handle competing agencies: but the continuation of separate buying organizations in Britain incurred a heavy penalty. It meant that the strength of the Corporation as a buyer was not mobilized. The dissemination of buying staffs in different parts of London and Liverpool was an error, and the failure to bring the directors and their personal staffs together in one place was a source of weakness.

The weaknesses of central organization and control ought to have been solved before the vast programme of acquisitions was undertaken. Many of the companies which were bought were owned but not managed. In so far as the acquisitions were manufacturers of merchandise which the Corporation hoped to sell in Africa, the basic philosophy was wrong. The Corporation made the same mistake as so many latter-day critics of the colonial system, when they speak of merchant houses providing outlets for manufacturing interests. That kind of vertical integration is not helpful to a merchant. Burdened with it, he must always be at a disadvantage compared with his rival who has free access to all sources of supply. The manufacturing concerns in the bundle which the Corporation acquired were, on the whole, not successful. Curiously, the two which directly competed with Lever Brothers were perhaps the ones with the best record. T. H. Harris has already been mentioned. The other, the oil crushers Loder and Nucoline, maintained an interesting business. But it is astonishing that none of the nine companies in the textile industry seems to have made any impact at all on the West African trade. This is all the more surprising since the Corporation was the leading merchant in textiles in West Africa, largely owing to its excellent relations with Dutch manufacturers, and it had the best possible access to sources for designs and information about fashion trends. It must be concluded that the management structure for communicating those advantages to the manufacturing units had simply not been created.

In matters of employment, however, there is much to be said for the African and Eastern. Many of the men whom they recruited for service in Africa had, later, outstanding careers in Africa. The Corporation had a non-contributory fund out of which pensions were provided for expatriate staff,[20] at any rate for some of them at the discretion of the board. This had been started by the African Association. If there was no systematic policy of bringing Africans into management, the old Swanzy stalwarts continued to be employed, while Grey and Bolliger took a personal interest in African students and in young African members of the staff. However, improved health conditions had removed the imperative which had opened up promotion to Africans in earlier decades.

Finally, there was the basic financial weakness. The warning of 1921 was not taken to heart. In the light of what happened in 1928, the distribution of the eight per cent dividend through the years 1922 to 1927, together with large expenditure on acquisitions, must be seen as a failure to create reserves which were adequate for such a risky business.

Nevertheless, the business in the Gold Coast had continued to be profitable, and it may be of interest to record General Grey's views on how it was done:

> We are not in Africa to sell goods at a loss and if opponents are prepared to cut our trade by losing money they may do so being confident that we can get the trade back when they come to their senses or disaster whichever may be first. This is the policy which has always been followed on the Gold Coast by the African and Eastern Trade Corporation and has been successful. Price wars may be necessary between companies which deal in one class of business but they are suicidal when carried out by merchant companies handling thousands of different articles and having no interest in their manufacture.[21]

This was part of Grey's defence of his performance, after the storm had burst. Others, however, might have made the comment that though there might have been thousands of different articles in the trade, there was just one which might make the difference between profitable and unprofitable trade in the Gold Coast, and that was the Dutch wax block. This merits a chapter for itself, and the chapter follows next.

[20] Rankin, p. 115.
[21] Grey, W. W. H., Memorandum to the directors of the United Africa Company, 29 December 1930.

2 1

Dutch Wax Blocks

The West African trade has known a vast number of different styles of cloth, and many of these have borne exotic names which have occurred on earlier pages of this book; but of all the cloths that have gone into West Africa, none has caused greater excitement in the markets, and none has earned larger profits for the merchants and market traders, than the Dutch wax block. (An example of a traditional design of Dutch wax blocks will be seen at the end-papers, inside the front and back covers.)

The African and Eastern Trade Corporation inherited from Swanzys and from Millers many hundreds of credit customers, nearly all of whom were women. They bought merchandise from the Corporation at wholesale prices, and sold it in the markets at retail prices. When the Corporation acquired the unique trading asset of the Dutch wax blocks, it was a natural decision for the Corporation to sell this product through the women traders. The scenes that sometimes were witnessed when bales of Dutch wax blocks were opened for the inspection of the designs in the Corporation's trading premises, were most unusual and very exciting. The women traders, substantial in every sense of the word, would struggle with each other to get a hand first into the bale, or to attract the attention of the manager. No holds were barred, and attempts to impose discipline and order were resented as an interference in restraint of trade. Many of these women became well-to-do and a few gained great riches. The most successful were regularly consulted regarding designs, and if a trader could arrange for the printing of a design and reserve that cloth exclusively for herself, it was a high status symbol. As for credit terms, it was well understood that every trader paid on the last day of the month for the supplies which she had drawn during the month. She normally made settling day the occasion for drawing new supplies, on the following month's account. No interest was charged for this credit. Many women traders asked the Corporation to hold deposit accounts for them.

In the days of the African and Eastern Trade Corporation, wax block prints were produced only by two manufacturers in Holland. They employed skilled Dutch craftsmen and the process involved some operations which were secrets jealously guarded by the manufacturers.

What was a wax block print? What made it different from ordinary roller prints? A basic pattern was applied in wax on both sides of the cloth whereupon it was immersed in a bath of indigo. That part of the cloth covered by wax resisted the indigo dye, so when the wax was removed after the indigo bath dipping there was an identical indigo-dyed design on both sides of the cloth. Subsequently some of the undyed (white) areas of the cloth were filled in with colours applied by means of wooden blocks which were manipulated by hand.

Handling the cloth subsequent to the application of wax, and before the indigo dipping took place, caused hair cracks to appear in the wax through which the indigo seeped during the dipping process. This was known as the indigo crackle and was highly regarded as one of the characteristics of the Dutch wax article. Other cherished features were the irregularity of the colour blocking unavoidable in the application of colour by hand blocking to an outline design in indigo, and the colour penetration which could be secured by hand blocking. No colour is absolutely fast, but the Dutch always used the best dyes available to secure the most satisfactory resistance to light, washing, perspiration, and rubbing, under African conditions.

The designs owed much to *batik* themes from the East Indies. The object in *batiking* is to preserve the design in white while the fabric is being dyed or otherwise coloured. Recurring motifs are peacocks, dragons, snakes, tigers, flowers, and quaint objects symbolizing luck.[1] The designs were popular with African soldiers who had served in the Dutch forces in the East Indies.[2] The preference for Dutch designs in the Gold Coast was established before 1823, for in that year merchants were advised that goods suitable to barter for gold and ivory on the Gold Coast would include red and blue bejutapauts, 'Dutch pattern best', and neganipauts,[3] 'Dutch pattern

[1] Van Vlissingen and Company, *Gerdenbock 1846–1946* (Helmond: 1948) p. 84.

[2] Rodenburg, G. H., 'Dutch Wax Block garments' in *Textielhistorische bijdragen 8 Jaarverslag over 1966* (Hengelo: Stichting Textielgeschiedenis, 1967) pp. 42–3.

[3] Bejutapauts and neganipauts. When the Dutch replaced the Portuguese in the spice trade between Europe and the East Indies (late sixteenth century) Dutchmen travelling in the East were delighted by the beauty of the clothes of the people. These were of woven cotton, printed with batik designs in fast dyes. Trade developed in the importation of such

best'.[4] The Dutch government left the Coast in 1872 (chapter 3) but Dutch designs of printed textiles remained, for a century, essential and profitable in the import trade of the Gold Coast and Ghana.

The wax blocking process was not invented until about 1882. Naamlooze Vennootschap Haarlemse Katoend-Maartschappij were the first to produce wax blocks in Holland. They made their first export to Africa in 1893. This company ceased production in 1912–1914. The works were acquired by the town planners of the time, and attempts to get started elsewhere failed.

The Corporation developed the closest connection with two Dutch companies which carried on the production of wax blocks after the Haarlem company had given up, namely Ankersmit's Textielfabrieken N.V. of Deventer, and P. F. Van Vlissingen and Company of Helmond. In view of the importance of these firms in the Corporation's story it is appropriate that something should be said of their origins.[5]

The firm of P. F. Van Vlissingen and Company of Helmond, founded in 1846, had established its imitation sarongs in the Indies and was able to take advantage of the developing trade in the Gold Coast. The development of the wax block process by Van Vlissingen belongs to the period 1900–1909.[6]

When Van Vlissingen began to make wax blocks, he sold them at first in part through a merchant in Amsterdam, Haykens and Company, and in part through his own agent in Manchester. However, by 1914 he had established a connection with F. and A. Swanzy. His supplies to Swanzy at that time were all thirty-six inches in width. When the African and Eastern Trade Corporation came into being in 1919 it was clear to Van Vlissingen that the Corporation dominated the print trade in British West Africa, and selling arrangements were progressively developed, so that by 1929 Van Vlissingen was selling only through the Corporation, with the single exception of the Belgian Congo. However, there was never

---

cloth from the Far East to the Netherlands. In 1687 Jacob ter Gou and Hendrick Popta established the first 'calico printworks' at Amersfoort in Holland, and began to manufacture comparable cloth in Europe. By 1750 no less than a hundred factories in Holland were specializing in this trade (Rodenburg, op. cit.). Taking their techniques and designs from the Far East, they also adopted many names, of which bejutapaut and neganipaut are examples. A few such names survive in modern English, such as bandanna, calico, chintz, and sarong.

[4] Adams, J., *Remarks on the country extending from Cape Palmas to the River Congo* (London: Whittaker, 1823) p. 235.

[5] Rodenburg, op. cit., p. 49.

[6] ibid.

any written agreement between Van Vlissingen and the Corporation. The exclusivity accorded by Van Vlissingen was simply something which he recognized as being in his interest: because for the manufacture of high-priced fashion goods it is essential to be sure that the goods are marketed with skill and discretion. Tom, Dick, and Harry can soon ruin such a trade. The exclusivity arrangement was not even reciprocal, for the Corporation never ceased to handle the products of Ankersmit, who was a competitor of Van Vlissingen.

The firm of Ankersmit opened in Deventer in 1798 as indigo dyers, Hendrik Jan Ankersmit I supplied yarn to handloom weavers in their cottages, and collected the cloth from them for dyeing. His son, Henrik Jan II, built a steam-driven weaving mill. It was ready in 1862 but owing to the Civil War in America there was no cotton, so it did not start work until 1865. Its products included blue baft, sucretons, and 'Guinee Holy Shandora',[7] which were exported to the Netherlands East Indies and to Africa. The famous 'Blue Men' of the desert, the Touaregs, dressed themselves in indigo-dyed cloth from Deventer. Special care was taken to dye in such a way that the colours would rub off on the wearer, which gave the desired copper sheen to the skin.

In 1899 the fourth generation entered the firm, among them Hendrik Jan IV, a chemical engineer, who studied in Zürich. He started the wax block printing. The idea was first discussed with a representative of the Basel Mission. This was a society which engaged in trade in the Gold Coast and Togo, using the profits to support evangelical and educational activities. This society wished to buy wax blocks, and Ankersmit started production for them in 1912. The first two designs were 'linoleum pattern' and 'pelican'. Dr. H. J. Ankersmit visited the Gold Coast in 1912. However, the trade came to an end on the outbreak of war, when the Basel Mission was considered by the British government as an enemy company and sequestrated. In 1919 Ankersmit wrote to Swanzy, 'Knowing that you are one of the most important firms, who also have many dealings in wax prints, we would suggest to you to enter into relation with our firm as makers of this article'. It was not long before Cottrill of Swanzy was in Deventer, and an agreement was reached under which Swanzy acquired the exclusive right to market

---

[7] Baft is unprinted white (or off-white) cotton cloth. The word, which comes from Persian and means 'woven', is still current in the West African trade. Blue baft is simply baft dyed solid blue. 'Shandora' is a word of eastern origin, but 'sucreton' appears to be connected with the French 'cretonne', a word derived from Creton, the name of a village on the River Eure.

Ankersmit products for the whole of West Africa with the exception of the Ivory Coast and Portuguese Guinea, for five years.[8]

Thus, the Corporation was handling the whole production for West Africa of both Ankersmit and Van Vlissingen. A good design of 'Dutch wax block' might sell in the market for about twice as much as a good design of Manchester print. It became the prime object of the Corporation textile managers to preserve the prestige of Dutch wax blocks, and with it, of course, the price premium.

Millers introduced wax blocks to Nigeria, and although they did not become so popular there as in the Gold Coast, they were a valuable article of trade, especially at Onitsha and Warri.

[8] From records kindly supplied by Texoprint N.V., Helmond.

22

Plantations, Timber, Ranching

While Lever was creating a palm-oil industry in the Belgian Congo, interesting plantation developments were taking place in Nigeria without his assistance. Each of these stories has its dominating note. The dominant note in Nigeria is the successful introduction into West Africa of the modern scientific techniques of rubber and oil-palm cultivation. The dominant note in the Congo is development by private enterprise, which, as well as creating a new source of palm products for international commerce, created many thriving communities with their churches, schools, hospitals, roads, shops, cinemas, bathing pools, sports facilities, and other infrastructure, of which an interesting feature was the local production of foodstuffs.

Nigeria, plantations

Since the Nigerian story started first in time, it can come first in this chapter.

In 1887 Alexander Miller, Brother and Company received a recruit. His name was Alexander A. Cowan, and it has already occurred in these pages. The remarkable progress of the business during the 1890s and later was due in large measure to Cowan. His career in Nigeria, spent at various places, lasted until about the end of the century. For many years afterwards, while resident in Liverpool, he paid frequent visits to Nigeria.

An important piece of pioneering stands to the credit of George Miller. In the year 1900 Miller approached Sir Ralph Moor, the High Commissioner for Southern Nigeria, on the subject of interesting Africans in the cultivation of rubber. He asked if land would be available and he endeavoured to make it clear that his object was to benefit the people. He offered to distribute plants free. Authority replied with an emphatic 'no'. The policy of the Nigerian government was to maintain the communal ownership of the land, an institution which was regarded as vital to the well-being of the population.

Regretfully Miller dropped his project. One evening in 1904 Cowan was talking to Mr. (afterwards Sir Walter) Egerton, the successor of Sir Ralph Moor as High Commissioner. Egerton had come from Malaya, where he had seen the beginning of rubber planting. 'What a pity,' he remarked to his guest, 'that there is so little initiative among the mercantile community in this part of the world!' Cowan proceeded to relate what the reader has just learned. Egerton asked, 'Do you think Mr. Miller is still disposed to carry out that scheme?' Cowan answered affirmatively. 'In that case,' said the High Commissioner, 'he shall have the land *tomorrow morning*.' A lease was granted of 500 acres of land at Sapele, fronting the river, the site being Cowan's selection. The acreage was later increased. Miller's Nigerian rubber estates proved a success and African farmers took up the industry exactly as George Miller had foretold.

Owing to the policy of the government, referred to above, there was little land in Nigeria which could be rented for plantation work, but there were a few areas which resulted from land transactions carried out by African chiefs before the policy of the protectorate government had been well established. Miller was able to acquire rubber plantations at Ikotmbo and Qua Eboe in the period between 1905 and 1907. The firm of W. D. Woodin secured a plantation at Bai about the same time, and this became the property of Millers when they bought Woodin.

In the early years of the century a man named Cranston, whose main activities were in cutting and exporting mahogany, acquired an area at Sapobah, where he made a rubber plantation which was acquired by MacIver, the company which was Lever's first acquisition in Nigeria. A fine plantation of rubber had been created on the Jamieson River in Nigeria by I. T. Palmer, a Sierra Leonean who served with distinction as a political agent for the Royal Niger Company. On his death the Niger Company acquired the plantation. One substantial rubber estate at Sapele was, up to 1929, in the ownership of a Nigerian, J. A. Thomas. At the sale of enemy properties in West Africa which took place in 1924, the African and Eastern Trade Corporation (of which by now Millers formed a part) purchased estates at Ndian in what was then the British mandated territory of Cameroon.

The comfortable belief that West Africa's natural palmeries made that country secure as the main supplier of palm oil and palm kernels for all time received a rude shock in the second decade of the present century. In Sumatra the first planting of palms on a commercial scale took place in 1911. Between 1911 and 1936 exports of palm oil from the Far East rose from nil to 170,000 tons, while Nigeria's progress during the same period was from 85,000 tons to 163,000 tons. Cowan, who visited the Far East in 1925–6, saw evidence there that, to maintain West Africa in the position of the leading supplier of palm produce, plantations were a matter of vital and immediate urgency. He pressed that conclusion upon his colleagues on the board of the African and Eastern Trade Corporation and the decision was taken that the cultivation of oil palms on the most scientific lines should be carried out at Ndian. The clearing of bush and the cultivation of seedlings in a nursery began in 1926, and the first planting of oil palms took place in 1928.

It must be emphasized however, that the total area of all these Nigerian plantations, whether for rubber or for palm products, and even including Ndian, was very small, amounting to no more than 14,556 acres.[1]

Plantations in Gold Coast and Sierra Leone

The attempt of Lever Brothers to develop a concession area for palm fruit around Yonnibannah in Sierra Leone has been mentioned (chapter 14). It appears that in 1917 staff were moved from Yonnibannah to manage a palm-oil plantation at Sese in the Gold Coast. Just what the nature of the Lever interest in this estate was, is not clear, but from the fact that they operated under the name Palm Oil Estate Managers (P.O.E.M.) it may perhaps be deduced that they were not the owners. The estate produced palm oil of a special quality, which commanded a premium price. This was due to its high content of B-carotin, the pro-vitamin of vitamin A. The oil was used to produce a vitamin concentrate which, when used in the margarine mix, improved the health value of the product and gave it the colour of butter. This was of special value in several countries where the dairy farmers' lobby had secured the enactment of legislation preventing the use of colouring matter and synthetic adjuvants. However, the manager of the estate found that he could improve on selling his oil at a premium price on the international market. He developed a local trade in palm oil, packing it in four-gallon petrol tins; by 1929 a high proportion of the Sese oil was sold that way.[2]

[1] Hancock, Sir Keith, *Survey of British Commonwealth Affairs* (Oxford: Clarendon Press 1942) II. 2, p. 192.
[2] Sir Malcolm Knox, diary, 1 January 1929.

In another part of the Gold Coast the Niger Company, before it was acquired by Lever Brothers, had acquired the lease of a narrow strip of land three miles long, on the Birim river, at a place called Bunso. This land was leased with a view to its mineral possibilities. Holes were dug, seeking gold, and a dredge was imported and set to work in the river; but the amount of gold that it recovered was not enough to pay expenses, so it was abandoned; the cost of moving it somewhere else would have been more than it was worth. After this disappointment, plots were planted with rubber trees and kola nut trees. In 1921, shortly after the Niger Company had been acquired by Lever Brothers, William Lever's associate Greenhalgh visited Bunso and on his instructions the rest of the estate was planted with cocoa. However, by 1928 it had become necessary to admit that the cocoa had been planted without proper agricultural advice. A second effort was undertaken, using cocoyams and plantains to provide shade for the young plants, and devoting more attention to the control of insect pests.[3]

In Sierra Leone the African and Eastern Trade Corporation contributed £6,000 in 1926 to assist the establishment of a plantation of oil palms by the Department of Agriculture at Masanki. This was in conformity with the policy on which the Corporation was working in Nigeria, aiming at developing plantation techniques in order to preserve the competitiveness of West African palm oil under the attack from the plantations of the East Indies.

Huileries du Congo Belge

Very early in the century Lever had approached the Nigerian government for concessions of land which would have enabled him to organize native palmeries, as he later did in the Congo, with a view to developing plantations. The reader will appreciate that this happened many years before the altercation with Sir Hugh Clifford to which reference has been made in chapter 14. Since the government of Nigeria was not favourable towards Lever's proposals, his attention was drawn to the Belgian Congo and it was there that he put forth his effort.

The epic of the Congo venture has been told by Charles Wilson, and briefly mentioned in chapter 14. It is not necessary to repeat here the story of the political complications, the formidable physical difficulties, the extensive commitment which was undertaken to-

---

[3] Sir Malcolm Knox, diary, 3 January 1929.

wards the welfare of the local populations, and the heroic journeys of Lever and his wife into the interior of the Congo.[4]

The profusion of wild palms in the Belgian Congo was such that cultivation was not considered a matter of urgency, and attention was centred on the collection of fruit from the large territory of the concession, the erection of mills, and the scientific extraction of the oil.

The competition from the plantations in the Far East, which had impressed Cowan so much, now became a serious threat to the survival of the enterprise in the Congo. Managers reported that, even after the greatest efforts towards economy and efficiency, they could not foresee the possibility of producing palm oil at a cost lower than £18 per ton, F.O.B. Matadi: and this at a time when eastern palm oil was available at £11 per ton! If that opinion had been accepted, it would have been necessary to close the business.

It was now seen that the reliance on natural palmeries, although it had provided a good basis for the Huileries to get started quickly in 1911, could not hope to provide a permanent basis for competing with the Far Eastern plantations. The Nigerian (Cameroon) plantations started by the African and Eastern Trade Corporation had eyes on the Far East, and had taken up all ideas of plant breeding, improved agricultural methods, and manuring. The Huileries had concentrated on engineering. In the mechanical treatment of the fruit, it had much to contribute to the industry.

SEDEC

The Société des Entreprises Commerciales au Congo adopted SEDEC as its telegraphic address, and by that name it was known. It was set up by Lever Brothers in 1912 when they began to develop the Huileries du Congo Belge. It was to provide shops in the communities brought together by the Huileries, and at the same time to engage in two-way trade, exporting produce and importing merchandise. In these activities it had to compete with two powerful groups, one sponsored by the Société Générale of Belgium and the other by the Bank of Brussels. There were also many Greek and Portuguese firms, but these were small men trading with their own capital, and they therefore assisted in maintaining good margins. Because of its connection with the Huileries, SEDEC operated in the centre and the north of the country, and did not at first attempt

[4] Wilson, C., *History of Unilever* (London: Cassell, 1954) vol. I, pp. 167–79, 289–90.

any penetration of the rich mining area, Katanga, in the south. Its trademark was a blue diamond. Throughout the 1920s this company incurred heavy losses.

Timber

The export trade in timber developed rapidly in the first quarter of the twentieth century, as the following figures show:

	Exports in £000	
	Nigeria	Gold Coast
1911	56	139
1929	243	207

It was characteristic of the merchant companies in West Africa that they were anxious to engage in every activity which held out an opportunity of profit, and it is therefore not surprising that both the Corporation and the Niger group had interests in the timber trade.

Millers established a sawmill at Koko on the Benin river in 1903[5] and they added a second sawmill at Sapele, which was already in existence in 1917.[6] Millers, when they acquired the firm of Woodin, also took over the African Mahogany Association Limited which was a Woodin subsidiary. The African and Eastern Trade Corporation, in its first year 1919–1920, bought a firm called the Standard Mahogany Company[7] of which nothing is known, and it also bought McNeill Scott and Company, well known as exporters of logs from Nigeria.[8] In the Ivory Coast the Corporation had the Société d'Exploitation des Acajous de Bassam, for which the Corporation built a little railway to carry logs to the sea at Half Assini.

The Niger group had the Société Forestière du Niari, which was associated with Lord Leverhulme's concession in French Equatorial Africa; and MacIver was active in the timber trade both before and after its acquisition by the Lever group.

In those days all felling was carried out with the axe. The African axeman used a five pound axe head, which was sent out from the United Kingdom without a shaft. He preferred not to use a shaped axe shaft, but a longer and more pliant shaft which he cut for himself from the forest. Many of the forest trees are provided with powerful buttresses at the base, up to fifteen feet high, which resemble the

[5] Thorpe, E. to Pedler, 24 July 1970.
[6] United Africa Company of Nigeria, *Link*, 1970, p. 5.
[7] Rankin, p. 95.
[8] Howarth to Pedler.

buttresses of the Eiffel Tower. These buttresses stand out from the main trunk, and render the bottom part of the tree unusable in the sawmill or the plywood mill. As a consequence, such trees were felled above the buttresses, and a platform was erected to enable the axemen to cut into the trunk at the appropriate height. As the tree gave its final groan and began to fall, they would all come scrambling down from their platform to get clear.[9]

There was no mechanical hauling machinery in those days, and the logs were drawn by manpower from the forest to the water-side. A large log, weighing several tons, might require the strength of as many as a hundred men. One can picture the long tug-of-war teams, pulling huge logs over rollers; little boys seizing a roller as the log passed and whizzing round to the front with it; and a jolly man seated on top of the log, drumming to encourage the rhythmic heaving of the others, who sing as they lug.

Ranching

Millers had a concern called 'African Ranches' in northern Nigeria,[10] and after Millers became part of the African and Eastern Trade Corporation a tannery was added. This, like so many of the Association's activities, may well have been stimulated by their desire to compete with the Lever group in every field, for, as mentioned in chapter 14, the Niger Company had a tannery. The Association's tannery, like that of its rival, made a heavy loss.[11] Could it have been that two tanneries were one too many? When Lord Leverhulme visited Jebba during his tour of Nigeria in 1925, the installation was still described as 'the tannery', but the notes of the tour record, 'they merely cure and clean the hides and do not tan them. The process is simply one of dipping and is accompanied by a certain amount of smell.'

[9] United Africa Company, *Statistical and Economic Review*, no. 10, September 1952.
[10] Hartje, H. G. and Watson, G., oral.
[11] Mars, J., in *Mining Commerce and Finance in Nigeria*, vol. 2 of Perham (ed.) *The Native Economies of Nigeria* (London: Faber, 1946).

23

Motors

Before the outbreak of the First World War in 1914 only very few motor vehicles had been imported into West Africa. The pioneer work of Cato in taking his Model T Ford across the Volta has already been noted in chapter 8. In Nigeria an early pioneer was the commander of the Southern Nigeria Regiment, Trenchard.[1] The motor bicycle afforded an improved method for patrolling the roads which he was building in the south-eastern part of the country. 'I brought out motor bicycles from England,' he wrote, 'and I remember putting my cook on one on the barrack square. He went round and round, gripping the handle bars, with his eyes starting out of his head, until the petrol ran out. We yelled at him all round every time he passed us to shut off the throttle. It was no good.'[2]

Four years of war delayed the development of motor transport, but when the fighting was over manufacturers turned their attention from military work to civilian needs, and the vast potential of Africa did not escape their notice.

Merchants and manufacturers

In the importation into Africa of motor vehicles the trader was very dependent on the manufacturer. The pattern of the trade required that the merchant should undertake, by agreement with the manufacturer, to provide certain services; to hold stocks, not only of capital units but of spare parts; to honour such guarantees as were offered by the maker to the customer; and to provide repair and service facilities. Most manufacturers made it a condition that their representative should handle no competing product. In return, the manufacturer would normally undertake not to supply his product to any other merchant (or customer) within the area to which the agreement related. Such agreements varied one from another, and

[1] Later Marshal of the Royal Air Force, the Viscount Trenchard, G.C.B., G.C.V.O., D.S.O.
[2] Trenchard, unpublished autobiographical notes, p. 57.

even the names were numerous and confusing: agencies, distributorships, dealerships, franchises, and concessions. The trade attracted vigorous competition between powerful merchant organizations backed by powerful manufacturers. In this competition the manufacturer had to move ahead of his rivals in technological progress, and the merchant had to win the customer's confidence in his service and spare parts organization.

The Congo Basin treaty system resulted in the admission of American and other foreign vehicles into Nigeria and the Gold Coast under the same terms as British vehicles. In the years between 1920 and 1930 the American vehicles, built for the rough roads and farm tracks of the Middle West, were more suitable for African conditions than the British vehicles, and also they were cheaper. Only America made the 'kit-car', which was the 'maid-of-all-work' for the coaster.

The African and Eastern Trade Corporation begins to deal in vehicles

In 1920 Millers[3] held the Ford franchise in Lagos, for which they provided 'an excellently equipped establishment' in Davies Street. For Millers to be first in the field was very much in keeping with their thrusting tradition. The African and Eastern Trade Corporation (of which by this time Millers had become a founder-member) formed a company named Nigerian Motors Limited with premises in Tinubu Street, Lagos, and this took over the Ford business from Millers. By 1925 it had branches in Kano, Jos, Ibadan, Aba, and Sapele. Nigerian Motors were also sole distributors of Albion trucks and represented Dunlop tyres. They held a franchise for the products of the General Electric Company (England) and engaged actively in wiring contracts.

In Freetown in 1920 the African and Eastern Trade Corporation appears to have been the only firm engaged in the motor trade. At first it handled several makes of cars and trucks, but by 1925[4] all had been given up save Dodge, and before 1929 that too had been given up in order that the Corporation might be in a position to distribute Chevrolet cars and trucks, products of the General Motors Corporation of America.

[3] MacMillan, A., *Red Book of West Africa* (London: Collingridge, 1920).
[4] Goddard, T. N., *The Handbook of Sierra Leone* (London: Grant Richards, 1925) p. 193.

One of the companies in the African and Eastern Trade Corporation group in Nigeria bore the name African Traders, and through this subsidiary the Corporation began, in 1927, to import from America General Motors' cars and trucks, and Buick cars. This arrangement appears to have been connected with the withdrawal by Ford of his famous Model T. The Ford factories which made that vehicle discontinued production for about a year while they re-tooled for the new Model A. The hiatus was unwelcome to Ford distributors, and the African and Eastern reacted as described; but it did the Corporation no good with Ford. That company was not disposed to employ a distributor who was not wholly devoted to its interests, and therefore it transferred its franchise in the British colonies to another firm.[5] The Corporation's connection with Ford survived only in the Spanish colonies. Under the names of its subsidiaries, Ambas Bay Trading Company[6] in Fernando Po, and Hatton and Cookson in Spanish Guinea, the Corporation continued to hold the Ford franchise.

Thus in Nigeria and in Sierra Leone about the same time contacts were made with General Motors.

In the Gold Coast the African and Eastern Trade Corporation appears to have left the motor vehicle trade to others in the early years; or perhaps other firms were quicker in securing the popular agencies, for in 1920 three firms were in this trade in Accra, none of which had any connection with the Corporation. About 1923, however, a motor business was opened under the name Swanzy Motor Transport. The main purpose was to operate trucks for bringing cocoa to the Corporation's buying stations. There were at that time no roads connecting Kumasi with Sekondi or with Accra. The function of the motor vehicles was therefore to concentrate the cocoa at points on the railway and particularly at Kumasi, which was served by feeder roads. The vehicles employed for this purpose by Swanzy Motor Transport were the Autocar and the Guy. The Autocar was an American product with a two-cylinder engine, and it carried a ton of cocoa. The Guy truck was made at Wolverhampton in England, and also carried one ton. In addition to this in-company service, Swanzy Motor Transport imported the Morris bull-nosed two-seater passenger car, and sold it to the public for less than £100.

The African and Eastern Trade Corporation no doubt hoped

---

[5] Dunnet, D. D. to Pedler, 1 July 1970 and 23 November 1970.
[6] McKendrick A. T. to Pedler, 16 October 1972 and 20 October 1972.

that, in providing the companies of their group with an in-company service for transporting cocoa, they would establish an advantage over their competitors. However, the shipping company, Elder Dempster, set up a competitive organization, Elders Road Transport. This was a typical example of the competitive relationship which existed between the Corporation and the shipping company at that time, which will be further noted in the next chapter. As so often happens when investment is made in the equipment of a new branch of technology, Swanzy Motor Transport paid the penalty of the pioneer and became encumbered with out-of-date material. Elders Road Transport introduced the Albion truck which carried two tons, and in 1926 Swanzy followed that example, ceasing to import Autocars and Guys.

By 1928 Elders Road Transport had greatly reduced its activity, and in that year Swanzy Motor Transport ceased to reserve its commercial vehicles for companies of the Corporation group, and offered sales and service to the public, not only of Albions but also of International lorries. The Studebaker car (imported in the name of Miller) and the Essex car were added to the range.[7]

Ships could not come alongside at the small harbour at Accra and therefore the crates containing cars and lorries (like all other cargo) were discharged from steamers anchored out at sea beyond the breakers. The crates were loaded on to two surf boats, lashed alongside one another, the crates being lowered by the ship's derricks and placed at right angles upon the two surf boats. This was no easy business with a heavy sea running, and it was not uncommon for a crated vehicle to go to the bottom. The surf boats were paddled away from the steamer to the little harbour jetty, where the cases were lifted by a crane and loaded on flat railway trucks which were shunted along the sea front to a site opposite the Korle Bu lagoon. Here the cases were lifted by a mobile railway crane on to the sand, and there the initial stage of assembly had to be undertaken. With lorries, front and rear axles, wheels, and steering gear, were unpacked and mounted, and with passenger vehicles it was just a question of fitting the wheels. All the work at the beach had to be carried out under a shower of surf spray and in the stink of fish. Then the units were towed to the motor department for the work to be completed. This was done in Swanzy's transport shed on the sea front to the west of the Accra lighthouse. Salt spray was constantly blown into the building, promoting rust and corrosion.[8]

[7] Roberts, W. W. to Pedler via Denys Hall, 23 September 1970.   [8] ibid.

The Niger Company enters the trade

The Niger Company was in no hurry to invest in the trade in motor vehicles. The reasons for hesitation are not difficult to divine. This trade was hungry for capital. Specialized premises, expensive tooling, stocks of spare parts, demanded investment in both fixed and working capital, which in relation to turnover was higher than anything of which the old trading companies had experience. The moral commitment to provide service for customers imposed formidable problems of recruiting, training, and accommodating technical staff; staff of a kind that was not available in Africa at all. Clearly it was not a venture to be entered light-heartedly; and the Niger Company, following its acquisition by Lever Brothers, was for some years not encouraged to commit more capital.

In 1925, however, Lord Leverhulme personally visited Nigeria and here he made the acquaintance of George Weekes. Before the war of 1914–1918 George Weekes was in the service of the Qua Iboe mission as a handicraft instructor. In the war he served in the Royal Navy, and when it was over he returned to the Aba area, bringing with him a cinematograph outfit and a lorry. He went from village to village showing his moving pictures in court houses or in the open air. After the show the audience had need for conveyance back to their villages, which he provided, using the lorry which carried him and his apparatus. He realized that the transport opportunities were more attractive than the cinema, and set up a passenger business. He employed European drivers and paid them the same as a European assistant earned from the trading companies. The business was successful, and when Lord Leverhulme visited the country Weekes was engaged to provide road vehicles for him and his staff. George Weekes personally drove Lord Leverhulme, and as a result of this association Lord Leverhulme bought Weekes Transport, retaining Weekes as general manager.[9] Thus the Niger group found itself with a transport business, and this may well have influenced it in setting up West African Motors Limited as a subsidiary company in 1926. It secured concessions for Brockway trucks (American), Fiat and Austin cars, Triumph motor cycles, Lucas/C.A.V./Girling electrical equipment, and Goodyear tyres. In 1929 it also represented Morris.

[9] Dunnet, D. D., as 5 above.

Petroleum

It may not be generally appreciated that there had been considerable imports into Africa of a petroleum product from America for a long time before the first internal combustion engine reached the shores of Africa. The product was kerosene, and it became important in the 1860s as a fuel for lamps.[10] It was imported in tins containing four American gallons, and these tins were packed in pairs in wooden boxes. This form of packing was so valuable that African retailers would frequently deal in the fluid kerosene without taking any margin, in order to earn profit by the sale of the tins and the wooden box. The tins were used to supplement the home-grown calabashes as water pots, and they became the usual receptacle for taking palm oil and groundnut oil to the markets when those products were sold locally for edible purposes. When the tin had served its time as a container, and had developed a leak, it was beaten out flat and used as a roofing tile.

The internal combustion engines made it necessary to import petrol, and at first this product came in exactly the same kind of packages as the kerosene. There were no facilities for handling petrol in bulk, and the day of the 44-gallon drum had not yet dawned.

The African and Eastern Trade Corporation held the agency for the Socony Vacuum Oil Company (which changed its name to Mobil many years later) in Nigeria, Gold Coast, and Sierra Leone (though not elsewhere), and the Niger Company was agent for Shell throughout the whole of West Africa, British, French, Belgian, and Spanish. Socony Vacuum had been very successful in West Africa and held more than half of the market. Shell, Atlantic, and Texaco shared the balance, Atlantic being represented by Patterson Zochonis in most places, and Texaco by the Compagnie française de l'Afrique occidentale.

Under the agency agreement the packages became the responsibility of the agent when they crossed the high tide mark. In those rare ports which provided a deep-water quay, delivery to quay was deemed to be 'crossing the high water mark', but at many places on the African coast the packages were landed from surf-boats on the beaches.

[10] Hancock, Sir Keith, *Survey of British Commonwealth Affairs* (Oxford: Clarendon Press, 1942) vol. II part 2, p. 159.

24

Relations with the Shipping Conference

Navigation in West Africa differed from that in most other parts of the world. The ports of call were numerous. Many of them were open roadsteads, with heavy surf through which produce and merchandise had to be conveyed from shore to steamer and vice versa in large wooden boats manned (usually) by a dozen paddlers and a coxswain, who negotiated the perilous surf with marvellous skill.

Other ports were situated far up rivers. These rivers had many sharp turns, and sometimes a steamer would fail to make the turn and ram the bank. A traveller who underwent such an experience wrote:

> With a crash of splintering timber, the iron bows ploughed right into forest. The mangroves went down before them, groaning and creaking in a heap of sap-filled fragments; crawling roots rose up and rasped the rusty sides; while, resistlessly forging ahead, the steamer buried perhaps thirty feet of her length in the quagmire, for she was built light-draughted and with a cutaway forefoot. Then the whirl of the reversed propeller made itself felt, and the mud, when the wash seethed among it, made one gasp for breath. Nor was this the worst. Red mangrove flies, whose bite leaves a wound which often remains unhealed for days, venomous spiders, and legions of ants, shaken from the branches ripped off by shroud and stay, which strewed the deck, commenced to stir themselves in search of prey.[1]

It must have been very uncomfortable and, for the uninitiated, rather alarming. Yet in fact, ramming a mangrove swamp was comparatively unalarming to the seamen in charge of the ships, who knew well the greater perils of the bars which formed where these

[1] Bindloss, H., *In the Niger Country* (London: Blackwood, 1898) p. 140.

rivers met the sea, the treacherous movements of the sand-banks in the estuaries, and the dangers of mists and mirages on a coast where there were hardly any aids to navigation.

Because of these dangers, added to West Africa's reputation as the white man's grave, the area was unpopular with tramp steamers, whose owners often refused to accept charters to West Africa, and if they did accept, the rates were high. This circumstance alone would have provided valuable protection for liner companies which kept their ships regularly on the route; and those liner companies found even more protection in owning the wooden boats at the surf port, and employing the pilots on the bars and estuaries. Without the use of facilities which were reserved by the liner companies for their own ships, it was impossible in many of these ports for tramp steamers to discharge or receive cargo.

Notwithstanding these rigorous conditions, the regular steamer services in the latter part of the nineteenth century and in the early part of the twentieth century enjoyed a general reputation for efficiency. They were provided by the British lines, welded together and managed by the firm of Elder Dempster; by the Woermann line of Germany; and by the Holland West Africa Line. These lines co-operated with each other in the West African Shipping Conference, which was formed in 1895. The unsuccessful challenge to that conference by the African Association in 1896 (chapter 10) followed immediately. The command of the sea remained with the conference. As already explained, if the merchant houses wished to take advantage of the deferred rebates offered by the conference, they had to pledge themselves to an agreement which it was impossible for them to discontinue without incurring very severe financial penalties in the loss of accumulated rebates. They would forfeit the deferred rebates offered if they acquired a ship either by purchase or charter. As may be imagined, this system produced an uneasy relationship between the merchant houses (particularly the larger ones) and the conference. The larger merchant firms particularly resented the policy adopted by the conference, of according exactly the same rate of rebate to all shippers, however large or small. It seemed to be contrary to the normal practice in commerce, under which the largest customers secure the most favourable terms. The conference companies defended their policy by asserting that they had a responsibility to ensure fair competition. The merchant companies found it odd that the shipping companies, which had organized themselves as a tight ring which prevented anyone else from placing a ship on the route, should set themselves up as the guardians of free and fair competition.

The conference system was generally adopted throughout the world in the liner shipping trade, and in 1906 the British government appointed a Royal Commission on shipping rings. The West African merchant companies, large and small, laid their complaints before the commission. The three merchant companies which had recently set up the Bank of Nigeria (chapter 13) declared in evidence that they had felt obliged to do this, because the shipping companies controlled the Bank of British West Africa, and manipulated its financial services to the disadvantage of any trading houses which dared to dispute the wishes of the conference. In spite of the vigour with which the merchants urged their case, the West African Shipping Conference emerged from this inquiry unscathed.[2]

Sir Alfred Jones, chairman of Elder Dempster until his death in 1909, managed these arrangements on behalf of the conference with great skill. He cultivated the friendship of the merchants, made himself popular with the smaller houses by convincing them that they were as dear to his heart as their larger competitors, and to all he rendered service with an efficiency which they were forced to admit and to esteem, even if they chafed at what it cost. Sir Alfred tolerated a little chartering by the Niger Company each year at the height of the produce season, and regularized this by an agreement in 1908 (chapter 12). There was a minor challenge to the conference by W. B. MacIver shortly before that company was acquired by Lever Brothers, which Sir Alfred Jones overcame by negotiation.[3]

On the death of Sir Alfred Jones in 1909 the four companies which were in the Nigerian pool agreement—the African Association, the Niger Company, Miller Brothers (of Liverpool) Limited, and the Company of African Merchants—tried to form a consortium for the purpose of buying the Elder Dempster steamers which were engaged in the African trade. However, they were unsuccessful. The whole of the Elder Dempster shipping interests were acquired by Lord Pirrie (chairman of Harland and Wolff, shipbuilders) and Sir Owen Philipps (chairman of the Royal Mail Shipping group, later Lord Kylsant). They continued the conference system in the West African trade and as a gesture of goodwill

[2] McPhee, A., *Economic Revolution in British West Africa* (London: Routledge, 1926) pp. 95–8.

[3] Davies, P. N., *The Trade Makers* (London: Allen and Unwin, 1973) pp. 131, 136.

towards the merchants they discontinued certain trading activities in which Sir Alfred Jones had engaged[4] (*see* chapter 10). Despite this gesture of goodwill, John Holt challenged the conference by buying two ships and Millers were beginning to charter[5] when in 1914 War broke out. Lever Brothers, as noted in chapter 14, were prevented by the conference from chartering an oil tanker.

On the outbreak of the War the conference immediately ceased to exist because the Germans were eliminated and Elder Dempster were unable to maintain the deferred rebate system because they could not provide enough ships to carry the trade. Therefore Lever Brothers' intervention as shipowners during the War (chapter 14) under the name of Bromport Steamship Company did not involve a fierce contest with the established shipping line. After the end of the War in 1918 Lever Brothers continued to run their ships to Africa, and when in 1920 they acquired the Niger Company these ships became associated with the Niger group. Both the Niger group and the African and Eastern Trade Corporation chartered ships at that time to cover part of their requirements. This prompted Sir Owen Philipps, chairman of Elder Dempster, to state in a speech in 1922 that if the merchants intended to carry their own cargoes, the steamship owners would have to become merchants. The close connection which Sir Owen had then recently established with the merchant house of G. B. Ollivant (*see* chapter 7) added point to this threat.

In 1924 Sir Owen Philipps (or Lord Kylsant as he was now) entered into agreement with the Dutch and German shipping lines to re-activate the conference, which now adopted the name, 'West African Lines Shipping Conference'. This had the curious sequel that the Niger Company ceased to own ships while the African and Eastern Trade Corporation began to own ships. Lever Brothers were still in a fairly tight position financially, largely as a result of their purchase of the Niger Company, and they did not want to put more capital into West African activities. When Lord Kylsant offered to buy their ships and to allow them a preferential rate with the conference, they readily agreed. The African and Eastern Trade Corporation, on the other hand, decided to own ships and to charter others as required. It was influenced in that direction by the firm of Henry Tyrer and Company, which had been managing agents for

---

[4] Parliamentary Committee, *Edible and oil-producing nuts and seeds* (London: H.M.S.O., 1915) Q 5992.

[5] As note 2 above.

Lever Brothers' Bromport Steamship Company. When that business ceased, Tyrer offered his services to the African and Eastern, and became the managing agent of the Corporation's ships. The Corporation, at the same time, was successful in making an agreement with the conference as to the terms on which it might use the conference lines. Thus the conference accorded to the two largest merchant companies the principle that their large size entitled them to special treatment.

The Niger group, however, did not for long remain content. In 1928 it acquired an ocean-going steamer and called it the *Ars*. This may seem a curious name for a ship, but it was symbolic and was certainly intended to be so. The motto of the Niger Company was '*Ars Jus Pax*', and in selecting a name which formed the first word in a series of three, the company gave an indication of its further intentions; it may also have been symbolic, that *Pax* would not come until the third of the series was reached.

25

Competition and Combination

The course of trade in West Africa, throughout the period with which this book is concerned, oscillated between wild competition and ambitious combination.[1] It would be inappropriate in a book, the purpose of which is to trace the story of certain companies, to attempt any general treatment of that oscillating process: but it may be useful to gather together in one chapter information as to how these companies were affected by the process, or contributed to it. Some of the information will be new to the reader, but part of it will necessarily be a recapitulation of details which have been spread over earlier chapters.

This chapter will not, however, be concerned with the kind of combination which consists of amalgamations and take-overs, because that has been the theme of several chapters already. This chapter is concerned rather with agreements between firms which retain their independence; agreements therefore of a more or less temporary character, which result in arrangements which are described by various names, such as cartels, pools, rings, oligopolies, and oligopsonies. All these names seem to have acquired a pejorative connotation in the latest age, although they may have sounded sweeter to the ears of earlier generations. Perhaps the name most commonly now employed to describe agreements between firms is 'monopoly'; but this is an inexact and, indeed, improper use of that word, which ought to be reserved for situations in which there is only a single seller; and no agreement which was ever made between firms in West Africa produced such a situation.

Competition was maintained by a great many firms, and whatever steps they may have taken to modify the competition between themselves by making agreements from time to time, these were constantly upset by the arrival of new firms which were not parties to them. The first appearance of many such newcomers has been described in these pages; but besides those firms which have been

[1] For an authoritative treatment of the subject *see* Hancock, Sir Keith, *Survey of British Commonwealth Affairs* (Oxford: Clarendon Press, 1942) vol. II part 2.

identified as predecessors of the United Africa Company, there were many others, some of which have survived, while others have disappeared. The most powerful competitor, taking West Africa as a whole, towards the end of the period, was the Compagnie française de l'Afrique occidentale. A second French company was established in many places, the Societé commerciale de l'Ouest Africain. In Senegal and the Gambia there were also several French firms with headquarters in Bordeaux, such as Maurel et Prom, Maurel Frères and Vézia Frères. A Dane named V. Q. Petersen, who had made his reputation and acquired his experience as the manager of the Palmine Company in the Gambia, had set up his own company with headquarters in Dakar, and had quickly secured a substantial share of the trade in that area. Other new trading organizations had been established and grown at an impressive rate, among which mention may be made of Saul Raccah in Kano and Sarkis Madi in the Gambia. John Holt, after leaving the African Association, had built up his family firm to a position of great strength. The other leading British-based company was Paterson Zochonis of Manchester. Gaiser of Germany and the Deutsche Kolonialgesellschaft had resumed activity after the war. The Union Trading Company of Basel, a Swiss company, was in some measure the successor to the Basel Mission (*see* chapter 21). In the Congo there were trading organizations backed by the Société Générale de Belgique and by the Bank of Brussels. There was not at that time much American competition in trading, though the firm of Ambrosini, established in Kano, had its headquarters in the United States. With all these competitors and many more, the competition was hot.

The spirit of intense competition was attributable not only to the number of firms engaging in the trade, but to the sort of people whom they employed. The competition for produce was terrific, insane, and inexplicable in rational terms. The blame lay partly on company head offices. While discountenancing the irregularities, they regarded a good trader as one who could buy produce, and the only way to buy produce where competition existed was by paying 'over the bar', that is to say, over the authorized limit, or by giving advances which were likely to result in bad debts. Many a young man went wrong over produce, gambling on a rise when a fall took place. The conscientious, neurotic, or anxious ones suffered badly under these conditions. The more robust ones regarded it as a grand game, and it was these who made the pace; a tiny community of youngish men, in the forest or the savannah, out of reach of supervision save on the occasion of a brief monthly check, accustomed to meet together each Sunday afternoon for groundnut soup or palm-oil chop, and all engaged in the fun of beggar-my-neighbour. The gentlemen who wore top hats and pin-striped trousers in the offices in Europe acquired a habit of describing the competitive tricks of these front line operators as 'abuses'; and from time to time agreements were made to put an end to 'abuses'; but the so-called abuses were the young men's articles of gamesmanship. The agreements notoriously failed to work.

Curiously enough, the earliest example of a major 'agreement' which these chapters have recorded was not between European firms, but between the African Association and the African middle-men of the Niger delta. Its purpose was to compel Alexander Miller Brother and Company to withdraw from its inland stores, and this was achieved by means of a boycott (chapters 8 and 10). The government was powerless to intervene even had it wished to do so; it was of course a very new government, hardly more than an embryo, for these events took place in 1893.

In 1899, relations between the African Association and George Miller had improved, and a closer understanding was felt by both parties to be desirable. The Royal Niger Company's charter was about to be withdrawn. That event, it was apparent, would have an important influence on the relations between the Niger Company, the African Association, and Alexander Miller Brother and Company. The Miller Company was of course a founder-shareholder of the Niger Company, and Alexander Miller was a managing director of that company; so relations between those two organizations were at all times close. On the other hand, bitter hostility had existed between the Niger Company and the Association; but it had ceased in 1893 when the Association sold its posts on the Niger to the Royal Niger Company in exchange for shares. Since that transaction, there had been a community of interest between the former rivals. What was to happen when the charter lapsed? Would the Niger Company, having become a simple trading concern, invade the territories where its two friends enjoyed the ascendancy? Would its two friends, with or without such provocation, go north into country where the Niger Company had been able to maintain a practical monopoly of trade, but which in future might be open to all on equal terms?

Sir George Goldie, George Miller, and Stanley Rogerson who was the chairman of the Association, entered into discussions with a view to averting such competition. From these discussions there emerged an agreement. It included not only the three large firms but also the Company of African Merchants, a small concern in which Lever had recently acquired a minority interest (chapter 14). Just why the big three included this small firm is not known. There were several other small firms in the area, but only this one became a party to the agreement; it may well be that Lever's shareholding was the reason. The big three may have had the foresight to recognize Lever as a potential danger. If they took this action with a view to neutralizing Lever's first step into West Africa, they had every reason to be content with what they did, for Lever sold his shares and it was some years before he was seen in those parts again.

The Niger Company undertook not to trespass on the territories of the other parties, which lay on or near the seaboard, and the other parties gave a reciprocal pledge with reference to the markets which had hitherto belonged to the Niger Company. All four companies agreed to pool profits, which were to be divided in specified proportions. Each company was otherwise to remain independent, managing its own affairs. It was recognized, however, that the four would constantly have to meet and confer on questions of common interest, and a committee was set up, called the Committee of Control, of which Lord Scarborough (*see* chapter 13) was appointed president. The agreement was to come into force on 1 January 1900, and remained in force for ten years.

The name 'Committee of Control' was perhaps ill-chosen. At any rate, it disturbed Sir Ralph Moor, High Commissioner of the Protectorate of Southern Nigeria,[2] who seems to have entertained apprehensions that the committee might intend to interfere with the government. Moor suggested to Mr. Joseph Chamberlain, the Secretary of State for the Colonies, that he would be well advised to find out what was going on. Chamberlain had occupied his position for some years and had already acquired the reputation for which he is so deservedly remembered. He had revolutionized the attitude of the British government towards the colonies. In his speeches the idea was introduced to the British public that they had some responsibility for developing the colonies. Development was now official policy. Money was made available for 'infrastructure'—railways and

---

[2] From 1891 to 1899 British authority in the Delta region was represented by the Commissioner and Consul-General for the Oil Rivers and Niger Coast protectorate, who also held the office of consul for Fernando Po. In 1900 the Protectorate of Southern Nigeria was proclaimed, with a High Commissioner.

roads—in the form of grants or loans. Research was put in hand in agricultural and medical institutes. He was certainly not a person to be trifled with.

Chamberlain invited the Committee of Control to send a deputation to Downing Street to confer with him. The delegates found Moor in attendance on Chamberlain, who opened the proceedings with an appeal for frankness. He reminded them that he had himself been a business man. He alluded to his deep interest in the welfare of Africa. The representatives of the Committee of Control were able to satisfy the minister that they were not engaged in any conspiracy to attain objects incompatible with the well-being and prosperity of the Protectorate. Chamberlain expressed himself as reassured and thanked the deputation.[3]

The machinery for operating the pool was primarily an accounting arrangement between the head offices of the contracting parties. At agreed dates, they declared their profits to each other; and then those companies whose share of total profit was higher than their 'agreed' percentage, made an appropriate payment to those companies whose profit lagged behind their 'agreed' share. But the intention of the pool was, that competition between the contracting parties should be moderated; and this could only be achieved by giving instructions to agents in Africa, and taking disciplinary measures to enforce the observance of those instructions. Therefore it became normal for the head offices to instruct their local agents, in places where two or more of the agreed firms were established, to meet from time to time and contrive arrangements with a view to 'modifying competition'. The local agents then encountered the difficulty, that usually there were other firms in the locality whose head offices had not instructed them to co-operate, and who were only too eager to buy additional tonnage by offering just a little more than any price established by the agreed firms. So in each area, there were discussions with a view to persuading other companies to co-operate on a purely local basis. Sometimes these overtures met with some success, but more often they did not. However, there emerged a situation in which local arrangements were constantly being made, and very often abandoned. These local arrangements sometimes took the form of agreeing on physical shares of produce; on the accounting date an 'over-bought' firm transferred actual produce to an 'under-bought' firm, at the 'agreed' price. They also often took the form of mutual undertakings by the firms to suppress 'abuses',

[3] Rankin, p. 85.

by which generally they meant, dodges for giving inducements to middlemen which breached the spirit of the agreement by adding some additional consideration to the 'agreed' price.[4]

The original pool had reference only to Nigeria but, since it brought the African Association and the Glasgow house of the Miller brothers close together, its influence naturally extended to the latter's London house also. The co-operation between Millers and the Association was a factor in the foundation of the Ashanti Obuasi Trading Company. Obuasi in the Gold Coast was the centre of a large area, in which the Ashanti Goldfields Corporation Limited, formed in 1897, enjoyed an exclusive concession both for mining and for trade. Experience convinced the directors of Ashanti Goldfields Corporation that the two activities could not be carried on to the best advantage by a single concern.

Alexander Miller was asked if he would take over the trading side of the Corporation. The Ashanti Obuasi Trading Company Limited was incorporated in 1903. The subscribers were Millers Limited, the African Association, and F. and A. Swanzy. An allotment was made to the Ashanti Goldfields Corporation in consideration of the ceded trading rights.

A Gold Coast pool was a logical sequel to the Nigerian pool. It followed in 1905. The parties to it were the African Association, Millers Limited, and F. and A. Swanzy. It was an agreement which, like the Nigerian pool, involved placing profits in a common fund from which they were re-distributed in predetermined percentages. Thus, no party to the agreement could derive advantage from competitive measures directed against other parties to the agreement.

When the Nigerian pool expired in 1909 it was re-negotiated, and the four partners agreed to continue on the same basis for a further period of twenty years. This was generally referred to in trading circles as the 'second pool'. On the renewal of the pool some modifications were made with a view to avoiding controversies. The principle that each company should conduct its affairs as it thought fit was, however, preserved; though it was precisely that clause which had caused trouble in the past. There was only one effective remedy, and that was amalgamation. A draft agreement was printed in 1915. It provided for a merger of the African Association, Miller Brothers (of Liverpool), the Company of African Merchants, and the Niger Company; but the project fell through.

The failure of the negotiations did not improve relations between

---

[4] Hartje, H. G. and Crookenden, H. C., oral.

the Niger Company and its partners in the pool. The African Association and Miller Brothers were on the best of terms. In 1917 Alexander Miller resigned his directorship of the Niger Company. Age rather than the events related here seems to have induced him to take that decision. He was nearly 80. However, his departure removed a link which had connected the Millers with the Niger Company and its predecessors for thirty-eight years.

In that year the African Association and Miller Brothers felt that the pool situation had become intolerable. In the Niger Company's territory competition was still less intense than in that of the others, who therefore expected from the Niger Company a correspondingly large contribution to the pool, but, instead of that happening, they found themselves called upon at every settlement to hand over a considerable sum to the Niger Company. The invasion of the Niger Company's territory by some Lagos firms brought things to a head. The African Association and Miller Brothers believed they could deal with such competitors more effectively than the Niger Company and asked to be allowed to lend a hand. Their offer was rejected. The Niger Company insisted on the strict observance of the partition of territory established by the agreement. Though little more than a third of the period for which the agreement had been renewed had expired, the African Association and Miller Brothers decided to break with their partner. The break was sudden and violent. The Association and Miller each opened stations at places situated deep in the Niger Company's territory, such as Zaria and Kano. The Niger Company regarded their action as an illegal trespass and sought an injunction. The court, however, refused to grant it. The three parties then formally declared the agreement at an end.

Britain had already been at war with Germany for three years. West African produce was essential in war-time not only for feeding the army and the civilian population but also for the manufacture of munitions. Yet the European staffs of the trading companies were much reduced, both in Britain and in Africa. In 1914 many men had simply left their appointments to join the army as volunteers. At a later stage of the war conscription was applied to the staffs in Britain and more men had to go. Some firms were unable to carry on with their depleted staffs. However, the firms which survived the first shock discovered that in the war economy (high prices and assured market) profits were easy to make; though the cream was skimmed off by Excess Profits Duty. These circumstances tended to restrain competition and promoted trade agreements the purpose of which was to regulate the purchase and division of produce. Other influences, besides the staff shortages and the desire to co-operate in support of Britain's war effort induced the conclusion of agreements between firms in these days of war. There was a common interest in dealing with the assets of enemy companies, to which reference has been made. When war broke out Kano was just settling down from the excitements of the scramble for position which characterized the first two years of the groundnut trade. The Niger Company had bought nuts at prices which could not be recovered in the international trade, in order to make good its position. The other firms had been obliged to follow the price up, or rest content with small shares. Now that the shares had been established and that, for the time being, they were recognized as reflecting the comparative strength of the antagonists, it was time for every firm to rest on its share and make profits by keeping the local price in line with the international market price. The Niger Company worked out a 'schedule' in which an appropriate sum was allowed for every item of cost between the purchase of nuts on a weigh-scale in Kano and the delivery of the nuts to the customer in a European port; and it invited its partners in the agreement to regulate the price which they paid in accordance with the schedule. (This was very similar to the system which the government marketing boards in later years established for their licensed buying agents.)

Groundnuts were also of importance in the Gambia. The trade had been almost entirely in French hands, but for reasons which have already been explained, early in the war it passed almost entirely into British hands. The companies engaged were in several cases the same as those which had concluded the agreement at Kano, and it was therefore natural for them to extend that agreement to Gambia.

In Sierra Leone also there were special reasons why the firms welcomed an agreement to cover the trades in palm oil and palm kernels at this time. Lever Brothers, by their purchase of Peter Ratcliffe in 1912, had signified their interest. The established firms were very pleased to make an agreement assuring a share of ten per cent to Lever Brothers, but limiting them to that figure. It suited everybody; Levers secured ten per cent without having to fight for it, and the established firms kept ninety per cent between them, which was more than they would have dared to hope if Levers had attacked with their strength.

The groundnut pool in the Gambia broke down owing to the

intervention of the Maypole Dairy Company through its subsidiary Palmine (*see* chapter 15). The groundnut pool at Kano came to an end in 1918 owing to the intervention of Jurgens (chapter 15) and competition was unrestrained until 1923, when an agreement was operated, but without the participation of Jurgens. This arrangement was short-lived, but in 1927 ten firms began again to operate an agreement. This consortium included the Niger Company, the African and Eastern Trade Corporation, Ollivant, and three other British firms, two Germans and two Swiss, but as before the Dutch retained their independence and the two French companies refused to join.[5]

Another agreement in which a number of large firms, including both the Niger group and the African and Eastern Trade Corporation, participated for a number of years following the war of 1914–1918 and prior to 1929, was the All-Africa Agreement, which was colloquially described in trading circles as A.A.A. Its members seem to have been mainly concerned with the trade in palm oil and palm kernels, but they also discussed matters related to the sale of imported goods. Indeed, in those days when straight barter was carried on in some areas, while even in places where cash was used traders bringing in produce for sale would expect to return to their homes with loads of imported goods, it was hardly possible to discuss the terms of purchase of produce without discussing the terms of supply of the merchandise which was the counterpart of the produce.

The gentlemen at the head offices were very anxious to suppress 'abuses'. They exhorted one another not to permit their local managers to supply free transport for produce, nor free delivery for merchandise. They wished to abolish 'touting' for produce, and the practice of setting up scales by the roadside. They were very much opposed to the custom of giving 'tops and dashes', which were presents to the seller after he had received the price agreed. In making stock declarations, it was said, no produce should be declared as stock which was not actually in the firm's premises. In general they wanted to establish the principle that produce should be bought at a certain price, without any artful extras which would escape the control of head offices. Some of them even wished to suppress the use of credit in the sale of merchandise, but this was generally held to be impossible.

The discriminating reader may have difficulty in accepting all the practices in the list as 'abuses'. While it is obviously bad practice to

[5] Hancock, op. cit. p. 215.

declare stocks which do not exist, it is not so obviously bad practice to provide free transport. Indeed, it might be regarded as a legitimate method of competition: while going to meet the producer on the roadside might, in another day and age, have been praised as healthy propaganda, or (by those who disapprove of middlemen) as 'getting nearer to the producer'. However, readers will have no difficulty in recognizing all these practices as dodges for evading a price-fixing agreement; ways of offering additional inducements while keeping within the strict letter of the law.

In 1927 they really did succeed, at any rate, in some areas, in stopping the old trade custom of giving 'dashes'. The evidence for this is found in the report of a government commission which was set up to investigate the causes of the 'women's riots' which took place in Aba and the adjacent area in 1929. The commission found that the main cause was the taxation policy of the government, but it also listed a number of minor, subsidiary causes; and among these was the fact that the trading firms had stopped paying 'dashes'.[6]

Within the general scope of the A.A.A., local agreements were made in some places. Possibly the most effective of these was in Cameroon. It was supported by the Niger group (trading as Richard and William King), by the African Association (trading under three different names), and by five other firms. For details of that agreement, the reader may refer back to chapter 11.

The arrangement between the Niger group and the African and Eastern Trade Corporation for dealing in cocoa (chapters 14 and 20) was intended to co-ordinate the actions of the two firms on the terminal markets in London, New York, and Hamburg. Their basic problem was, of course, that as merchants they were obliged to accumulate a very large stock of cocoa during the annual marketing season, whereas the effective demand from the chocolate manufacturers was spread more or less evenly over the twelve months of the year. The arrangement never achieved any success and was abandoned after four years.

The pros and cons of inter-company agreements have been much debated both in Africa and in Europe. Their basic purpose was to increase the profits of the participants: but commerce is not a zero sum game[7] in which anything won is subtracted from a pre-existing value. Commerce, by placing the right things in the right places at

---

[6] Commission of Enquiry into the Aba riots, *Report* (Lagos: Government printer, 1930) p. 93 and annex I paras. 211, 220, 240–52.

[7] Nwankwo, G. O. in *West Africa*, 14 July 1972.

the right times, creates value which would otherwise not exist. Such created value is normally divisible between the two parties to a transaction, and the merchant's profit is part of it. Competition between merchants has the effect of reducing the merchants' share of the value added. Theoretically therefore, an agreement between firms in restraint of competition would have the effect of increasing the merchants' share of the value added. This must be to the detriment of the other parties to trading transactions, that is, to the suppliers of produce and to the purchasers of merchandise, *unless* the agreement between the firms also has the effect of increasing the total value added so that both parties to the transaction may benefit absolutely. This would be the case, for instance, when trading firms, acting in agreement, took defensive action against other trades which were organized in cartels. If the suppliers of important staple merchandise entered into rings or cartels, the ability of the main merchant companies to join together and fight the cartel in the interests of lower prices might be of advantage to the African consumer. This was the main basis of the merchants' hostility towards the shipping conference. If it was in the public interest for the shipping companies to co-ordinate their activities, surely it was no less in the public interest for the trading companies to take parallel action with a view to securing cheaper freights.

The firms which formed the pools and agreements were not trading with primary producers. It must have been very unusual for a farmer, or for a gatherer of forest fruit, to present his own produce for sale at one of the firms' establishments. The trade was done with middlemen, and these were professional traders of experience and resourcefulness, no less capable than the expatriate traders of combined action.

In Africa the trading companies had come under much criticism, mainly from government officers after the establishment of the colonial administration, on account of alleged trickery and dishonesty in their trading methods. Trickery was of course a feature of unregulated competition, and in trying to suppress 'abuses' the members of the A.A.A. endeavoured to suppress dishonest practices. Trading men with memories are still prepared to maintain that the agreements played their role in establishing a better trading climate.

No agreement between firms eliminates all competition, nor is designed to do so. The intention is that competition shall continue within the rules laid down. It creates the condition which economists call 'imperfect competition', though commercial men may take a different view of perfection. It is obvious, however, that firms acting in agreement cannot regulate prices unless they succeed in keeping out non-agreed competitors; and that the only method by which they can discourage non-agreed competitors is by the use of the price mechanism. That is to say, the agreed firms must either keep prices generally at a level which renders the trade unattractive to other firms, or they must take specific action to undercut competitors who defy them. There seems every reason to suppose that this represented the policy of the Nigerian pool in the decade 1900 to 1910, and that it met with considerable success in northern Nigeria. In the Delta it was less successful because there were many firms outside the agreement, and in Lagos it was irrelevant because many newcomers established their businesses in that developing city. However, even in the north there was the London and Kano Trading Company, which was not prevented by the agreed firms from opening in 1905 and maintaining its position. The policy of the firms in agreement, as has been described, broke down after 1911 when many new competitors invaded the north of Nigeria.

The usual result of agreements which were designed to regulate prices was, to 'hold an umbrella' over some enterprising competitor who saw his opportunity in trading at prices just slightly more favourable to the supplier of produce, or to the purchaser of merchandise. This is exactly what Birtwhistle, in his letter to Jurgens mentioned in chapter 15, said he intended to do. It was a major factor in facilitating the rapid growth of the businesses of Saul Raccah and of Sarkis Madi, in the groundnut trade in Kano and Bathurst respectively.

26

G. and A. Baker

Once upon a time there was a little boy named George Baker and he lived in a large house at Guildford. He had a nasty stepmother, so at the age of twelve he ran away, with a shilling in his pocket. When night fell he slept in a conservatory belonging to a nursery gardener. The owner, William George Middleton, found him there and kept him as an apprentice gardener. It was 1834. George Baker studied landscape architecture and secured employment at the Kew Botanical Gardens, and later in the Office of Works. He never spent his shilling, and it hung from his watch-chain until the day he died.

About 1848 he was sent by the Office of Works to lay out new embassy gardens in Constantinople. This work occupied him until 1853, when he was instructed to extend the gardens by taking in an ancient Turkish cemetery. With five years of experience, Baker adopted a different view from the ambassador as to the canons of diplomatic behaviour in a Moslem country, and rather than desecrate the holy ground he resigned. In fact, the cemetery remained inviolate. Baker married and secured employment in improving the gardens of the Sultan's palace. This enabled him to enjoy a special position at the Ottoman court, and he began to import Irish linen for the ladies of the harem. This was the beginning of Bakers as a trading firm. It was in 1854, and the Crimean War had broken out. Baker became a local supplier to the British army in Constantinople. He must have done well, for he was able to send five sons and two daughters to be educated in England. Louisa, the eldest child, secured notoriety by sending a Valentine to the Pope. The Pope was enchanted and sent his blessing, but Louisa's name appeared in the papers and the headmistress was not amused.

In 1869 the Empress Eugénie of France passed through Constantinople on the way to the opening of the Suez Canal. The Sultan made a palace available for her, and 10,000 tulip bulbs were imported from Holland to decorate the palace gardens. It is believed that Baker handled this business.

Meanwhile, in 1867, the Sultan had visited England and had

ordered a cruiser. This was designed by a naval architect named Charles Reed Edwards. Edwards went to Turkey to teach at the naval college, and continued to design ironclads. He married Louisa, the lady of the Valentine, in 1872. He formed with George Baker the partnership of Baker and Edwards, and, in addition to continuing the general trade which Baker had established, the firm became a supplier to the Turkish naval and mercantile marines. The firm began to export Turkish carpets to England. George Baker had five sons. Two of the boys formed companies of their own in London, one under the name of G. P. and J. Baker Limited, and the other under the name of the Oriental Carpet Manufacturers Limited. These companies handled the London end of the produce and carpets exported by Bakers of Constantinople. Son Henry ran a flour mill on the Golden Horn, while son Arthur remained with his father in the main business.

In 1890 George Baker and Charles Edwards separated and set up two firms. It is not known why they took this decision. They had worked in agreement for almost twenty years and their sons got on well together. George Baker took his son Arthur into partnership and G. and A. Baker was formed.

George Baker's affection for the country grew and he was continually finding ways of improving Anglo-Turkish relations. He had his reward. Not only was he decorated by the Turkish authorities, but one evening the palace dragoman pounded on the door of his house and presented Baker with a *firman* from the Sultan, offering him any concession he wished to choose. He decided on a cold store for fish and meat. The cold store was built by the Golden Horn, a separate company being formed—The Constantinople Cold Storage Society. It was not a success; storage of food-stuffs by freezing appeared to the local people to be an invention of the devil. It was in advance of the times.

George Baker died in 1905 and Arthur, carrying on the business, opened two large department stores in the Grande Rue de Péra. Shortly before the First World War he added a third. He also did business in supplying to the Turkish War Department cloth for army uniforms, boots, and saddlery. Henry Baker died of cholera in 1906 and Arthur made arrangements for the flour mill to continue. Arthur Baker's son, Arthur Warden Baker, joined the firm before 1914.

In 1912 Arthur Baker received a silver tea service from England which the Sultan had ordered. Unfortunately, when it arrived it was discovered that the spout of the tea kettle portrayed a human face and therefore could not possibly be given to the Sultan. Arthur Baker promised a quick replacement from England; the court chamberlain cheerfully accepted his apologies and graciously bestowed the tea service as a wedding present from the Sultan to Arthur's daughter. In view of these happy relationships with the Turkish court, it was a great tragedy that all the Bakers and Edwardses had to leave Turkey when war broke out. Arthur Leavitt, Arthur Baker's American son-in-law, was with the American embassy and stayed on until the United States entered the war in 1917. He was able to give an eye to the family affairs.

When Charles Edwards separated from George Baker in 1890 he formed a company called Edwards and Sons. When he died, his son Middleton Edwards took over the business. He bore the name of the kind nurseryman who had helped his grandfather. Edwards and Sons exported Turkish products and ran a general merchant business. They were contractors to Turkish government departments, railways, and steamship lines. In 1907 Middleton Edwards' sister Edith married Cuthbert Evelyn Binns, and Binns joined the company. He played a leading part in Bakers in later years.

G. and A. Baker and Edwards and Sons built up a large export trade in carpets. They started with used carpets, in which the colours had often mellowed with time. However as demand increased they began to deal in newly manufactured Persian carpets. Many of these were extremely bright in colour and ingenious methods were used to mellow them. Some of the carpets were placed on the ground in the bazaars to be trampled underfoot by the heavy traffic, whereas others were exposed to the scorching sun and sprinkled daily with watering cans. One blue silk Bokhara carpet was even nailed to the roof of the bridgehouse of a coastal steamer for six months. Although these various methods were successful, it was eventually found that the simplest and best way of mellowing carpets was to wash them with wood ash.

In 1919 Middleton Edwards returned to Constantinople as also did Arthur Baker with his son Arthur Warden Baker. Cuthbert Binns followed after a short spell at the Peace Conference in Paris. The war had caused havoc in Turkey. Prices soared and necessities of life were scarce. The firms of Baker and Edwards set about trying to meet some of this demand. In the main they handled different lines. Apart from the retail stores, there was a substantial wholesale trade in woollen and cotton piece goods and haberdashery.

Medicines, household requirements, and many other items, were imported, and exports included carpets, tobacco, and other products.

During his war service Arthur Warden Baker had met Major-General W. W. H. Grey, who was a director of the African and Eastern Trade Corporation Limited.[1] Arising out of this contact, the African and Eastern took a shareholding in the Constantinople companies in 1919. Two new limited liability companies were formed in London with branches in Constantinople. They were G. and A. Baker Limited, and Edwards and Sons (Near East) Limited. Both companies had similar boards. The shareholders were the African and Eastern Trade Corporation Limited, F. and A. Swanzy Limited, and members of the Baker, Edwards, and Binns families. They operated separately for seven years, and then, for reasons of economy and taxation, G. and A. Baker Limited absorbed Edwards and Sons (Near East) Limited. F. and A. Swanzy Limited acted as buying and selling agents in the United Kingdom.

The African and Eastern Trade Corporation proceeded to ship to Constantinople all kinds of goods, including large quantities of cotton and woollen goods. The cottons were to a large extent Manchester stocks originally bought for West Africa. They had been purchased without local consultation and were not suitable for the Turkish market. Shortages in Russia resulted in Russian buyers snapping up their requirements on the Constantinople market, and consequently much merchandise was dumped in the transit depots there in anticipation of quick sales to Russia. However, as the Bolsheviks extended their grip over southern Russia, this trade dried up and large stocks lay unsold in Constantinople. Efforts were made to seek outlets, not only throughout Turkey but in the Balkans and in the Caucasus. Branches were set up in Sofia and Varna, Bucharest and Galatz, Sevastopol in the Crimea, Novorossisk in southern Russia, at Batum and Tiflis in the Caucasus, and at Trebizond, Samsoun, and Gallipoli, in Turkey. The Sevastopol branch was stuck with a lot of stocks and debts and Cuthbert Binns went there to see what he could recover. It took a long time and the daily visits to officials made great demands on his patience, but in the end he obtained his permit to leave with the right to take anything he could carry.

It was decided to start a motor business, and the first motor vehicle establishment in Turkey was constructed. It was known as the Grand Garage. Agencies were secured for Essex, Ford, Chev-

[1] W. W. H. Grey has previously been mentioned in chapters 8 and 20.

rolet, Erskine, and Studebaker. In 1922 Turkey boasted a total of seventy-five cars. In this year Bakers secured the Dunlop tyre agency.

Mustapha Kemal raised his banner in the Black Sea port of Samsoun and declared Ankara the capital. The Greeks invaded the hinterland of Smyrna and fighting covered large areas. By 1922 the position had become so acute that Bakers and Edwards made preparations for evacuation. They contemplated packing up and removing from the country all valuable stock. A ship was chartered and stood by for a month. But the crisis passed, peace was made between Turkey and the Western Powers at Lausanne in 1923, and the Sultan with all his entourage disappeared.

By 1925 all branches with the exception of Sofia had been closed and the large shipments of Manchester cotton and woollen goods had been liquidated at heavy loss.

The four-floor retail store at No. 370 on the Grande Rue de Péra was the only real department store in the country. It sold ladies' and gentlemen's clothing and shoes, perfumes, hosiery, haberdashery, toys, bicycles, bed linen, suitcases and leather goods, and furniture. It supplied shoes and suitings to President Atatürk (Mustapha Kemal). In 1924 it became the first to adopt a customers' credit system. In 1927 a radio department was added, but it survived only two years.

In the four years to 1929 every department except the garage had made a loss: then Bakers, like many other companies, was badly hit by the 1929 crash; and the African and Eastern Trade Corporation was hardly in a position to help. The Turkish currency depreciated badly. The tremendous slump in prices of produce put Bakers in terrible financial straits. Staff members were cut and salaries reduced. The last branch in Sofia was shut down, the Grand Garage sold, the readymade clothing building was closed, and all other activities greatly restricted. Small offices were found. Of the directors, only Cuthbert Binns and Middleton Edwards remained to run the business.[2]

[2] Binns, V. M., *The Evolution of G. and A. Baker Ltd.* (privately circulated: 1968).

27

Extension into East Africa

The African and Eastern Trade Corporation, as part of its great programme of expansion in 1919–20, announced its intention of establishing a business in East Africa, and in 1921 it bought the firm of Bullows and Roy in Nairobi, Kenya. The main asset of the business was a department store in the main street of Nairobi. Some attempt was also made to do wholesale business in imported goods, but the emphasis was on the retail trade. It was in fact the leading European-owned shop in Nairobi, but it had to meet very vigorous competition from a great many Indian shopkeepers who encouraged the habit of haggling over prices and made it extremely difficult for Bullows and Roy to adopt a price-ticketing policy on European or American lines.

In 1927 the African and Eastern Trade Corporation extended its investment in East Africa by buying the firm of Rosenblum. This was a business of long standing in Tanganyika where it was engaged in the purchase and export of produce. Its staff included a substantial element of Austrians. The combined businesses were now registered under the name, Rosenblum, Bullers, and Roy, and this was one of the predecessor companies of the United Africa group.

The other was Gailey and Roberts. In 1897 D. O. Roberts joined the survey staff of the railway which was being built in fulfilment of Joseph Chamberlain's policy of providing infrastructure to promote development. It had started at Mombasa on the coast of the Indian Ocean. Shortly after, James Hamilton Gailey took service in the same capacity. When they completed their contracts with the railway, they set up in partnership as estate agents and surveyors. They did business in the lobby of Nairobi's only hotel.[1]

In 1903 Gailey sent an enquiry for ploughs to his London cousins, George McArthur Scales and Harold John Scales, and from this grew the business of Gailey and Roberts Limited, which subsequently became very well known throughout East Africa. The

[1] *Progress*, Spring 1964.

following year[2] they opened a trading business in a wood and iron shack in Government Road, dealing in farm implements, saddlery, seeds, picks, paint, and barrows. As engineers and surveyors they were well qualified to cater for the needs of a developing country. For the accounting side they engaged G. E. Ramsey, who had also worked on the railway. In the same year two farmers joined Gailey and Roberts. They were R. Hancock and Alan Thompson, friends who helped to lead the company for many years. The company held the agency for Lloyds, for the German East African shipping line, for W. and A. Gilbey the wine and spirit firm, and for the Royal Exchange Insurance Company. It was a banker's agent and a contractor for railways and other public works. It built dams and houses. It is evident therefore that the partners showed infinite adaptability and were prepared to undertake any service for which there was a demand.

On the outbreak of war in 1914 both Gailey and Roberts joined the armed forces which were engaged against the Germans on the southern frontier of Kenya. During the campaign Roberts contracted blackwater fever and died. In 1921 James Gailey married Mrs. Roberts, the widow of his partner, and she was known affectionately for the rest of her life as Mrs. Gailey and Roberts.

The firm opened at Nakuru in 1921. Further branches followed in other towns of Kenya. In 1927 Gailey and Roberts secured the agency for the Caterpillar Company of Peoria, Illinois, and the sale and servicing of their equipment was henceforth to be the most important item in the company's business. The spare parts were entrusted to Fred Cogle, whose reminiscences describe the state of affairs then prevailing as follows:

When I took over Caterpillar spare parts in 1927, we had just taken over the agency from Carr Lawson and Company, and had about two hundred spare parts housed in two wooden bins and recorded in one small ledger. At this time the tractors were called the 2-ton, 5-ton, and 10-ton. There were only a few in the field. Once we had the agency, sales became very brisk, all in the agricultural and timber field. We were selling up to seventy-five 2-ton tractors in a season, mostly in the Nakuru and Eldoret districts. There was no road construction machinery at this period. All the tractors were petrol driven, converted to burn

[2] *Short History of Macdonald Scales and Company Limited 1843–1968* (London: privately produced, 1969).

kerosene. The machines were painted battleship grey. When the diesel tractor was introduced, Caterpillar yellow became the colour. We also handled Adam's road graders, subsequently made by Caterpillar. These graders were hauled by tractors. Gailey and Roberts were the pioneers in the introduction of road making machinery to east Africa. We faced considerable difficulty in persuading the public works department and district councils to purchase, but the resistance was eventually overcome.

The business in mechanical equipment was hungry for space, and a huge depot was built in Nairobi to accommodate the technical service departments and their stores of spare parts. This kind of activity required the investment of a great deal of capital, and by 1929 Gailey and Roberts had grown to a size which fully justified the partners in giving thought to the question, how they might secure for their company a firmer financial foundation.

28

Trade Without Profit
is Madness

The Hausa have a proverb, *Ciniki babu riba hauka ne;* which being translated means that trade without profit is madness. That might have been the motto of all the merchant firms. They went to Africa to earn profit by trade. How did they fare? The Royal Niger Company maintained a dividend of six per cent. The African Association did badly from 1889 to 1896, incurring loss in 1892 and 1895. From 1897 to 1918, on the other hand, it made profits with the exception of one year, 1908; the yield on the ordinary shares gradually improved, rising to twenty per cent in 1917 and thirty per cent in 1918. The Niger Company paid to its ordinary shareholders dividends of ten per cent except in 1914, when they had no dividend.[1] The Niger group made losses from 1920 to 1924, and then for five years made modest profits which at last in 1929 enabled a dividend of five per cent to be paid. The African and Eastern Trade Corporation declared a dividend of thirty per cent for its first year, nothing in its second year, and thereafter maintained its dividend at eight per cent until the crash came in 1928. Of the smaller companies little information is available: the Lagos Ready Money Store Company paid dividends of $7\frac{1}{2}$ per cent in 1890 and of ten per cent in 1891. The Cavalla River Company made losses in its first four years and then for four years made profits which could be reckoned as an average of $17\frac{1}{2}$ per cent on its capital; it then became part of the Niger group.

---

[1] In 1918 W. B. MacIver and Company paid to Lever Brothers (by whom they were wholly owned) a dividend of 125 per cent (interview with Timberlake recorded at Port Sunlight, 13 July 1948, Unilever secretarial department). However, this may be more an indication of the cash-flow policy of the Lever group at that time than an index of the yield on capital invested in African trade. The great expansion of MacIver in the preceeding eight years had been financed by loans from Lever Brothers so that by 1918 the registered and issued capital was highly geared.

Ambas Bay Trading Company Limited paid dividends as follows:

for year to April 1904	6 per cent
for year to April 1905	6 per cent
for year to April 1906	7½ per cent
for year to April 1907	10 per cent
for year to April 1908	10 per cent
for year to April 1909	10 per cent
for year to April 1910	10 per cent
for year to April 1911	10 per cent
for year to April 1912	10 per cent
for year to April 1913	nil
for year to April 1914	nil
for year to April 1915	20 per cent
for year to April 1916	nil
for year to April 1917	nil
for year to April 1918	6 per cent[2]

A rare example of really large profit was the £8,000,000 of Lever's money which the shareholders of the Niger Company received in 1920. That was a capital profit taken with consummate skill in most exceptional circumstances.

The general level of annual profits was modest, and the risk of incurring losses and falling into the hands of creditors was always a real one. Forster and Smith became a casualty; Irvine and Woodward failed in 1881; the River Gambia Trading Company Limited passed into the hands of the Official Receiver in 1886; MacIver was declared bankrupt in 1900; F. and A. Swanzy collapsed a couple of years later; in 1905 G. B. Ollivant and Company was taken over by its creditors; and the African and Eastern Trade Corporation had to submit to the control of the banks in 1928.

The story of this book lends little support to the theory that powerful financial interests were anxious to place capital in West Africa. It is true that Forster and Smith, in addition to setting up their own organization in Bathurst, acted as financiers for other merchants. Later in the century, James Finlay, the East India merchant, placed a financial stake in the Bathurst Trading company, and Elder Dempster, the shipping line, acted as a financial backer for G. B. Ollivant. Lever made a large capital investment in building

[2] Minute book of the Ambas Bay Trading Company Limited: United Africa Company records.

up the Niger group and in creating the plantations in the Congo. However, all these placements of capital were associated with the actual management of enterprises. The export of capital was a consequence of the enterprise, not a prime motive. For an example of 'the superabundance of capital in the metropolitan countries looking for higher profits overseas',[3] attention can only be directed to the *concessionnaires* in the French Congo in the 1890s; but that was an episode in which the companies considered in this book did not participate until Lever tried to pick something out of the ruins of the concession policy in 1910.

As stated in chapter 1, palm oil was the basis of the trade for many years; how splendidly it performed in the seventy-five years from 1785 to 1860! On the average, the quantity imported into Britain from West Africa doubled every ten years: rapid growth indeed! As is to be expected in periods of rapid growth, the price was high. Opening in 1785 around £40 per ton c.i.f. British port, it held that figure until 1854 when it rose to its peak, £48. For the next fourteen years the average price was £43·60.

After that palm oil came under severe competition from other oils and fats, animal, vegetable, and mineral, largely from Australia and America. Its price fell by about fifty per cent to around £20 in the decade 1881–1890. Since at that time palm oil was the only significant export, there resulted a period of depression. The total trade of the British dependencies (import and export) which had exceeded £3,000,000 a year in 1875–1885, fell to £2,700,000. After 1890 it revived. Goddards and their French competitors were opening up the Gambia River again after the religious wars (chapter 4); the Gold Coast was booming owing to gold and colonial government expenditure (chapter 8); and the Royal Niger Company was developing trade on the Nigerian rivers (chapter 9). In the first decade of the twentieth century came the remarkable growth of the cocoa and cotton trades, and in the second decade the 'groundnut explosion' in northern Nigeria. The result was that in the period 1890 to 1914 total trade increased at a rate of approximately a hundred per cent each decade.

Throughout the period from 1807 to 1929 the prime concern of British merchants in West Africa was to buy raw materials. In this

[3] Gann and Duignan (eds.) 'Imperialism and the Scramble for Africa' in *Colonialism in Africa 1870–1960* (Cambridge: University Press, 1969) vol. I, p. 104, referring to Hobson, *Imperialism: a study* (1902) and Helphand, *Marinenforderungen, Kolonialpolitik und Arbeiterinteressen* (1898).

Palm Oil[4]

		Tons	Value £	Average price per ton c.i.f. U.K. port £	Average price in Africa £
1785	imports to Liverpool from West Africa	55	2,224	40+	—
1810	imports to U.K. from West Africa	1,000	—	—	—
1815	,,	2,000	—	—	—
1826–9	annual average exports at port of shipment	—	150,000	—	—
1830	imports to U.K.	10,000	—	—	—
1839	exports from W. Africa	—	500,000	—	—
1840	imports to U.K.	16,000	—	—	—
1842	imports to U.K.	20,000	—	—	—
1849	—	—	—	42	20
1851	imports to U.K.	30,000	—	40	25
1854	—	—	—	48	
1855	exports from W. Africa	40,000+	1,000,000	—	—
1856–99	annual average exports from Nigeria, Gold Coast, and Sierra Leone	50,000	—	—	—
1856–60	—	—	—	43·6	—
1861–5	—	—	—	37·2	—
1866–70	—	—	—	38·4	—
1871–5	—	—	—	34·2	—
1876–80	—	—	—	33	—
1881–90	—	—	—	20·4	12
1891–5	—	—	—	23·6	—
1896–1900	—	—	—	21·4	—
1911	exports from Nigeria, Gold Coast, and Sierra Leone	—	1,896,000	—	—
1913	imports to U.K. from W. Africa	—	2,400,000	30	—
1929	exports from Nigeria, Gold Coast, and Sierra Leone	—	3,782,000	33·2	—

[4] The tables in this chapter have been made up with figures drawn from the following sources: Schlote, W., *British Overseas Trade from 1700 to the 1930s* (Oxford: Blackwell, 1952) pp. 156–7; McPhee, Alan, *Economic Revolution in British West Africa* (London: Routledge, 1926); Hancock, Sir Keith, *Survey of British Commonwealth Affairs* (Oxford: Clarendon, 1942) vol. II part 2; United Africa Company, *Statistical and Economic Review*, no. 4, September 1949, no. 5, March 1950, and no. 7, March 1951. *See also* Newbury, Colin W., 'Trade and Authority in West Africa from 1850 to 1880', and Pedler, Sir F. J., 'British Planning and Private Enterprise in Colonial Africa', both in Gann and Duignan (eds.) *Colonialism in Africa* (Cambridge University Press., 1969–74).

respect the trade was an extension of the industrial revolution in Britain. The concentration on raw materials enabled the merchants to stimulate and assist peasant producers to create great export industries, for palm products, groundnuts, cocoa, cotton, and rubber.

Palm kernels

Value of exports from Nigeria, Gold Coast, and Sierra Leone

1911	£3,321,000
1929	5,237,000

The two essential elements in this growth were the farmers and the merchants, and their co-operation has been noted in several chapters. However, it could not have happened so quickly nor so plentifully without the provision of ports and railways by the colonial govern-

Groundnuts

	Gambia exports Tons	£	Nigeria exports Tons
1835	47	—	—
1851	12,000	—	—
1875–90 annual average	15/20,000	100/150,000	—
1910	—	—	1,179
1911	48,000	437,000	2,518
1912	—	—	19,288
1913–14 annual average	—	—	9,000
1915–19	—	—	41,000
1920–4	—	—	44,300
1922	64,800	—	—
1925–9 annual average	—	—	117,100
1929	56,000	766,000	—

Tonnage figures for Nigeria and Gambia are not comparable without adjustment, since exports from Gambia at that time were always made in shell, while the exports from Nigeria consisted of decorticated nuts. The shell accounted for approximately thirty per cent of the weight of an undecorticated nut.

ments, and it was much assisted by the excellent shipping service: for, in spite of the complaints of the merchants about high freight charges, the cost of transport was considerably reduced during the period, which did something to compensate for the low price of palm oil.

Thomas King was in the trade from the earliest beginning; but, apart from his temporary personal commitment as captain of Sydenham Teast's *African Queen*, he plied the African trade as a sideline. He was a wealthy merchant ship-owner, able to engage in many trades, and so long as the African trade was a matter of scrambling for a share of less than 10,000 tons of palm oil, he did not devote to it his full resources of capital or management. In the

Cotton exports from Nigeria

1868–70, from Lagos, a million lbs. worth £60,000 f.o.b. each year for three years. This trade arose because exports from the U.S.A. ceased during the Civil War and for some years thereafter. When the American cotton plantations came into production again the Lagos producers could not compete, and exports ceased.

	Quanity in 000 bales of 400 lbs. annual average	Value in £000 f.o.b. annual average
1905–9	8	62
1910–14	11	114
1915–19	12	223
1920–4	22	503
1925–9	34	641

1830s however the growth of the trade was so spectacular that his sons, Richard and William, were tempted to become African specialists. Their father supported their decision by selling them his share in the *John Cabot* (1833). Within the decade, they had Thomas Harrison and Hatton and Cookson in Africa, competing with them.

Cocoa production

	Quantity in tons, Gold Coast	Value in £000 Gold Coast	Nigeria
1891–5 annual average	5	—	—
1900	536	—	—
1906–10 annual average	14,784		
1911	—	1,613	165
1912	38,647	—	—
1914	52,888	—	—
1921	133,195	—	—
1926–30 annual average	218,895	—	—
1929	—	9,704	2,306

The Swanzys were different. They had been in the slave trade and when it was suppressed in 1807 they had to adjust themselves to the new situation, in which they succeeded better than any other. Forster and Smith, wealthy ship-owners like Thomas King, turned to West Africa because they held the 'abolitionist' view that new opportunities would follow the suppression of the slave trade. The 'tropical treasure house' theory of Africa[5] may have weighed with

[5] Gann and Duignan, op. cit., p. 100.

them. Ollivant started in 1858 when the prosperity of the palm-oil trade was at its high point. In the period 1864 to 1869, although the price of palm oil had declined to £37 or £38, the major fall in price had not yet occurred, and this is the decade when the reduction in

Hides and skins, Nigeria

	Exports Number ooos	Value £ooo
1910	176	—
1911	332	28
1912	813	—
1913	1,128	—
1914	2,764	—
1915	1,651	—
1916	3,609	—
1917	4,120	—
1918	4,051	—
1919	5,959	—
1922	3,022	335
1929	—	889

transport costs made its greatest impact. This quinquennium witnessed the arrival in Africa of

The West Africa Company	1864
John Walkden	1865
Roebuck Pickering	1868
Millers	1868
Holland Jacques and Company	1869

No doubt they were encouraged by the steamship services. Woodin followed in 1882, Lagos Stores in 1884, and Gottschalck in 1896.

Tonnage of British shipping visiting West Africa

1854	57,000
1864	113,000
1874	504,000
1884	1,157,000
1894	2,269,000
1904	4,674,000
1914	5,360,000

The early trade depended on substantial African operators who were able to handle credit and whose transactions were of a size to enable a trading ship to sell out her import cargo and load produce without too much delay; though, as Harford found at Duala, it did not always work that way. There are indications, however, that in the seventh and eighth decades of the century, a more sophisticated type of African merchant was engaging in the import and export trades, in competition with the European firms established in Africa, and in correspondence with import/export houses of Liverpool and London. Indeed, Ollivant, Walkden, the Lagos Stores, and possibly

Trade of British West Africa

	Imports £000	Total imports and exports £000	Exports £000
1787 from U.K. to all W. Africa	584	—	—
1856–60 annual average	—	915	—
1861–5 ,,	—	664	—
1866–70 ,,	—	1,272	—
1871–5 ,,	—	2,322	—
1875–80 ,,	—	3,020	—
1881–5 ,,	—	3,028	—
1886–8 ,,	1,179	—	1,328
1886–90 ,,	—	2,707	—
1891–5 ,,	—	4,166	—
1895–1900 ,,	—	6,266	—
1901–5 ,,	—	9,708	—
1906–10 ,,	—	16,314	—
1911–13 ,,	13,074	—	13,072
1912 ,,	—	25,309	—

Roebuck Pickering, started in just that way, as correspondents of African merchants. They later established positions in Africa by acquiring the businesses of some of their opposite numbers. There were two ways of doing this, one being outright purchase and the

Nigeria and Gold Coast

Annual Averages			
Imports £M		Non-mineral exports £M	
1900–9	4·5	1901–10	4·1
1910–19	10·2	1911–20	11·9
1920–9	22·5	1921–30	21·1

other, foreclosure or mortgage. The action of Tomlinson, founder of the Lagos Stores, is an example of the former method. He built up his firm by putting together three African-owned businesses. It is of interest that the second and third of these were acquired from eager sellers, and that in order to raise money to buy them out, Tomlinson formed a limited liability company in Britain. This exemplifies an important advantage which the British-based merchant enjoyed over the Africa-based house, namely, access to capital markets. It is not difficult, however, to surmise other reasons why the number of African import/export firms declined towards the end of the century. The profits of such trade were at best moderate, and in that boom period when towns were being built and cocoa farms were being created, there were for African investors more profitable ways to employ their money, ways in which they enjoyed a natural protection from expatriate competition: and that is no doubt why some of them were anxious to see the colour of Tomlinson's money.

French West Africa total of imports and exports £ooo

1895	3,148
1900	5,192
1905	6,120
1910	11,132
1912	10,128

In other cases, the British-based firm was obliged to foreclose the assets of an Africa-based firm which was unable to discharge its obligations. G. B. Ollivant and Company appear to have acquired property in Africa in this way, and very likely Walkden did so too.

Such businesses could be taken over by an expatriate firm because they were completely unpolitical. They were in fact 'modern' businesses of private enterprise, independent of the government. They were one of the fruits of colonial government because under the pre-colonial systems on the coast of Africa, political power and trading activity were closely associated and no African would have been able (nor probably would he have wished) to establish a business save in the closest association with, and under the protection of, authority. Many of the largest traders were themselves potentates such as King Gezo of Dahomey and King Ja-Ja of Opobo. Other traders were habitually referred to as 'chiefs' and their trade debts were 'guaranteed' by a superior chief. This suited everybody well in the early days. Richard and William King moved east from the Gold Coast because they preferred that type of trade to the conditions under a colonial government. But as trading methods became more sophisticated, it became inconvenient to mix up state authority with commercial activity. (You can neither refuse credit to a Head of State, nor dun him for debt.) Such changes usually take place gradually without anybody noticing exactly when they occur, but there is an interesting example of the specific recognition of this process when a new Ologun, Docemo, was installed at Lagos in 1853. Some European traders made an agreement with the new Ologun, undertaking to pay him a duty on exports, namely two 'heads' of cowries (worth eight shillings) on a puncheon (120 gallons) of palm oil, and two 'strings' of cowries (worth 2½ pence) on a pound of ivory, in return for which the Ologun agreed to 'relinquish trading on his own account', which his father had done.[6] Curiously, the Royal Niger Company put this process into reverse, combining rule with commerce, uncharacteristically, in European hands.

As time went on, the European firms were all the more set apart from the colonial governments because they rarely had any opportunity of selling anything to them. The British colonial governments bought all their imported supplies through the Crown Agents for the Colonies in London. The only significant exceptions were coal and cement, of which the shipping companies made themselves the sole suppliers by reserving for their own cargoes special rates of freight.

The owners of the firms' capital looked for profit, but what motives prompted their employees to take service in the white man's grave at such rates of remuneration as £6 per month (all found but subject to deduction for stock shortages)? To some, Africa offered an escape from poverty and a squalid home.[7] But others were impelled by very different motives. Thomas King, for instance, was the only son of a well-to-do merchant of Bristol, and he had a doting mother. He did not need to go to Africa to escape from bad conditions, nor even to earn his living. He went to Africa for adventure. Equally Harford, nearly a hundred years later, went to Africa for adventure, loved it, and embarked upon private hostilities against Ja-Ja with real zest. Batty, when he persuaded Alexander Miller to allow him to go to Cape Coast, was driven by ambition. Another young man, 19 years of age, went to Africa in 1913 for W. D. Woodin and Company. He had been a junior salesman in a fashionable Regent Street store, but he left that job to sign an agreement with Woodin, to work as a clerk for three years on a salary rising from £50 to £70 a year, all found; and he described his motive quite simply as 'adventure'.[8] Geoffrey Watson in 1923 joined the African

---

[6] Newbury, C. W., *The Western Slave Coast and its Rulers* (Oxford: Clarendon Press, 1961) p. 60.

[7] Stuart-Young, J. M., *Coaster at Home* and *Iniquitous Coaster* (London: Stockwell, 1916 and 1917).

[8] Taylor, H. R., *Jungle Trader* (London: Jarrolds, 1939).

and Eastern Trade Corporation for the sake of his interest in polo and Hausa. The elder Hartje was tricked into employment in Africa, because he did not read the 'small print' in the ship's articles which he signed; or if he read them, he had not understood how they might be used against him. But he came to like the job. He, and Frost senior, recommended their sons to follow them into a career of employment in Africa. The African and Eastern Trade Corporation had a manager at Opobo in the 1920s whose name was P. H. Davey, and he was the third generation of his family to occupy that kind of position. He claimed that his grandfather had been the first European to sail up the Opobo River in charge of a sailing vessel, and his father had managed the Sierra Leone Coaling Company in Freetown. None of these men made a fortune, but each of the fathers achieved that kind of 'job satisfaction' which makes a son admire his father and follow his footsteps. Sons followed fathers in Africa in the families of Swanzy and Chadwick, but those families had an interest in the ownership of the firm, which the Daveys, Frosts, and Hartjes never had. Cotterell took service in Africa because he liked what he saw when he visited the Delta, working as a steward in a sailing vessel; he was ambitious to earn more money, and in this he was successful.

The willingness of such people to face the health hazards may be set against the grim conditions of English seaport towns in the nineteenth century; all things are comparative: but many of these men simply enjoyed taking risks, as is manifested by the zest with which (like the crew of the *Fighting Téméraire*) they engaged in hostilities. In addition to Harford's private war, the reader will recall Francis Swanzy's expedition against Ahanta, Hineson's affrays with the Itsekiri on behalf of Thomas Harrison, and Cockshut's 'fine fight' on the Ngunie River on behalf of Hatton and Cookson. An extreme example was the determination of McEachan and others to take their ships up the Niger even though it could only be done by engaging in artillery duels. It is hard to believe that the expense of such operations could be borne by the profits of trade.

The greatest fighter of them all was Sir George Goldie, but he had started life as a professional soldier. It is to his enduring honour that when the Royal Niger Company sent its forces to fight Nupe and Ilorin, he did not direct the campaign from an arm-chair, but went with the troops. He is an example of the investor who personally went to Africa, like Thomas King, the early Swanzys, Macgregor Laird, and the Chadwicks. It is however interesting to recall that Alexander and George Miller never visited Africa, nor did any of the proprietors of Gottschalck; yet both of those businesses were very successful.

Another investor who personally went to Africa was Lord Leverhulme. His enthusiasm for the continent increased with the size of the difficulties which he encountered. His experience in Africa might be represented as a series of mistakes and failures. Yet in the final balance, his instincts and hunches must have been more often right than wrong, for the group which he brought together survived and became the strongest commercial organization in Africa. Still, it is interesting to consider his mistakes and misfortunes. The fear that there would be a shortage of vegetable oils and fats proved to be unfounded. It did not happen in his lifetime and it has not happened since his death. The attempt which was made by himself and his lieutenant, Greenhalgh, to secure land for oil palms in Nigeria was unsuccessful, in spite of the fact that Millers, Woodin, and Mac-Iver, were able to secure land for rubber plantations. This is hard to understand, but in view of the diplomatic gaffe which was committed in Liberia when the government of that independent republic was asked to follow the example of the colony of the Belgian Congo, it is permissible to doubt whether the application to the government of Nigeria was well expressed. The Congo enterprise, wonderful though it was, continued to depend for too long on natural palmeries, allowing the Dutch in the Far East to gain eighteen years' start with cultivated palms, and permitting even the African and Eastern Trade Corporation in Nigeria to become the pioneer in Africa of the new plantation methods. The Kouilou–Niari investment was a fiasco. The West African Oil Mills (kernel-processing factories) failed and had to be abandoned. The Lever Stores ('Woolworth in Africa') became a laughing stock. The purchase of the Niger Company was made at an exorbitant price without any prior examination of the accounts, and the bid for the African and Eastern Trade Corporation could not be carried through. Notwithstanding all these setbacks, he sailed up the Congo River for the second time in October 1924 at the age of 73. Twelve years had passed since his previous visit, and he was able to see that his dream had come true and that his faith had been rewarded; not, so far, in terms of profit, but in terms of physical development and social welfare. In the five concession centres thriving communities of Africans had been created, with houses, gardens, churches, hospitals, and schools. One of these townships had been named Leverville. The experience lifted up his heart, and his enthusiasm for the Congo knew no bounds. It provoked some private comments from his personal secretary, who kept a diary:[9]

> Left Kinshasa 6.30 a.m. on sail up river. Lord Leverhulme said after we had been six hours under weigh that the trip up the Congo was the finest yachting trip in the world. I am not sure that I can agree, though my knowledge of the world is infantile compared with the old man's. I admit that the Congo is longer, that its magnificence is therefore greater in quantity than anything else I have seen from a boat; but for real beauty and grandeur I am bound to say that I prefer the Rhine gorge and, in some ways, Loch Fyne . . .
>
> 31st January 1925. At Onitsha (Nigeria) all day. Since Lord Leverhulme is writing today to everybody to say that the Niger is not as delightful or as interesting or as magnificent as the Congo, I think it worth while to record my opinion that it is infinitely more interesting, and therefore more delightful. It may not be as big, but that does not trouble me. It resembles the Kasai in some ways. Lord Leverhulme says that there are not so many crocodiles as there are in the Congo. I have seen more crocodiles on the Niger in as many days as we had weeks in the Congo. He says the same about hippos, and I saw as many hippos at Bonny in one day as I saw all the time on the Kasai.

Leverhulme was primarily an industrialist and he was the first investor to create modern industrial enterprises in tropical Africa. The extraction units in the palmeries were large mechanical installations. The West African Oil Mills were fully industrial, even though they failed. The soap factories in the Congo and Nigeria did not fail and survived to become the nuclei of impressive manufacturing businesses.

It would probably be incorrect to suggest that William Lever's decisions to combine the production or purchase of raw materials with the manufacture of industrial products were based upon a theory of vertical integration, because his decisions appear to have been intuitive. However, it looked to others like a policy of vertical integration, and Lever's example was followed by both his Dutch competitors, by his English competitor Bibby in the alliance with Ollivant, and in reverse by the Niger Company when it acquired the De Bruyn business, and also in reverse by the African and

[9] Sir Malcolm Knox, diary.

Eastern Trade Corporation when it bought numerous factories in Europe. None of these alliances between manufacturers and merchants appears to have conferred advantages on either side. The merchant who is tied to one source of supply must become uncompetitive with any rival who has access to all sources of supply. The manufacturer equally must insist on access to all sources of supply for raw materials, and his sales manager will hear nothing of limiting sales to such outlets as can be commanded by one tied customer.

After the acquisition of the Niger Company by Lever Brothers, one of its managers wrote, 'The *raison-d'être* of our business is the purchase of cash wherewith to buy produce.'[10] However, that was not the view of Bell and Snelling as senior executives of the Niger group. Snelling especially viewed the merchandise business as one to be made profitable in its own right. By 1929 it was seen in Lever Brothers and in the Niger group that an integral operation of the raw material supply line from the merchant to the factory suited neither party. The Niger group desired freedom to determine its own selling policy, feeding the market with small lots when prices were low, and selling largely (perhaps selling forward more than it held in stock) when prices were high. Lever Brothers equally wanted liberty to do precisely the opposite, to buy quantities and qualities to suit their needs, at the lowest prices.

In financial stability, however, the union with Lever Brothers turned out to be of great value to the Niger group. A merchant almost necessarily trades with borrowed money, and it was of vital importance to the Niger group to enjoy the financial support and the credit guarantee of Lever Brothers. Under that financial shelter the group was able to reorganize and consolidate.

[10] Sir Malcolm Knox, *Report to the Board on a Visit to West Africa 1929*, unpublished.

29

Half and Half

It was to be expected, from the facts which were related in chapter 20, that Sir Robert Waley Cohen, the new chairman of the African and Eastern Trade Corporation, would sound the chairman of Lever Brothers, the owners of the Niger Company, on the subject of amalgamation, and that the proposal would be received favourably. It was in fact welcomed, but it was soon apparent that there would be difficulty in settling terms. On behalf of the Niger Company it was made clear that nothing less than an equal division of assets, profits, and control would be acceptable. This claim implied equality of earning power between the two parties. The implication was hardly borne out by their respective trading histories, and the directors of the Corporation thought the demand unreasonable and resisted it strongly.

In February 1929 the plenipotentiaries of the two sides met at the Savoy Hotel. The Niger Company was represented by D'Arcy Cooper, Hyslop Bell, and McDowell, and the Corporation by Waley Cohen, Cowan, Grey, and Nicholl. Evening came without agreement. After dinner discussion was resumed but at midnight the parties were still divided. It was decided to adjourn the conference. All were disappointed but all were too tired to argue any further.

D'Arcy Cooper resided at Reigate and he did not look forward with pleasure to his long journey home in the cold early hours of the mid-winter morning. Waley Cohen had not so far to go. He lived no farther away than Highgate. He invited D'Arcy Cooper to spend the night, or rather the remaining morning hours which divided one working day from another, at Caen Wood Towers. Cooper gladly accepted. When, refreshed by a few hours slumber, host and guest sat down to breakfast, they saw things in a different light. They devised a formula which was satisfactory to themselves and would, they believed, be satisfactory to their colleagues. Their expectations proved correct. Negotiations proceeded rapidly to agreement. The United Africa Company was formed on 3 March 1929.[1]

This story must swing between Europe and Africa. That day happened to be the first day of a match in Accra in which the Gold Coast was playing against Nigeria at cricket. A number of commercial managers had been selected to play, and that evening at dinner they were told of the formation of the United Africa Company. They were all, unexpectedly, members of the same firm. Someone said, 'What an awful name! It sounds like a football club.'[2] In fact the name was an historic one revived with slight alteration. The 'United African Company' had been the original title under which fifty years earlier the four British firms on the Niger had combined under the influence of Goldie Taubman (chapter 9). The letter N was dropped from the 1879 name in 1929. The Niger Company and the African and Eastern Trade Corporation, ceasing to be trading companies, merged as equal holding companies in the new trading company called the United Africa Company Limited. The capital was £13,000,000, almost immediately increased to £14,200,000 in fully paid ordinary shares, which were allotted in equal number to the holding companies. The transfer of the businesses of the African and Eastern Trade Corporation and of the Niger Company to the United Africa Company formally took place on 30 April 1929, and the trading career of the United Africa Company began on 1 May.

Between them the African and Eastern Trade Corporation and the Niger Company operated at over a thousand places in Africa, and in several other parts of the world. In the four British Colonies of West Africa their combined exports were estimated at sixty per cent of the palm oil, forty-five per cent of the palm kernels, sixty per cent of the groundnuts, and fifty per cent of the cocoa. Their combined imports were on a scale which gave them a corresponding proportion of the totals. (It is perhaps as well to draw attention to the fact that, large as these proportions were, they fell short in all cases of monopoly.) There were other important activities, among them being plantation development, timber production, ocean steamers, lighterage, and river and motor transport. The Niger Company also received income from mining royalties in Nigeria.

The fixed assets, including land and buildings, were spread over Africa. A physical valuation of the fixed assets was deemed im-

---

[1] Rankin, pp. 110–12.
[2] From Sir Patrick FitzGerald, who was one of those selected to play for the Gold Coast.

practicable as a preliminary to forming the merger. Each company transferred all its assets in Africa, fixed and floating, and its
goodwill with certain reservations, to the United Africa Company
in exchange for the shares received. The lack of a physical valuation
of assets however proved to be a misfortune. The United Africa
Company (like any other merchant) had to finance its trade with
borrowed money, and its debts had to be guaranteed by its two
shareholders, the Corporation and Lever Brothers, in exactly
equal sums. The uncertainty about the value of the assets damaged
the creditworthiness of the United Africa Company as prime
borrower and also the creditworthiness of the Corporation as
guarantor. In the end, when the reconstruction of the United
Africa Company had to be undertaken in 1931, the assets were
valued and the valuation was used as a basis for the plan of reorganization.

The Huileries du Congo Belge did not come into the merger,
and nor did their soap-making offshoot. The remaining Lever
enterprises in the Congo did: which meant, in effect, that SEDEC
the trading company became part of the United Africa Company.
All other purely oil-extracting and soap-making concerns of Lever
Brothers elsewhere in Africa were excluded from the transfer. Such
were the Niger Company's reservations. Those of the African and
Eastern Trade Corporation were Africa House, T. H. Harris and
Son Limited, soap manufacturers, and Loder and Nucoline Limited, oil-crushers. These two enterprises were soon afterwards sold
for cash, the former to Lever Brothers, and the latter to Unilever
Limited, Lever Brothers having, between these two transactions,
amalgamated with the Margarine Union to form Unilever Limited.

The Niger Company had debentures. The African and Eastern
Trade Corporation had remained free from this encumbrance.
Naturally the Niger Company's debentures could not be transferred to the partnership. Here the Niger Company's fairy god-
mother stepped in. Lever Brothers guaranteed the debentures both
as to principal and interest.

Effect was given with meticulous exactitude to the principle of
equality between the two parties. It was provided that the Corporation and the Niger Company should appoint to the board of the
United Africa Company an equal number of directors, and that if
for any reason this principle should cease to obtain in practice, the
voting power of the two sets of nominees should be exactly equal.
The chairman should have no casting vote. There were provisions

for arbitration in case of a deadlock. Waley Cohen, chairman of the African and Eastern Trade Corporation, was the first chairman of the United Africa Company. The directors on his board were:

F. D'Arcy Cooper
Lt.-Col. E. H. L. Beddington, C.M.G., D.S.O., M.C.
A. A. Cowan
H. R. Greenhalgh
Maj.-Gen. W. W. H. Grey, C.B., C.M.G.
John McDowell
Lt.-Col. W. Nicholl, T. D.
V. B. Powis
Sir Edgar Sanders

and the secretary was E. A. Enfield.

Perhaps the most remarkable thing about the board was that it did not include either the chairman or the vice-chairman of the Niger Company, E. Hyslop Bell and W. E. Snelling. After all, the Niger Company at the time of the merger was more successful than the Corporation, and Lever Brothers might have been expected to back the head men of their side for high posts in the new organization. But Francis D'Arcy Cooper evidently entertained no such feelings towards Bell and Snelling. They (the latter perhaps more than the former) had run the Niger Company at arm's length from Lever Brothers. They were offered the choice of two courses: either that they should become directors of the new company, serving under Waley Cohen as chairman, and continue to receive the remuneration which was due to them under service agreements which had still more than two years to run, or that they should retire and receive compensation for the premature termination of their service contracts. They chose the second of these courses. It then came to light however, that while they had held office as chairman and vice-chairman of the Niger Company, they had engaged in some private transactions involving the purchase and sale of cocoa. It may be doubted whether Lever Brothers, left to themselves, would have taken Bell and Snelling to law on the matter. The transactions in question were neither very large nor very recent, but the Corporation people took a most serious view of the matter. The Niger Company and the Corporation had been parties to a cocoa agreement at the time, and if these transactions could have been held to have been made on behalf of the Niger

Company, they might have formed the basis of a claim by the Corporation against the Niger Company. Lever Brothers sued Bell and Snelling for the recovery of payments made to them in compensation for their removal from the board. The case went on appeal to the House of Lords. In some of the points at issue the case went in favour of Lever Brothers, while on other points the final judgment was in favour of Bell and Snelling; but they kept the money.[3]

The board consisted in theory of five from each side, but when an analysis is made of the nucleus which could be available to take decisions, the position looks very different. The Niger Company's five directors started with D'Arcy Cooper, McDowell, and Greenhalgh, all directors of Lever Brothers. Cooper, an accountant by profession, had been brought into Lever Brothers by Lord Leverhulme and had created the business organization which took over from Leverhulme's personal autocracy. He had visited Africa with Leverhulme. McDowell had great abilities as a lawyer, but he knew nothing of Africa, and by this time his energies were mainly engaged in the collection of china and in the study of Shakespearean drama. Greenhalgh had made a prospecting tour for Lever in Africa in 1903, and had visited Africa on several subsequent occasions. His particular function on the board was to ensure co-ordination with the other activities of Lever Brothers in Africa. Then there were Powis and Sanders, both of whom had been directors of the Niger Company since it was taken over by Lever Brothers in 1920. However, Powis was ill at the time of the merger and died shortly after. Sanders, also a distinguished lawyer and the author of a text-book on the criminal law, at first represented the United Africa Company on chambers of commerce in London, Liverpool, and Manchester, and on the joint West Africa Committee of those three chambers. He continued to take an interest in the mining activities, which included the Seychelles Company. However, he does not appear to have enjoyed good personal relations with the chairman, who appointed a newly recruited manager to replace him on the various chambers of commerce, without troubling to tell Sir Edgar or to explain the situation to the chairmen of the various chambers. As may be supposed, a number of embarrassing situations resulted.

The Corporation's five members included, of course, the chairman, Waley Cohen. Then there were Cowan, Grey, and Nicholl.

---

[3] For the judgment, reference may be made to the law reports; for the interpretation of the situation, I am indebted to Lord Cole.

Cowan had gone out to the Oil Rivers in 1887 for Millers, and he continued to take a great interest in plantations in Nigeria which he had initiated. Nicholl had been a managing director of the African Association before 1919, and had served on the board of the African and Eastern Trade Corporation since its formation in 1919. There seems to have been some arrangement that he should take a special interest in the ships. Grey had a deep experience of Africa. His walk from Lagos to Kano has been noted. He at any rate was prepared to commit himself fully to the new company and to be a working director. He was named as joint managing director, the other being the non-starter, Powis.

The Corporation's fifth member on the board was Beddington. He had held a regular commission in the Sixteenth Lancers and in the war of 1914–1918 he rose to the position of first general staff officer of the Fifth Army. He became managing director of Abdullah Limited (a cigarette company) in 1920, and later the chairman of that company. He was brother-in-law to Waley Cohen and it is perhaps understandable that in assuming chairmanship Waley Cohen should bring in a close friend in whom he had confidence, and who was not emotionally committed to either of the merging companies, and who was prepared to work as an active manager. However, Beddington knew nothing of Africa. He was engaged in public life in Hertfordshire for many years, as Deputy Lieutenant, Justice of the Peace, and member of the county council. He was appointed managing director, in succession to Grey, in May 1930. From the inception of the United Africa Company he took particular interest in the factories in Britain which the United Africa Company had inherited from the African and Eastern Trade Corporation, and which were listed in chapter 20. Everyone in the company liked him, but they all wondered why he had been appointed.[4]

Such a board must necessarily depend very much on its chairman, and in order to understand the strange tragedy of the first twenty-one months, it will be helpful to know what kind of a man he was. Robert Waley Cohen, born in 1877, was the son of wealthy parents. He took a degree at Cambridge and then went to work in the Shell Transport and Trading Company.[5] In 1906 at the age of 28 he was appointed a director of that company, and he played a

---

[4] Henriques, R., *Sir Robert Waley Cohen 1877–1952* (London: Secker and Warburg, 1966) p. 305.

[5] ibid., pp. 32, 87, 89.

critical role in the creation of the Royal Dutch–Shell group. He received his knighthood 'for services in connection with the war'. After the war, as one of the managing directors of the Royal Dutch–Shell group, he made a further contribution to building up that great company; but he had serious disagreements with the chairman.[6]

It was in these circumstances that Waley Cohen left the oil business in 1928 at the age of 51, intending apparently to devote his life to his numerous voluntary activities, such as the interests of the Jews in Palestine, education, motoring, and local government. Why, a few months later, did he take on African and Eastern and the United Africa Company? He must have felt the urge to hold top command, something that had eluded him in Shell. Clearly he underestimated the size of the job, thinking it could be 'a short-term commitment', and even in the short term permit him to pursue his other interests.[7] He combined natural charm with the capacity to be devastatingly rude—as for instance to Sanders, as noted above. He took personal command of the United Africa Company and frequently issued instructions without consulting anybody. He visited Africa at the beginning of 1930, taking with him Cowan, a director of the United Africa Company and of the African and Eastern Trade Corporation, and T. M. Knox, whom he had appointed as his private secretary.[8]

Waley Cohen and his colleagues would have liked to extend the merger to include all the other British trading companies that were significant in West Africa. Approaches were made to John Holt, London and Kano, Paterson Zochonis, and Ollivant, but all replied that they preferred to retain independence. On the other hand, an approach which was received from Maurel and Prom, a leading Bordeaux company active in Senegal and the Gambia, was not considered interesting. Almost immediately after the merger, two small concerns known as the Anglo-Guinea Produce Company Limited and Thomas Welsh and Company Limited fell into difficulties and were bought.[9]

---

[6] ibid., pp. 125, 129, 242, 251–2, 296.

[7] ibid., pp. 301, 308.

[8] Thomas Malcolm Knox, a Niger Company man, had accompanied Leverhulme on his African tour in 1925, as mentioned in chapter 28. He later became Professor of Philosophy and Principal of Saint Andrew's University, and is now Sir Malcolm Knox. Sir Malcolm has kindly gone over the draft of this chapter with me.

[9] Minutes, United Africa Company board and executive committee. The acquisition of the Anglo-Guinea Company by the U.A.C. was also minuted by the Unilever Joint

When Waley Cohen met the shareholders of the African and Eastern Trade Corporation at Liverpool three weeks after the formation of the United Africa Company, he was asked to promise that the headquarters would be at Liverpool. He refused to do so, and about a month later those members of the Liverpool staff of the two companies whose services it was decided to retain were nearly all transferred to London. The Liverpool business was accommodated in the smaller premises in Mersey Street, already mentioned in chapter 6. The fine building in Kingsway, London, also previously described, became the head office of the United Africa Company. The Corporation, it will be remembered, was the owner of Africa House, which had been reserved at the amalgamation, and the Corporation leased it to the United Africa Company. It was necessary to discharge many employees, whom the merger rendered redundant. Though the times were bad, those of long service and retiring age were pensioned. Where the age was not considered such as to justify a pension, compensation was granted in a lump sum. The management of the French business was concentrated in London, and such functions as had to be carried on in France were centralized in Paris under the direction of Amedée Thube, who came to the group through NOSOCO. The headquarters of the trading businesses in the Congo were, however, established in Brussels. They consisted of SEDEC, which had belonged to Lever Brothers, and of the posts which had belonged to the African and Eastern Trade Corporation under the names Hatton and Cookson, and African Association.

Immediately upon the formation of the company, instructions were issued that notices reading 'Branch of the United Africa Company Limited' should be affixed to all premises below the names of the existing companies, and Sanders made haste to design the notice. The board also charged Nicholl to design the United Africa Company flag. The question of the extent to which the name of the United Africa Company should be used concurrently with, or in substitution for, the names of existing trading units, was left to be discussed at a later date. It was then seen that, in order to take advantage of off-setting past losses against future profits for pur-

directors' committee on 25 June 1930. This company had a share of thirteen per cent of the cocoa pool and they had sold their business to the U.A.C. on the basis that they were to receive the profits that might be made on the Anglo-Guinea's percentage of the cocoa pool over the ensuing ten years. No other payment was to be made to them. They gave up their assets to the U.A.C. and the U.A.C. undertook to discharge their liabilities.

pose of tax, the old companies would have to continue trading in Africa for four years. Since in the second year of the United Africa Company further losses were made, the necessity of retaining the old names continued for six years after the company's formation. So it was not until 1935 that the general use of the United Africa name became official.[10] Even after that, local managers retained the old names in many places.

What was called inter-competition (two or more branches of the same concern operating in the same place under different names) had existed both in the Corporation and in the Niger group. The union of the two groups accentuated the anomaly. It was imperative to see which stations should now be closed and what reductions could be made in staff in the interests of economy but without sacrificing trade. This difficult and disagreeable mission was confided to Grey for the Gold Coast and to Bates for Nigeria.

Major Cecil Bates, D.S.O., M.C., had become a director of the African and Eastern Trade Corporation in 1927. He had been in the regular army and had served in India, and after that he had worked in Nigeria for the London and Kano Trading Company. In the weeks immediately preceding the merger, he had been touring Nigeria with a view to the reorganization of the Corporation's activities in that country. His report, dated 5 April 1929, was critical of the way the business had been run in Nigeria. It was immediately available to the United Africa Company. After a good deal of discussion, to which Cowan contributed much, the main lines of the report were approved, and Bates was asked to go back to Nigeria and put his ideas into effect, bringing the ex-Niger group within the scope of his activities. He was accompanied by Sloss, who had been the head buyer for the African and Eastern Trade Corporation in Liverpool, and by Beaumont (*see* chapter 14). Bates' name became a legend in Nigeria. A pennant with '*Ars Jus Pax*' on one side and 'Your money or your life' on the other was worn on his car. He quarrelled with senior government officials at the Lagos Club. The reorganization which he carried out permitted the reduction of the European staff from 547 to 419, so Bates had to sack a great many men. The ex-Niger Company staff considered that he showed favouritism for the ex-African and Eastern men, but the latter also felt that they had raw treatment. Major Bates had been given large discretionary powers, and while he put up much excellent work, he failed to maintain the

[10] Minutes, United Africa Company board and executive committee.

human touch with the personnel of the company. As a result, the personnel came to look on him as ruthless, and there can be no doubt that in this way he allowed himself to be seriously misunderstood. The fact remains that serious disorganization resulted where steady re-organization was aimed at, and for a time the company was actually going back rather than forward.'[11] However, he did the job: it had to be done, and it was hardly likely to gain popularity. Furthermore, with hindsight it is clear that the survivors of this exercise were able and willing to respond to the calls which were made upon them. Bates reported to the board on 28 January 1930, and described how he had divided Nigeria into districts with one man in charge of each, and specialized managers of particular lines of business in the districts. However, his 'specialization' was a very tentative and partial beginning, and the lines of administrative responsibility were far from clear.[12]

When Bates went to Nigeria, Grey was asked to do a similar job in the Gold Coast, Togoland, and Ivory Coast. He left in August 1929, accompanied by Bolliger,[13] H. N. Phillips,[14] and Arthur Smith.[15] Grey seems to have found a way of carrying out his disagreeable duties without causing too much upset. In any case he was a man who personally commanded respect in Africa. In the course of his travels he decided to take a weekend off to relax in the old Swanzy fortress at Dixcove. His staff were entertained, that same weekend, fifteen miles away on the plantation at Sese. They were out for a stroll on Sunday morning when they saw Grey walking up the old path which had connected Dixcove, via Sese, with the gold mines. It was apparently his idea of a Sunday morning's relaxation. Having completed his task in the Gold Coast, he went on to the Ivory Coast, accompanied by Smith. They crossed the border in a Morris Isis, driving along the firm sand of the beach at low tide.[16]

The massive reduction of the European staff was carried out in the interests of economy, but it laid the foundation for a policy of Africanization. Europeans were cleared out of the middle grades of

[11] Cowan, A. A., to Muir, R. H., 31 May 1937, on file of papers left by Rankin.

[12] United Africa Company, board memorandum, 28 January 1930.

[13] see chapter 8.

[14] H. N. Phillips joined the A. & E.T.C. in 1927 and was appointed assistant chief accountant of U.A.C. in 1929. After the war he joined the U.K. Food Executive of Unilever as commercial officer, from which post he retired in 1960.

[15] Later Sir Arthur Smith, chairman of the United Africa Company and director of Unilever.

[16] From Sir Arthur Smith, oral.

commercial activity in sales, storekeeping, and clerical posts. The employment of Africans in senior positions was already well established in the Gold Coast. In Nigeria, the reorganization lists show that many Africans were employed in sole charge of trading posts and that some of these were interchangeable with junior Europeans. In the Benin area a number of African book-keepers were rendered redundant by the concentration of accounting arrangements, and these men were placed in trading posts which had previously been held by Europeans.

It was necessary to convince the management staff in Africa that the United Africa Company would be a good employer. One of the first improvements of conditions of service was, to pay to European managers when on leave the same salary as they received in Africa (May 1929).[17] Then Waley Cohen addressed himself to the task of making proper provision for retirement. The matter was tackled with such energy that a provident fund for European employees was announced in August 1929, and it took effect from May 1929, so that the staff knew about it when Bates and Grey were on their travels.

Waley Cohen believed that the new company would need new men of the first quality, both in London and in Africa, and his recruitment policy marks him out as a man of great perception. It must have been difficult to overcome the resistance against such recruitment in a company which was engaged in massive reductions of staff and which was very poor. In London he brought in Muir and Samuel, of whom more later; but if Waley Cohen had never done anything else for the United Africa Company, this alone would have earned him a high place in its annals. Rollo Mellor[18] was engaged and to him Waley Cohen entrusted the responsibilities of recruitment, and of improving relations with governments. For Africa, six university graduates were engaged. In his days with Shell, Waley Cohen had known Roberts of the Cambridge University Appointments Board, and now he turned for

---

[17] United Africa Company board minutes.

[18] Aubrey Rollo Ibbetson Mellor, M.C., commanded his battalion in the war at the age of 24 and then served in the Egyptian Civil Service, at first on the financial side, but latterly in political affairs. He joined the staff of the United Africa Company in 1930 and was asked by Waley Cohen to devote his attention to government relations and the recruitment of management staff. He was appointed secretary of the company in 1931. He was not a trading man, nor ever tried to be one, but he thought deeply abut the problems of staff and public relations. He was a director of the United Africa Company from 1941 to 1957. He has given me much valuable help in the preparation of this and the ensuing chapter.

help to him and to the Oxford University Appointments Board. It must have been like manna from heaven to the appointments boards, for jobs were terribly hard to find in 1930. They produced men with high academic honours, of whom in later years two were to become directors of the company, while a third became a general manager. They did not have an easy time in winning acceptance, and the hostility of some of their colleagues was not diminished when it became known that they were being paid a bit extra 'at home' in addition to their salaries in Africa.[19]

The African and Eastern Trade Corporation owned four ocean-going steamers, and the Niger Company had as recently as 1928 acquired one. Some chartering was done by both companies, but the greater part of their cargoes was carried by the conference lines, that is to say, Elder Dempster, the Woermann Line, and the Holland West Africa Line. Both the Corporation and the Niger Company had contracts with the conference lines. It was expected that they would be replaced by a contract between the United Africa Company and the conference lines, and negotiations for it began. Almost at once important differences of opinion revealed themselves. The dispute went far beyond questions of money. It brought under discussion the whole philosophy of competition and combination. The conference lines believed that they had a public duty to promote competition, by which they meant granting the same freights to all traders, large and small. The United Africa Company replied that the merchant houses were as fully entitled as the shipping lines to set their affairs in good order: the United Africa Company wanted, in effect, to form a 'conference' of merchants. To indicate what impact the United Africa Company made in its first year, and what a weight of negotiation fell upon Waley Cohen, it is appropriate to mention that, when discussions with the conference ran into difficulty, a minister of the Dutch government intervened at the instance of the Dutch member of the shipping conference; Mr. J. H. Thomas as Secretary of State for the Colonies, Lord Inverforth, and the managing director of the North German Lloyd Line, all took a hand in trying to influence the parties towards a settlement. Eventually negotiations were broken off and the parties separated in a spirit far from friendly. Steamers were bought and chartered.

In its first year the United Africa Company involved itself in a project for trading in local food. This had some public repercus-

[19] Stanbury, R. W. W., oral.

sions in Nigeria, and in Britain it provided the occasion for a
decision about policy within the board of the company, which
helped to shape the future. The enthusiast behind the scheme was
T. M. Knox. 'We ought to endeavour,' he wrote, 'to do a trade in
local produce. We should try to buy groundnuts from Northern
Nigeria or the Upper Benue and sell Onitsha Area edible palm
oil in tins in exchange . . . It is a long time now since I first recommended that we should go into this business and put a trade mark
on the tins of palm oil. The mark which I suggest is a striking one
used by H.C.B. in the Congo and which is now actually used by
P.O.E.M. on the Gold Coast for the considerable local sales of
palm oil which they make there. I have referred already to the
shortage of native foodstuffs which is bound to arise as more and
more people are induced to give up work on the farms.'[20] This
was a prophetic remark in view of the massive imports of basic
foods which developed over the next thirty years. Waley Cohen was
impressed by his secretary's enthusiasm, and during his visit to
Africa he discussed the matter with government and company
people. On his return he had some difficulty in winning his colleagues to his ideas, but it was agreed that he should write to the
Governor of Nigeria, explaining what he had in mind. The Governor
replied in cordial terms.[21] Area native foodstuff officers were
appointed by the company. In Lagos palm oil was placed on sale
by the bottle, and groundnuts by the cigarette tin. The market
women resented it bitterly, and the Acting Chief Secretary of the
government warned the company's Lagos agent that it might lead
to riots.[22] There was, of course, no consumer council to speak up
for cheap food. The new men who were taking over in London
did not believe in this kind of business. Muir, at that time, was
convinced that Africans would quickly take over the ordinary
buying and selling functions in their own countries, and that his
job was to find other things for the company to do. With such a
philosophy, it did not make sense to invest resources in trading in
local foods. It is not clear whether the decision to stop was taken
before the government's warning became known; but the project
had no support on the board after the changes of personnel

---

[20] Knox, T. M., *Report to the Board on Visit to West Africa 1929* (24 May 1929) unpublished
p. 18.

[21] United Africa Company board minutes.

[22] Crowder, M., *West Africa under Colonial Rule* (London: Hutchinson, 1968) p. 301:
and Burns, Sir Alan, to Pedler, 14 October 1969 and 18 October 1969.

towards the end of 1930.[23] Perhaps the United Africa Company missed a chance to be on the side of the angels. If marketing facilities for food crops had been provided, as efficient as the marketing facilities for export crops, Africa would have been more prosperous in the following forty years. The light in Knox's eye was the light which had been in Clifford's eye in 1925, when he expressed the intention to stimulate the production of crops not dependent on export. Could it be that Knox, Leverhulme's secretary, had been impressed by Clifford's philosophy?

In its first trading year, ended in April 1930, the United Africa Company made a profit of £24,143: which, for a concern of that size, was very disappointing.

[23] I have been fortunate in being able to discuss this matter with three of the principal actors; with Sir Malcolm Knox who initiated the policy, with Sir Alan Burns who communicated the government's view to the United Africa Company, and with R. H. Muir who was responsible for abandoning the policy.

30

Disaster and Reconstruction

On 2 September 1929, that is to say four months after the United Africa Company started, Lever Brothers Limited agreed to amalgamate with the Margarine Unie, a Dutch company, and with its English counterpart, the Margarine Union. The company which resulted from this merger was registered, in England, under the name Lever Brothers and Unilever Limited; hereinafter it will be referred to as Unilever.[1]

Unilever now became the joint guarantor, with the African and Eastern Trade Corporation, of the debts of the United Africa Company Limited. The two partners guaranteed the debts of the United Africa Company, and any liability which might have to be met under the guarantees would be shared equally between them; but Unilever's guarantee would 'cease to apply if the guarantors were ever called upon for an amount in excess of the whole resources of either'. However, the Corporation was not in a position to guarantee very much. Its credit had collapsed in 1928, and the only assets which had been reserved from the amalgamation were Africa House and the two factories, Harris the soap maker and Loder the oil-crusher.

It is normal for merchant houses to finance the greater part of their stocks and debts (by which is meant, mainly, the credit which they have advanced to middlemen) by borrowing. The United Africa Company was no exception, and being a very large merchant it needed very large loans. It became involved, immediately upon its formation, in difficult negotiations with banks and credit houses, with a view to raising finance. The cloud of imminent bankruptcy overhung the African and Eastern Trade Corporation, one of its guarantors. The Niger Company's trading results over the previous nine years showed a substantial excess of loss over profit. True, it had made a profit in each of the preceding five years, but these profits had been small. Such records did not inspire lenders with confidence. A tremendous amount of management time was

[1] Wilson, Charles, *History of Unilever* (London: Cassell, 1954) vol. II, p. 301.

taken in arranging credits, switching from overdrafts to acceptance bills and then back again, and arguing about rates of interest. However, they managed to get along until the autumn of 1930, when produce prices came crashing down: the United Africa Company made heavy losses, and lenders showed great anxiety. Lloyds Bank and the Eastern Bank asked the company to close its account. The Bank of the Belgian Congo asked SEDEC to reduce its overdraft. Sir John Caulcutt, on behalf of a group of banks, asked the company for a statement of the debts owed to it by its customers, suggesting that the figure had not declined though turnover had fallen dramatically. The United Africa Company fortunately was able without undue delay to present Sir John with a statement showing that the total debts were, on the average, turning over three-and-a-half times a year, and he was satisfied—apparently with some surprise. It all involved an exercise in brinkmanship which could not form a stable basis for trade, and at length in November 1930 Unilever grasped the nettle; they offered to take full responsibility for finance; and they demanded full control.

The Margarine Union, which amalgamated with Lever Brothers in 1929, was itself the result of a merger which had taken place as recently as 1927 between the firms of Jurgens and Van den Bergh. Under the terms of its merger with Lever Brothers, the Margarine Union put into the United Africa Company the five businesses which it owned in Africa. Those enterprises have been mentioned in chapter 15, but it may be convenient to give the names again:

> Syndikat für Ölpalmenkultur
> Jurgens Colonial Products
> Standard Company of Nigeria
> Palmine
> Nouvelle Société Commerciale Africaine.

The transfer of these assets took place on 1 January 1930, and the Margarine Union received payment in the form of 1,531,600 shares of the nominal value of one pound each of the United Africa Company. The capital of that company was thereby increased from £14,200,000 to £15,731,600. The participation in the profits by the African and Eastern Trade Corporation was accordingly reduced to a fraction over forty-five per cent, while that of Unilever became fifty-four and a fraction per cent. However, the right of the African and Eastern Trade Corporation to a half share of the control of the United Africa Company, so carefully provided in the first instance, was preserved. The Corporation retained equality of control. It was made a condition of the entry of the Margarine Union into the United Africa Company that the combined voting power of the Corporation's directors on the United Africa Company board, be their number what it might, should be equal to the combined voting power of all the other directors.[2]

In January 1930 the board was augmented by the addition of three directors representing the Margarine Union; Anton Jurgens, Albert van den Bergh, and Paul Rijkens. They 'attended by invitation of the chairman' until they were formally elected in the following September; but until the beginning of April the chairman was not there—he was in Africa. Anton Jurgens was in effect the head of the Margarine Union. His position received formal recognition in the following year, 1931, when he became the chairman of the Dutch Unilever company. He was 'a man of immense ability . . . always expressionless . . . the coldest and most ruthless man on earth';[3] 'autocratic personality'.[4] He had formed a poor view of the United Africa Company's prospects and of Waley Cohen's methods of management. D'Arcy Cooper, by virtue of his long association with Waley Cohen, whose guest he had been at Highgate on several occasions, must have been disposed to give him the benefit of any reasonable doubt, and furthermore his own reputation as a chooser of men was at stake in Waley Cohen. Anton Jurgens was not inhibited by any of those considerations. It is probable that his clear foresight made him a frightened man; he feared that the United Africa Company might go bankrupt and lead Unilever into terrible trouble.

Waley Cohen, on returning from Africa in April 1930, was confronted with a demand that he should give up his personal method of management. There was a period of intense discussion during which several different proposals were produced. What came out of it was an executive committee of the board consisting of Waley Cohen, D'Arcy Cooper, Anton Jurgens, and Beddington. It was to meet frequently and to be the effective decision-making organ. Waley Cohen was to preside over meetings but Beddington was to

---

[2] The Corporation's copy of the agreement is held by the Unilever secretarial department. It bears the date 13 September 1929 and the parties were the United Africa Company Limited, Margarine Union Limited, N.V. Margarine Unie, African and Eastern Trade Corporation, and the Niger Company Limited.

[3] Henriques, R., *Sir Robert Waley Cohen 1877–1952* (London: Secker and Warburg, 1966) p. 308.

[4] Wilson, op. cit., vol. II, p. 312.

be sole managing director, and he was the only member of the committee who was entitled to hand down executive instructions to members of the staff. Beddington as sole managing director lasted only from May to October, when three joint managing directors were named, Knight,[5] Muir,[6] and Samuel.[7] In preparation for this

[5] Jasper W. Knight (see plate 22) was a little over 50 years of age when he joined the board of the U.A.C. In his younger days he had enjoyed a reputation as a boxer and oarsman. He was senior partner in Nicholl and Knight, produce brokers and merchants, until 1919 when he joined the board of Jurgens Limited and took charge of buying that company's raw materials. In 1929 he became the chief buyer for Unilever, a post which he relinquished on being appointed as a joint managing director of the U.A.C. He was named as an alternative director of the U.A.C. by Anton Jurgens in 1930. He frequently visited Africa. He acquired a reputation for toughness and for a nerve of steel in handling his produce trading risks: but he had all the magnanimity of a good sportsman and he was very generous in his attitude to young men.

[6] Rowland Huntly Muir (see plate 23) was born in 1889 and was educated at Wellington with the intention that he should enter the army. A slight affection of the throat frustrated that intention, so at the age of 18 he went to India. By the time he was 27 he was in charge of four jute mills employing 12,000 persons. He was with the well-known firm of Andrew Yule and in 1927 he received an offer to be the managing director of that company on a contract for seven years. But he had had twenty years of India and did not want to stay for seven more. He secured employment with a financial house in the City of London and while so employed he met Beddington who introduced him to Waley Cohen. He joined the staff of the U.A.C. in June 1929 and was appointed by Grey as his alternate director. In July he submitted his plan for the reorganization of the company in Britain. It was based upon the premises that the produce side should work within a cost figure of one half of one per cent of turnover, and that the merchandise side should work within a figure of two per cent. In August 1929 he was made responsible for the administration of head office, and he proceeded to achieve the objectives which he had set himself. However, he did not do it by grinding down the poor, for during the exercise he wrote, 'the lower grades of the staff are underpaid. Whatever the need of economy, I feel sure that a concern like ours would not wish to save on their lower paid men'. In November 1929 he was appointed a director of the U.A.C., being then 40 years of age. He left forthwith for Africa and thereafter frequently visited the company's places in that continent and in Asia. Muir was a man of few words and brilliantly concise as a draftsman. He is happily in the best of health at the time of writing and has given much valuable help in the compilation of this book. He cannot, however, remember a single occasion when he and his two colleagues had a difference of opinion, let alone any disagreement on a question of importance. He was the Carnot of the United Africa Company's revolution, the organizer of victory.

[7] Frank Samuel (see plate 24) was a little younger than Muir. He had been chairman and managing director of the forerunner of the Decca Gramophone Company. That business had been largely owned by himself and his relatives. It was sold to other trade interests, and Samuel set off with his wife to go round the world. They had reached the place which was then known as Batavia, but which is now called Djakarta, when he received a telegram from Waley Cohen inviting him to join the U.A.C. He was most excited and returned at once; for he was an excitable and emotional man. He joined the staff in October 1929, was named as alternate to Beddington, and went out at once to Africa. His personal generosity was enormous, but it was little known because his gifts were anonymous. His vibrant energy was tempered by a warmth of personal friendship which, as the years rolled on, endeared him to every member of the company's staff, and to every competitor. In 1953 John A. Holt conveyed to him the wish of members of the West African trade that he should be presented

change the board had, on 22 September 1930, resolved 'that the executive committee as a body shall decide the policy and managing directors shall be responsible to them alone, and no member of the board, in the course of interviews with the managing directors or staff, shall give instructions to them, otherwise than through the committee'. Cooper and Jurgens each had a deputy on the committee, namely McDowell and Rijkens. These two, from the passing of the resolution of 22 September, made a practice of attending the meetings of the committee, whether Cooper and Jurgens were able to attend or not. The company was incurring very heavy losses and everyone was frightened and tense. Obviously the scene was set for clashes of personalities.[8]

As early as 27 May 1930 the executive committee of the board discussed whether it was possible to introduce some new elements of control and discipline into the business of produce buying with a view to avoiding the repetition of past mistakes. The basis for the discussion was a memorandum by Frank Samuel, and it appears to have been his first contribution to the company's business. The need was felt for some forecast of prices which might serve as guidance to the company's agents. However it was decided that the exercise was too difficult and 'the matter was left for the chairman to deal with'. The premonitions which had underlain these discussions were unhappily shown to be well founded. The price index of Nigerian exports fell from 87 in 1929 (1926 = 100) to 74 in 1930 and to 47 in 1931. The fall in the price of cocoa, however, was more drastic than the average. As the 1930 crop moved forward into European and American markets, the ordinary prudent devices of hedging on the markets proved inadequate to meet the situation. At the same time, in Africa the low prices paid to producers caused such a shortfall in spending power that heavy losses were sustained in merchandise.

Up to September 1930 the United Africa Company had made a profit of £46,000 in the five months of its trading year, commenced in May. In October the position turned bad. For that one month the loss was £93,000: in the single month of November the loss

---

with a portrait of himself as a token of appreciation of all he had done to break down old antagonisms and engender friendly co-operation among the merchants. He was a great believer in promoting young men, and would sometimes say when such proposals were under discussion that youth was the one fault which time would certainly set right. He died in 1954.

[8] In this paragraph and in many following paragraphs I have made use of the minutes of the board of the U.A.C. and of its executive committee.

was £144,000. From December until April there were heavy losses every month, made worse by an item of more than £100,000 on the realization of New York market purchases of cocoa.

The circumstances in which this loss was incurred are extremely interesting. In 1929 the United Africa Company had made an agreement relating to the cocoa trade. The other parties to this agreement were Ollivant, Anglo-Guinea, Société commerciale de l'Ouest africain, Compagnie française de l'Afrique occidentale, and Union Trading Company of Basel. Buying and selling were to be controlled by a board, and any profit or loss was to be shared upon agreed percentages, that of the United Africa Company being 52·75 per cent. In June 1930 there was a long discussion about cocoa at the board of the United Africa Company. It was foreseen that the coming year would be disastrous in the sale of merchandise unless the price of cocoa went up, so that the producers of cocoa in Africa might have money to spend. The discussion ended with a decision to begin at once to buy cocoa on the terminal markets in New York at the rate of 300 tons a day. It was the reverse of normal practice, since the more usual operation on the terminal markets was that the merchant houses sold cocoa in advance of the season, so that they might have orders on their books against which they could make deliveries when the crop came in. The purpose of these purchases was to support the price, and those who were responsible for making them believed that the price was unnaturally low and might be expected to rise. This belief proved to be erroneous. Furthermore, the general idea that a major seller of cocoa could support the price by acquiring more cocoa was almost certainly mistaken. Subsequent experience was to demonstrate that the accumulation of large stocks of cocoa would depress the market. Anyway, in 1930 the price did not rally; it fell further, and the cost of liquidating the purchases made in New York was over £200,000, of which the United Africa Company's share was 52·75 per cent.

At the close of the year it was clear that merchandise stocks had to be drastically written down in value, and when this had been done the accounts showed a loss of £1,288,123.

In December 1930 Samuel came forward with a proposal that the salaries of the directors, and of all managers receiving more than £500 a year, should be reduced. This was done, the directors' pay being cut by one-third. About the same time a recommendation was received from the general managers in the Gold Coast that reductions should be made in the salaries of all the company's employees in that country, and this was gratefully accepted. It appears that no such communication was received from Nigeria, but the salaries were reduced just the same. Furthermore, the number of European managers was again reduced.

In that same month of December Waley Cohen had to meet the shareholders of the African and Eastern Trade Corporation in their annual general meeting, and he made no pretence of being a happy man. He told them that the fall in the prices of produce had given the company a bad set-back, and that their duration could not be predicted. He lamented the fierce and short-sighted competition and the indifference to the advantages of co-operation which he had observed during his recent visit to Africa. He had confident hopes for ultimate success, but could offer no comfort for the immediate future. He announced that Africa House had been sold, at a price exceeding half a million pounds, the value which had been placed on this asset in the balance sheet. The disposal of Africa House had been consequent on a decision that the United Africa Company should share Unilever House with Unilever as soon as the reconstruction, already well under way, was completed. Waley Cohen then went on to tell the meeting something that was very important and extremely personal. At the instance of, or rather at the demand of Unilever, a drastic change had been made in the method of running the United Africa Company. It was the substitution, to use Waley Cohen's own expression, 'of committee management for personal management'. Three managing directors had been appointed and the daily control and conduct of the company's affairs was in their hands. Waley Cohen did not disguise his disagreement with this innovation. He had, he said, concurred in it reluctantly. On the other hand, he spoke with generous appreciation of the three men who had been selected to carry the responsibility, Knight, Muir, and Samuel. Those who heard the speech were not surprised when two months later Waley Cohen resigned.

Again in that same month of December, Grey made a final effort to resume command. He was not impressed by the new men. He addressed all members of the board in the following terms:

The present system of three managing directors is a compromise resulting from circumstances of which we are all aware and cannot be considered the best solution of the problem. It seems to me only a trial makeshift which may do the company harm as it does not appear, on the surface, to be of a permanent character . . . It was perhaps inevitable that new blood should cause new methods and new diseases; therefore I will not at present waste your time in labouring this opinion other than to say that new blood, in itself, is no remedy, its value depends upon the work it is capable of doing and, in our case, the new blood represented by experience which, in my view, cannot safely be applied in West African conditions without a mixture of knowledge of the practical work, which it does not possess and hitherto has tried to acquire by a system of trial and error, if continued is likely to be extremely costly . . . To sum up, my proposals are—Reduce director-managers from eight to three, including the chairman.[9]

The triumvirate, Knight, Muir, and Samuel were, however, firmly in the saddle. The only result of this memorandum was the departure of General Grey.[10]

The year 1931 witnessed a severe and widespread economic depression. The most drastic measures were taken by the British government. They included an increase of taxation, the utmost curtailment of public expenditure, pay cuts for all government servants and even for Members of Parliament, reductions in allowances to the unemployed, the formation of a coalition government, the abandonment of the gold standard, and the jettisoning of the policy of free trade.

Waley Cohen had been a party to the board resolution of 22 September but he simply could not abide by it. His personal interventions continued, and at a meeting of the executive committee on 12 January 1931 (the only occasion on which the cool D'Arcy Cooper was seen to lose his temper) he was challenged with having infringed the resolution of 22 September. T. M. Knox, secretary of the committee, was instructed to read that resolution. D'Arcy Cooper then asked Waley Cohen if he had complied with it, and Waley Cohen said he had not done so. There was a long silence. Knox was then asked to leave the room. What happened then was not recorded. Clearly, there was a tremendous clash of wills.[11]

[9] Grey, W. W. H., memorandum headed *The Directors, the United Africa Company Limited* (unpublished, 29 December 1930) pp. 6, 7, 10.

[10] Comment by T. M. (Sir Malcolm) Knox on his copy of the above.

[11] There has been much discussion about what exactly happened on this occasion. Henriques, in his biography of Waley Cohen, has given a dramatic account in which Anton Jurgens delivers the *coup de grace* to Waley Cohen. The minutes of the executive committee, however, do not support the view that Anton Jurgens was present on that occasion. Some

Waley Cohen went abroad for a holiday and tendered his resignation from the chairmanship and from the boards of both the United Africa Company and the African and Eastern Trade Corporation. His resignations were accepted.[12]

The new chairman succeeding Waley Cohen both in the United Africa Company and in the African and Eastern Trade Corporation was none other than Beddington. He had a task which called for great courage. He and his colleagues knew that the year's results were going to be disastrous.

The year ended at April 1931 showed a loss of £1,288,123. It had long been believed that the main obstacle to the progress of the Niger Company and of the Corporation had been their strenuous competition against one another. Their amalgamation had removed that obstacle, but the expected result had not followed. Things were not better but worse.

The situation called for drastic measures. No physical valuation, it will be remembered, of the fixed assets of either company had been made at the time of the merger. The combined fixed assets were now carefully valued and it was decided in consequence to write off the company's capital the large amount of £8,231,600, of which £6,967,620 was applied to reducing the value of fixed assets and investments, and the balance of £1,263,980 was used to cancel the net loss resulting from two years' trading. The capital, which had been raised to £15,731,600 at the entry of the Dutch, thus became £7,500,000, held by the partners in the same proportions as before.

But Unilever were not satisfied yet about the position. They thought that the United Africa Company should be provided with further liquid capital of £3,500,000. Unilever could put up their share of this large sum, fifty-five per cent for the reasons explained

---

friends of Paul Rijkens, who discussed the incident with him shortly before his death, gained the impression that Rijkens had spoken the final words of doom, in the absence of Anton Jurgens; but others, who were present on the same occasion, do not remember that Rijkens said that. Sir Malcolm Knox is of the opinion that it must have been Anton Jurgens, and that no record of the meeting was ever made: that is to say, that the meeting of 12 January which is on record took place earlier in the day, or that the incident which led to Waley Cohen's resignation may have occurred on 13 January.

[12] After his resignation, Sir Robert Waley Cohen received 'a handsome cheque' from Unilever (*see* Henriques, op. cit., p. 325). He immediately wrote a cheque for £1,000 and sent it to Rollo Mellor, asking him to use it in the relief of distress of those who had lost their jobs in the process of the reorganization following the merger, particularly in paying school fees for their children.

above. The Corporation would have to find forty-five per cent, nearly £1,600,000. But it possessed little money beyond the £500,000 which had been realized by the sale of Africa House. Unilever made a proposal. If the Corporation advanced £500,000, its maximum possible effort, Unilever would advance £3,000,000: but a condition was attached. The Corporation's share of the ownership and control should be reduced to twenty per cent, that of Unilever becoming eighty per cent.

The stipulation caused consternation to the Corporation's shareholders. It seemed to them inexplicable and incredible that their great organization should have reached this sorry pass. A single year, rather to be called unsatisfactory than very bad, as the loss had been trifling in comparison with the previous succession of profits, had caused disproportionate trouble, frightening the banks and credit houses and forcing the Corporation into a partnership, nominally with the Niger Company, but virtually with Unilever. There had been no humiliation for the Corporation in this arrangement, as it was a partnership on equal terms. Now, two years later, both humiliation and heavy material sacrifice confronted the Corporation. Its jealously guarded equality of control had to go; it was to sink to the status of a junior partner, and its share of the profits was to be reduced to a fifth. Bitter was the cup.

It was Beddington's thankless task to explain this state of affairs to the shareholders at the annual general meeting in Liverpool in December 1931. The shareholders concluded that the best course would be to sell their business to Unilever. Beddington was asked to invite Unilever to make an offer. The reply was received at an extraordinary general meeting on 30 December 1931. Beddington read a letter from Unilever. That company declined to make any offer of purchase. The letter presented the meeting with the alternatives of agreeing to Unilever's terms or going into liquidation; though there was, in theory, a third possible course. The shareholders of the Corporation or the general public might subscribe in cash the balance of the Corporation's share of the required new capital. Unilever had agreed, Beddington announced, that the offer would stand good until the end of February 1932, in order that there should be time for the Corporation to see if the additional money could be raised. Many very acrimonious comments were offered. After a great deal of discussion, ranging far afield at times, the decision of the meeting was that the board should try to procure fresh capital and that if they failed to get it they should accept Unilever's proposal. The attempt to raise new capital was made, and it failed. So Unilever's offer was, perforce, accepted.

The capital of the United Africa Company, written down as explained above to £7,500,000 by the revaluation of fixed assets and investments, was now increased by the new capital jointly subscribed by Unilever and the Corporation, £3,500,000, to £11,000,000. Twenty per cent was £2,200,000 and that became the Corporation's holding in the United Africa Company.

After the settlement with Unilever it became necessary for the African and Eastern Trade Corporation to reconstruct its own capital. Its issued capital was £7,366,180 and this was written down by £5,179,781. In other words, the shareholders were told that they had lost that sum. The surviving capital was £2,186,399. Nineteen shillings were written off each of the ordinary £1 shares, and considerable sacrifices were accepted by the preference share-holders.[13]

Bates, as a director of the African and Eastern Trade Corporation, strongly disapproved of the measures by which Waley Cohen was displaced from the chairmanship of the United Africa Company, and by which Unilever acquired control. He did not consider that Unilever's millions of pounds constituted a necessary rescue operation nor an act of faith in the future: he saw the transaction as a trick to get the Corporation's assets cheap.[14] He expressed that view in letters to Waley Cohen and D'Arcy Cooper, and took it with him into retirement early in 1932.

At the meeting which approved the necessary resolutions Beddington, as a variant to a long succession of disagreeable duties, had the pleasure of informing the Corporation's share-holders that in the year ended April 1932 the United Africa Company had earned a profit and declared a dividend. Profit and dividend were small, respectively £81,673 and a half per cent, but each was a pleasant surprise. The chairman did not neglect to express his thanks to the triumvirate, Knight, Muir, and Samuel.

---

[13] There were 300,000 'A' six per cent cumulative preference shares of £1 each, issued and fully paid. These were unaffected by the reconstruction. They retained their full value and also their cumulative character. On the other hand the holders of the 'B' six per cent cumulative preference shares of £1 each were asked, at a special meeting, to agree to the following changes; nine shillings were written off each of these £1 shares; all unpaid dividends on the said 'B' preference shares were cancelled; each of the 'B' preference shares was then exchanged for one twelve per cent non-cumulative preferred ordinary share and one ordinary share. The issued number of the 'B' six per cent cumulative preference shares of £1 had been 3,066,180 and at the special meeting the alterations were agreed by a large majority.

[14] Henriques, op. cit., p. 316.

They had indeed achieved something remarkable. In two years a complete reorganization had been carried out. The saving on annual working expenses amounted to no less than £1,400,000. Merchandise stocks had been brought down from over £4,000,000 to less than £2,000,000. Admittedly turnover had dropped from £12,000,000 to £7,750,000; this was in part due to the tumble in prices which had occurred but it also connoted a large loss in the share of the market. Part of this turnover was something which the group was happy to pass to other operators, for it had represented unprofitable trading. But even taking that into account, it was recognized that the group had retreated too far, and that a counter-attack was called for. After the measures which had been taken, the United Africa Company was stripped for action.

In 1939, the reconstruction of the United Africa Company was completed. Unilever made an offer to the shareholders of the African and Eastern Trade Corporation and bought them out. The ordinary stock of the Corporation was exchanged for ordinary stock of Lever Brothers and Unilever Limited at the rate of £1 (nominal) of the latter for every twenty units of one shilling (nominal) of the former; and so at last Unilever became the sole owner of the United Africa Company.[15]

15 Three companies whose antecedents have been noted in the text were not included in the amalgamation of 1929–31. Gailey and Roberts, of Nairobi (chapter 27) was bought in 1936. The partners who owned the firm were willing sellers, and they continued to be responsible for the management. G. Gottschalck and Company (chapter 18) was bought in 1939. Max Cohen, the chairman, died in that year, and although the business was sound, the surviving partners were not interested in trying to carry on under war conditions. Senior managers of the firm in Nigeria were promised that as long as they remained with the company a separate administrative channel for report to the board in London would be preserved, and that Gottschalck in Nigeria would never be administered as part of the United Africa Company. G. B. Ollivant and Company Limited had been greatly assisted by loans from Elder Dempster, but in 1930 Elder Dempster encountered difficulties, and the loan to Ollivant was withdrawn. Being unable to raise money to finance cocoa stocks, Chadwick, the chairman of Ollivant, turned for help to the U.A.C. A loan was granted, but there were other things to be financed as well as cocoa. Members of the staff were asked to wait for their salaries until a cargo of palm kernels could be realized. Chadwick turned to the U.A.C. for further help. The approach took the form of a visit by William Bibby to D'Arcy Cooper, chairman of Unilever (U.A.C. ex. co. mins. 18 July 1933 and memo. 1705. Unilever m.d. committee 27 July 1933). By agreement, G. B. Ollivant and Co. Ltd. went into voluntary liquidation and changed its name to L. C. Limited (from Leonard Chadwick the chairman). A new company was brought into being, called Ollivants (West Africa) Limited with a capital of £200,000, all subscribed by the U.A.C. This company changed its name to G. B. Ollivant Ltd. as soon as 'G. B. Ollivant and Co., Ltd.' was removed from the register at Somerset House. The new company took over from the liquidators of the old company all the assets at agreed valuation, but none of the liabilities except amounts owing to staff. Ollivant continued as a separate trading entity both in Africa and Britain. At Manchester the U.A.C. put in a managing director and an accountant, but L. Chadwick remained as

Why was the United Africa Company created? Lord Lever-hulme's motive for acquiring his group of African companies was clear enough; he believed in this way to increase and safeguard the supplies of raw materials for the manufacture of soap and margarine. However, by 1929 experience had taught Lever Brothers that there was no need to invest in African merchant firms for the purpose of safeguarding raw materials. The Far East had supplanted Africa as the principal source of supply, and it was easy to buy African commodities on the produce exchanges. The initiative which led to the amalgamation of 1929 between the African and Eastern Trade Corporation and the Niger Company was taken by the bank which had put in Waley Cohen to control the African and Eastern. Its motive was clearly defensive. On the Niger Company's side there is no evidence that either the chairman, Hyslop Bell, or the managing director, Snelling, was in favour of the merger; and there is much testimony that senior managers at the next level were opposed to it. The Niger Company had just begun to make profits, and they thought that they were beating the Corporation. To Lever Brothers, however, the shareholder of the Niger Company, the merger looked attractive. The defensive motive was strong in their case, though probably it did not weigh as much with them as it did with the Corporation's banker. Secondly, the deal which D'Arcy Cooper negotiated looked like good business, for the Niger Company secured half the equity of a concern to which its own contribution had been less than half of the assets at book value.

The disasters of 1930–1931 led to the reconstruction of the company, when Unilever put in £3,000,000 to keep the United Africa Company in existence. The triumvirate, Knight, Muir, and Samuel, had already been placed in charge; although the dates of their appointments were spread over some months, they were really all

---

chairman until 1946. The question of valuing the goodwill was covered by the terms of the agreement and it depended on the profits or losses in the eight years following transfer of ownership. The implementation of this agreement fell to Leonard's son, 'L.C.' or 'young Len', who had succeeded his father. After protracted discussions no progress was made towards a settlement, so in a reasonably friendly spirit (Lord Cole to Pedler, 6 December 1970) the parties came to the conclusion that they had better let the courts decide. In 1944 the House of Lords decided the case in favour of the U.A.C. There remained the problem of G. B. Ollivant and Company (Congo) Limited. Its shares were held equally by U.A.C. (through Ollivant) and by Bibby. The U.A.C. made Bibby an offer to buy his shares or to sell him the U.A.C.'s shares at the same price; the upshot was, that U.A.C. bought Bibby's shares (U.A.C. board memo., 2003, July 1946) and thus at last became owner of the whole of the Ollivant business. The U.A.C. then paid £44,000 as an act of grace for the benefit of the Chadwick family (U.A.C. board memo., 2004, July 1946).

part of one operation. At this stage, the principal architect of the new structure appears to have been Anton Jurgens, the Dutch leader. The experience of two years had shown that the United Africa Company was capable of running into heavy debts and incurring formidable losses, and that the financial responsibility inevitably rested upon Unilever, since the Corporation, although it owned forty-five per cent of the equity of the United Africa Company, had practically no other resources. It was felt to be essential therefore that Unilever, bearing the financial burden, should exercise control of the management and ensure that it was efficient.

It followed from the circumstances of the foundation and reconstruction of the United Africa Company that it never was used by Unilever as a special instrument for obtaining raw materials. So long as the shareholders of the Corporation continued to hold an interest (and that they had even after the reconstruction) it would have been inadmissible for Unilever to buy materials from the United Africa Company, or to employ its services, at any rates below full and fair market prices. There were agreements between Unilever and the United Africa Company concerning the trade in vegetable oils and oilseeds, but they were based on the principle of 'most favoured terms', and did not require either side to grant special or exclusive terms to the other.[16] The United Africa Company, never was the raw materials department of Unilever, and nothing was further from the policy of the raw materials department of Unilever than to be beholden to the United Africa Company. There were no arrangements with Unilever for integration, either vertical or horizontal. The United Africa Company as a trader in soap was not restricted to Unilever brands, and the Unilever companies exporting to Africa or manufacturing in Africa were not obliged to entrust the distribution of their products to the United Africa Company. In fact they always took the view that they needed a wider spread of sales outlets than the United Africa Company alone would be able to provide.

The function of the United Africa Company in Unilever was therefore simply to use the capital which had been entrusted to it for the purpose of making a profit. However, its size and character conferred upon it other attributes and functions, in a wider context. In several African countries it now occupied such a large

---

[16] Agreement *re* buying and selling of West African produce etc., with memorandum *re* Palm Oil endorsed and letter attached, 13 September 1929, in the records of the A. and E.T.C., now with Unilever secretarial department.

place in the economy, that it had to recognize and assume responsibilities towards society which could never have been imputed to
the constituent parts so long as they remained independent. With
that size and those responsibilities it became the target of attack
from those who disagreed with the way it ran its business, or with
the system which it represented. It was bound to be described as a
monopoly, even though this was far from the truth; for it had many
competitors, including several very substantial firms: such as
John Holt, Paterson Zochonis, Compagnie française de l'Afrique
occidentale, Société commerciale de l'Ouest africain, Maurel et
Prom, Union Trading Company of Basel, and G. L. Gaiser. In
competitive trades, however, there are often matters which affect
all the competitors, in which they find it convenient to act in
association. In such matters the United Africa Company would
now inescapably be the leader. Obviously, such matters would
usually be found in relationships with governments, metropolitan
or colonial. For the governments the United Africa Company was
a new phenomenon of considerable importance. They had not been
consulted as to its formation, but they were obliged to take account
of its existence. Was it to be welcomed as a powerful and responsible guardian of British commercial interests, or was it to be
regarded as an irresponsible and sinister monster? The relationship
would need to be worked out. For the company, two factors were
favourable towards long-term stable policies and responsible social
behaviour. The strong financial support which Unilever had so
amply provided created self-confidence within the company, and
confidence by others in the company. However, although Unilever,
as the majority shareholder, might be said to control the United
Africa Company, yet that 'control' did not take the form of setting
up an administrative department to supervise it. The link was in the
common membership of the two boards, that is to say, in the most
senior members of the Unilever board who were also members of
the Board of United Africa Company. Though the United Africa
Company 'reported' its results to Unilever at the year's end for
consolidation in the parent company's accounts, it did not report
to Unilever day by day nor even month by month.[17] This arm's-
length relationship with Unilever gave the United Africa Company
a sense of freedom in action, and enabled it to think of itself as a
company operating in Africa, bearing responsibilities towards
Africa, and depending for its success on the prosperity of Africa.

[17] United Africa Company board memorandum 1115 of May 1932.

Index